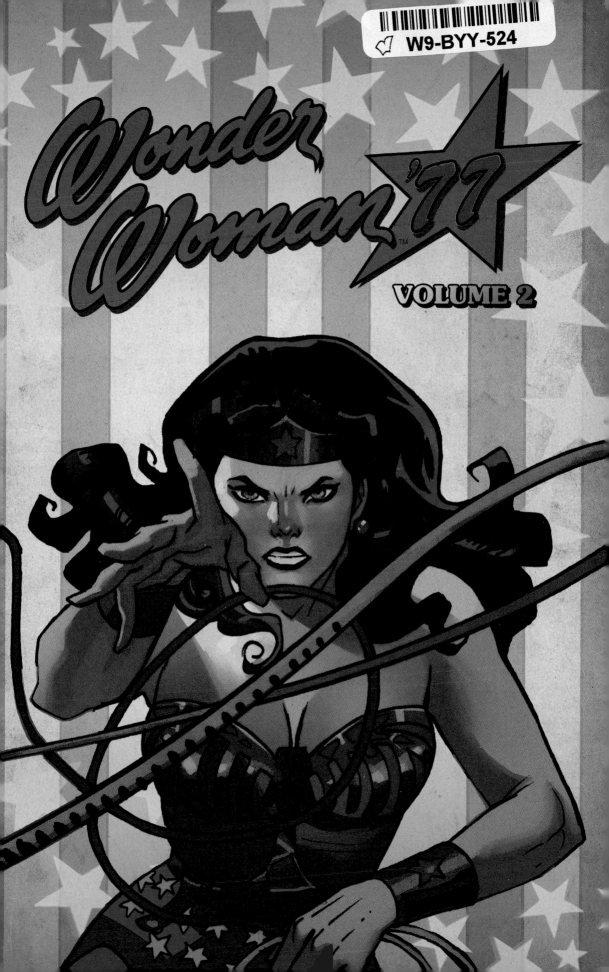

Wonder Woman '77

VOLUME 2

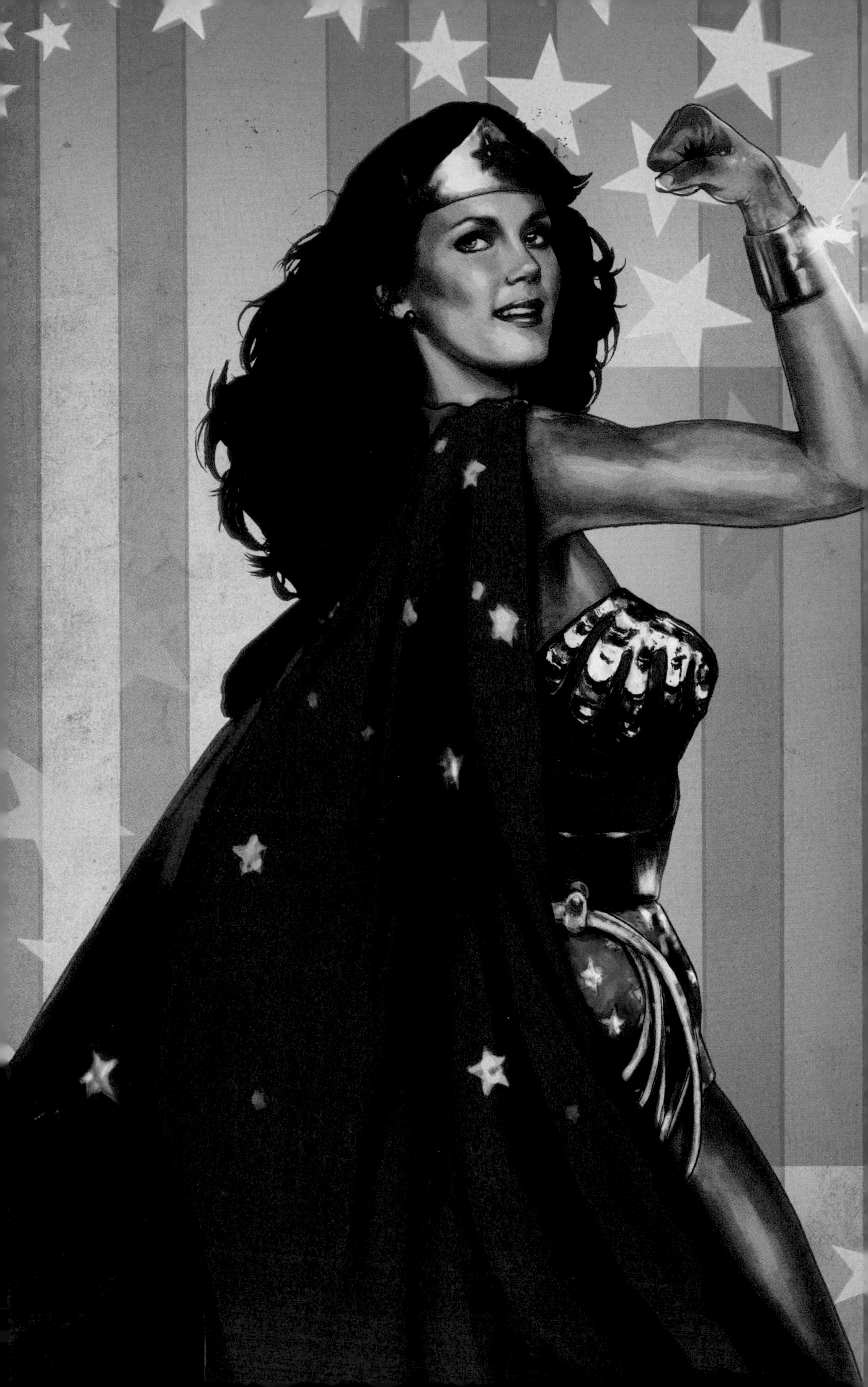

Wonder Woman '77

VOLUME 2

MARC ANDREYKO ★ CHRISTOS GAGE ★ RUTH FLETCHER GAGE
TRINA ROBBINS ★ AMANDA DEIBERT ★ AMY CHU
Writers

RICHARD ORTIZ ★ CHRISTIAN DUCE ★ DARIO BRIZUELA
ANDRES PONCE ★ CAT STAGGS ★ STAZ JOHNSON
WAYNE FAUCHER ★ TOM DERENICK ★ TESS FOWLER
Artists

ROMULO FAJARDO JR. ★ KELLY FITZPATRICK ★ LAURA MARTIN
CARRIE STRACHAN ★ JENN MANLEY LEE ★ WENDY BROOME
Colorists

WES ABBOTT
Letterer

JASON BADOWER
Collection Cover Artist

WONDER WOMAN created by WILLIAM MOULTON MARSTON

KRISTY QUINN Editor – Original Series
JESSICA CHEN Associate Editor – Original Series
JEB WOODARD Group Editor – Collected Editions
LIZ ERICKSON Editor – Collected Edition
STEVE COOK Design Director – Books
SARABETH KETT Publication Design

BOB HARRAS Senior VP – Editor-in-Chief, DC Comics

DIANE NELSON President
DAN DiDIO Publisher
JIM LEE Publisher
GEOFF JOHNS President & Chief Creative Officer
AMIT DESAI Executive VP – Business & Marketing Strategy, Direct to Consumer & Global Franchise Management
SAM ADES Senior VP – Direct to Consumer
BOBBIE CHASE VP – Talent Development
MARK CHIARELLO Senior VP – Art, Design & Collected Editions
JOHN CUNNINGHAM Senior VP – Sales & Trade Marketing
ANNE DePIES Senior VP – Business Strategy, Finance & Administration
DON FALLETTI VP – Manufacturing Operations
LAWRENCE GANEM VP – Editorial Administration & Talent Relations
ALISON GILL Senior VP – Manufacturing & Operations
HANK KANALZ Senior VP – Editorial Strategy & Administration
JAY KOGAN VP – Legal Affairs
THOMAS LOFTUS VP – Business Affairs
JACK MAHAN VP – Business Affairs
NICK NAPOLITANO VP – Manufacturing Administration
EDDIE SCANNELL VP – Consumer Marketing
COURTNEY SIMMONS Senior VP – Publicity & Communications
JIM (SKI) SOKOLOWSKI VP – Comic Book Specialty Sales & Trade Marketing
NANCY SPEARS VP – Mass, Book, Digital Sales & Trade Marketing

WONDER WOMAN '77 VOLUME 2

DC Comics, 2900 West Alameda Ave., Burbank, CA 91505
Printed by Solisco Printers, Scott, QC, Canada. 1/13/17. First Printing.
ISBN: 978-1-4012-6788-9
Library of Congress Cataloging-in-Publication Data is Available.

PEFC Certified

This product is from
sustainably managed
forests, recycled and
controlled sources

PEFC/26-31-02   www.pefc.org

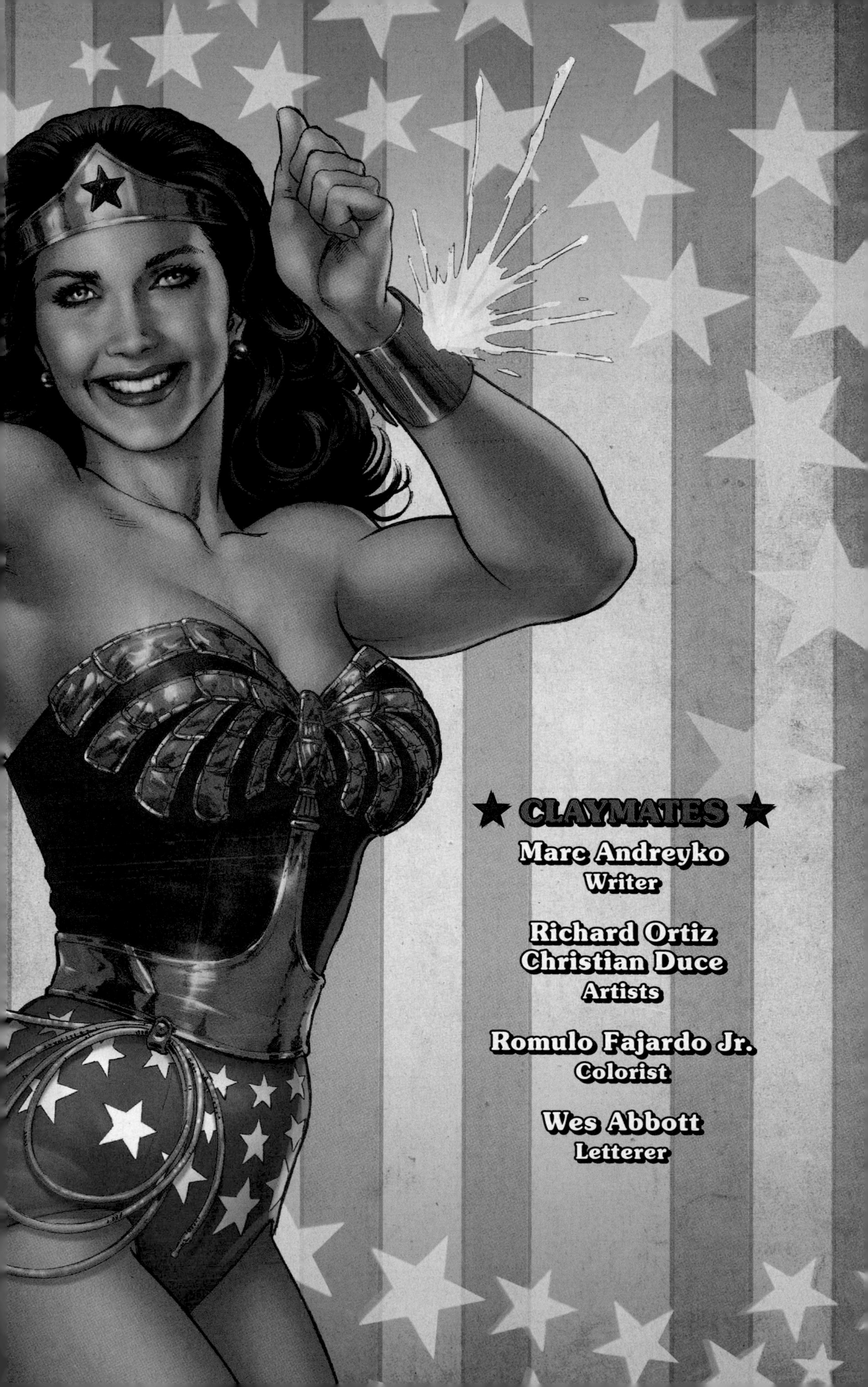
★ CLAYMATES ★
Marc Andreyko
Writer
Richard Ortiz
Christian Duce
Artists
Romulo Fajardo Jr.
Colorist
Wes Abbott
Letterer

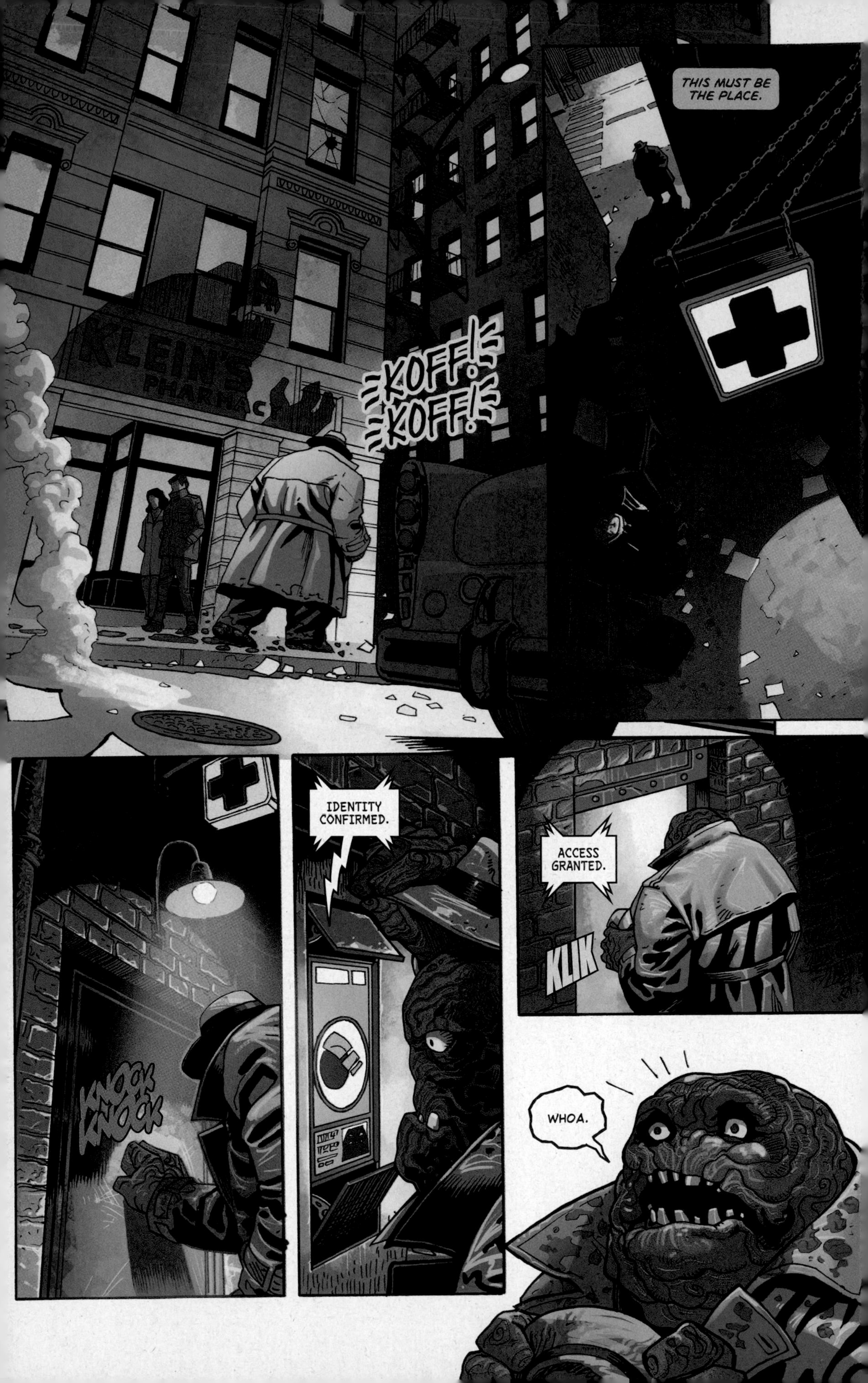
THIS MUST BE THE PLACE.
KLEIN'S PHARMAC
KOFF! KOFF!
KNOCK KNOCK
IDENTITY CONFIRMED.
ACCESS GRANTED.
KLIK
WHOA.

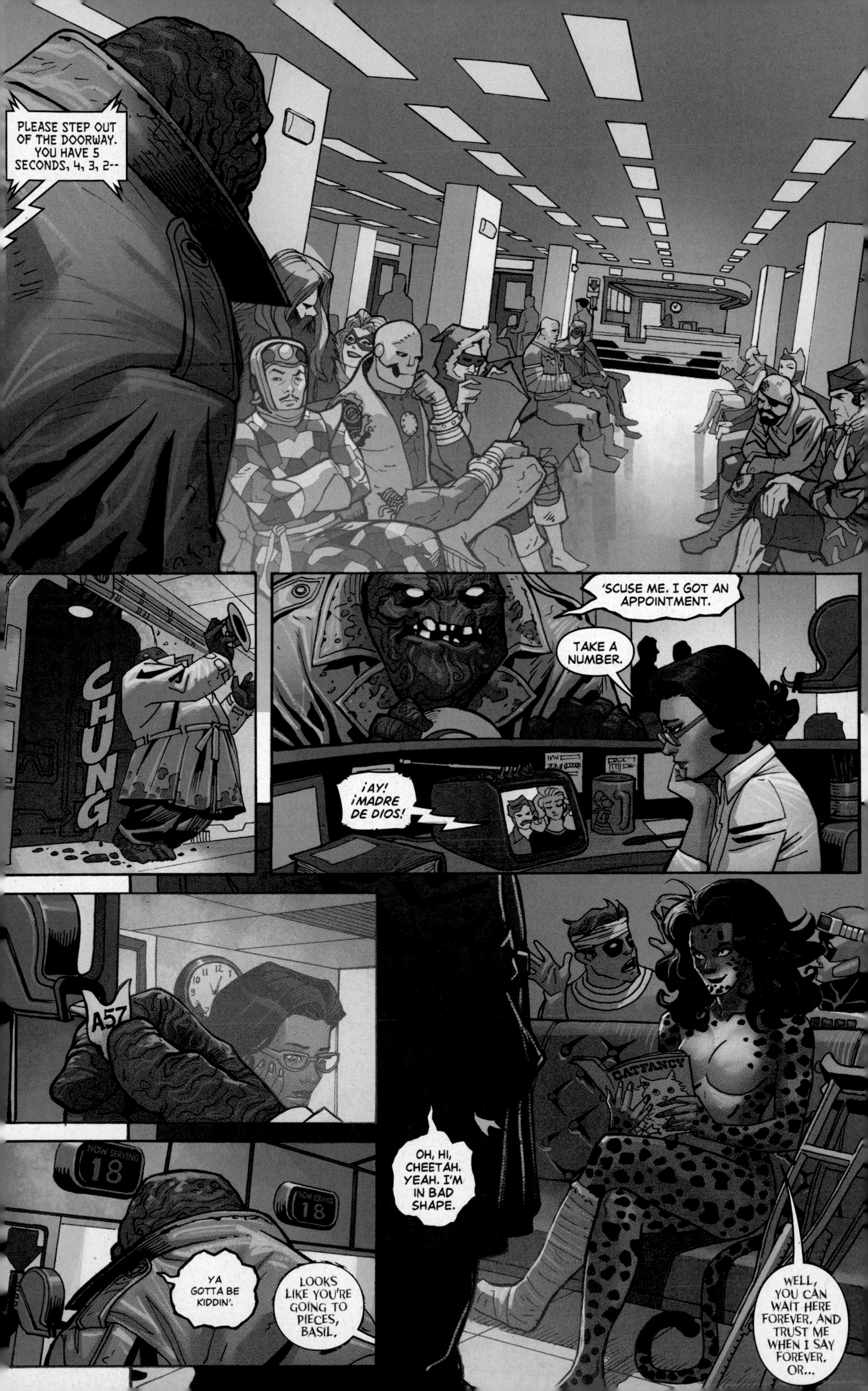
PLEASE STEP OUT OF THE DOORWAY. YOU HAVE 5 SECONDS, 4, 3, 2--
CHUNG
'SCUSE ME. I GOT AN APPOINTMENT.
TAKE A NUMBER.
¡AY! ¡MADRE DE DIOS!
A57
NOW SERVING 18
NOW SERVING 18
YA GOTTA BE KIDDIN'.
LOOKS LIKE YOU'RE GOING TO PIECES, BASIL.
CATFANCY
OH, HI, CHEETAH. YEAH. I'M IN BAD SHAPE.
WELL, YOU CAN WAIT HERE FOREVER. AND TRUST ME WHEN I SAY FOREVER. OR...

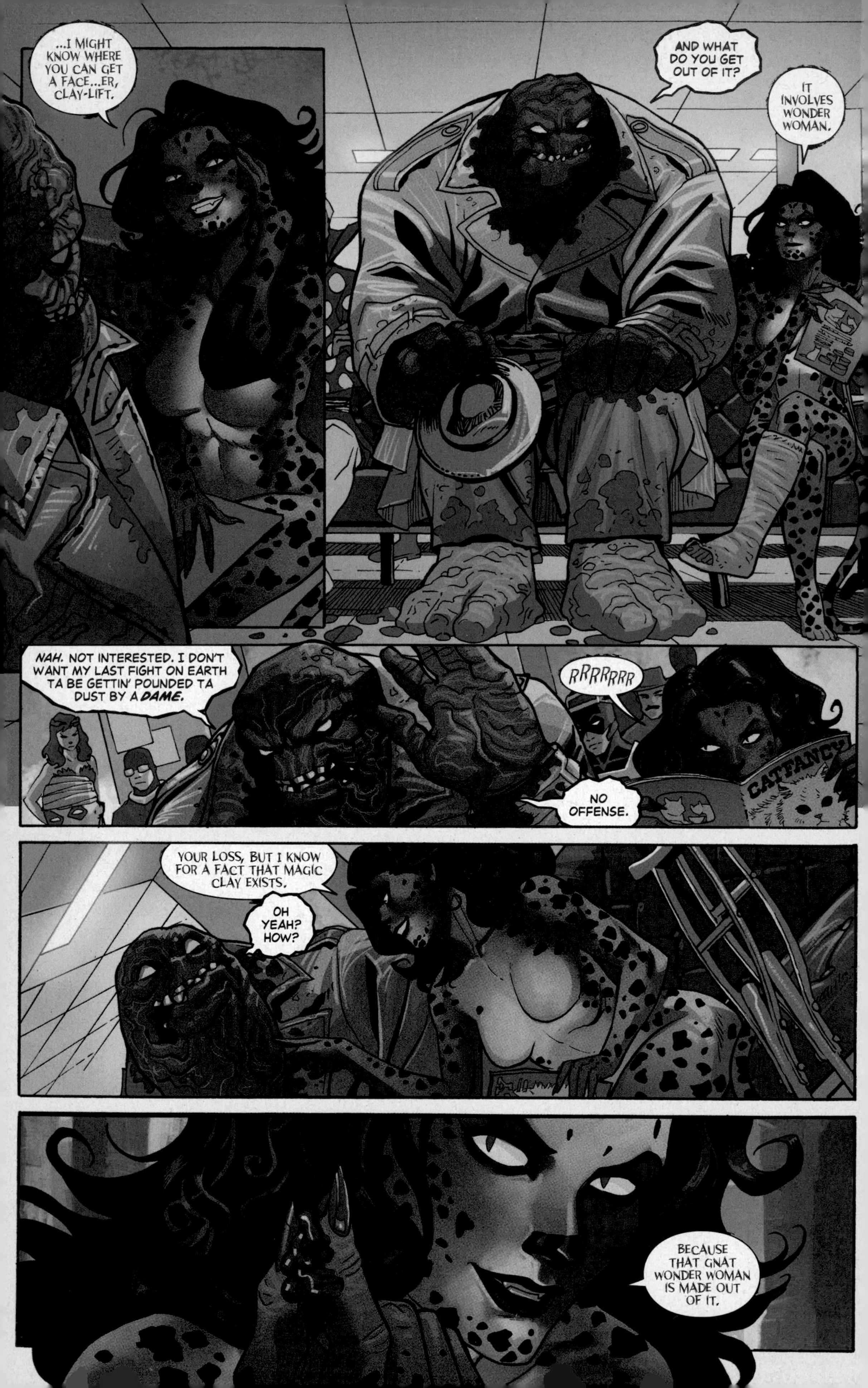
...I MIGHT KNOW WHERE YOU CAN GET A FACE...ER, CLAY-LIFT.
AND WHAT DO YOU GET OUT OF IT?
IT INVOLVES WONDER WOMAN.
NAH. NOT INTERESTED. I DON'T WANT MY LAST FIGHT ON EARTH TA BE GETTIN' POUNDED TA DUST BY A DAME.
RRRRRRR
NO OFFENSE.
CATFANCY
YOUR LOSS, BUT I KNOW FOR A FACT THAT MAGIC CLAY EXISTS.
OH YEAH? HOW?
BECAUSE THAT GNAT WONDER WOMAN IS MADE OUT OF IT.

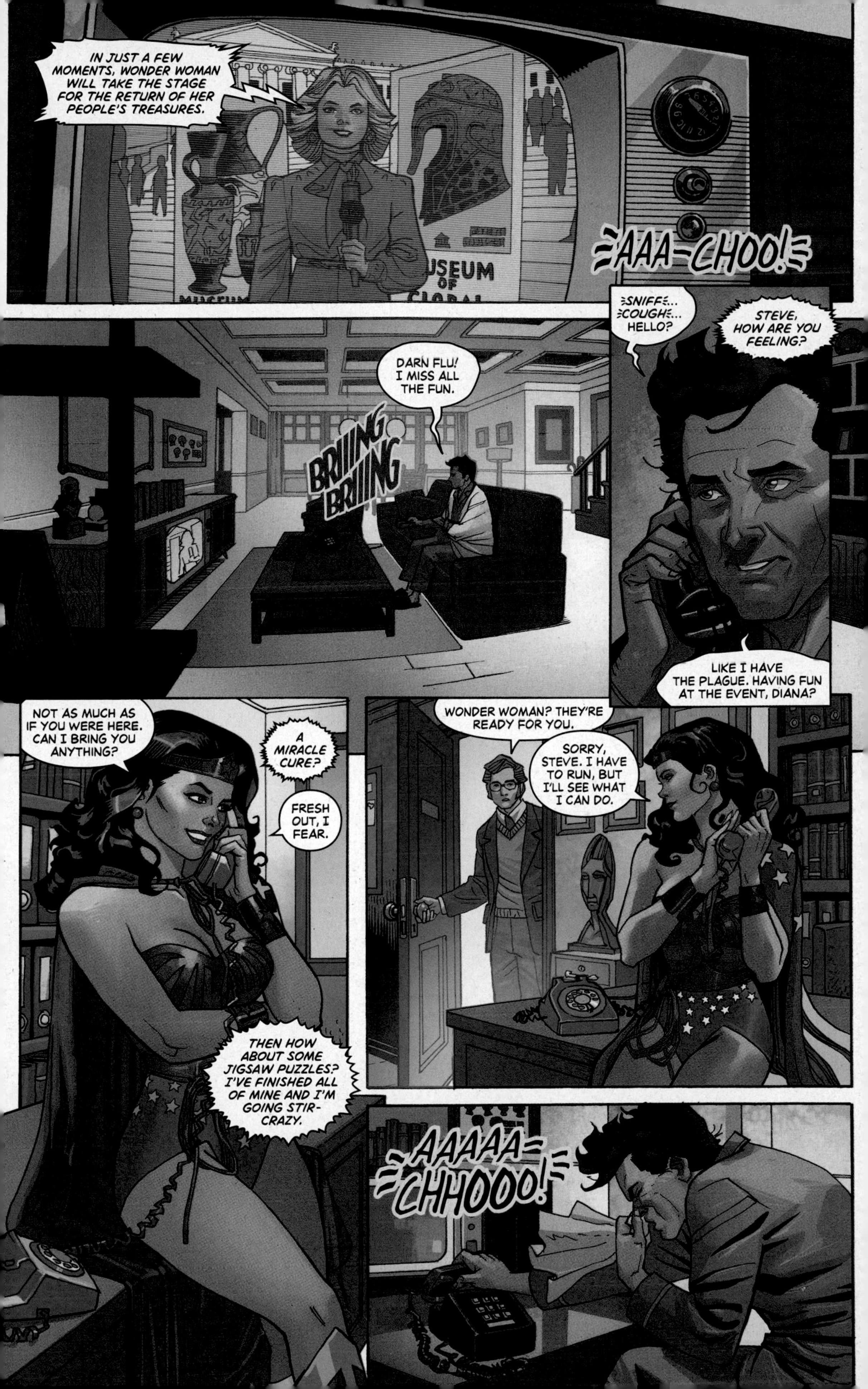
IN JUST A FEW MOMENTS, WONDER WOMAN WILL TAKE THE STAGE FOR THE RETURN OF HER PEOPLE'S TREASURES.
AAA-CHOO!
DARN FLU! I MISS ALL THE FUN.
BRIIING BRIIING
SNIFF... COUGH... HELLO?
STEVE, HOW ARE YOU FEELING?
LIKE I HAVE THE PLAGUE. HAVING FUN AT THE EVENT, DIANA?
NOT AS MUCH AS IF YOU WERE HERE. CAN I BRING YOU ANYTHING?
A MIRACLE CURE?
FRESH OUT, I FEAR.
THEN HOW ABOUT SOME JIGSAW PUZZLES? I'VE FINISHED ALL OF MINE AND I'M GOING STIR-CRAZY.
WONDER WOMAN? THEY'RE READY FOR YOU.
SORRY, STEVE. I HAVE TO RUN, BUT I'LL SEE WHAT I CAN DO.
AAAAA-CHHOOO!

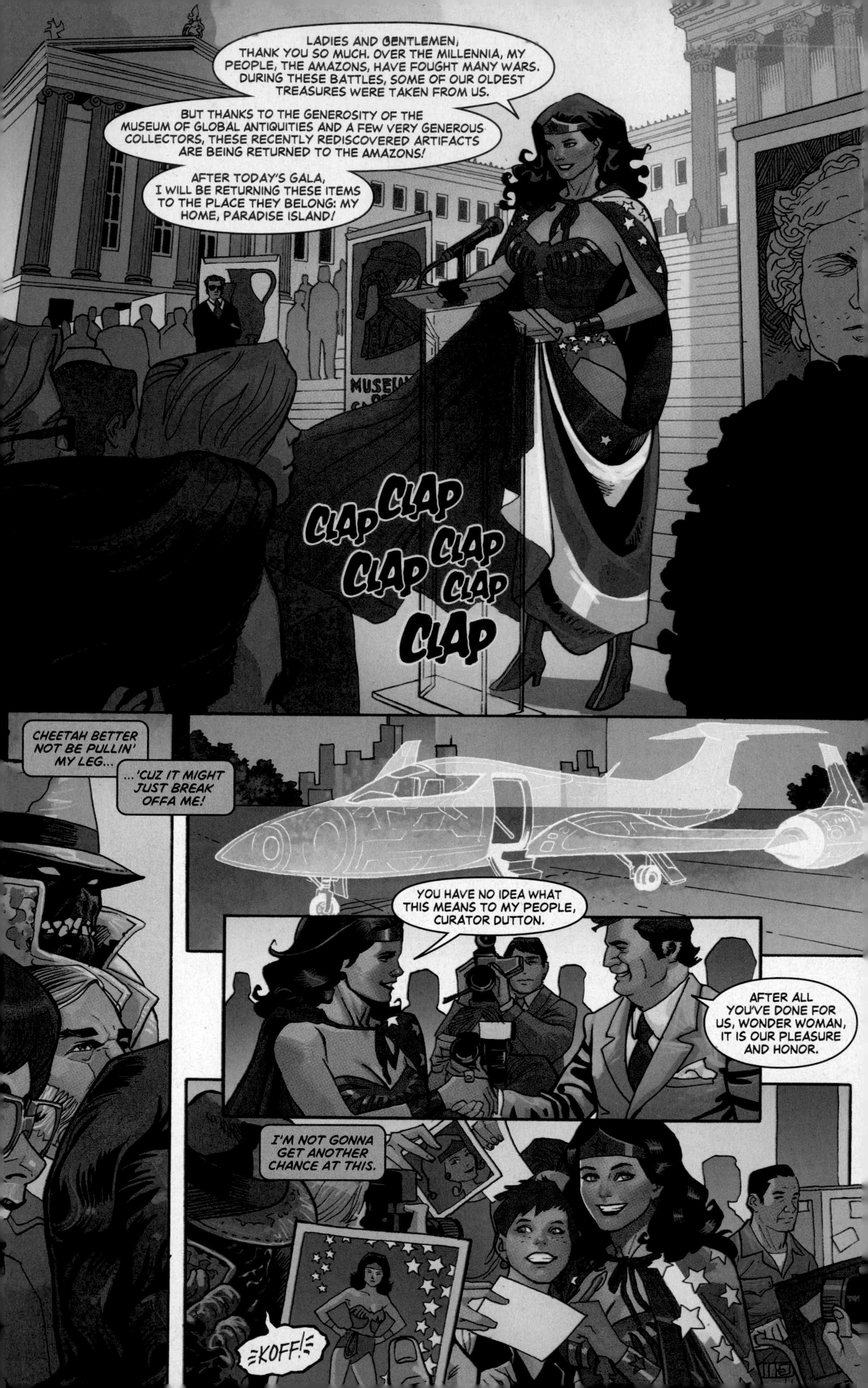
LADIES AND GENTLEMEN, THANK YOU SO MUCH. OVER THE MILLENNIA, MY PEOPLE, THE AMAZONS, HAVE FOUGHT MANY WARS. DURING THESE BATTLES, SOME OF OUR OLDEST TREASURES WERE TAKEN FROM US.
BUT THANKS TO THE GENEROSITY OF THE MUSEUM OF GLOBAL ANTIQUITIES AND A FEW VERY GENEROUS COLLECTORS, THESE RECENTLY REDISCOVERED ARTIFACTS ARE BEING RETURNED TO THE AMAZONS!
AFTER TODAY'S GALA, I WILL BE RETURNING THESE ITEMS TO THE PLACE THEY BELONG: MY HOME, PARADISE ISLAND!
CLAP CLAP CLAP CLAP CLAP CLAP
CHEETAH BETTER NOT BE PULLIN' MY LEG...
...'CUZ IT MIGHT JUST BREAK OFFA ME!
YOU HAVE NO IDEA WHAT THIS MEANS TO MY PEOPLE, CURATOR DUTTON.
AFTER ALL YOU'VE DONE FOR US, WONDER WOMAN, IT IS OUR PLEASURE AND HONOR.
I'M NOT GONNA GET ANOTHER CHANCE AT THIS.
KOFF!

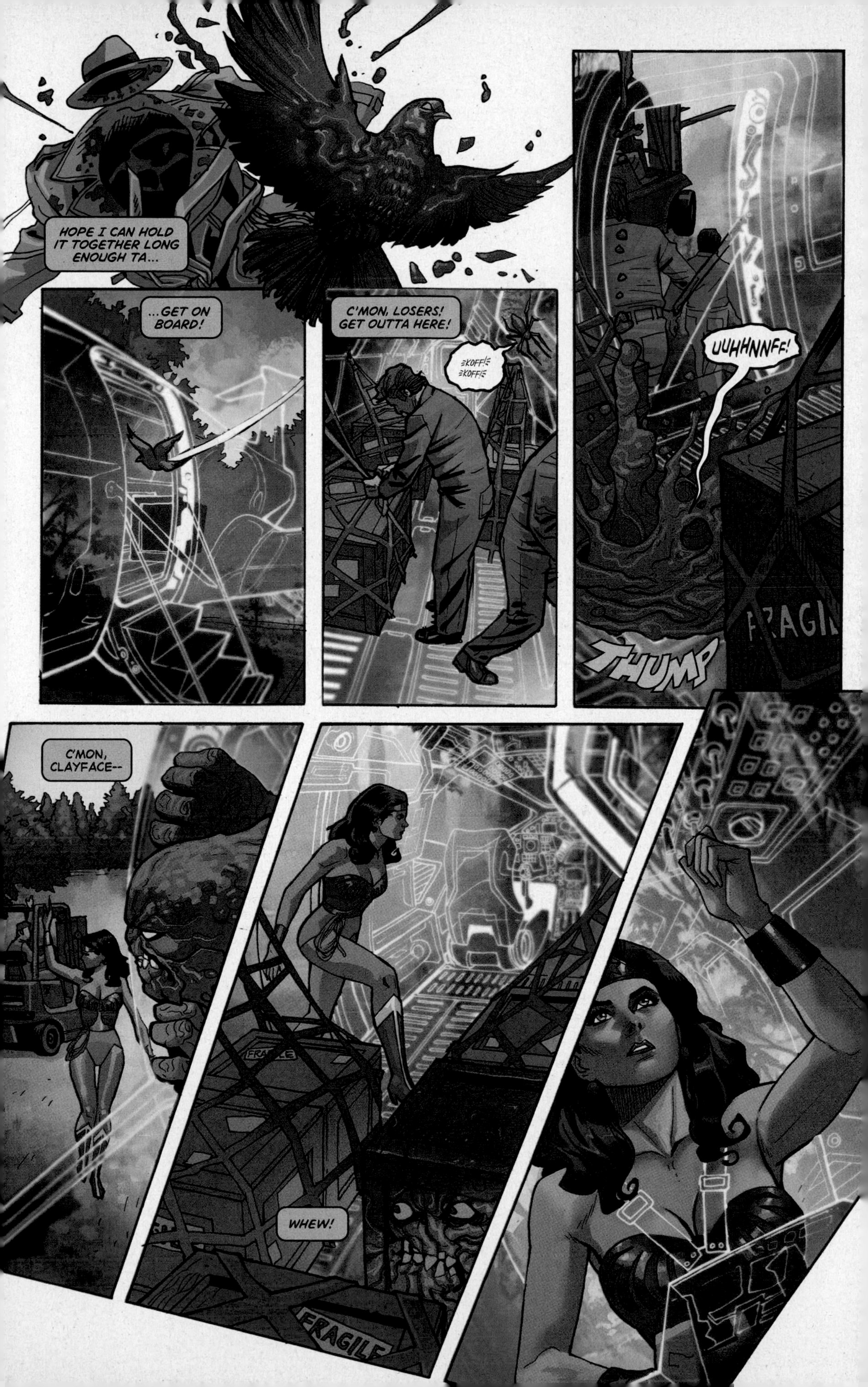
HOPE I CAN HOLD IT TOGETHER LONG ENOUGH TA...
...GET ON BOARD!
C'MON, LOSERS! GET OUTTA HERE!
KOFF! KOFF!
UUHHNNFF!
THUMP
FRAGILE
C'MON, CLAYFACE--
FRAGILE
WHEW!
FRAGILE

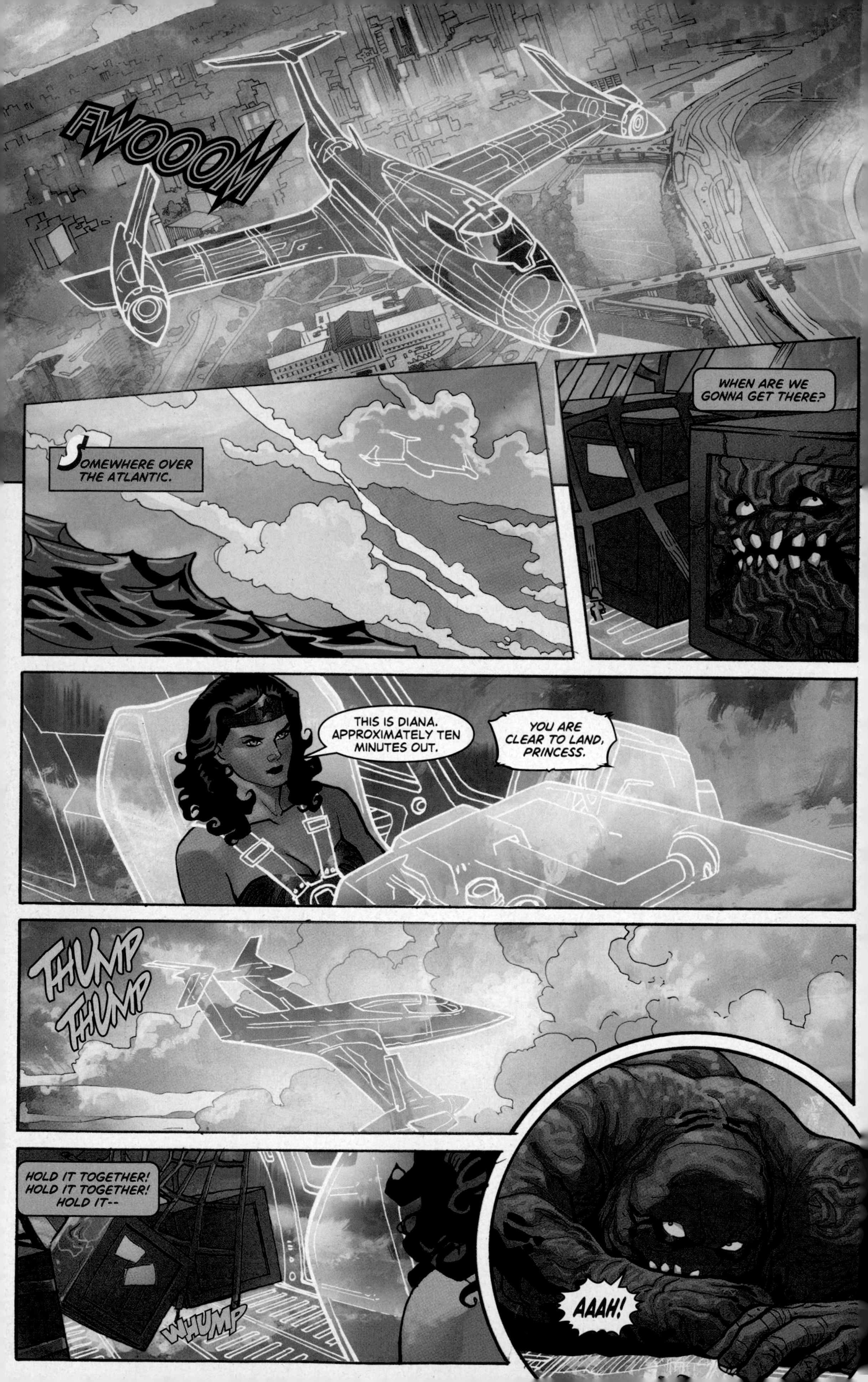
FWOOOM
SOMEWHERE OVER THE ATLANTIC.
WHEN ARE WE GONNA GET THERE?
THIS IS DIANA. APPROXIMATELY TEN MINUTES OUT.
YOU ARE CLEAR TO LAND, PRINCESS.
THUMP THUMP
HOLD IT TOGETHER! HOLD IT TOGETHER! HOLD IT--
WHUMP
AAAH!

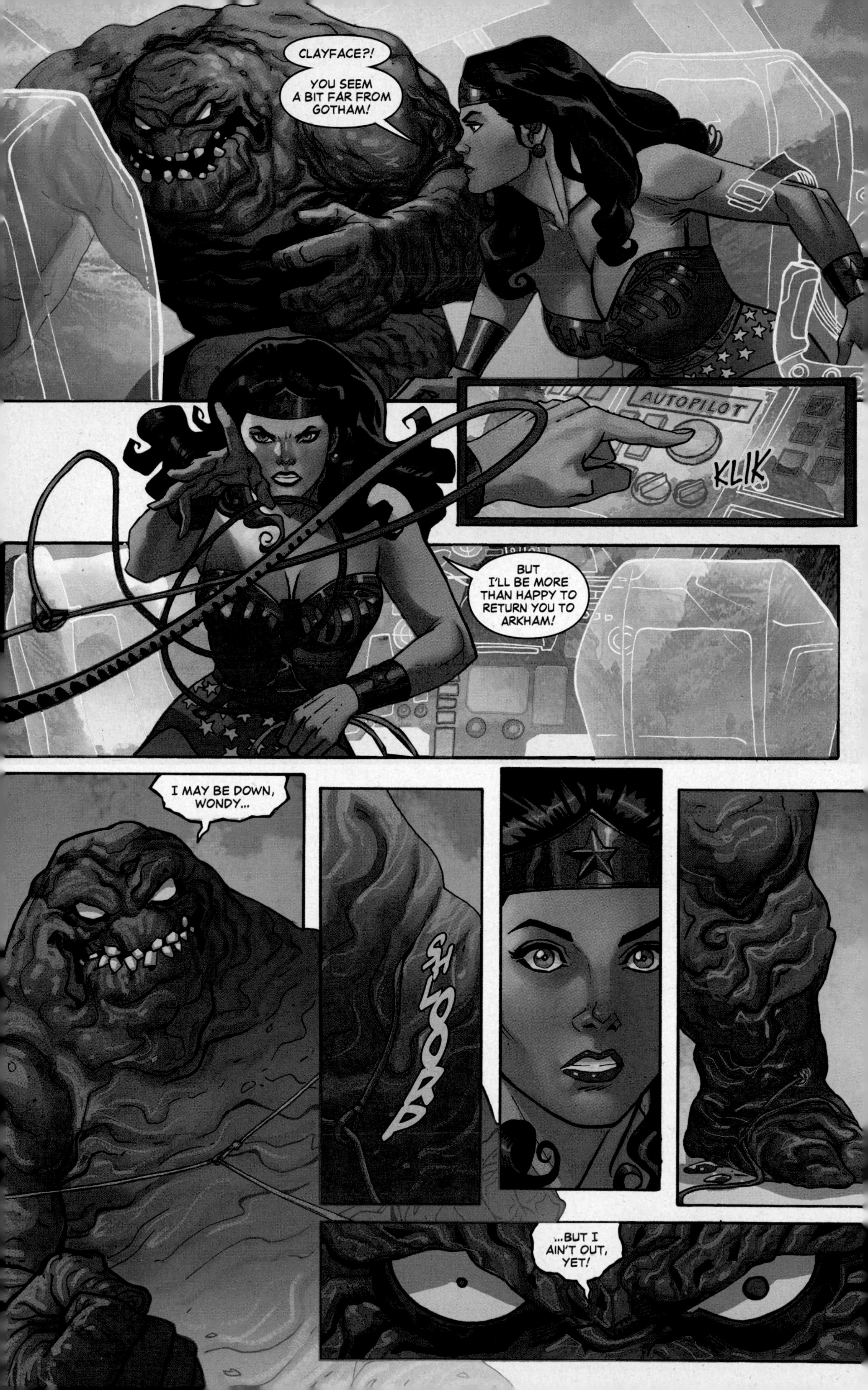
CLAYFACE?!
YOU SEEM A BIT FAR FROM GOTHAM!
AUTOPILOT
KLIK
BUT I'LL BE MORE THAN HAPPY TO RETURN YOU TO ARKHAM!
I MAY BE DOWN, WONDY...
SHLOORP
...BUT I AIN'T OUT, YET!

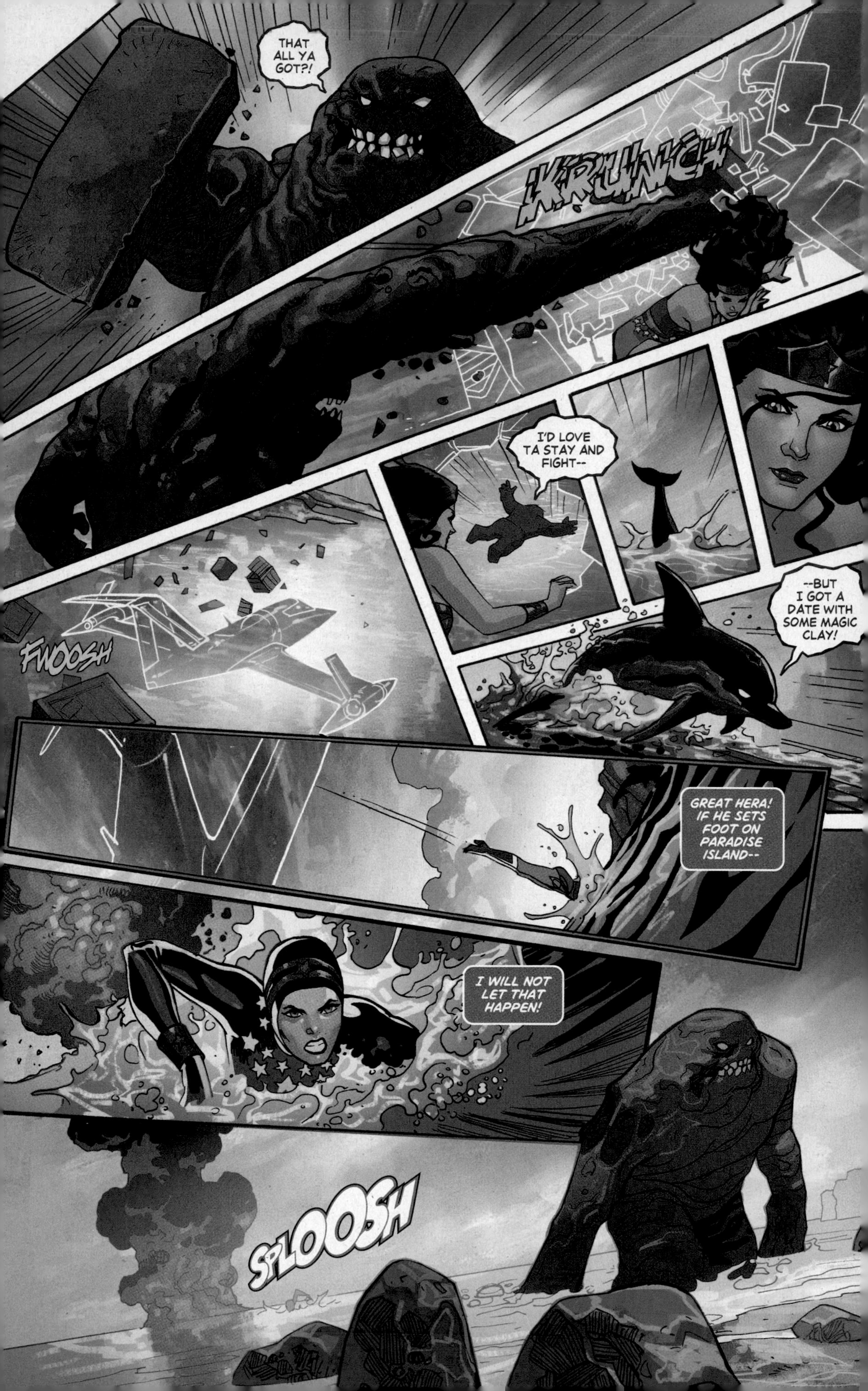
THAT ALL YA GOT?!
KRUNCH
I'D LOVE TA STAY AND FIGHT--
--BUT I GOT A DATE WITH SOME MAGIC CLAY!
FWOOSH
GREAT HERA! IF HE SETS FOOT ON PARADISE ISLAND--
I WILL NOT LET THAT HAPPEN!
SPLOOSH

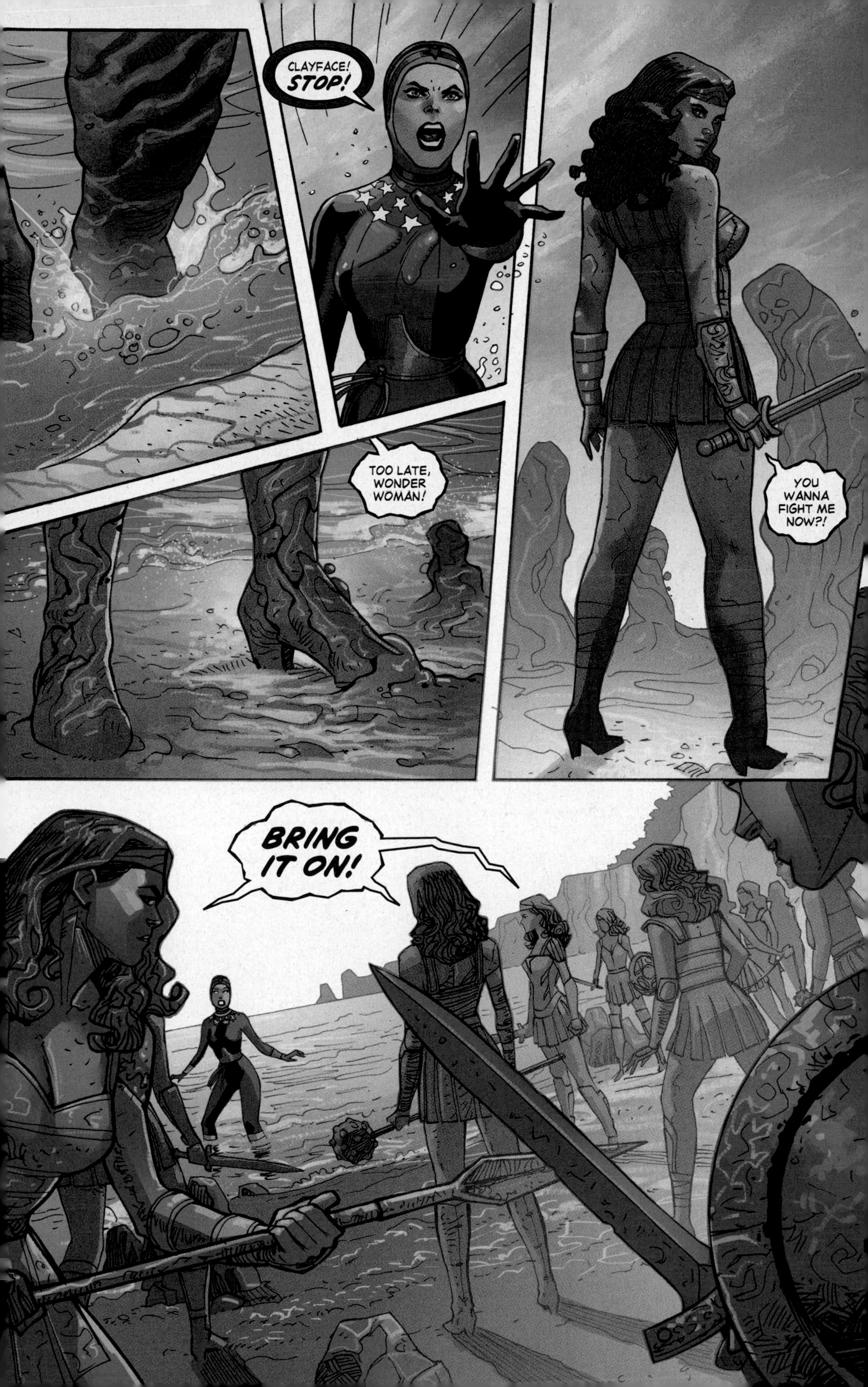
CLAYFACE! STOP!
TOO LATE, WONDER WOMAN!
YOU WANNA FIGHT ME NOW?!
BRING IT ON!

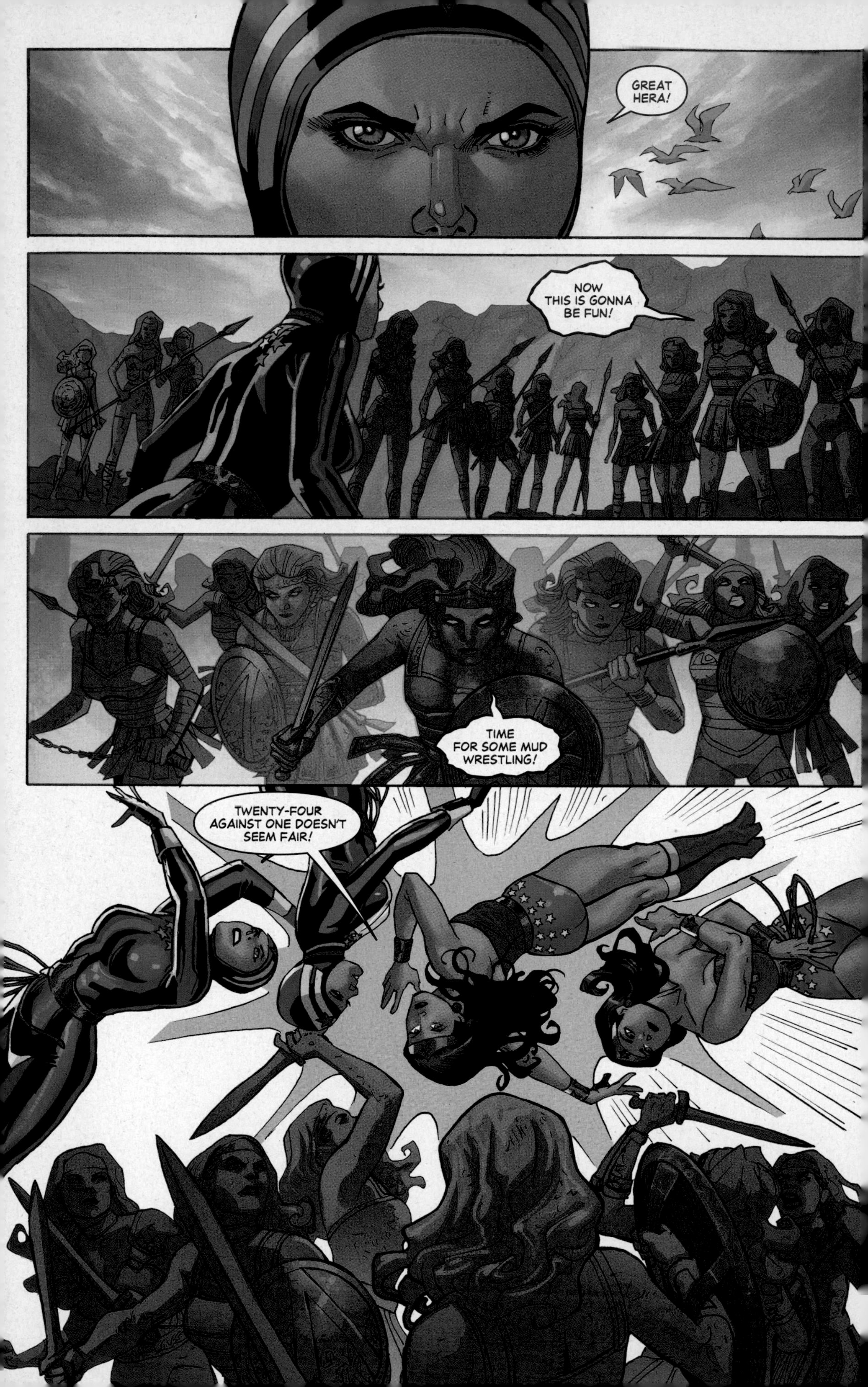
GREAT HERA!
NOW THIS IS GONNA BE FUN!
TIME FOR SOME MUD WRESTLING!
TWENTY-FOUR AGAINST ONE DOESN'T SEEM FAIR!

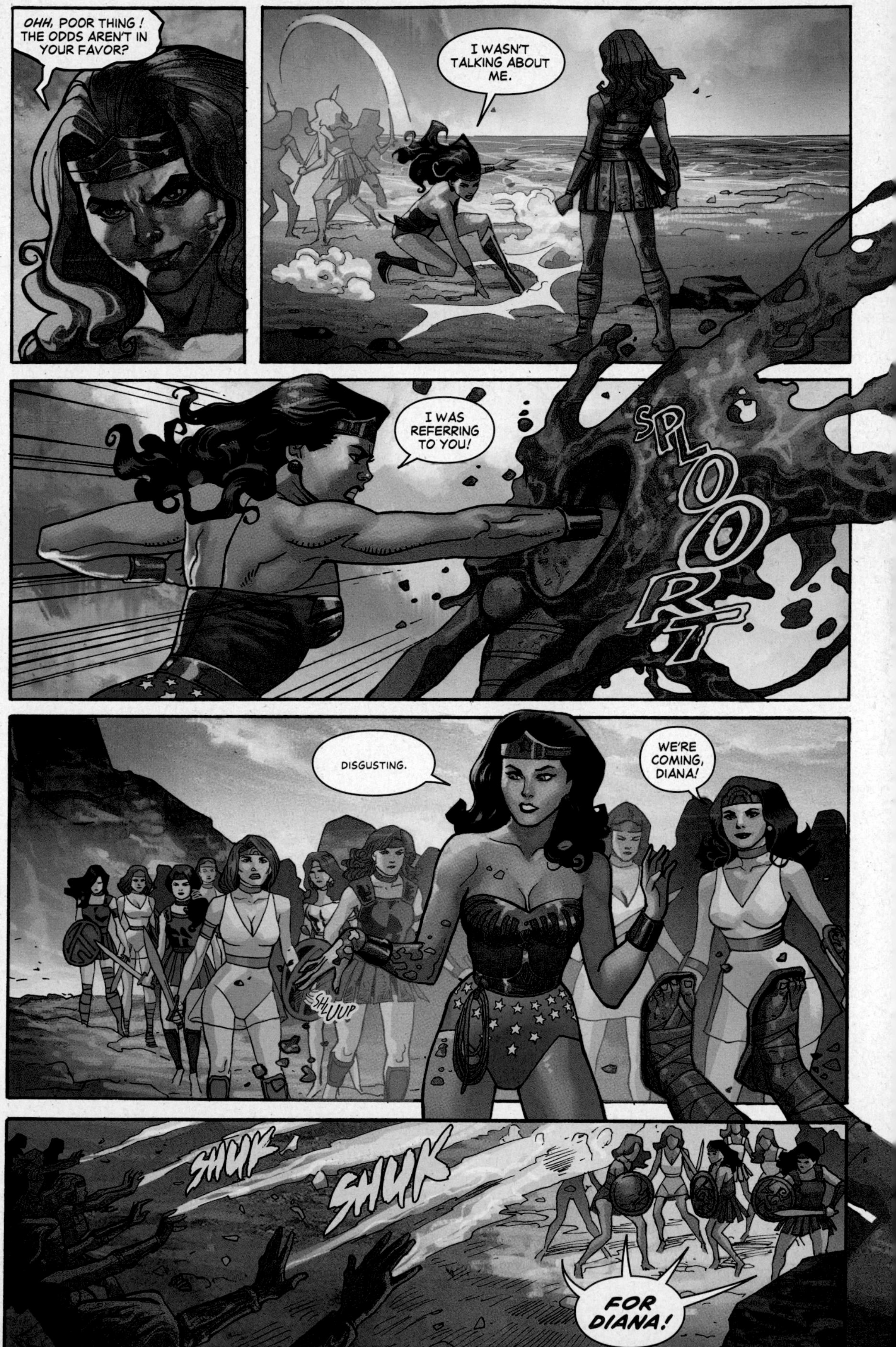
OHH, POOR THING! THE ODDS AREN'T IN YOUR FAVOR?
I WASN'T TALKING ABOUT ME.
I WAS REFERRING TO YOU!
SPLOOORT
DISGUSTING.
WE'RE COMING, DIANA!
SHLUUP
SHUK
SHUK
FOR DIANA!

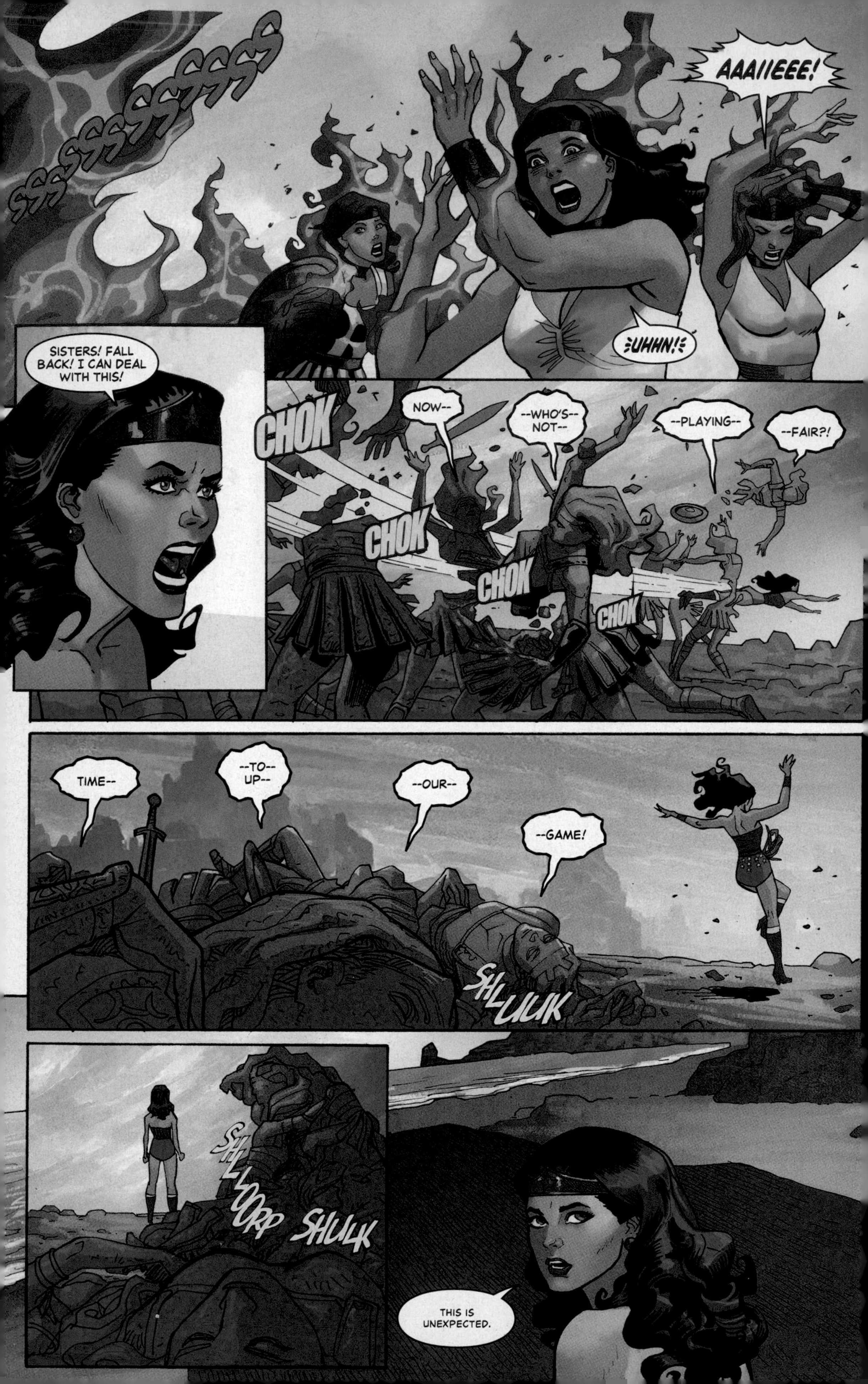
SSSSSSSSSSSSSS
AAAIIEEE!
UHHN!
SISTERS! FALL BACK! I CAN DEAL WITH THIS!
CHOK
NOW--
--WHO'S-- NOT--
--PLAYING--
--FAIR?!
CHOK
CHOK
CHOK
TIME--
--TO-- UP--
--OUR--
--GAME!
SHLUUK
SHLLOORP
SHULK
THIS IS UNEXPECTED.

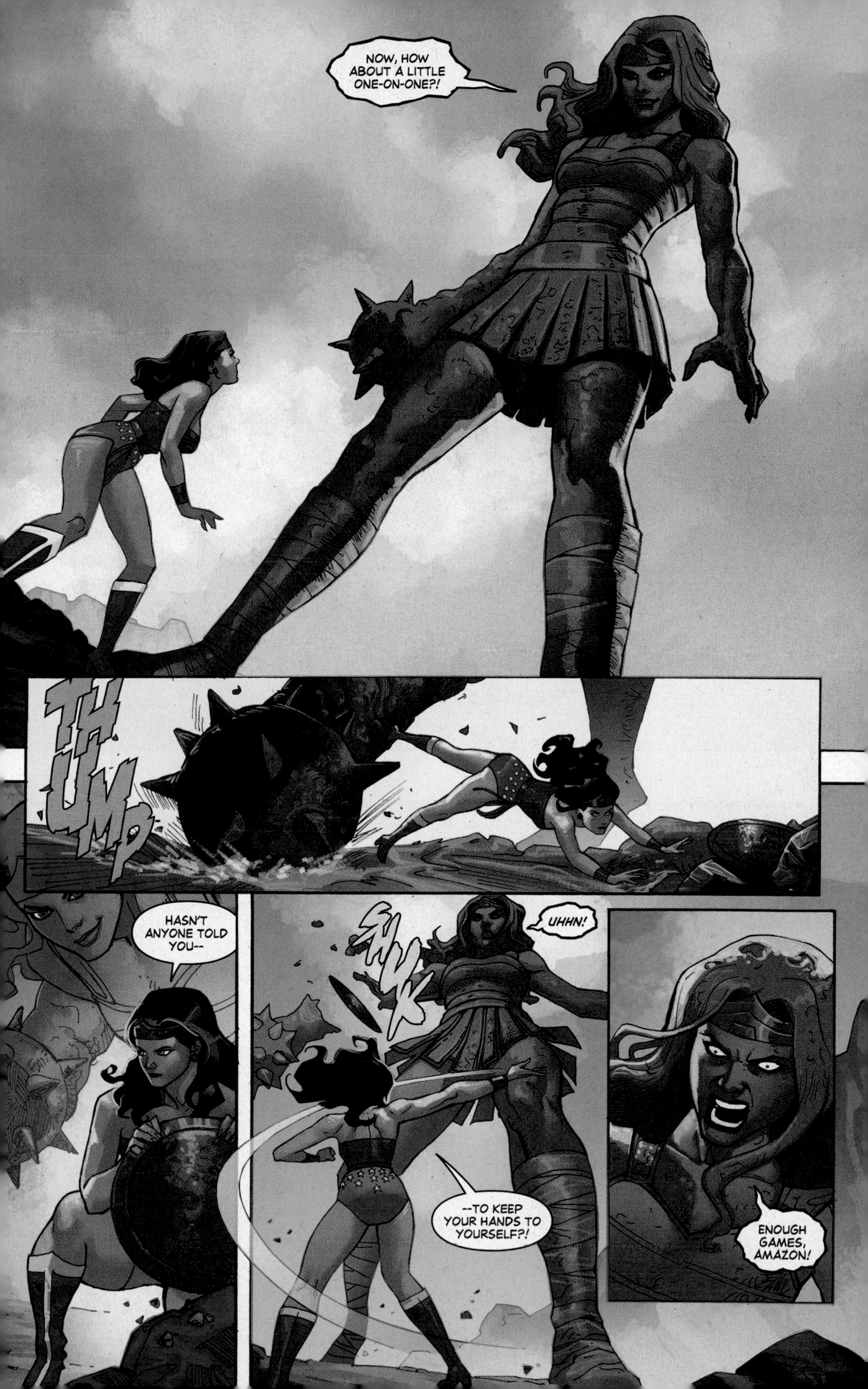
NOW, HOW ABOUT A LITTLE ONE-ON-ONE?!
THUMP
HASN'T ANYONE TOLD YOU--
SHUNK
UHHN!
--TO KEEP YOUR HANDS TO YOURSELF?!
ENOUGH GAMES, AMAZON!

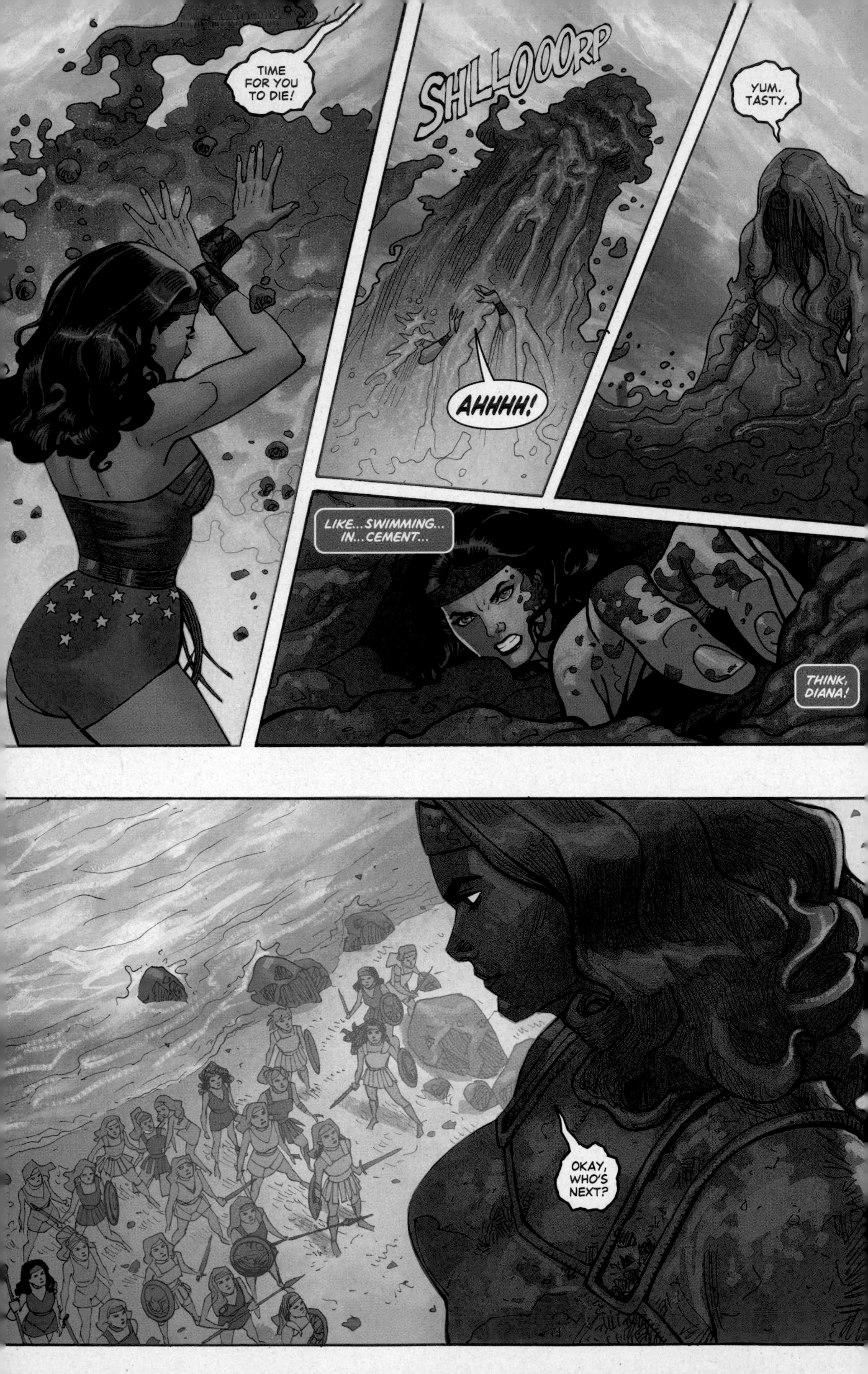
TIME FOR YOU TO DIE!
SHLLOOORP
AHHHH!
YUM. TASTY.
LIKE...SWIMMING... IN...CEMENT...
THINK, DIANA!
OKAY, WHO'S NEXT?

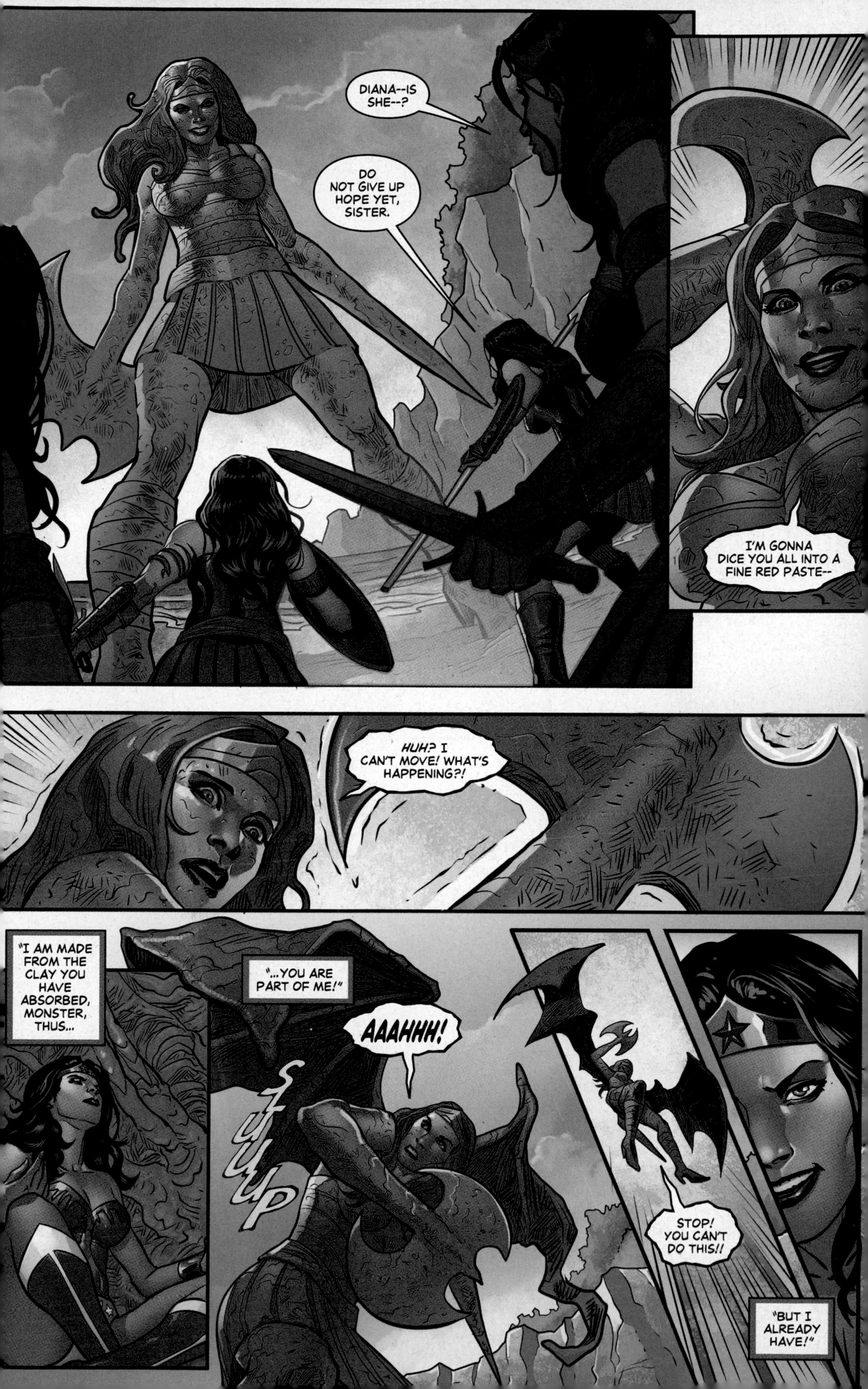
DIANA--IS SHE--?
DO NOT GIVE UP HOPE YET, SISTER.
I'M GONNA DICE YOU ALL INTO A FINE RED PASTE--
HUH? I CAN'T MOVE! WHAT'S HAPPENING?!
"I AM MADE FROM THE CLAY YOU HAVE ABSORBED, MONSTER, THUS...
"...YOU ARE PART OF ME!"
AAAHHH!
SHUUUP
STOP! YOU CAN'T DO THIS!!
"BUT I ALREADY HAVE!"

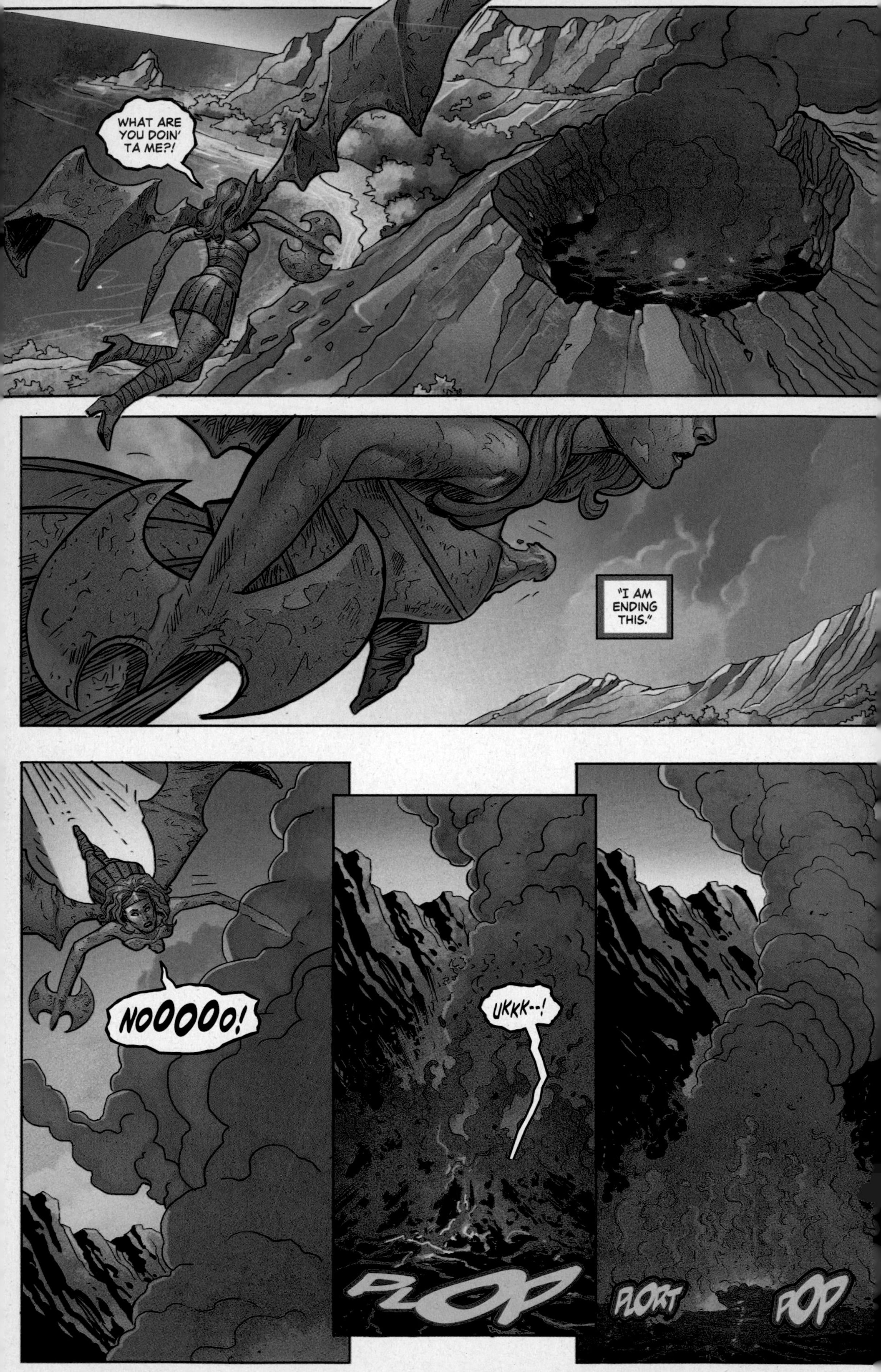
WHAT ARE YOU DOIN' TA ME?!
"I AM ENDING THIS."
NOOOOO!
UKKK--!
PLOP
PLORT
POP

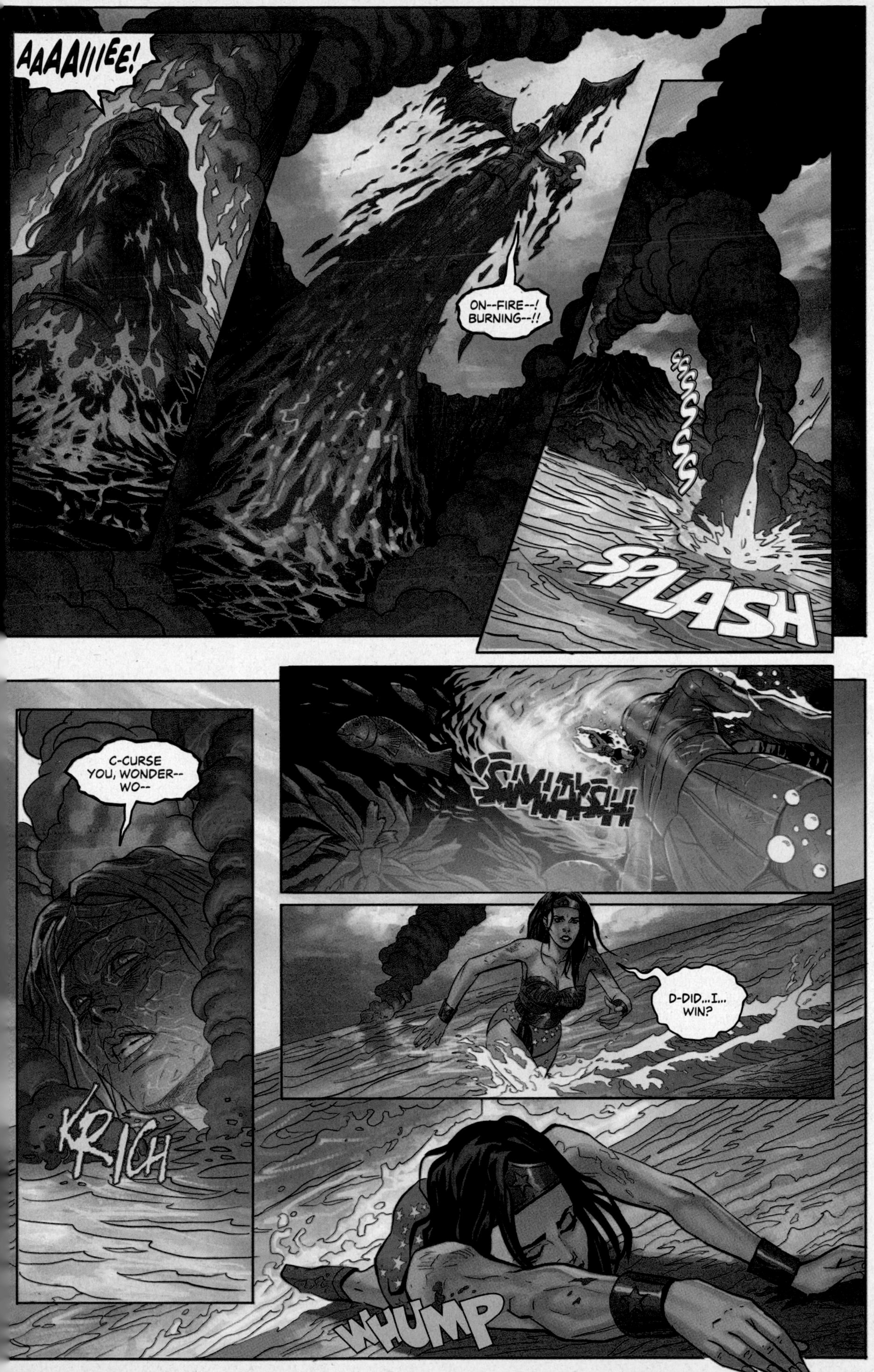
AAAAIIIEE!
ON--FIRE--!
BURNING--!!
SSSSSSS
SPLASH
C-CURSE YOU, WONDER-- WO--
KRICH
SHHHASH!
D-DID...I... WIN?
WHUMP

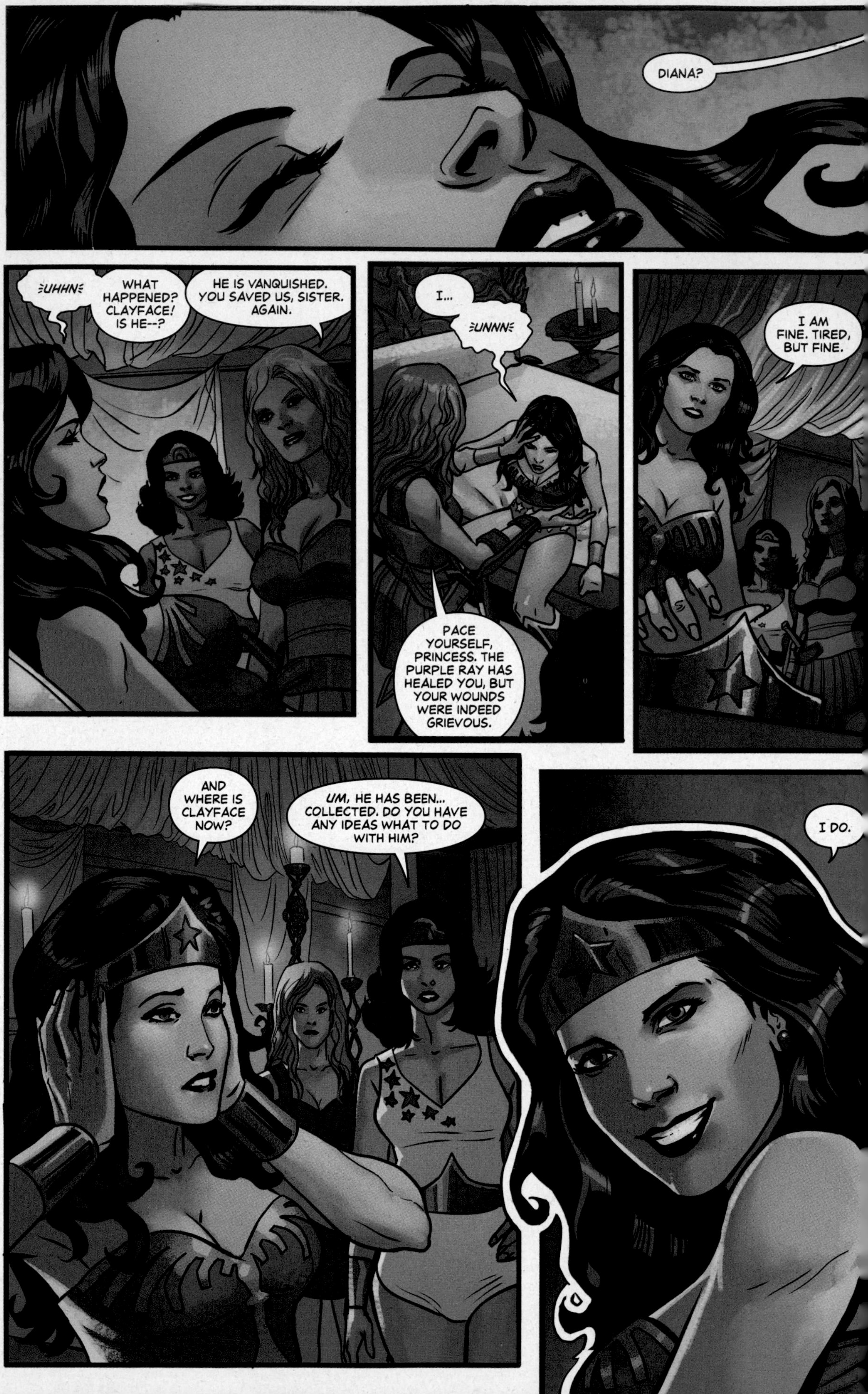
DIANA?
UHHN
WHAT HAPPENED? CLAYFACE! IS HE--?
HE IS VANQUISHED. YOU SAVED US, SISTER. AGAIN.
I...
UNNN
PACE YOURSELF, PRINCESS. THE PURPLE RAY HAS HEALED YOU, BUT YOUR WOUNDS WERE INDEED GRIEVOUS.
I AM FINE. TIRED, BUT FINE.
AND WHERE IS CLAYFACE NOW?
UM, HE HAS BEEN... COLLECTED. DO YOU HAVE ANY IDEAS WHAT TO DO WITH HIM?
I DO.

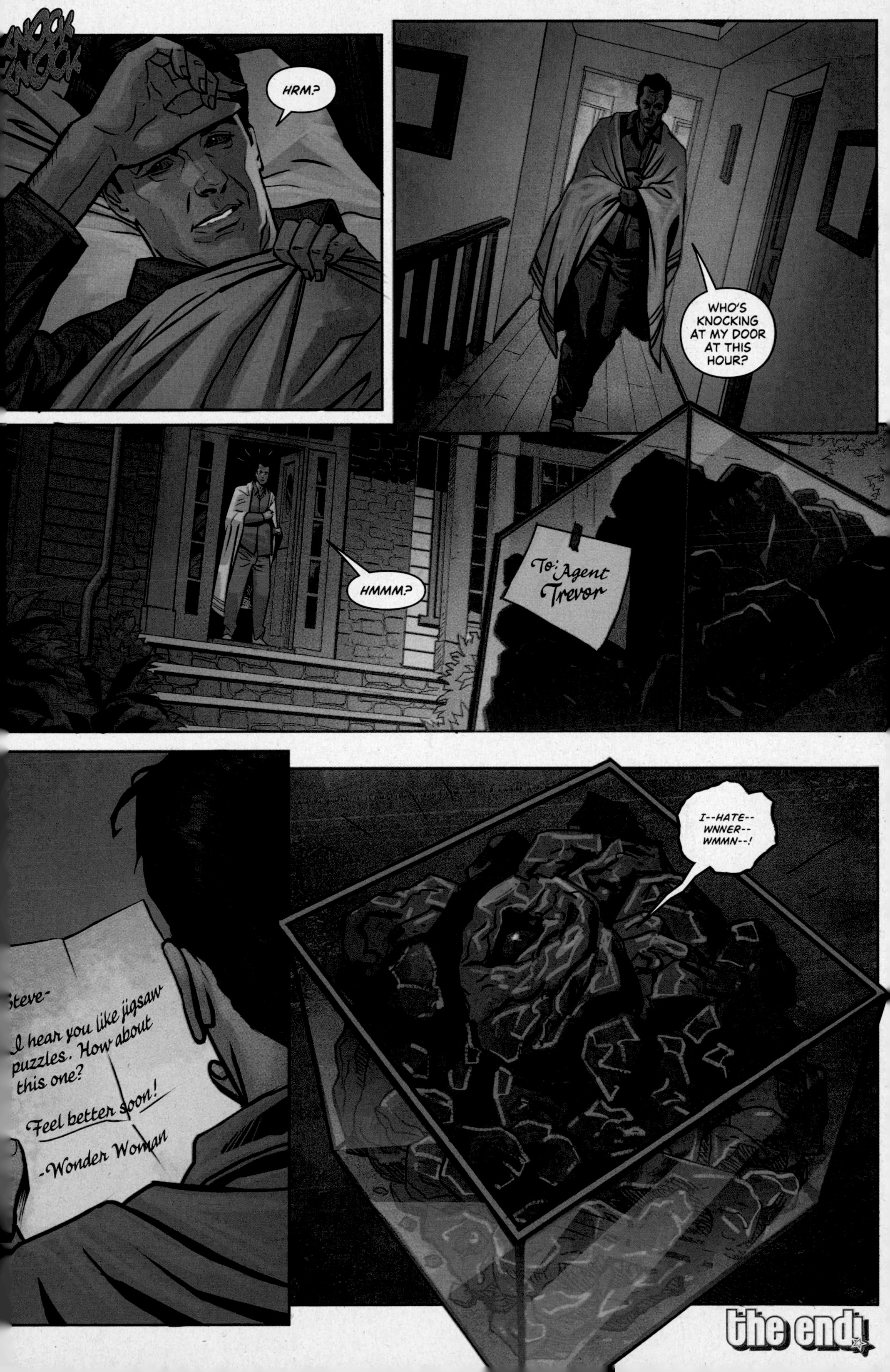
KNOCK KNOCK
HRM?
WHO'S KNOCKING AT MY DOOR AT THIS HOUR?
HMMM?
To: Agent Trevor
Steve-
I hear you like jigsaw puzzles. How about this one?
Feel better soon!
-Wonder Woman
I--HATE--WNNER--WMMN--!
the end

★ ORION THE HUNTER ★

Christos Gage
Ruth Fletcher Gage
Writers

Dario Brizuela
Andres Ponce
Artists

Kelly Fitzpatrick
Colorist

Wes Abbott
Letterer

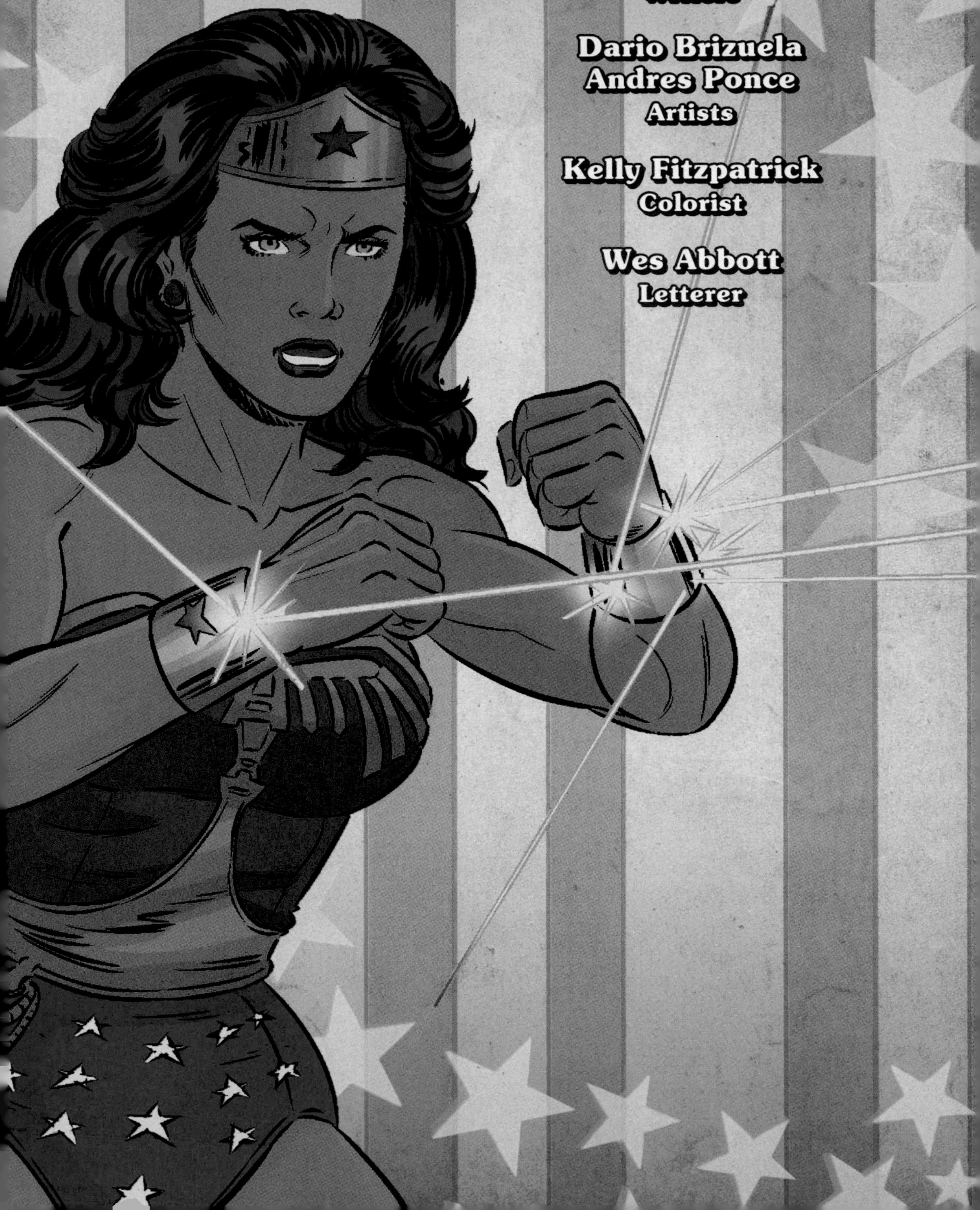

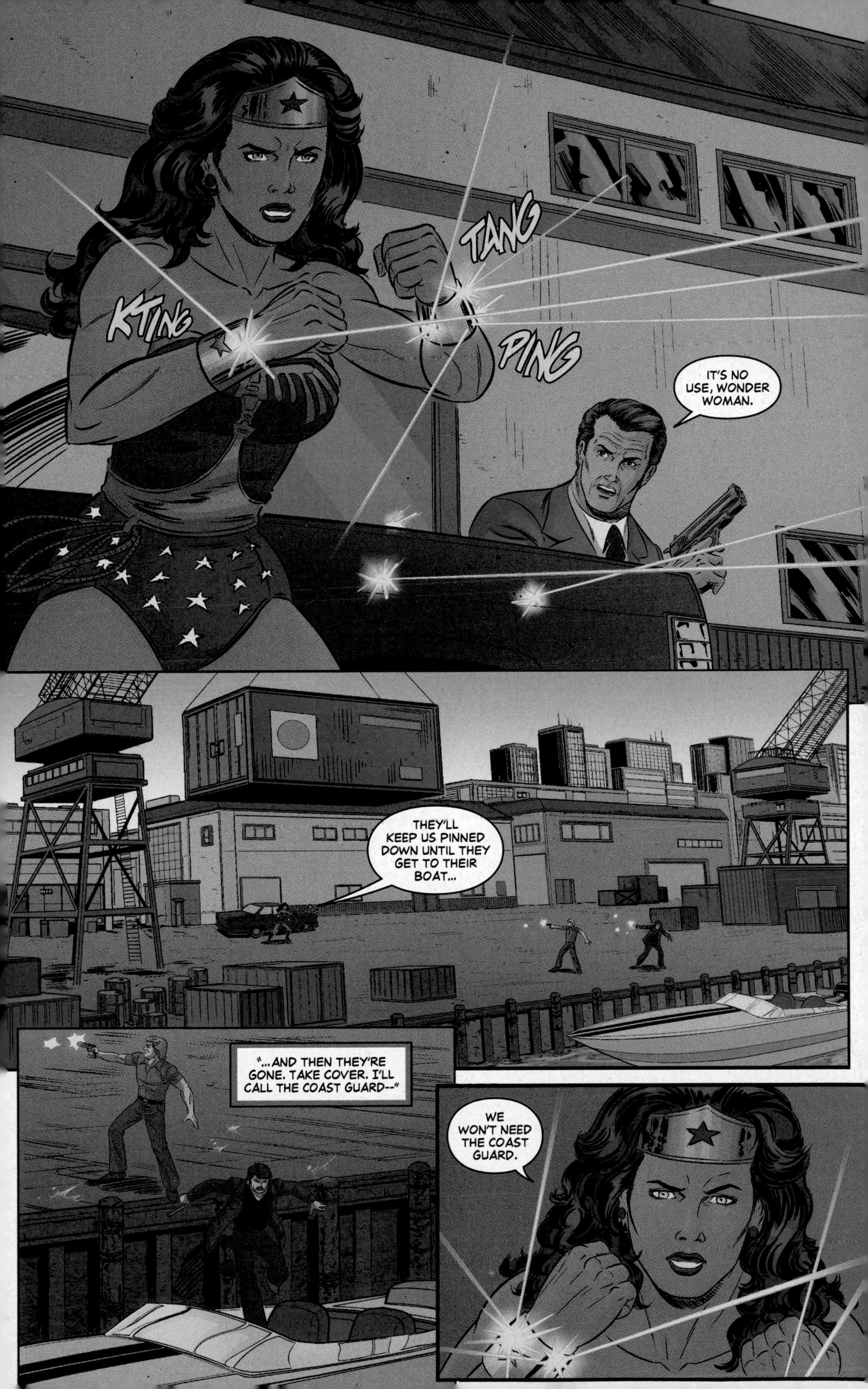
TANG
KTING
PING
IT'S NO USE, WONDER WOMAN.
THEY'LL KEEP US PINNED DOWN UNTIL THEY GET TO THEIR BOAT...
"...AND THEN THEY'RE GONE. TAKE COVER. I'LL CALL THE COAST GUARD--"
WE WON'T NEED THE COAST GUARD.

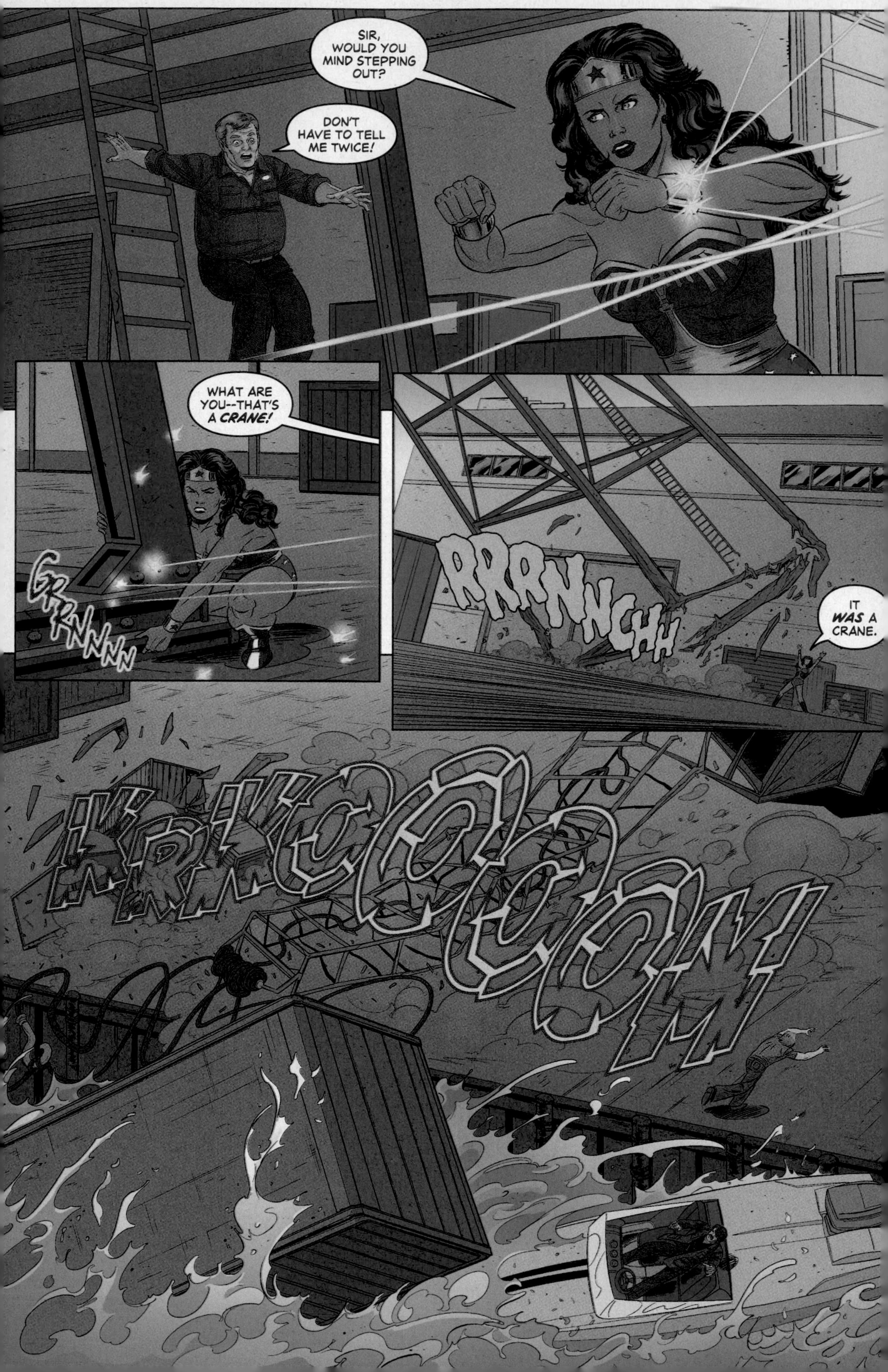
SIR, WOULD YOU MIND STEPPING OUT?
DON'T HAVE TO TELL ME TWICE!
WHAT ARE YOU--THAT'S A CRANE!
GRRNNNNN
RRRNNCHH
IT WAS A CRANE.
KRKOOOOOM

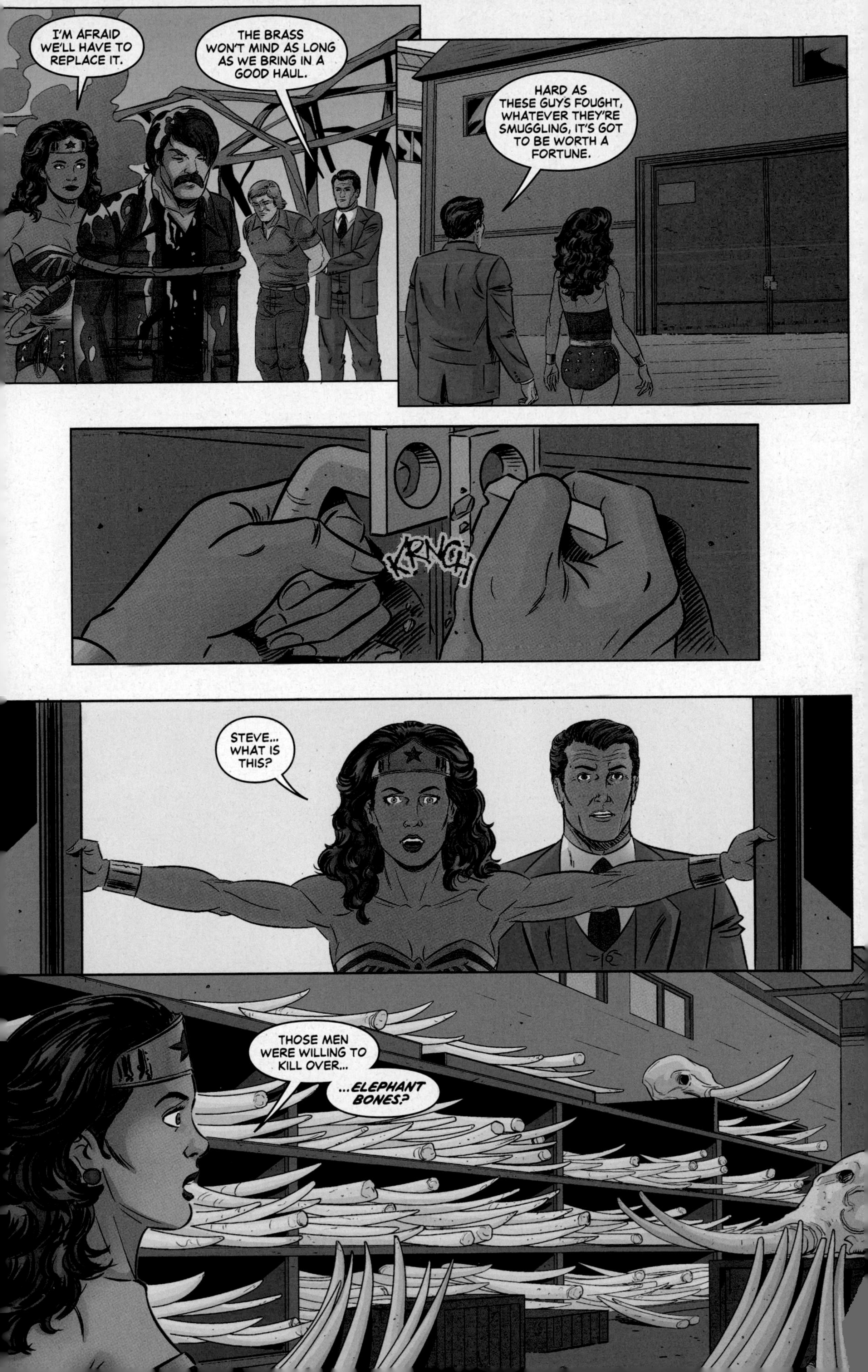
I'M AFRAID WE'LL HAVE TO REPLACE IT.
THE BRASS WON'T MIND AS LONG AS WE BRING IN A GOOD HAUL.
HARD AS THESE GUYS FOUGHT, WHATEVER THEY'RE SMUGGLING, IT'S GOT TO BE WORTH A FORTUNE.
KRNCH
STEVE... WHAT IS THIS?
THOSE MEN WERE WILLING TO KILL OVER...
...ELEPHANT BONES?

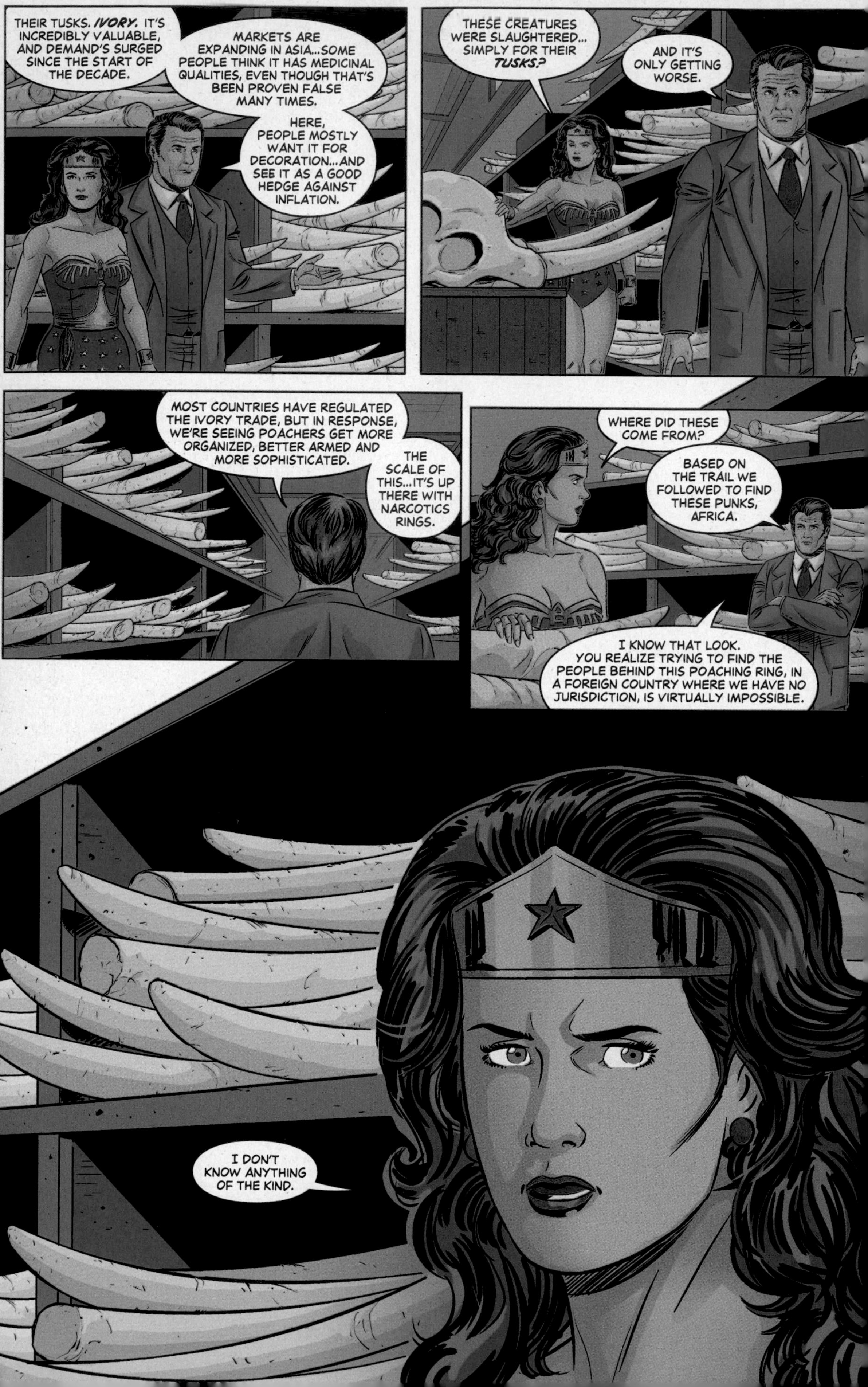
THEIR TUSKS. IVORY. IT'S INCREDIBLY VALUABLE, AND DEMAND'S SURGED SINCE THE START OF THE DECADE.
MARKETS ARE EXPANDING IN ASIA...SOME PEOPLE THINK IT HAS MEDICINAL QUALITIES, EVEN THOUGH THAT'S BEEN PROVEN FALSE MANY TIMES.
HERE, PEOPLE MOSTLY WANT IT FOR DECORATION...AND SEE IT AS A GOOD HEDGE AGAINST INFLATION.
THESE CREATURES WERE SLAUGHTERED... SIMPLY FOR THEIR TUSKS?
AND IT'S ONLY GETTING WORSE.
MOST COUNTRIES HAVE REGULATED THE IVORY TRADE, BUT IN RESPONSE, WE'RE SEEING POACHERS GET MORE ORGANIZED, BETTER ARMED AND MORE SOPHISTICATED.
THE SCALE OF THIS...IT'S UP THERE WITH NARCOTICS RINGS.
WHERE DID THESE COME FROM?
BASED ON THE TRAIL WE FOLLOWED TO FIND THESE PUNKS, AFRICA.
I KNOW THAT LOOK. YOU REALIZE TRYING TO FIND THE PEOPLE BEHIND THIS POACHING RING, IN A FOREIGN COUNTRY WHERE WE HAVE NO JURISDICTION, IS VIRTUALLY IMPOSSIBLE.
I DON'T KNOW ANYTHING OF THE KIND.

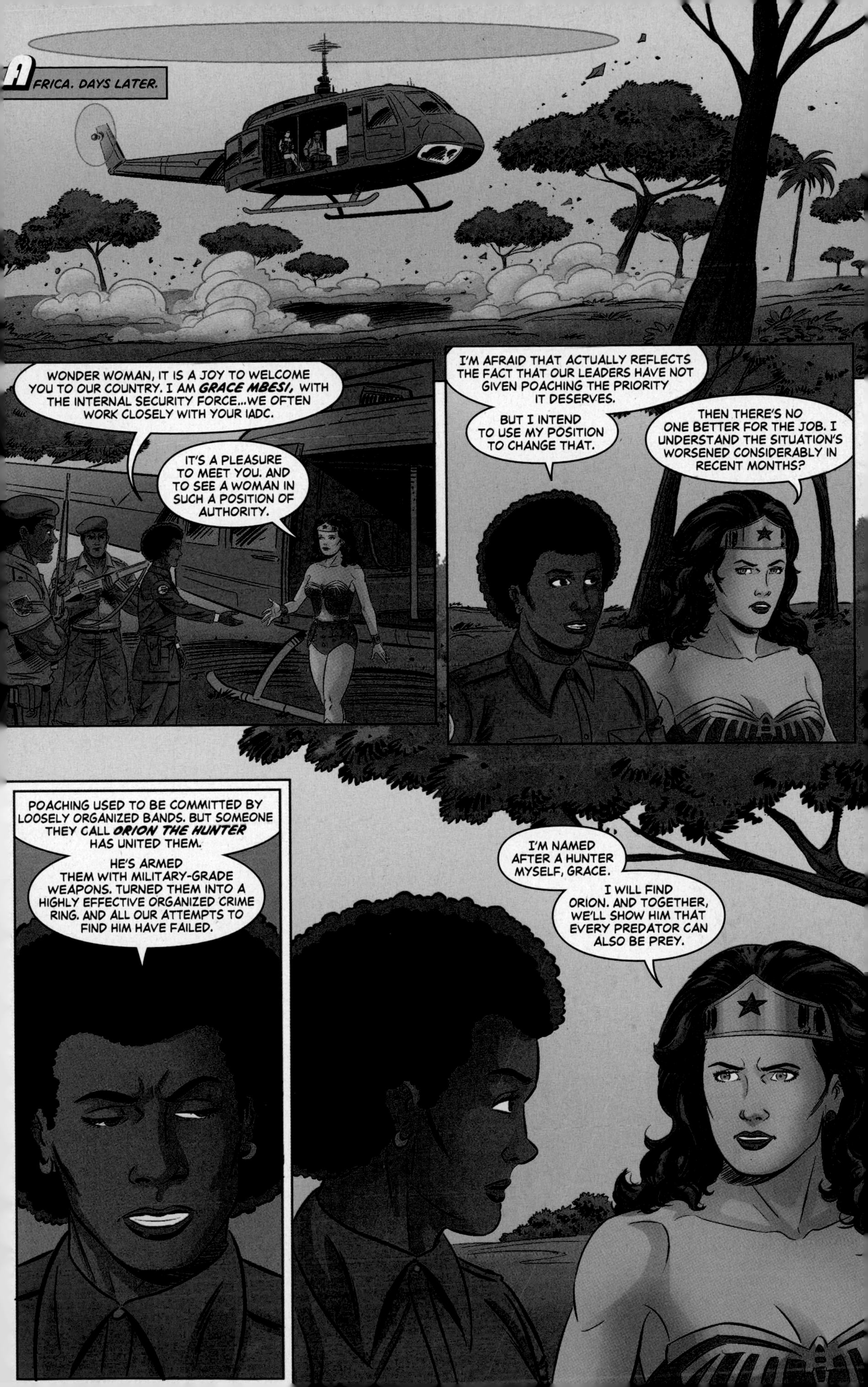
AFRICA. DAYS LATER.
WONDER WOMAN, IT IS A JOY TO WELCOME YOU TO OUR COUNTRY. I AM **GRACE MBESI**, WITH THE INTERNAL SECURITY FORCE...WE OFTEN WORK CLOSELY WITH YOUR IADC.
IT'S A PLEASURE TO MEET YOU. AND TO SEE A WOMAN IN SUCH A POSITION OF AUTHORITY.
I'M AFRAID THAT ACTUALLY REFLECTS THE FACT THAT OUR LEADERS HAVE NOT GIVEN POACHING THE PRIORITY IT DESERVES.
BUT I INTEND TO USE MY POSITION TO CHANGE THAT.
THEN THERE'S NO ONE BETTER FOR THE JOB. I UNDERSTAND THE SITUATION'S WORSENED CONSIDERABLY IN RECENT MONTHS?
POACHING USED TO BE COMMITTED BY LOOSELY ORGANIZED BANDS. BUT SOMEONE THEY CALL **ORION THE HUNTER** HAS UNITED THEM.
HE'S ARMED THEM WITH MILITARY-GRADE WEAPONS. TURNED THEM INTO A HIGHLY EFFECTIVE ORGANIZED CRIME RING. AND ALL OUR ATTEMPTS TO FIND HIM HAVE FAILED.
I'M NAMED AFTER A HUNTER MYSELF, GRACE.
I WILL FIND ORION. AND TOGETHER, WE'LL SHOW HIM THAT EVERY PREDATOR CAN ALSO BE PREY.

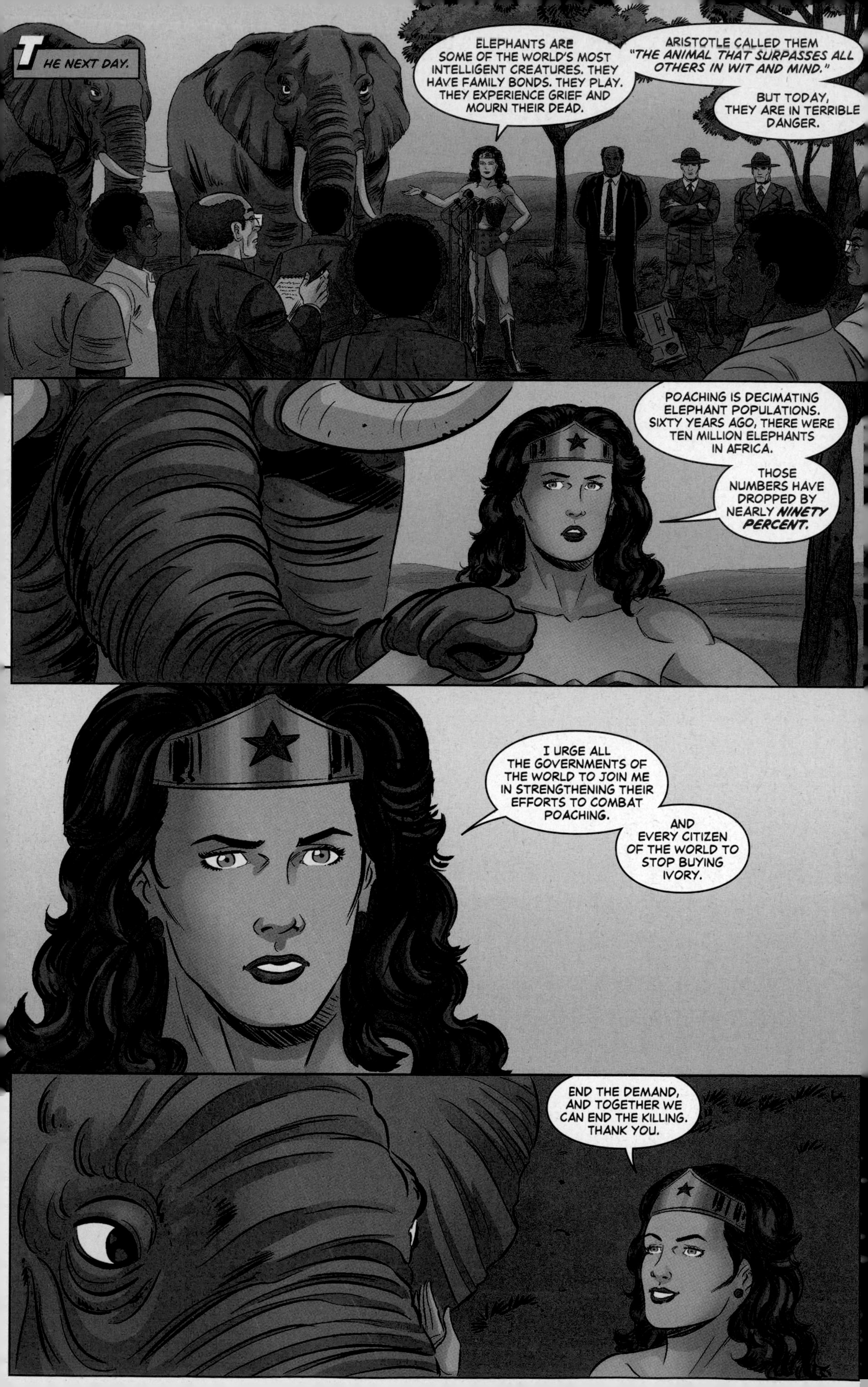
THE NEXT DAY.
ELEPHANTS ARE SOME OF THE WORLD'S MOST INTELLIGENT CREATURES. THEY HAVE FAMILY BONDS. THEY PLAY. THEY EXPERIENCE GRIEF AND MOURN THEIR DEAD.
ARISTOTLE CALLED THEM "THE ANIMAL THAT SURPASSES ALL OTHERS IN WIT AND MIND."
BUT TODAY, THEY ARE IN TERRIBLE DANGER.
POACHING IS DECIMATING ELEPHANT POPULATIONS. SIXTY YEARS AGO, THERE WERE TEN MILLION ELEPHANTS IN AFRICA.
THOSE NUMBERS HAVE DROPPED BY NEARLY NINETY PERCENT.
I URGE ALL THE GOVERNMENTS OF THE WORLD TO JOIN ME IN STRENGTHENING THEIR EFFORTS TO COMBAT POACHING.
AND EVERY CITIZEN OF THE WORLD TO STOP BUYING IVORY.
END THE DEMAND, AND TOGETHER WE CAN END THE KILLING. THANK YOU.

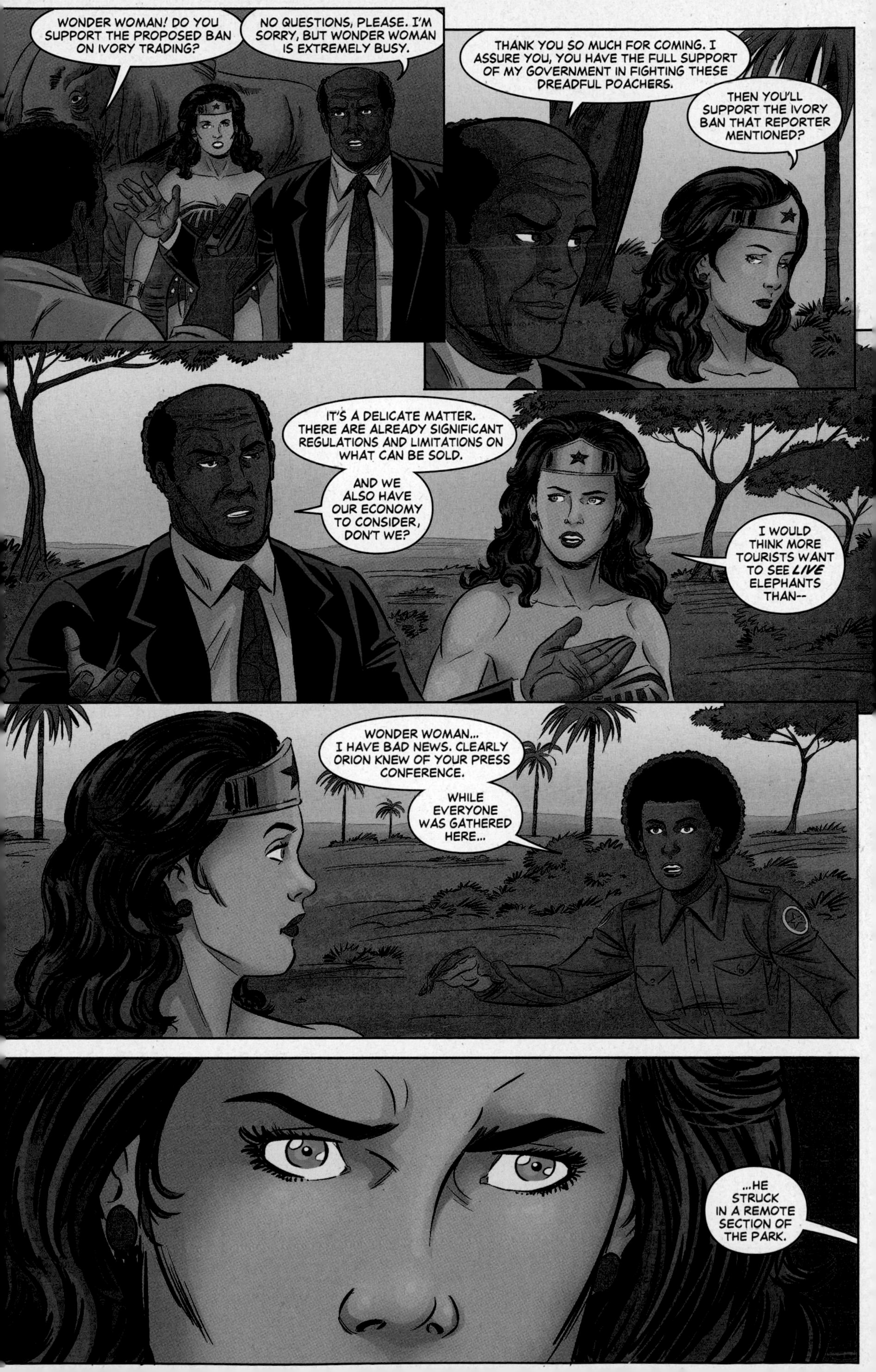
WONDER WOMAN! DO YOU SUPPORT THE PROPOSED BAN ON IVORY TRADING?
NO QUESTIONS, PLEASE. I'M SORRY, BUT WONDER WOMAN IS EXTREMELY BUSY.
THANK YOU SO MUCH FOR COMING. I ASSURE YOU, YOU HAVE THE FULL SUPPORT OF MY GOVERNMENT IN FIGHTING THESE DREADFUL POACHERS.
THEN YOU'LL SUPPORT THE IVORY BAN THAT REPORTER MENTIONED?
IT'S A DELICATE MATTER. THERE ARE ALREADY SIGNIFICANT REGULATIONS AND LIMITATIONS ON WHAT CAN BE SOLD.
AND WE ALSO HAVE OUR ECONOMY TO CONSIDER, DON'T WE?
I WOULD THINK MORE TOURISTS WANT TO SEE LIVE ELEPHANTS THAN--
WONDER WOMAN... I HAVE BAD NEWS. CLEARLY ORION KNEW OF YOUR PRESS CONFERENCE.
WHILE EVERYONE WAS GATHERED HERE...
...HE STRUCK IN A REMOTE SECTION OF THE PARK.

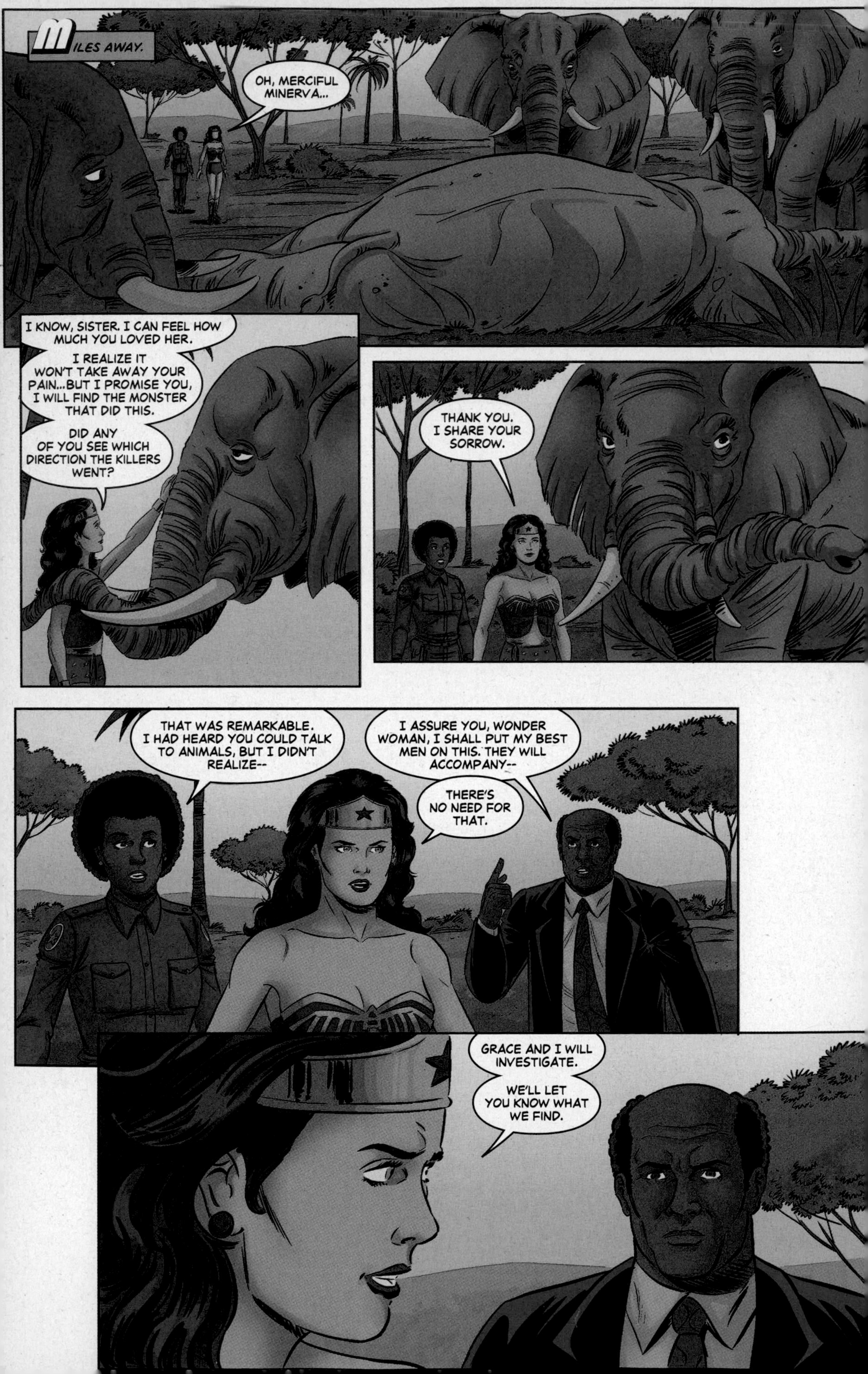
MILES AWAY.
OH, MERCIFUL MINERVA...
I KNOW, SISTER. I CAN FEEL HOW MUCH YOU LOVED HER.
I REALIZE IT WON'T TAKE AWAY YOUR PAIN...BUT I PROMISE YOU, I WILL FIND THE MONSTER THAT DID THIS.
DID ANY OF YOU SEE WHICH DIRECTION THE KILLERS WENT?
THANK YOU. I SHARE YOUR SORROW.
THAT WAS REMARKABLE. I HAD HEARD YOU COULD TALK TO ANIMALS, BUT I DIDN'T REALIZE--
I ASSURE YOU, WONDER WOMAN, I SHALL PUT MY BEST MEN ON THIS. THEY WILL ACCOMPANY--
THERE'S NO NEED FOR THAT.
GRACE AND I WILL INVESTIGATE.
WE'LL LET YOU KNOW WHAT WE FIND.

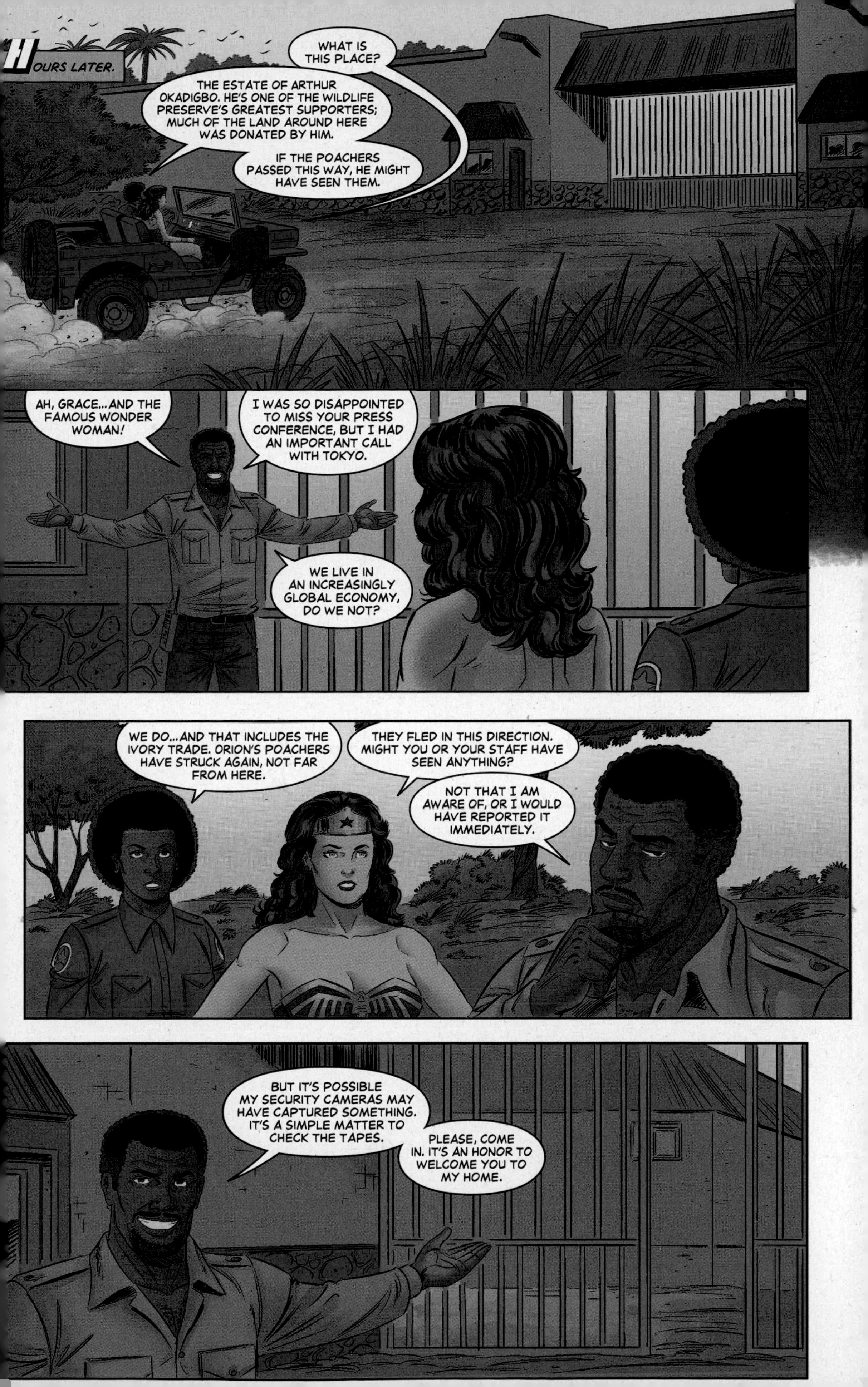
HOURS LATER.
WHAT IS THIS PLACE?
THE ESTATE OF ARTHUR OKADIGBO. HE'S ONE OF THE WILDLIFE PRESERVE'S GREATEST SUPPORTERS; MUCH OF THE LAND AROUND HERE WAS DONATED BY HIM.
IF THE POACHERS PASSED THIS WAY, HE MIGHT HAVE SEEN THEM.
AH, GRACE...AND THE FAMOUS WONDER WOMAN!
I WAS SO DISAPPOINTED TO MISS YOUR PRESS CONFERENCE, BUT I HAD AN IMPORTANT CALL WITH TOKYO.
WE LIVE IN AN INCREASINGLY GLOBAL ECONOMY, DO WE NOT?
WE DO...AND THAT INCLUDES THE IVORY TRADE. ORION'S POACHERS HAVE STRUCK AGAIN, NOT FAR FROM HERE.
THEY FLED IN THIS DIRECTION. MIGHT YOU OR YOUR STAFF HAVE SEEN ANYTHING?
NOT THAT I AM AWARE OF, OR I WOULD HAVE REPORTED IT IMMEDIATELY.
BUT IT'S POSSIBLE MY SECURITY CAMERAS MAY HAVE CAPTURED SOMETHING. IT'S A SIMPLE MATTER TO CHECK THE TAPES.
PLEASE, COME IN. IT'S AN HONOR TO WELCOME YOU TO MY HOME.

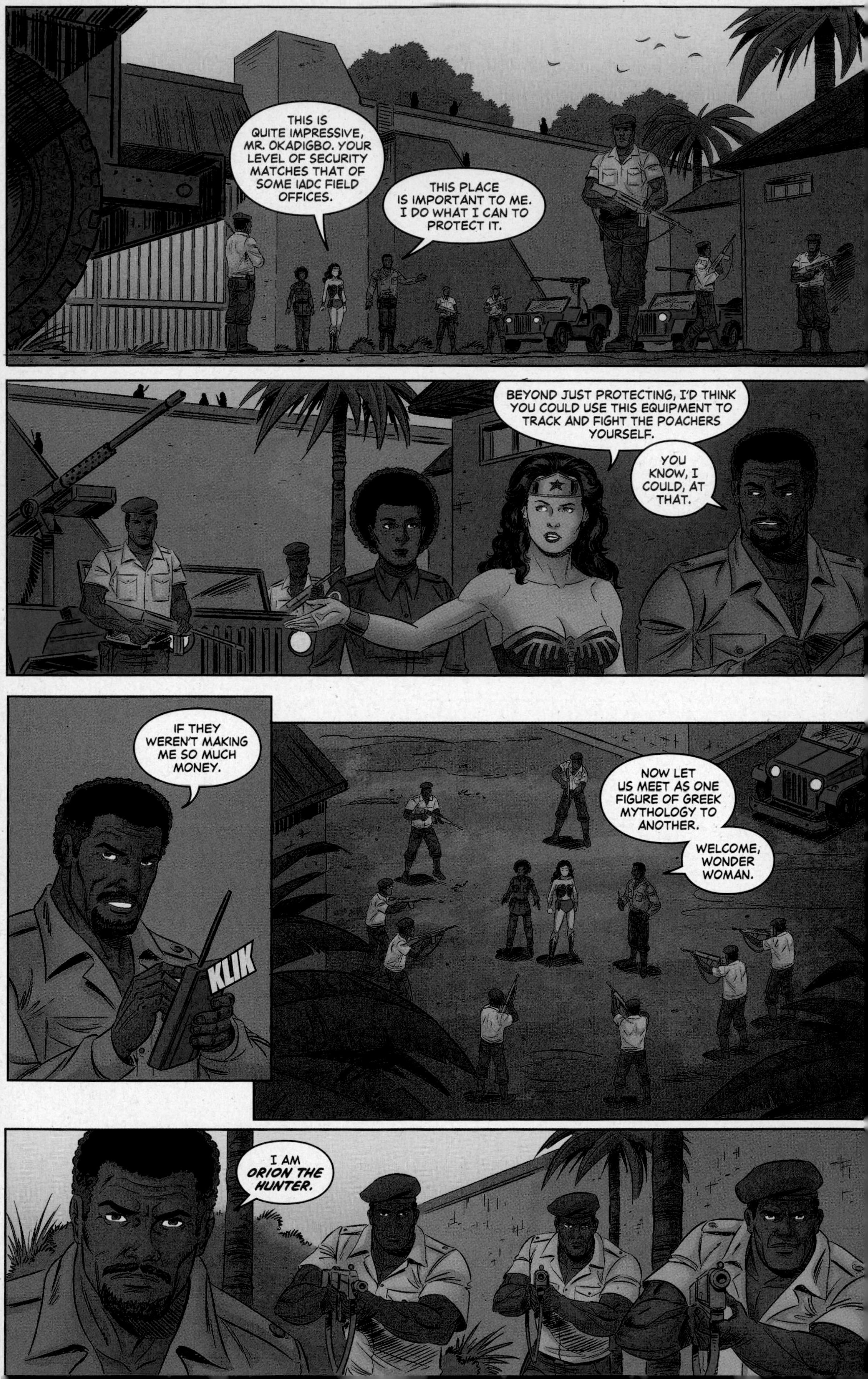
THIS IS QUITE IMPRESSIVE, MR. OKADIGBO. YOUR LEVEL OF SECURITY MATCHES THAT OF SOME IADC FIELD OFFICES.
THIS PLACE IS IMPORTANT TO ME. I DO WHAT I CAN TO PROTECT IT.
BEYOND JUST PROTECTING, I'D THINK YOU COULD USE THIS EQUIPMENT TO TRACK AND FIGHT THE POACHERS YOURSELF.
YOU KNOW, I COULD, AT THAT.
IF THEY WEREN'T MAKING ME SO MUCH MONEY.
KLIK
NOW LET US MEET AS ONE FIGURE OF GREEK MYTHOLOGY TO ANOTHER.
WELCOME, WONDER WOMAN.
I AM ORION THE HUNTER.

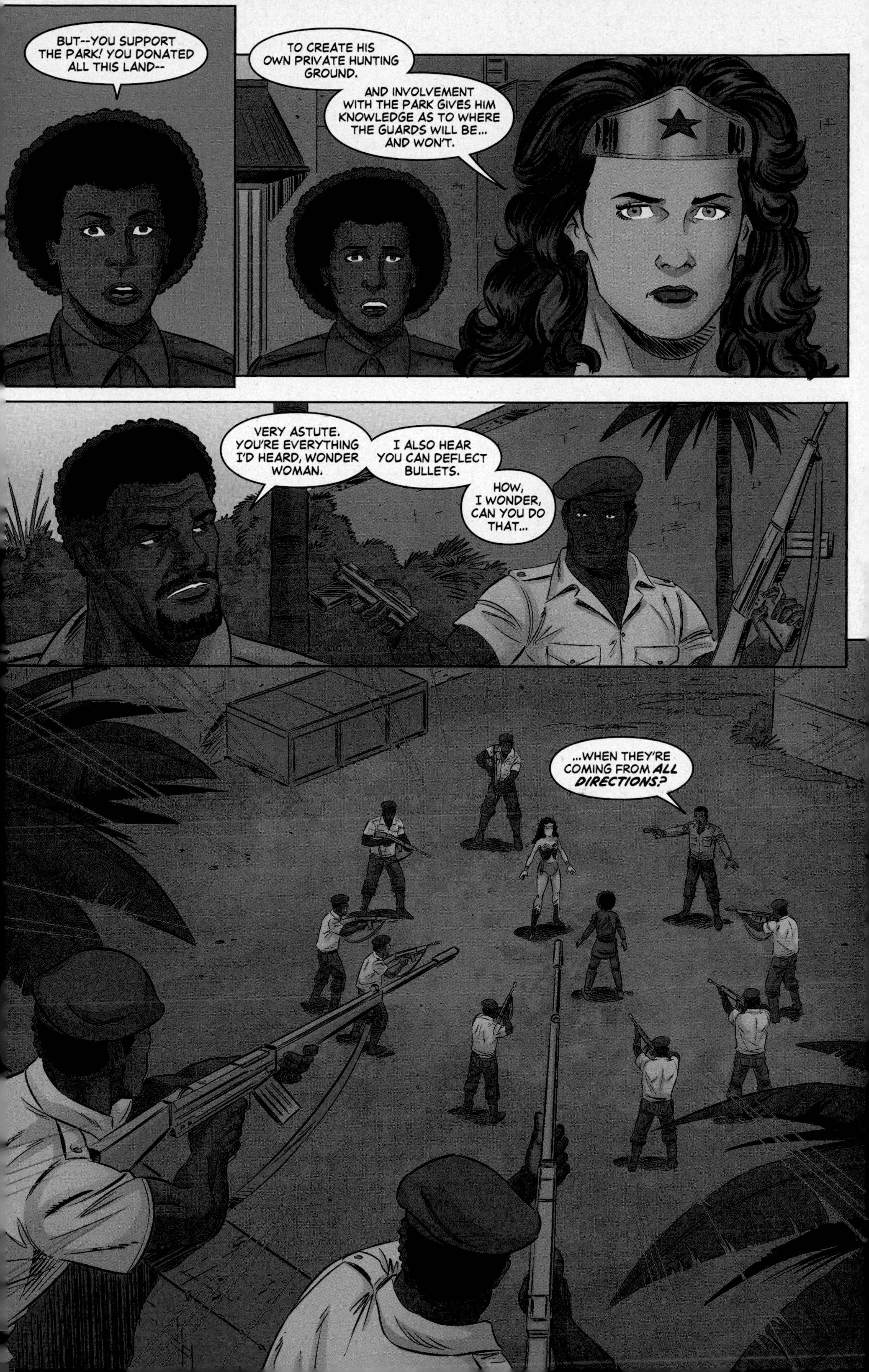
BUT--YOU SUPPORT THE PARK! YOU DONATED ALL THIS LAND--
TO CREATE HIS OWN PRIVATE HUNTING GROUND.
AND INVOLVEMENT WITH THE PARK GIVES HIM KNOWLEDGE AS TO WHERE THE GUARDS WILL BE... AND WON'T.
VERY ASTUTE. YOU'RE EVERYTHING I'D HEARD, WONDER WOMAN.
I ALSO HEAR YOU CAN DEFLECT BULLETS.
HOW, I WONDER, CAN YOU DO THAT...
...WHEN THEY'RE COMING FROM ALL DIRECTIONS?

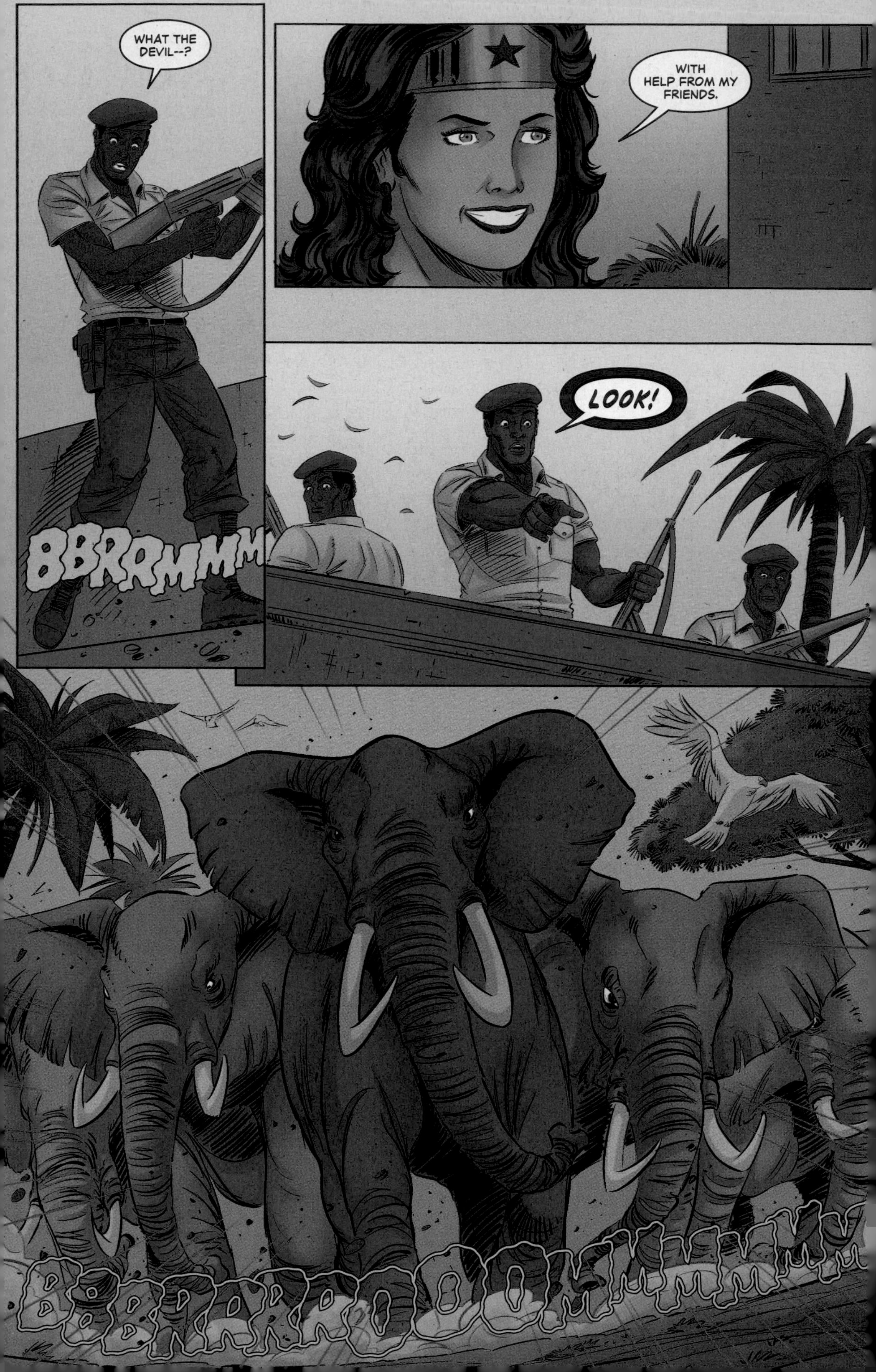
WHAT THE DEVIL--?
BBRRMMM
WITH HELP FROM MY FRIENDS.
LOOK!
BBBRRRRROOOMMMMMMM

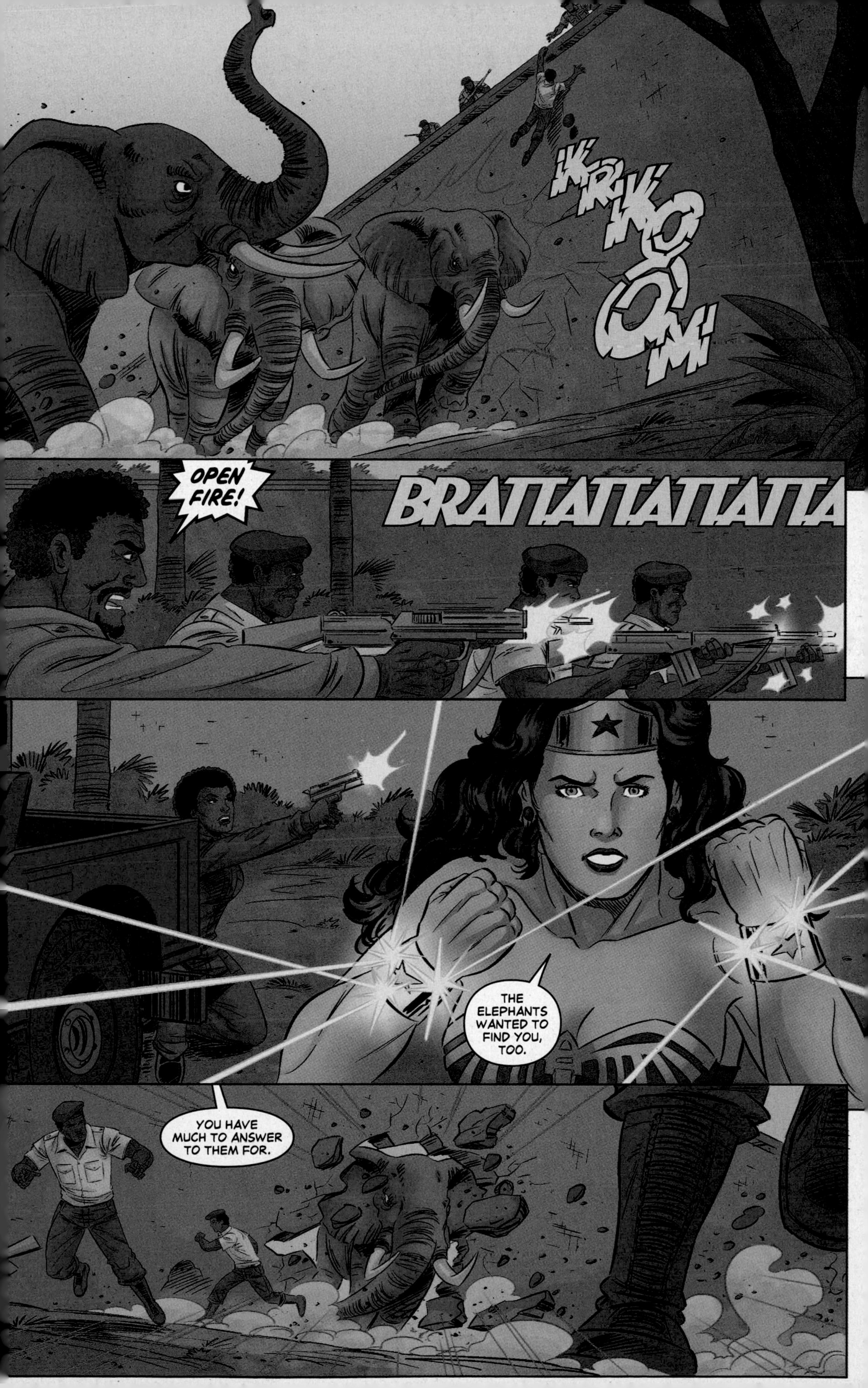
KRKOOM
OPEN FIRE!
BRATTATTATTATTA
THE ELEPHANTS WANTED TO FIND YOU, TOO.
YOU HAVE MUCH TO ANSWER TO THEM FOR.

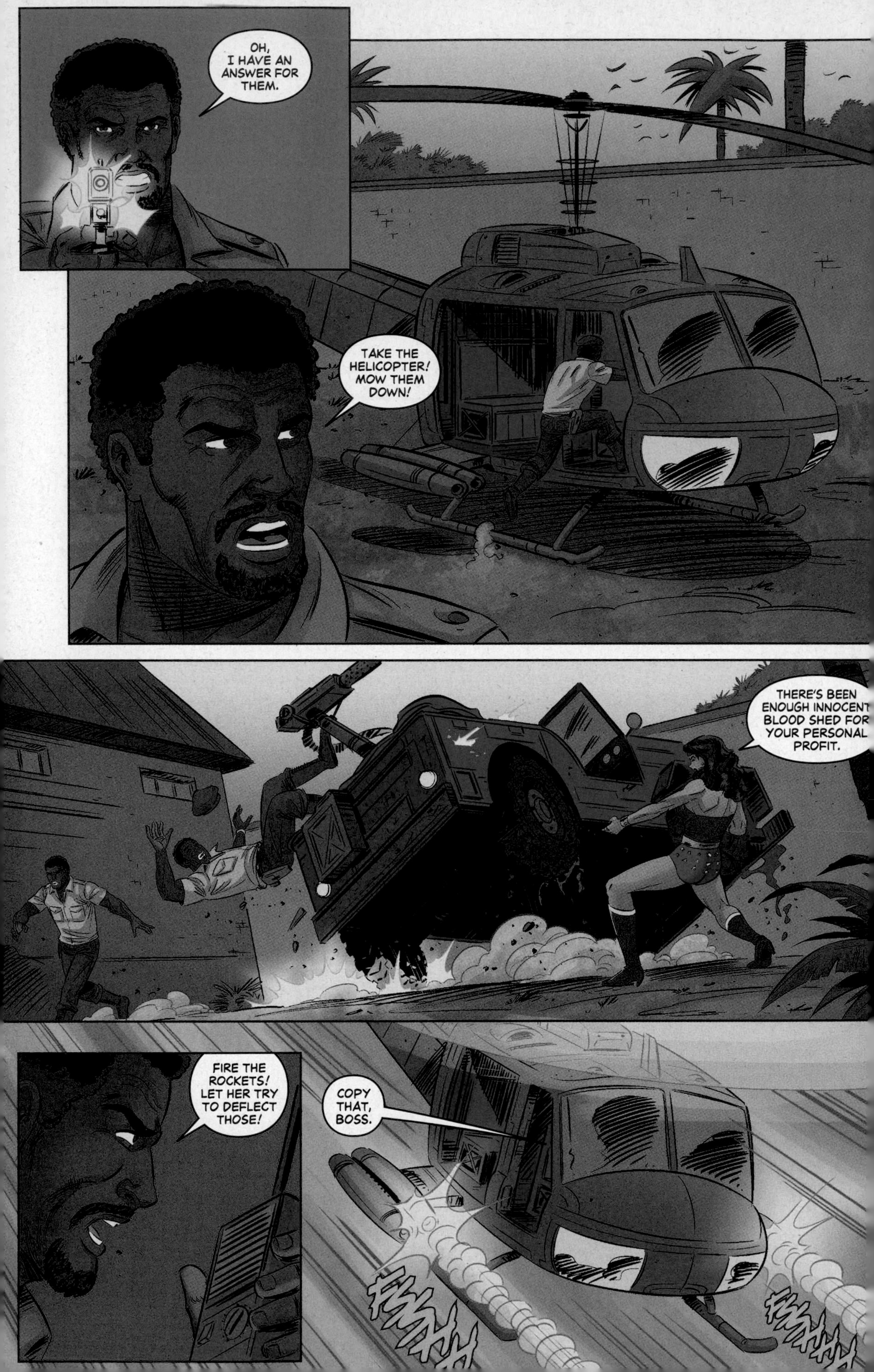
OH, I HAVE AN ANSWER FOR THEM.
TAKE THE HELICOPTER! MOW THEM DOWN!
THERE'S BEEN ENOUGH INNOCENT BLOOD SHED FOR YOUR PERSONAL PROFIT.
FIRE THE ROCKETS! LET HER TRY TO DEFLECT THOSE!
COPY THAT, BOSS.
FWHHH
FWHHH

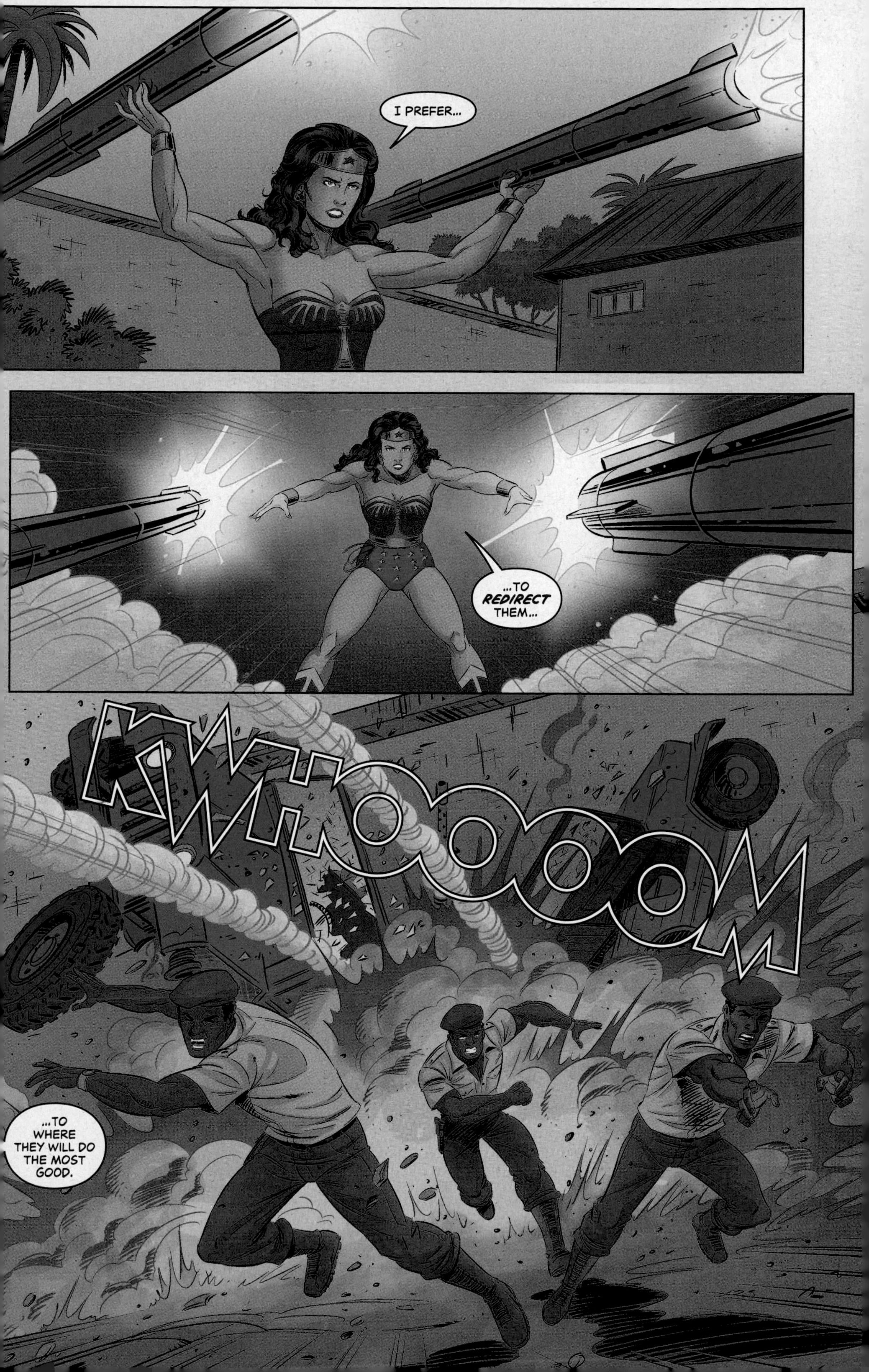
I PREFER...
...TO *REDIRECT* THEM...
KWHOOOOOM
...TO WHERE THEY WILL DO THE MOST GOOD.

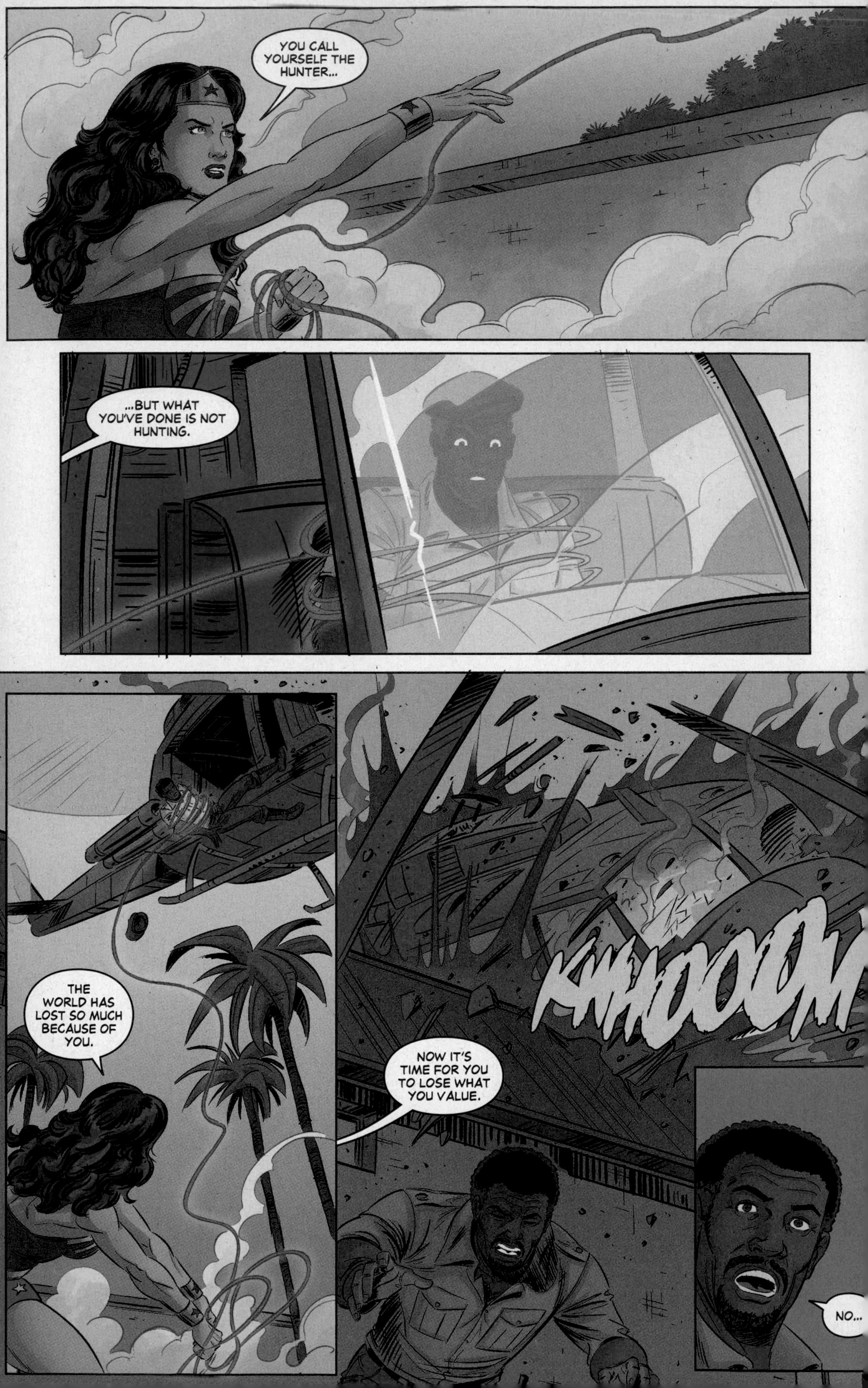
YOU CALL YOURSELF THE HUNTER...
...BUT WHAT YOU'VE DONE IS NOT HUNTING.
THE WORLD HAS LOST SO MUCH BECAUSE OF YOU.
KHOOOM
NOW IT'S TIME FOR YOU TO LOSE WHAT YOU VALUE.
NO...

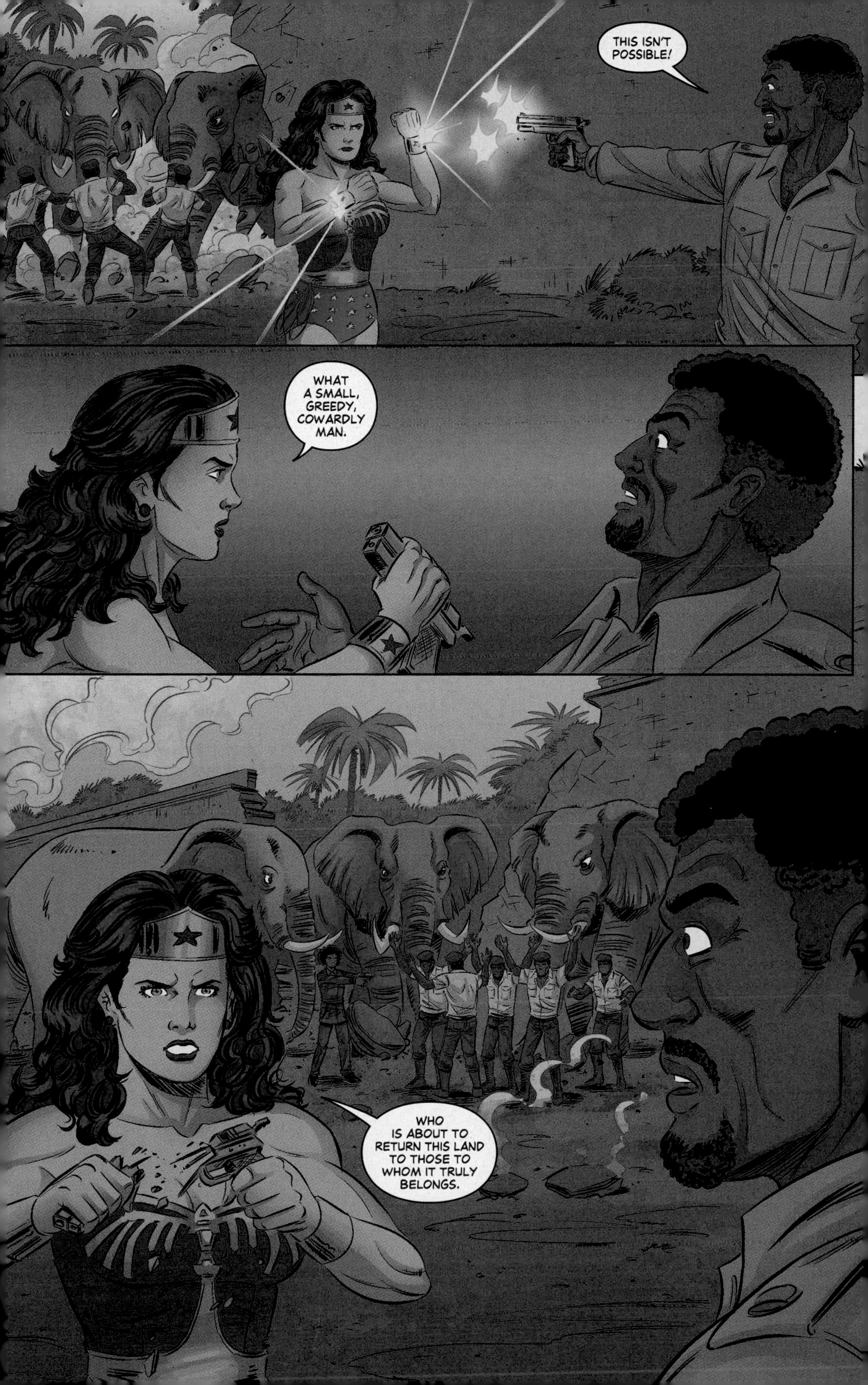
THIS ISN'T POSSIBLE!
WHAT A SMALL, GREEDY, COWARDLY MAN.
WHO IS ABOUT TO RETURN THIS LAND TO THOSE TO WHOM IT TRULY BELONGS.

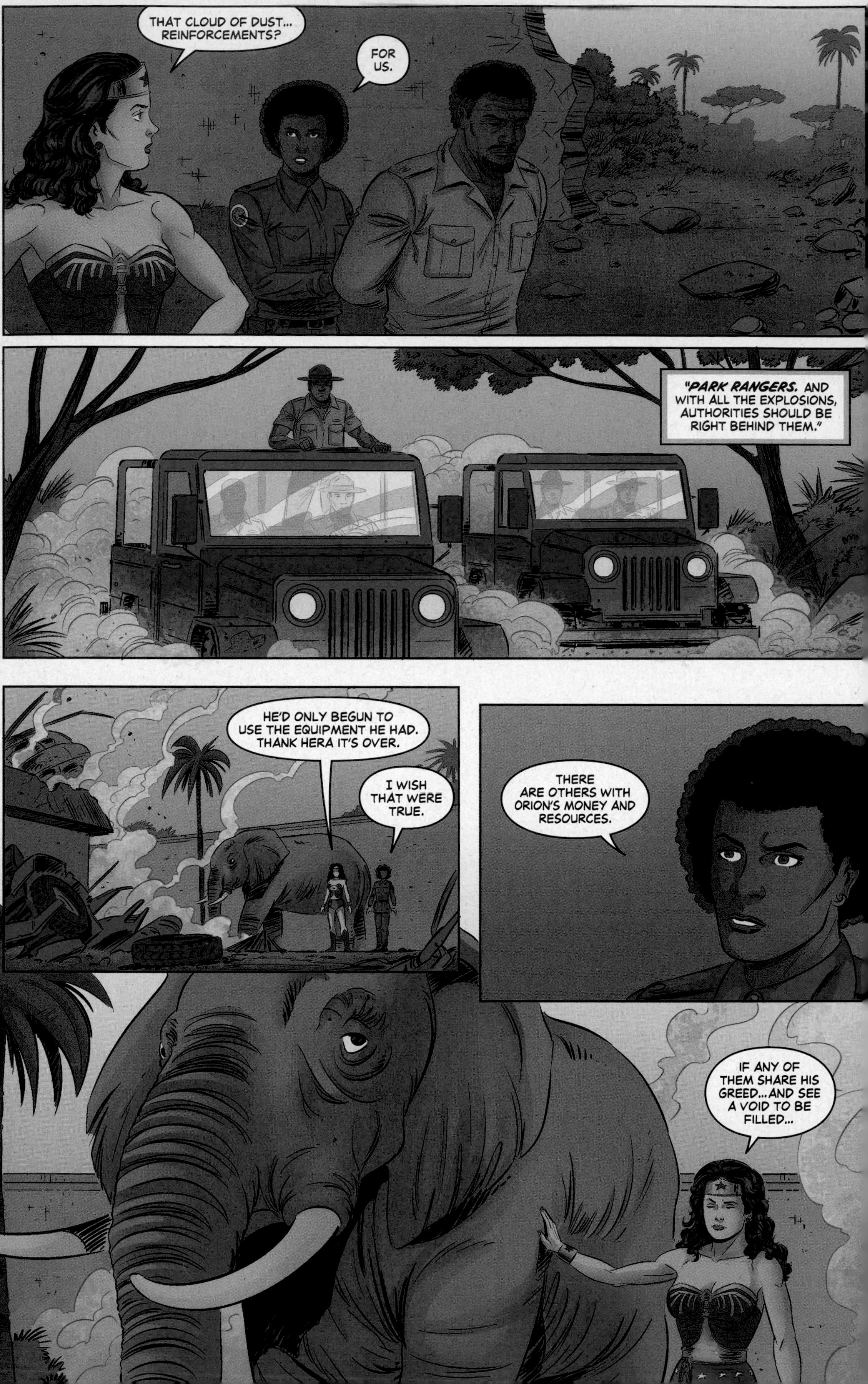

THAT CLOUD OF DUST... REINFORCEMENTS?
FOR US.
"PARK RANGERS. AND WITH ALL THE EXPLOSIONS, AUTHORITIES SHOULD BE RIGHT BEHIND THEM."
HE'D ONLY BEGUN TO USE THE EQUIPMENT HE HAD. THANK HERA IT'S OVER.
I WISH THAT WERE TRUE.
THERE ARE OTHERS WITH ORION'S MONEY AND RESOURCES.
IF ANY OF THEM SHARE HIS GREED...AND SEE A VOID TO BE FILLED...

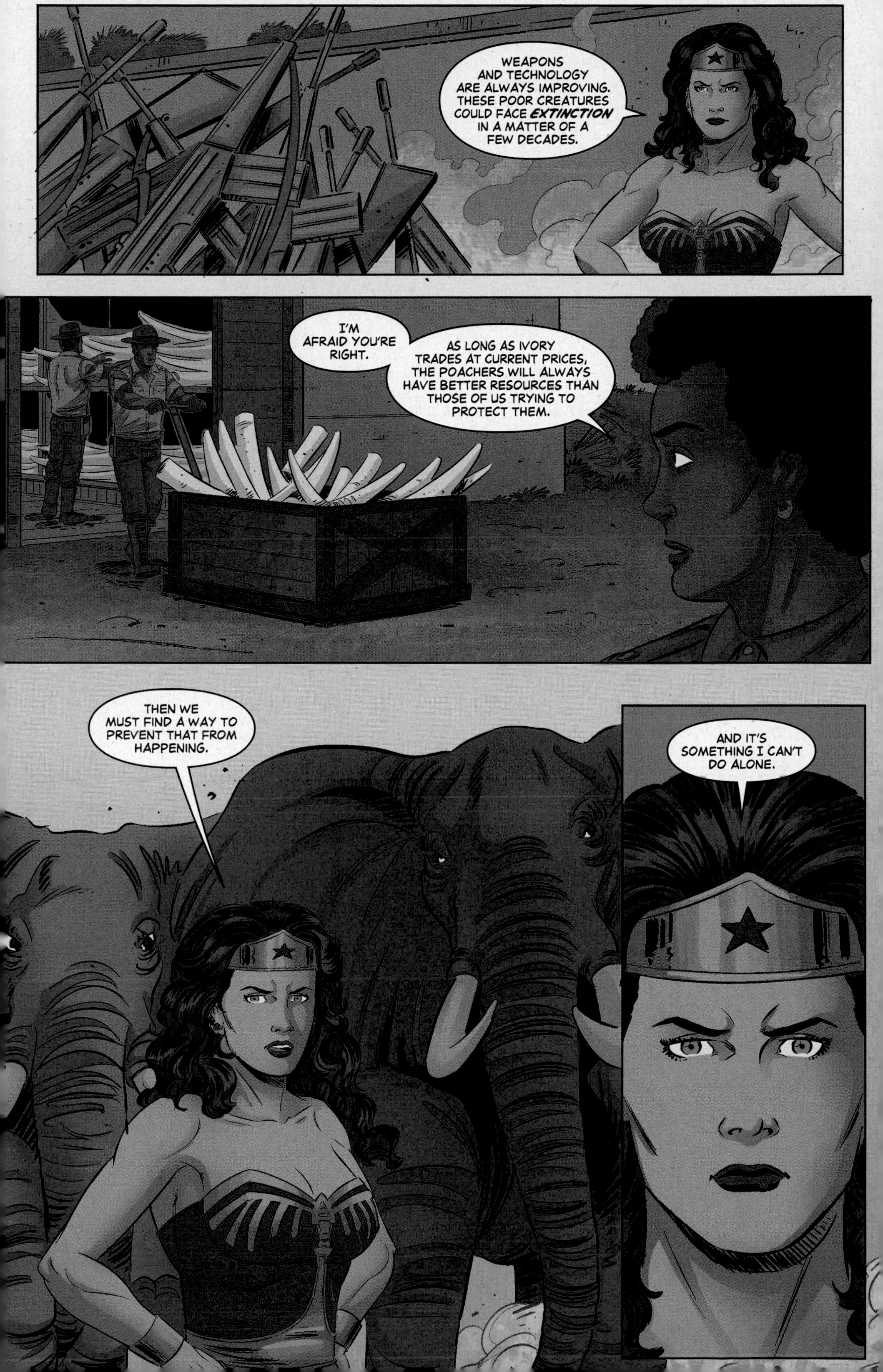
WEAPONS AND TECHNOLOGY ARE ALWAYS IMPROVING. THESE POOR CREATURES COULD FACE *EXTINCTION* IN A MATTER OF A FEW DECADES.
I'M AFRAID YOU'RE RIGHT.
AS LONG AS IVORY TRADES AT CURRENT PRICES, THE POACHERS WILL ALWAYS HAVE BETTER RESOURCES THAN THOSE OF US TRYING TO PROTECT THEM.
THEN WE MUST FIND A WAY TO PREVENT THAT FROM HAPPENING.
AND IT'S SOMETHING I CAN'T DO ALONE.

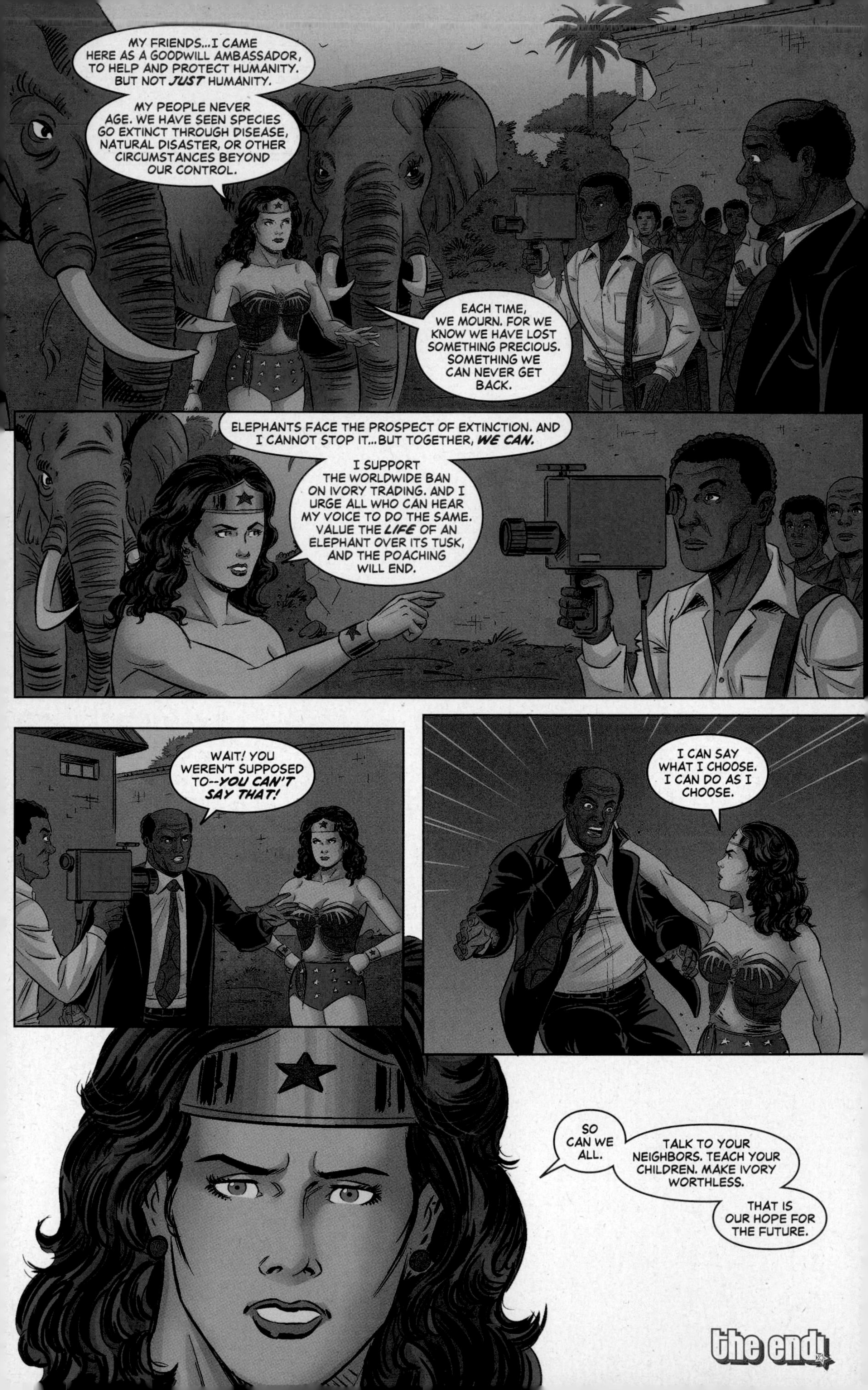

MY FRIENDS...I CAME HERE AS A GOODWILL AMBASSADOR, TO HELP AND PROTECT HUMANITY. BUT NOT JUST HUMANITY.
MY PEOPLE NEVER AGE. WE HAVE SEEN SPECIES GO EXTINCT THROUGH DISEASE, NATURAL DISASTER, OR OTHER CIRCUMSTANCES BEYOND OUR CONTROL.
EACH TIME, WE MOURN. FOR WE KNOW WE HAVE LOST SOMETHING PRECIOUS. SOMETHING WE CAN NEVER GET BACK.
ELEPHANTS FACE THE PROSPECT OF EXTINCTION. AND I CANNOT STOP IT...BUT TOGETHER, WE CAN.
I SUPPORT THE WORLDWIDE BAN ON IVORY TRADING. AND I URGE ALL WHO CAN HEAR MY VOICE TO DO THE SAME. VALUE THE LIFE OF AN ELEPHANT OVER ITS TUSK, AND THE POACHING WILL END.
WAIT! YOU WEREN'T SUPPOSED TO--YOU CAN'T SAY THAT!
I CAN SAY WHAT I CHOOSE. I CAN DO AS I CHOOSE.
SO CAN WE ALL.
TALK TO YOUR NEIGHBORS. TEACH YOUR CHILDREN. MAKE IVORY WORTHLESS.
THAT IS OUR HOPE FOR THE FUTURE.
the end

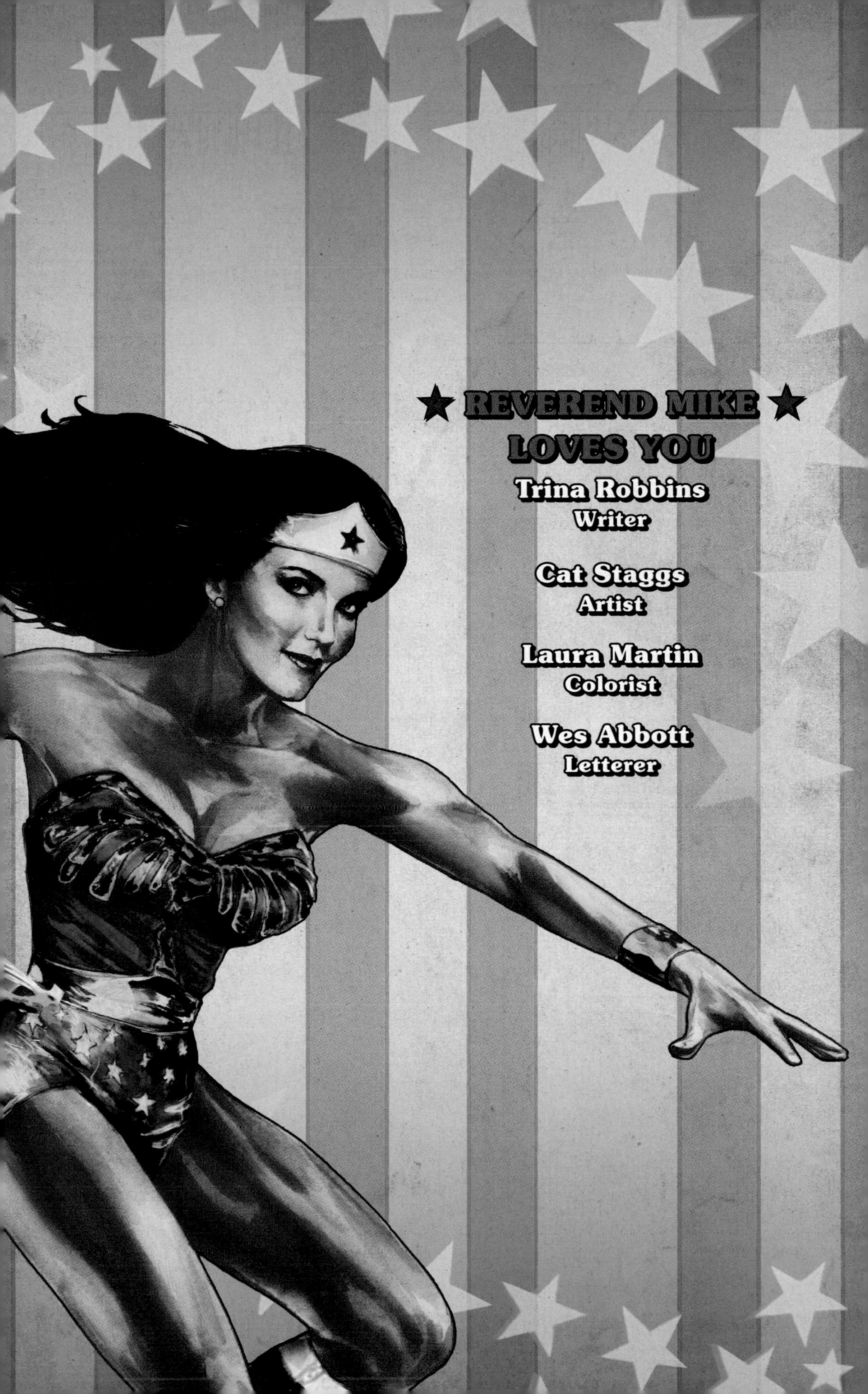
★ REVEREND MIKE ★
LOVES YOU
Trina Robbins
Writer
Cat Staggs
Artist
Laura Martin
Colorist
Wes Abbott
Letterer

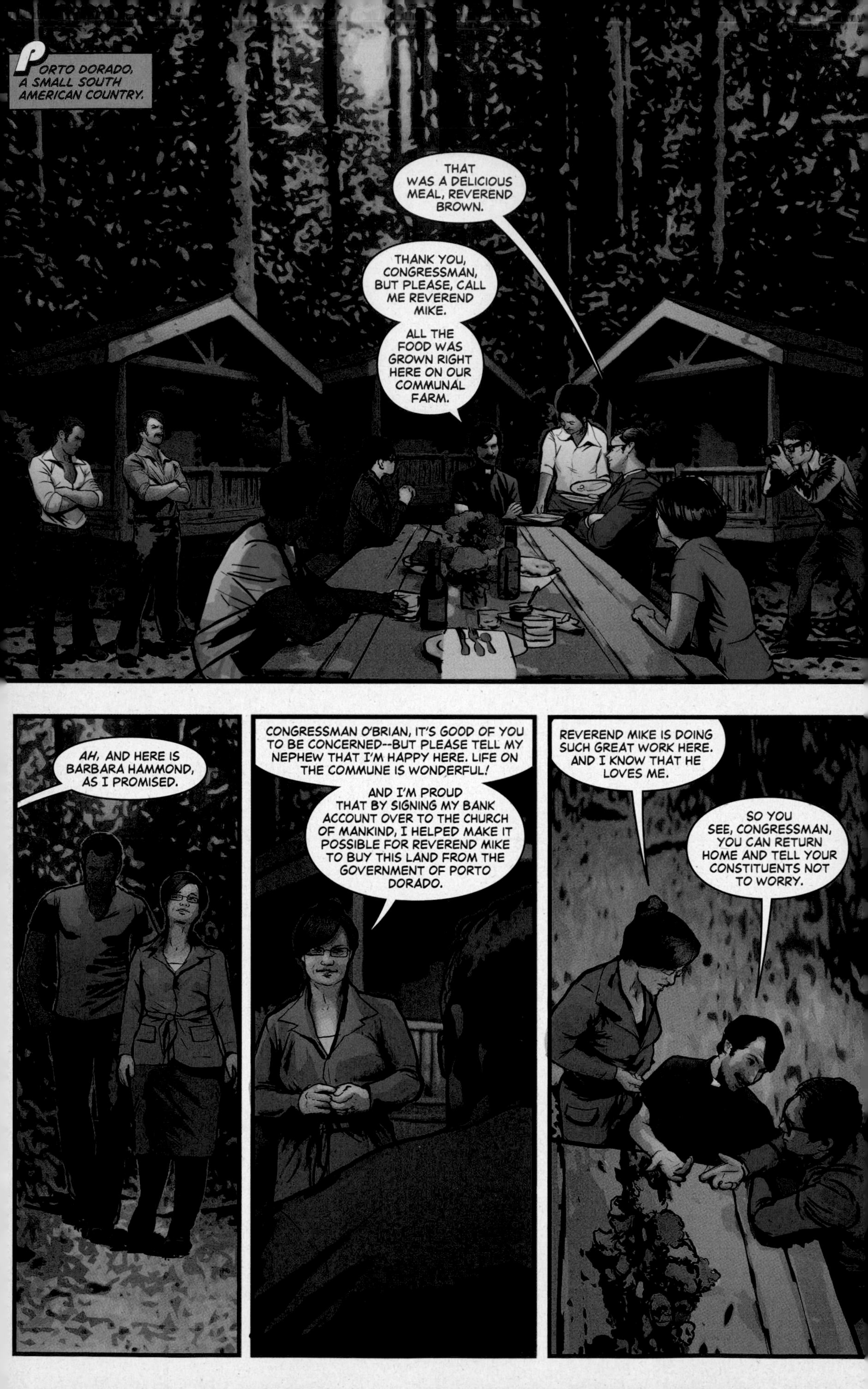
PORTO DORADO, A SMALL SOUTH AMERICAN COUNTRY.
THAT WAS A DELICIOUS MEAL, REVEREND BROWN.
THANK YOU, CONGRESSMAN, BUT PLEASE, CALL ME REVEREND MIKE.
ALL THE FOOD WAS GROWN RIGHT HERE ON OUR COMMUNAL FARM.
AH, AND HERE IS BARBARA HAMMOND, AS I PROMISED.
CONGRESSMAN O'BRIAN, IT'S GOOD OF YOU TO BE CONCERNED--BUT PLEASE TELL MY NEPHEW THAT I'M HAPPY HERE. LIFE ON THE COMMUNE IS WONDERFUL!
AND I'M PROUD THAT BY SIGNING MY BANK ACCOUNT OVER TO THE CHURCH OF MANKIND, I HELPED MAKE IT POSSIBLE FOR REVEREND MIKE TO BUY THIS LAND FROM THE GOVERNMENT OF PORTO DORADO.
REVEREND MIKE IS DOING SUCH GREAT WORK HERE. AND I KNOW THAT HE LOVES ME.
SO YOU SEE, CONGRESSMAN, YOU CAN RETURN HOME AND TELL YOUR CONSTITUENTS NOT TO WORRY.

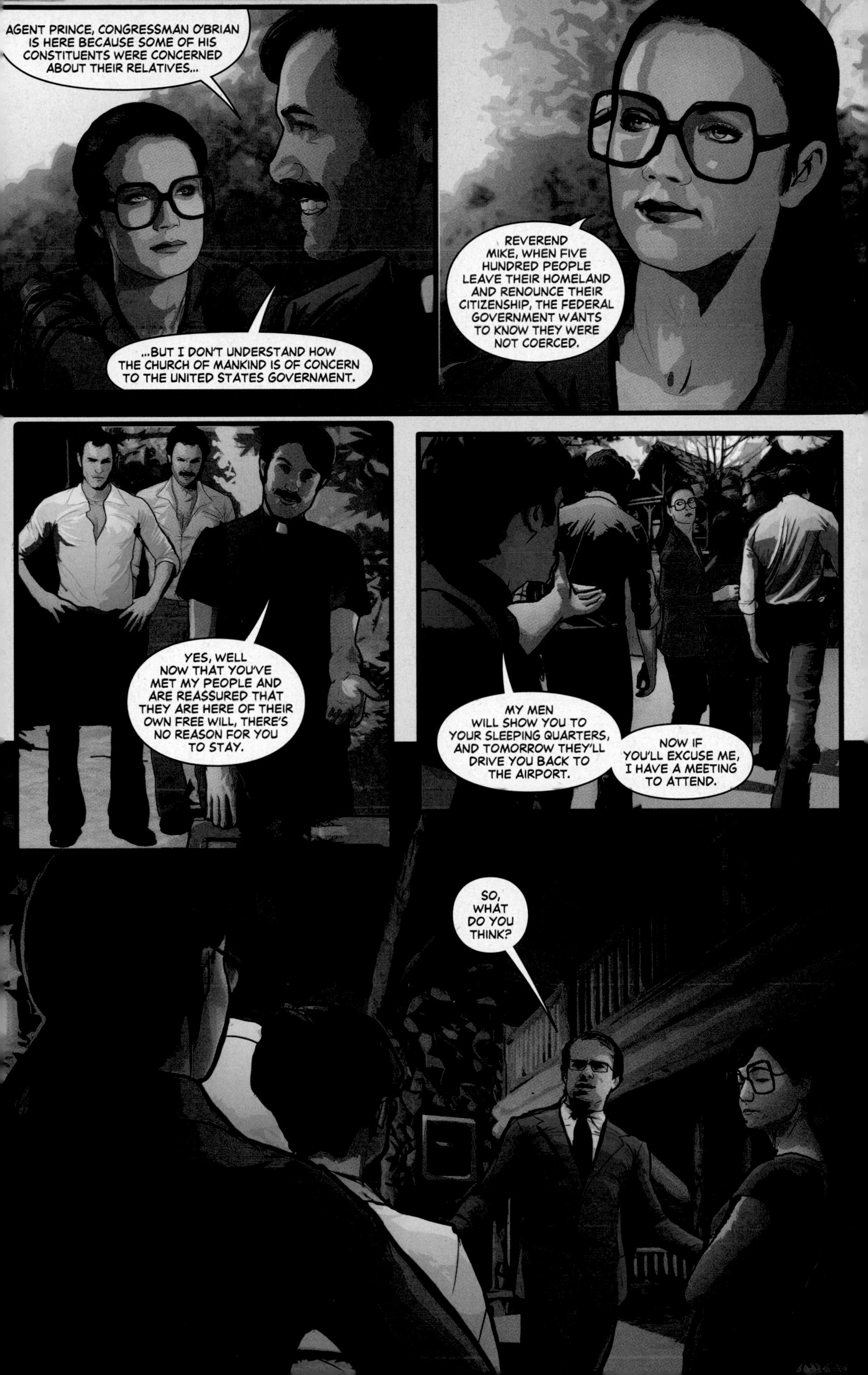
AGENT PRINCE, CONGRESSMAN O'BRIAN IS HERE BECAUSE SOME OF HIS CONSTITUENTS WERE CONCERNED ABOUT THEIR RELATIVES...
...BUT I DON'T UNDERSTAND HOW THE CHURCH OF MANKIND IS OF CONCERN TO THE UNITED STATES GOVERNMENT.
REVEREND MIKE, WHEN FIVE HUNDRED PEOPLE LEAVE THEIR HOMELAND AND RENOUNCE THEIR CITIZENSHIP, THE FEDERAL GOVERNMENT WANTS TO KNOW THEY WERE NOT COERCED.
YES, WELL NOW THAT YOU'VE MET MY PEOPLE AND ARE REASSURED THAT THEY ARE HERE OF THEIR OWN FREE WILL, THERE'S NO REASON FOR YOU TO STAY.
MY MEN WILL SHOW YOU TO YOUR SLEEPING QUARTERS, AND TOMORROW THEY'LL DRIVE YOU BACK TO THE AIRPORT.
NOW IF YOU'LL EXCUSE ME, I HAVE A MEETING TO ATTEND.
SO, WHAT DO YOU THINK?

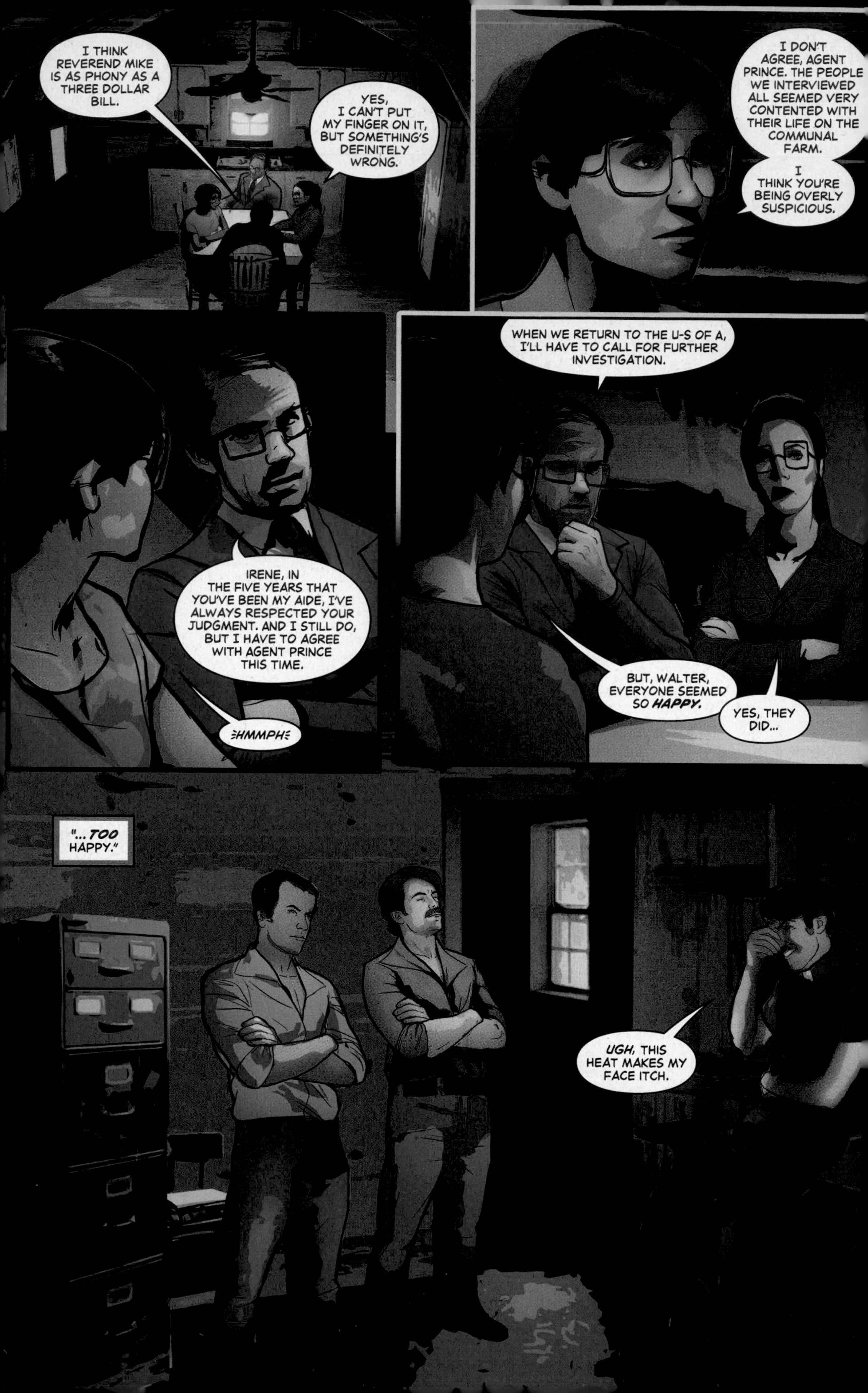
I THINK REVEREND MIKE IS AS PHONY AS A THREE DOLLAR BILL.
YES, I CAN'T PUT MY FINGER ON IT, BUT SOMETHING'S DEFINITELY WRONG.
I DON'T AGREE, AGENT PRINCE. THE PEOPLE WE INTERVIEWED ALL SEEMED VERY CONTENTED WITH THEIR LIFE ON THE COMMUNAL FARM.
I THINK YOU'RE BEING OVERLY SUSPICIOUS.
IRENE, IN THE FIVE YEARS THAT YOU'VE BEEN MY AIDE, I'VE ALWAYS RESPECTED YOUR JUDGMENT. AND I STILL DO, BUT I HAVE TO AGREE WITH AGENT PRINCE THIS TIME.
HMMPH
WHEN WE RETURN TO THE U-S OF A, I'LL HAVE TO CALL FOR FURTHER INVESTIGATION.
BUT, WALTER, EVERYONE SEEMED SO HAPPY.
YES, THEY DID...
"...TOO HAPPY."
UGH, THIS HEAT MAKES MY FACE ITCH.

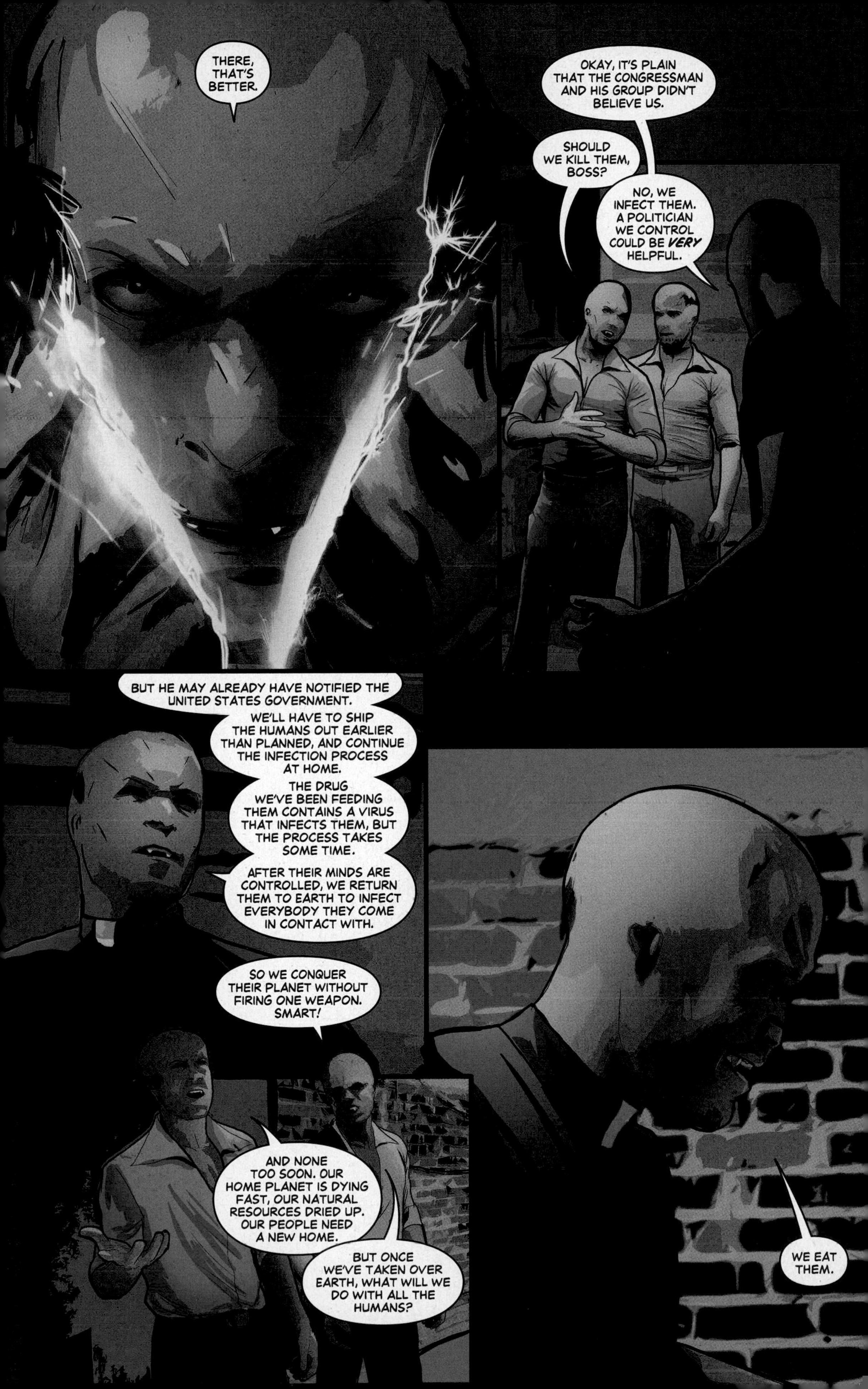
THERE, THAT'S BETTER.
OKAY, IT'S PLAIN THAT THE CONGRESSMAN AND HIS GROUP DIDN'T BELIEVE US.
SHOULD WE KILL THEM, BOSS?
NO, WE INFECT THEM. A POLITICIAN WE CONTROL COULD BE VERY HELPFUL.
BUT HE MAY ALREADY HAVE NOTIFIED THE UNITED STATES GOVERNMENT.
WE'LL HAVE TO SHIP THE HUMANS OUT EARLIER THAN PLANNED, AND CONTINUE THE INFECTION PROCESS AT HOME.
THE DRUG WE'VE BEEN FEEDING THEM CONTAINS A VIRUS THAT INFECTS THEM, BUT THE PROCESS TAKES SOME TIME.
AFTER THEIR MINDS ARE CONTROLLED, WE RETURN THEM TO EARTH TO INFECT EVERYBODY THEY COME IN CONTACT WITH.
SO WE CONQUER THEIR PLANET WITHOUT FIRING ONE WEAPON. SMART!
AND NONE TOO SOON. OUR HOME PLANET IS DYING FAST, OUR NATURAL RESOURCES DRIED UP. OUR PEOPLE NEED A NEW HOME.
BUT ONCE WE'VE TAKEN OVER EARTH, WHAT WILL WE DO WITH ALL THE HUMANS?
WE EAT THEM.

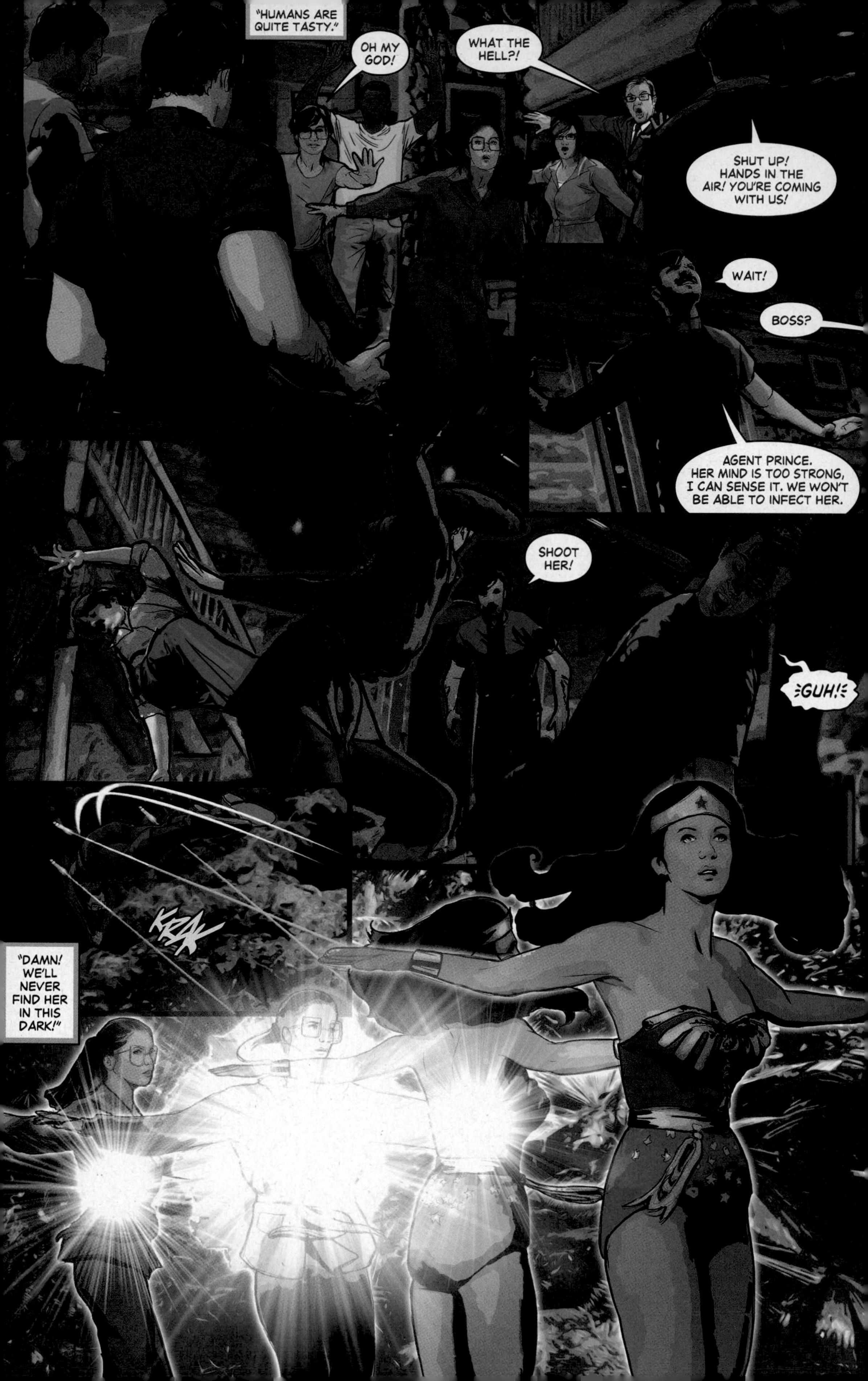

"HUMANS ARE QUITE TASTY."
OH MY GOD!
WHAT THE HELL?!
SHUT UP! HANDS IN THE AIR! YOU'RE COMING WITH US!
WAIT!
BOSS?
AGENT PRINCE. HER MIND IS TOO STRONG, I CAN SENSE IT. WE WON'T BE ABLE TO INFECT HER.
SHOOT HER!
GUH!
KRAK
"DAMN! WE'LL NEVER FIND HER IN THIS DARK!"

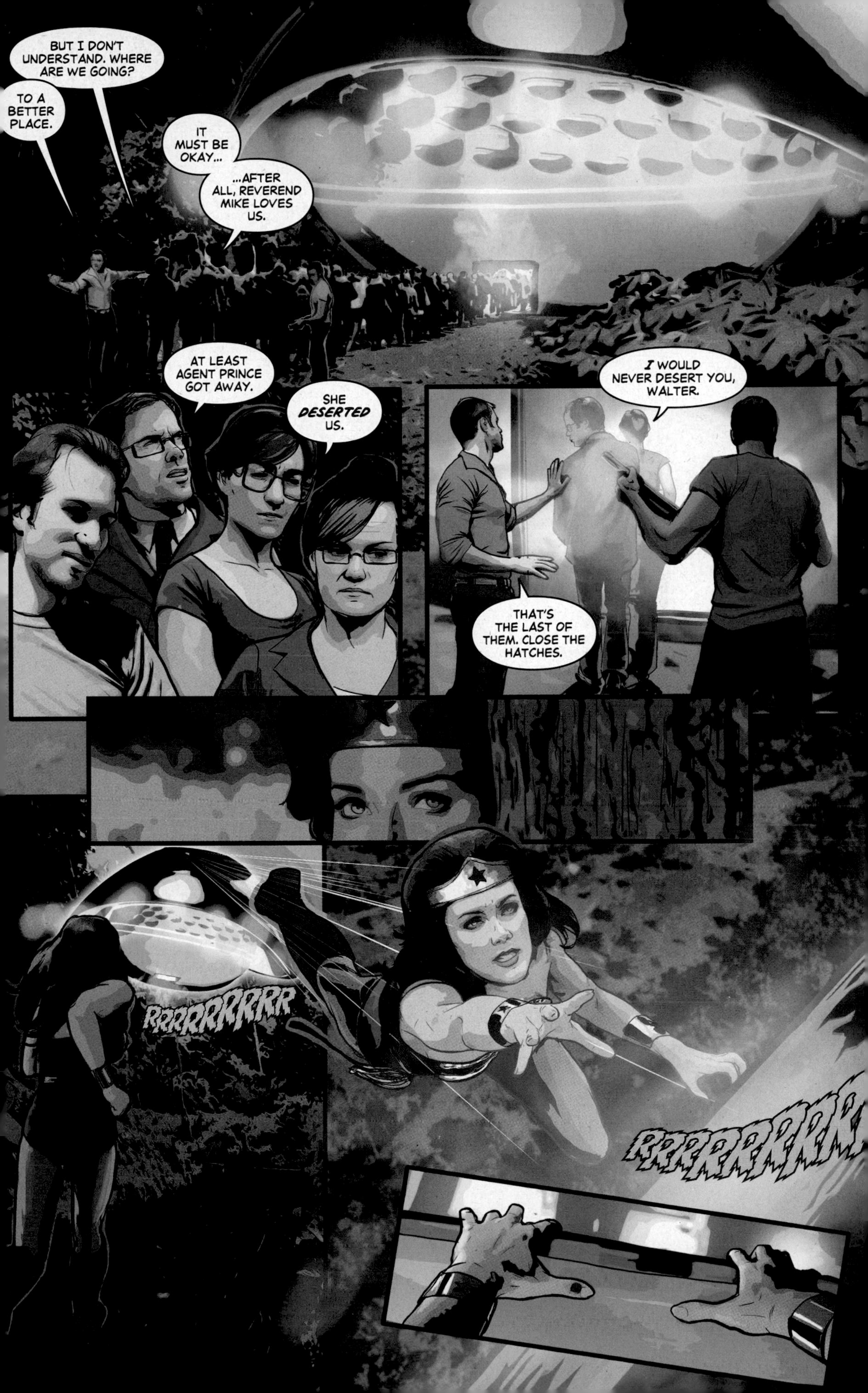
BUT I DON'T UNDERSTAND. WHERE ARE WE GOING?
TO A BETTER PLACE.
IT MUST BE OKAY...
...AFTER ALL, REVEREND MIKE LOVES US.
AT LEAST AGENT PRINCE GOT AWAY.
SHE *DESERTED* US.
I WOULD NEVER DESERT YOU, WALTER.
THAT'S THE LAST OF THEM. CLOSE THE HATCHES.
RRRRRRRRR
RRRRRRRRR

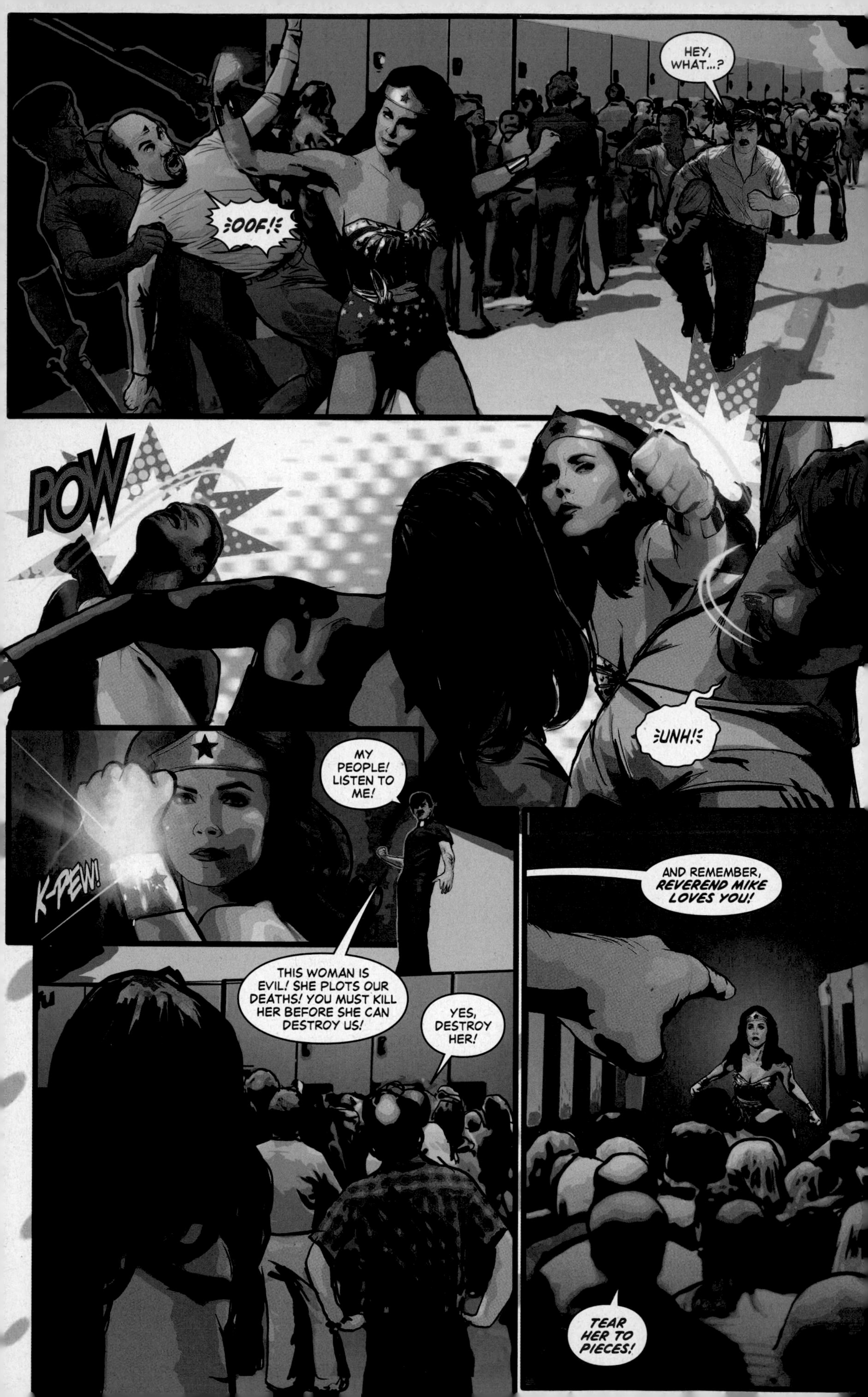
HEY, WHAT...?
OOF!
POW
UNH!
K-PEW!
MY PEOPLE! LISTEN TO ME!
THIS WOMAN IS EVIL! SHE PLOTS OUR DEATHS! YOU MUST KILL HER BEFORE SHE CAN DESTROY US!
YES, DESTROY HER!
AND REMEMBER, *REVEREND MIKE LOVES YOU!*
TEAR HER TO PIECES!

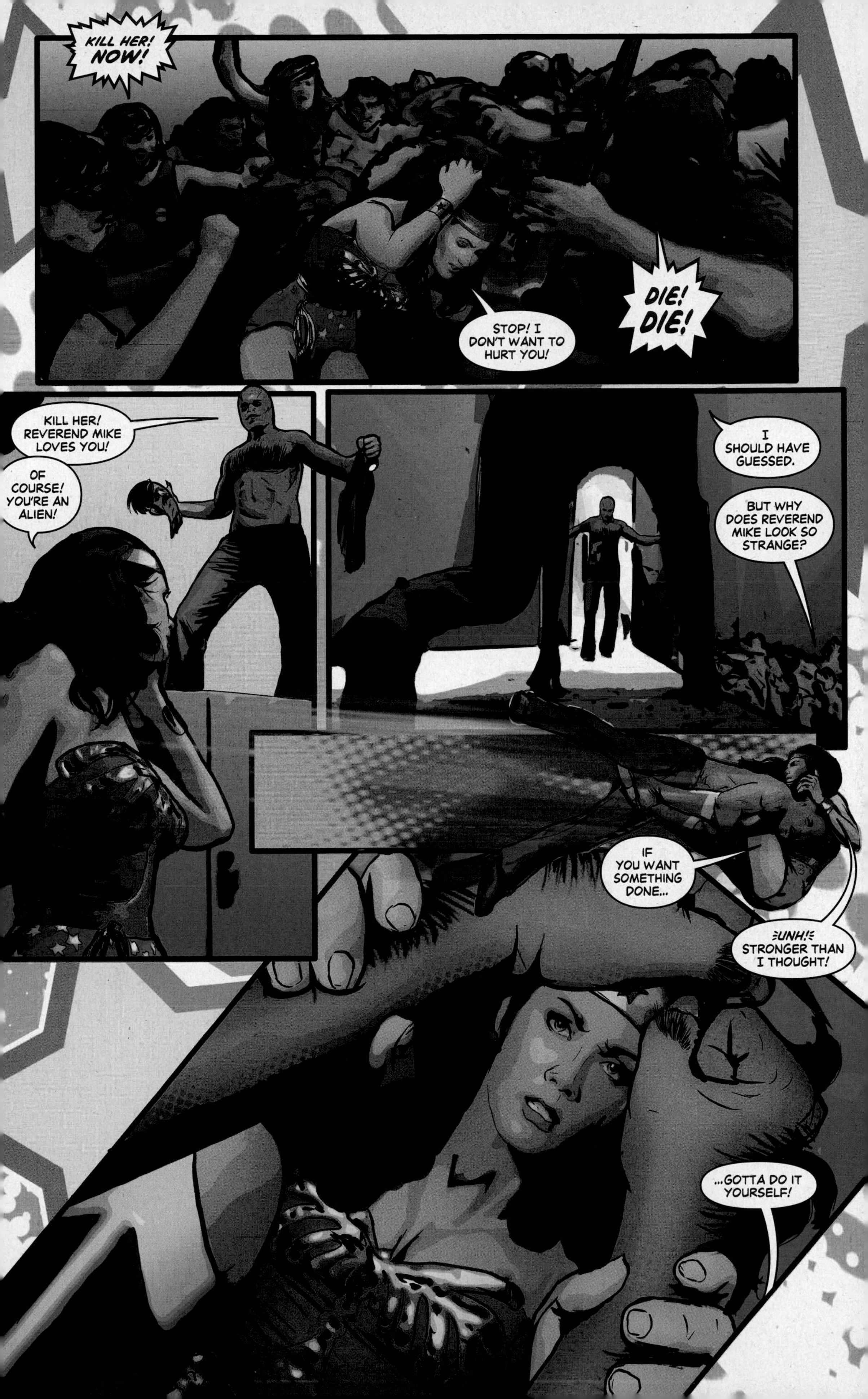
KILL HER! NOW!
STOP! I DON'T WANT TO HURT YOU!
DIE! DIE!
KILL HER! REVEREND MIKE LOVES YOU!
OF COURSE! YOU'RE AN ALIEN!
I SHOULD HAVE GUESSED.
BUT WHY DOES REVEREND MIKE LOOK SO STRANGE?
IF YOU WANT SOMETHING DONE...
UNH! STRONGER THAN I THOUGHT!
...GOTTA DO IT YOURSELF!

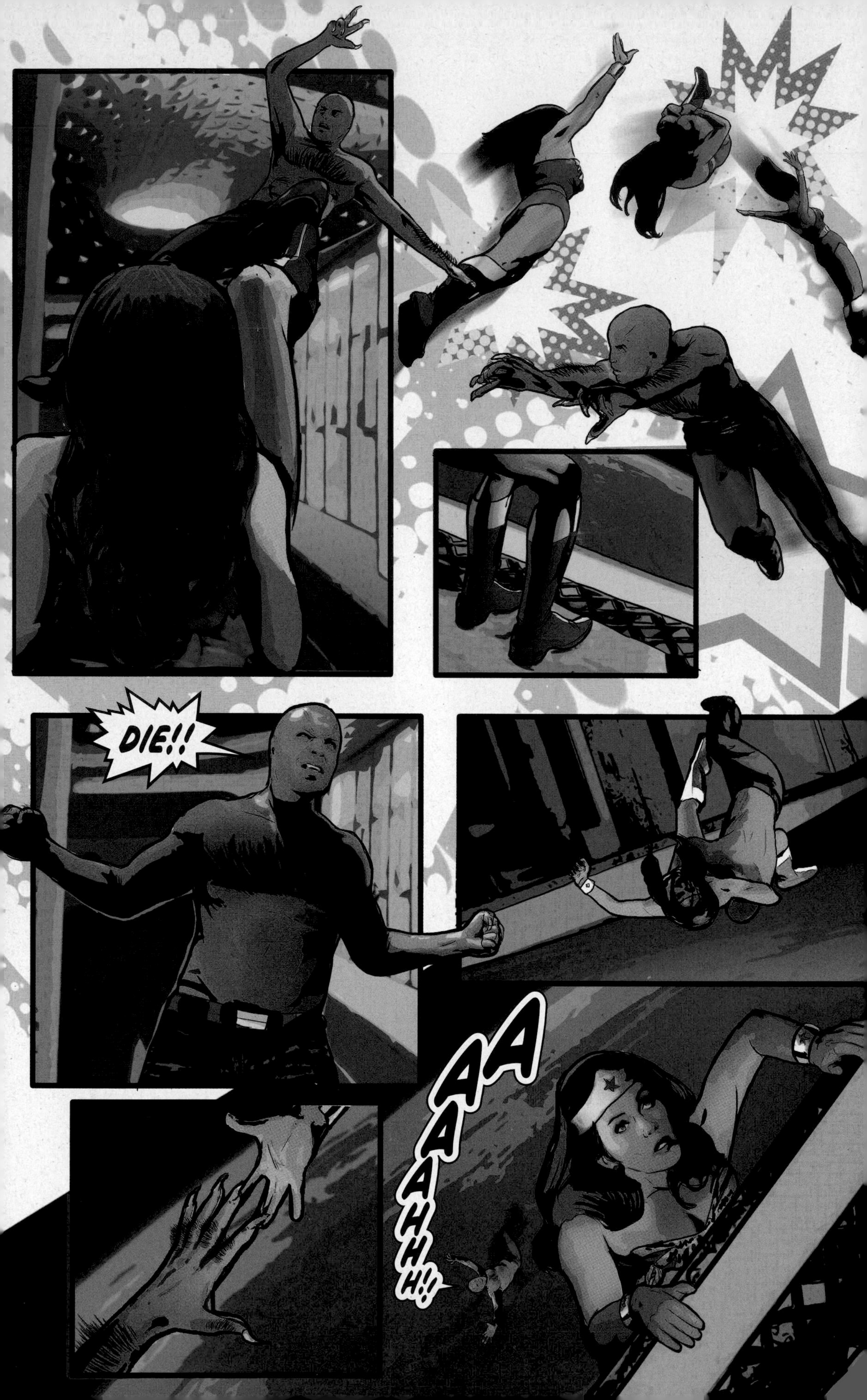
DIE!!
AAAAAAHHH!!

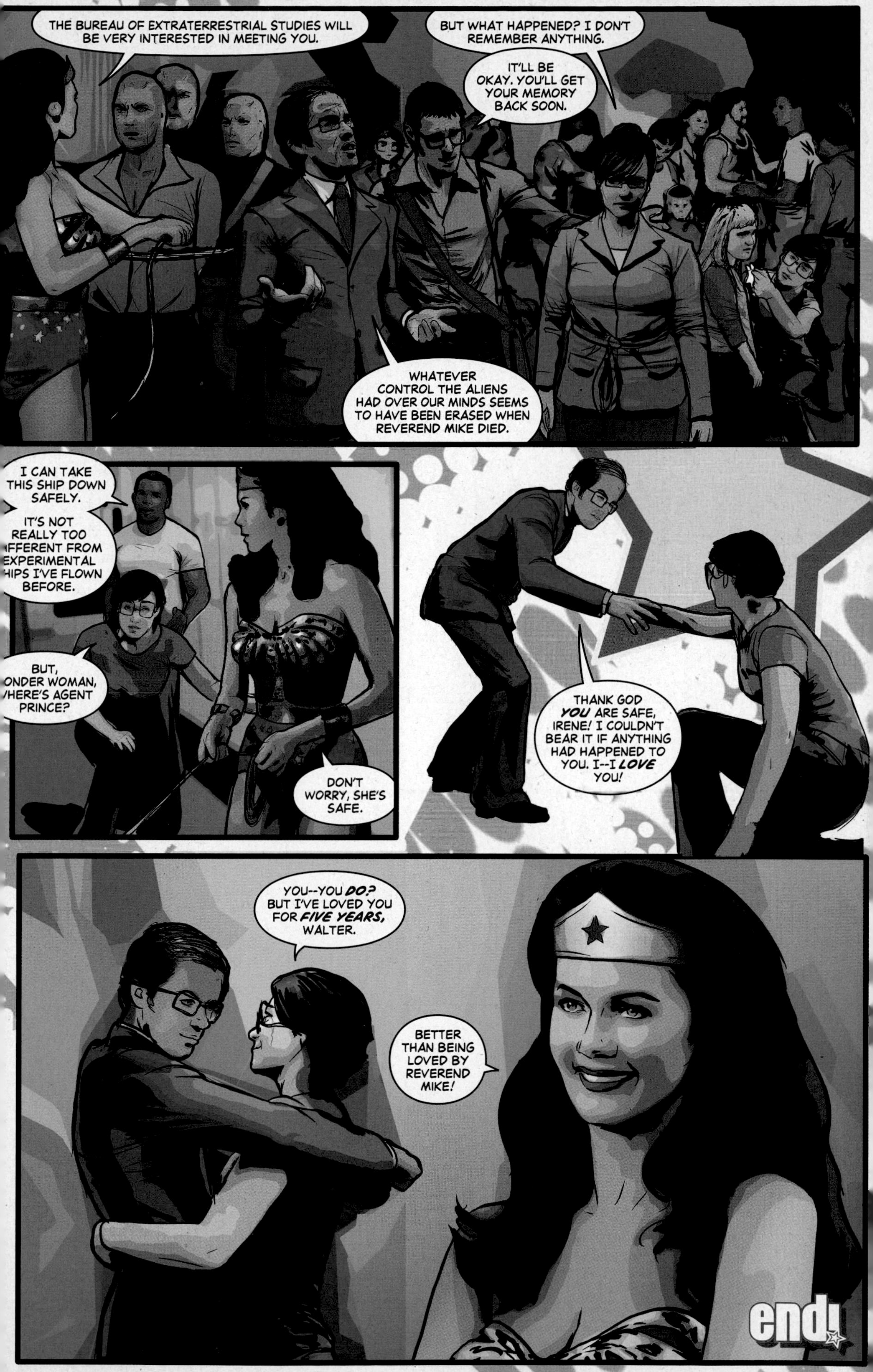
THE BUREAU OF EXTRATERRESTRIAL STUDIES WILL BE VERY INTERESTED IN MEETING YOU.
BUT WHAT HAPPENED? I DON'T REMEMBER ANYTHING.
IT'LL BE OKAY. YOU'LL GET YOUR MEMORY BACK SOON.
WHATEVER CONTROL THE ALIENS HAD OVER OUR MINDS SEEMS TO HAVE BEEN ERASED WHEN REVEREND MIKE DIED.
I CAN TAKE THIS SHIP DOWN SAFELY.
IT'S NOT REALLY TOO IFFERENT FROM EXPERIMENTAL HIPS I'VE FLOWN BEFORE.
BUT, ONDER WOMAN, HERE'S AGENT PRINCE?
DON'T WORRY, SHE'S SAFE.
THANK GOD *YOU* ARE SAFE, IRENE! I COULDN'T BEAR IT IF ANYTHING HAD HAPPENED TO YOU. I--I *LOVE* YOU!
YOU--YOU *DO?* BUT I'VE LOVED YOU FOR *FIVE YEARS,* WALTER.
BETTER THAN BEING LOVED BY REVEREND MIKE!
end!

★ OCEANS '77 ★

Amanda Deibert
Writer

Staz Johnson
Wayne Faucher
Artists

Kelly Fitzpatrick
Colorist

Wes Abbott
Letterer

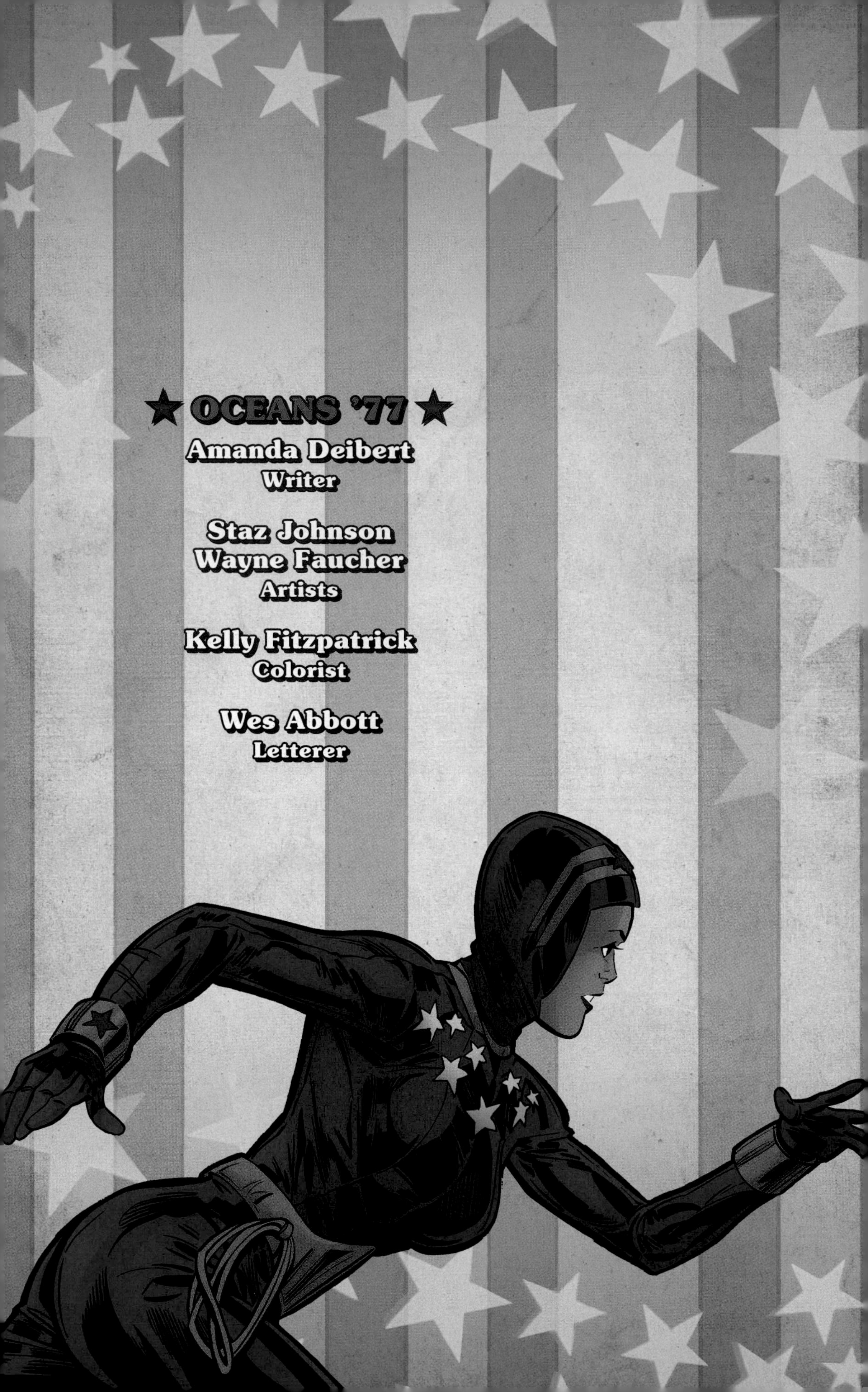

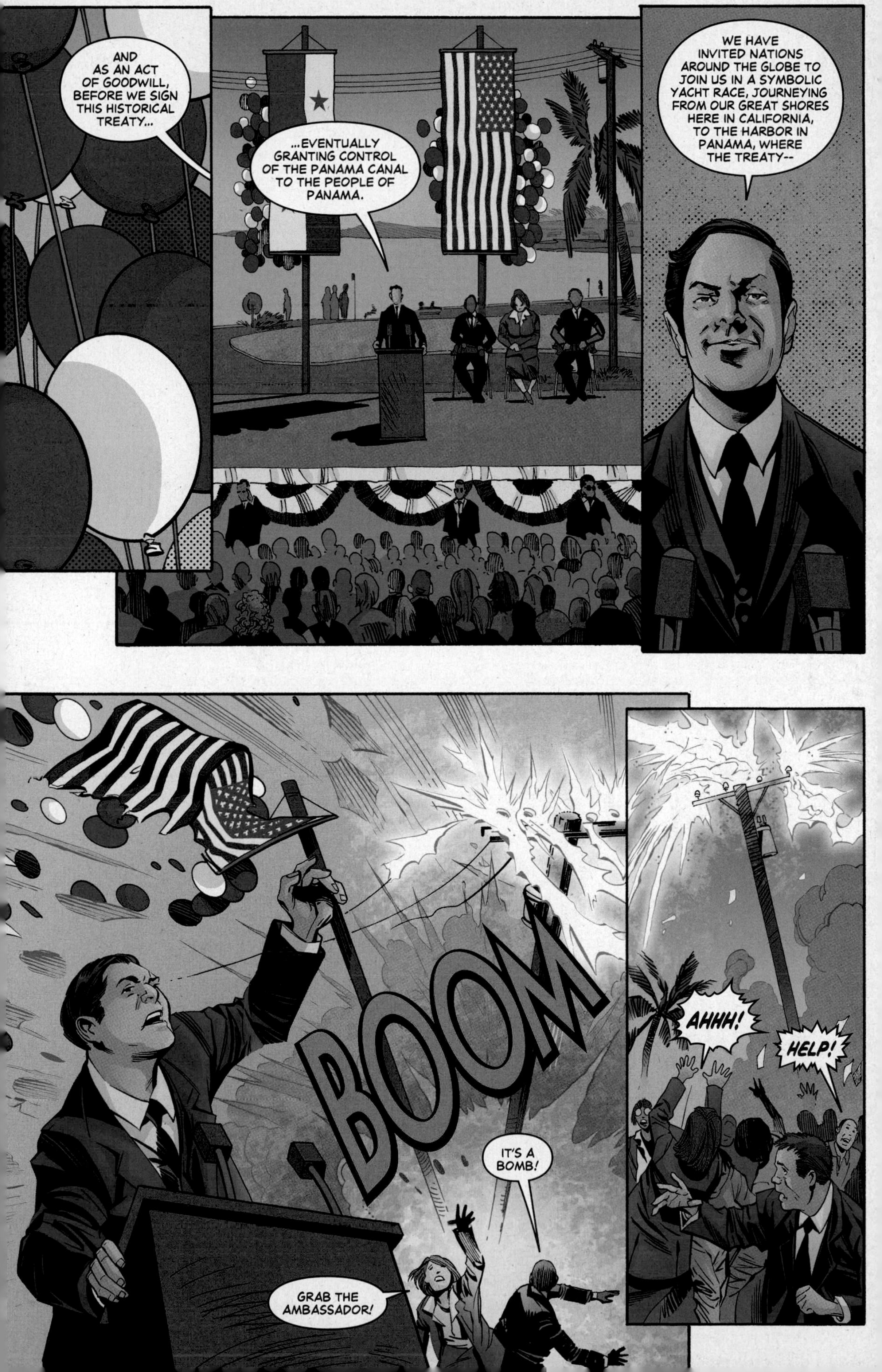
AND AS AN ACT OF GOODWILL, BEFORE WE SIGN THIS HISTORICAL TREATY...
...EVENTUALLY GRANTING CONTROL OF THE PANAMA CANAL TO THE PEOPLE OF PANAMA.
WE HAVE INVITED NATIONS AROUND THE GLOBE TO JOIN US IN A SYMBOLIC YACHT RACE, JOURNEYING FROM OUR GREAT SHORES HERE IN CALIFORNIA, TO THE HARBOR IN PANAMA, WHERE THE TREATY--
BOOM
IT'S A BOMB!
GRAB THE AMBASSADOR!
AHHH!
HELP!

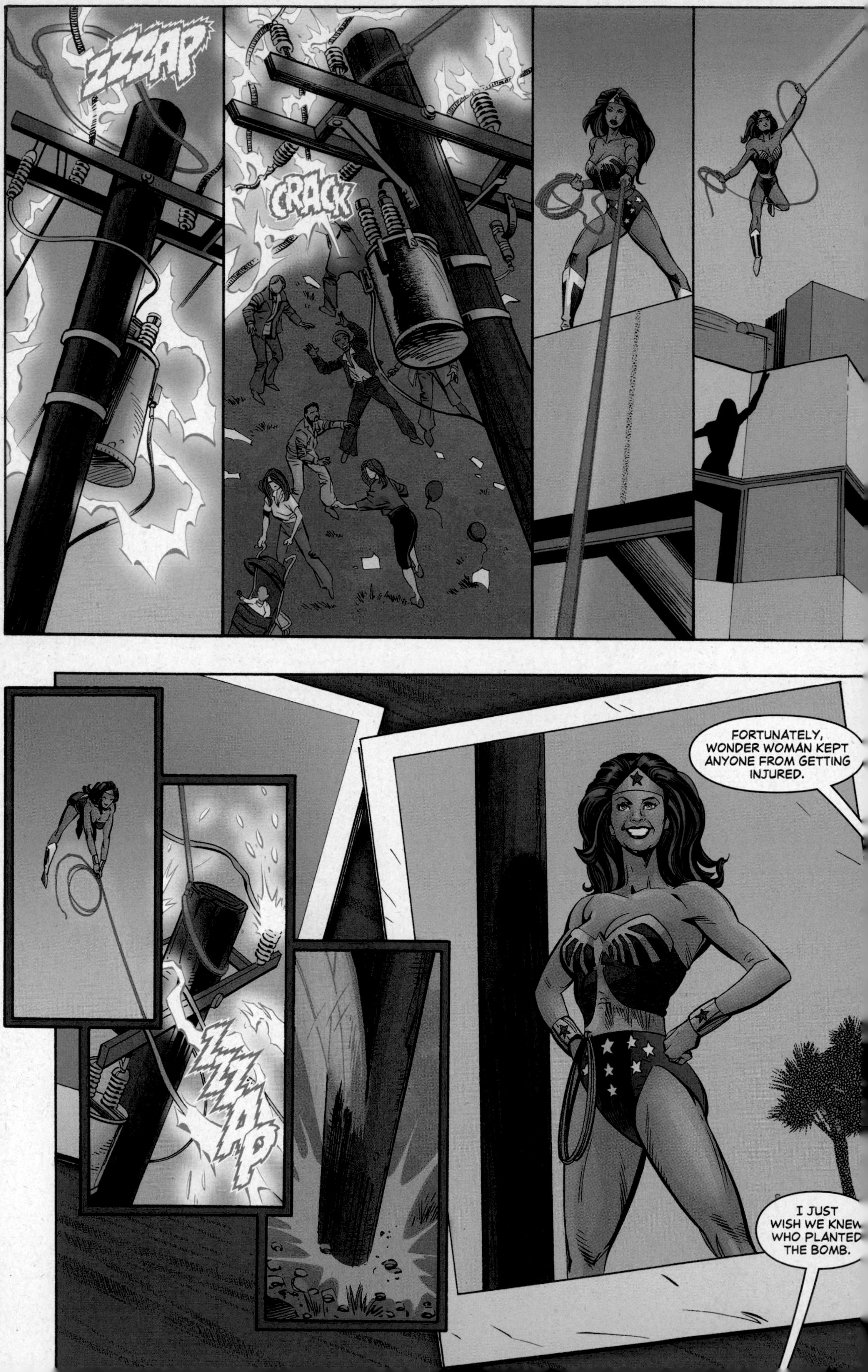
ZZZAP
CRACK
ZZZAP
FORTUNATELY, WONDER WOMAN KEPT ANYONE FROM GETTING INJURED.
I JUST WISH WE KNEW WHO PLANTED THE BOMB.

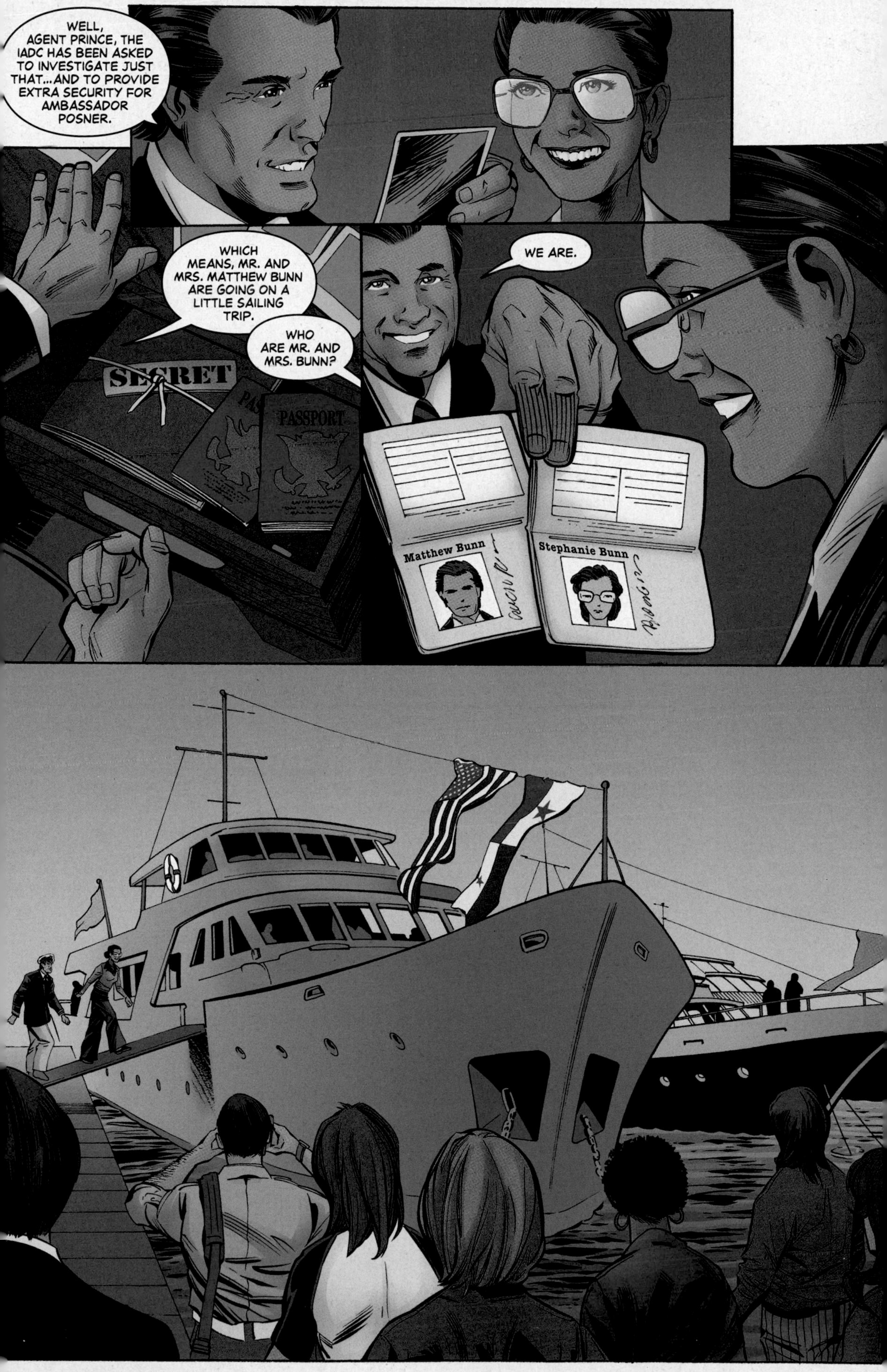
WELL, AGENT PRINCE, THE IADC HAS BEEN ASKED TO INVESTIGATE JUST THAT...AND TO PROVIDE EXTRA SECURITY FOR AMBASSADOR POSNER.
WHICH MEANS, MR. AND MRS. MATTHEW BUNN ARE GOING ON A LITTLE SAILING TRIP.
WHO ARE MR. AND MRS. BUNN?
WE ARE.
SECRET
PASSPORT
Matthew Bunn
Stephanie Bunn

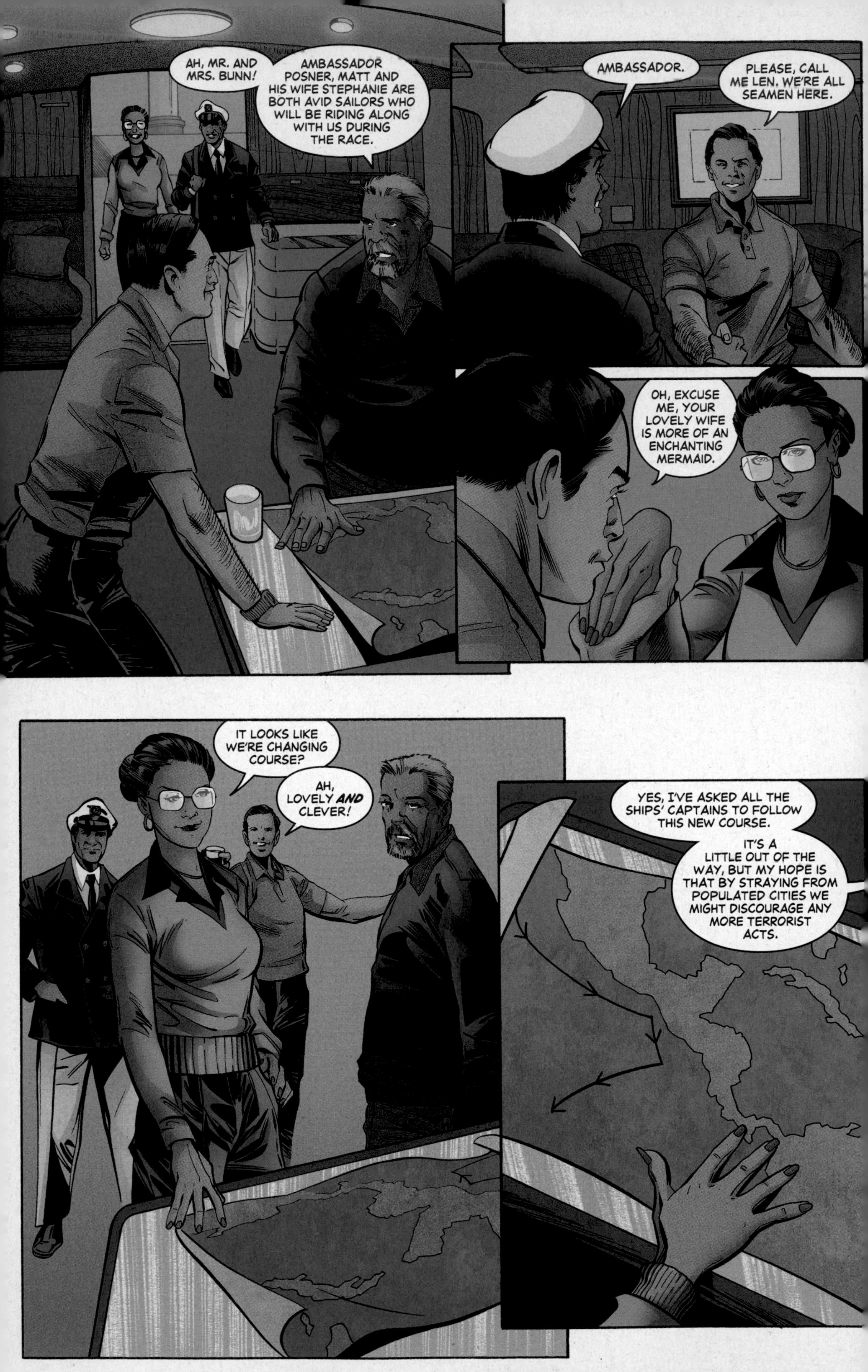
AH, MR. AND MRS. BUNN!
AMBASSADOR POSNER, MATT AND HIS WIFE STEPHANIE ARE BOTH AVID SAILORS WHO WILL BE RIDING ALONG WITH US DURING THE RACE.
AMBASSADOR.
PLEASE, CALL ME LEN. WE'RE ALL SEAMEN HERE.
OH, EXCUSE ME, YOUR LOVELY WIFE IS MORE OF AN ENCHANTING MERMAID.
IT LOOKS LIKE WE'RE CHANGING COURSE?
AH, LOVELY *AND* CLEVER!
YES, I'VE ASKED ALL THE SHIPS' CAPTAINS TO FOLLOW THIS NEW COURSE.
IT'S A LITTLE OUT OF THE WAY, BUT MY HOPE IS THAT BY STRAYING FROM POPULATED CITIES WE MIGHT DISCOURAGE ANY MORE TERRORIST ACTS.

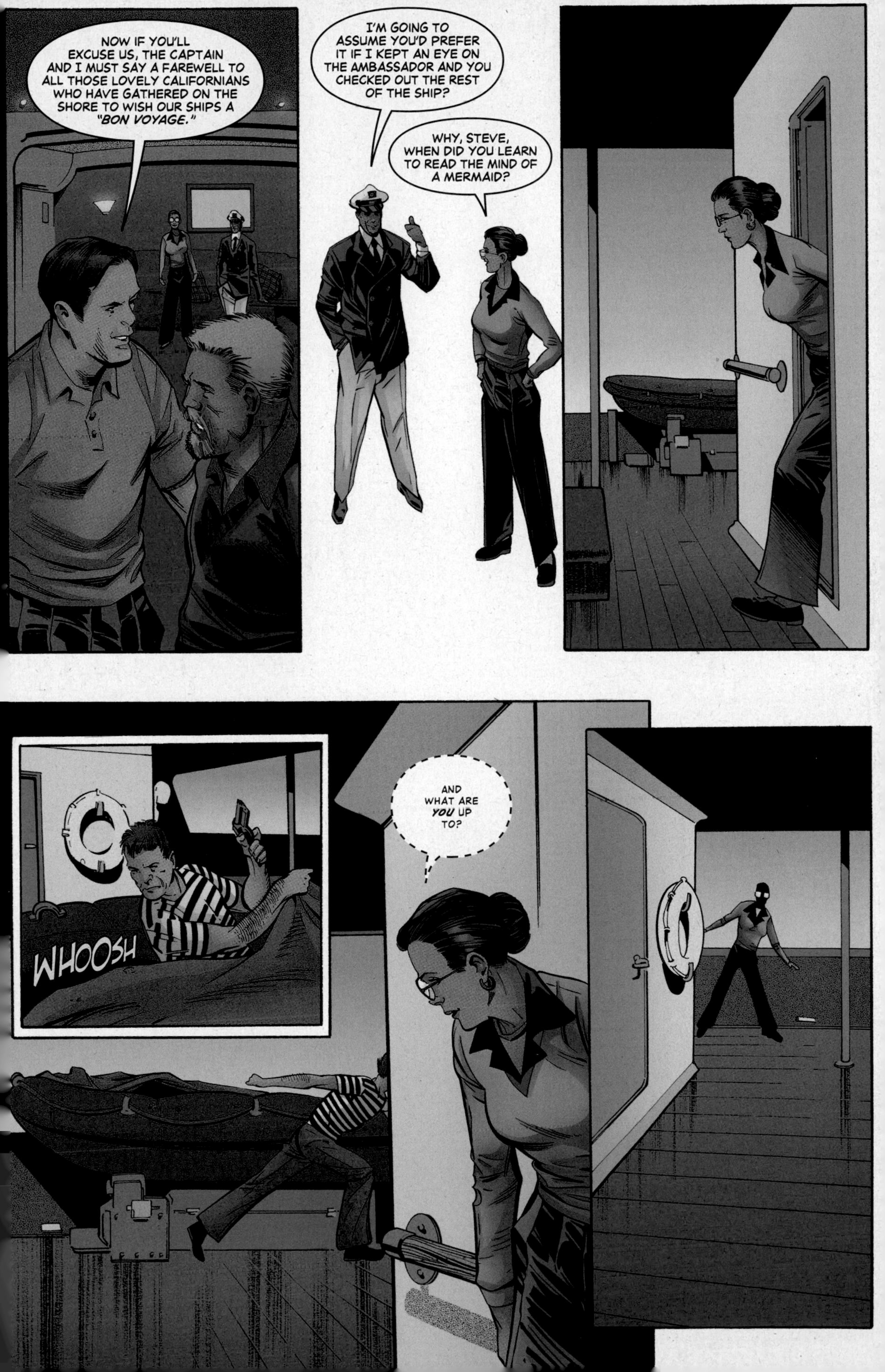
NOW IF YOU'LL EXCUSE US, THE CAPTAIN AND I MUST SAY A FAREWELL TO ALL THOSE LOVELY CALIFORNIANS WHO HAVE GATHERED ON THE SHORE TO WISH OUR SHIPS A "BON VOYAGE."
I'M GOING TO ASSUME YOU'D PREFER IT IF I KEPT AN EYE ON THE AMBASSADOR AND YOU CHECKED OUT THE REST OF THE SHIP?
WHY, STEVE, WHEN DID YOU LEARN TO READ THE MIND OF A MERMAID?
WHOOSH
AND WHAT ARE YOU UP TO?

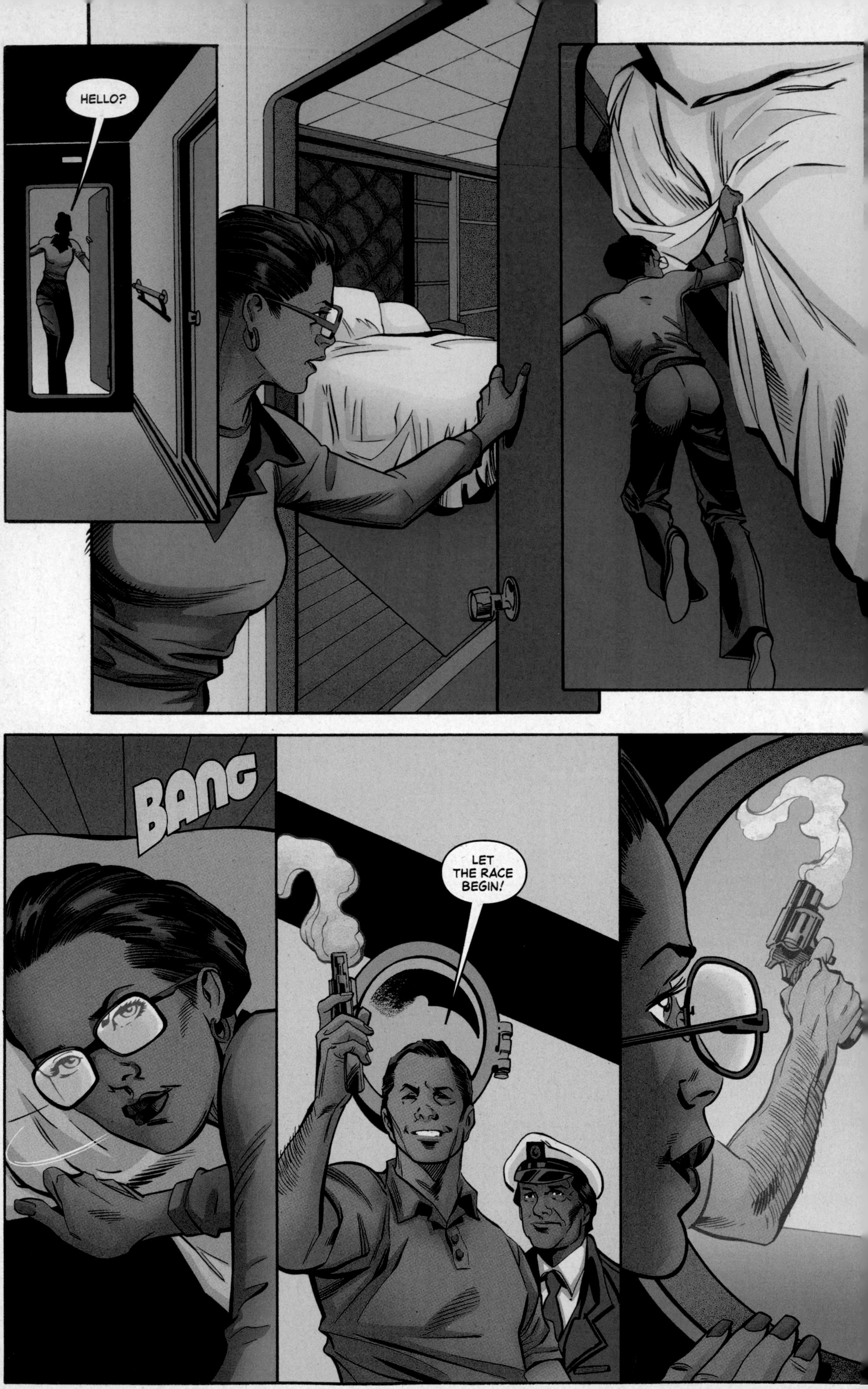
HELLO?
BANG
LET THE RACE BEGIN!

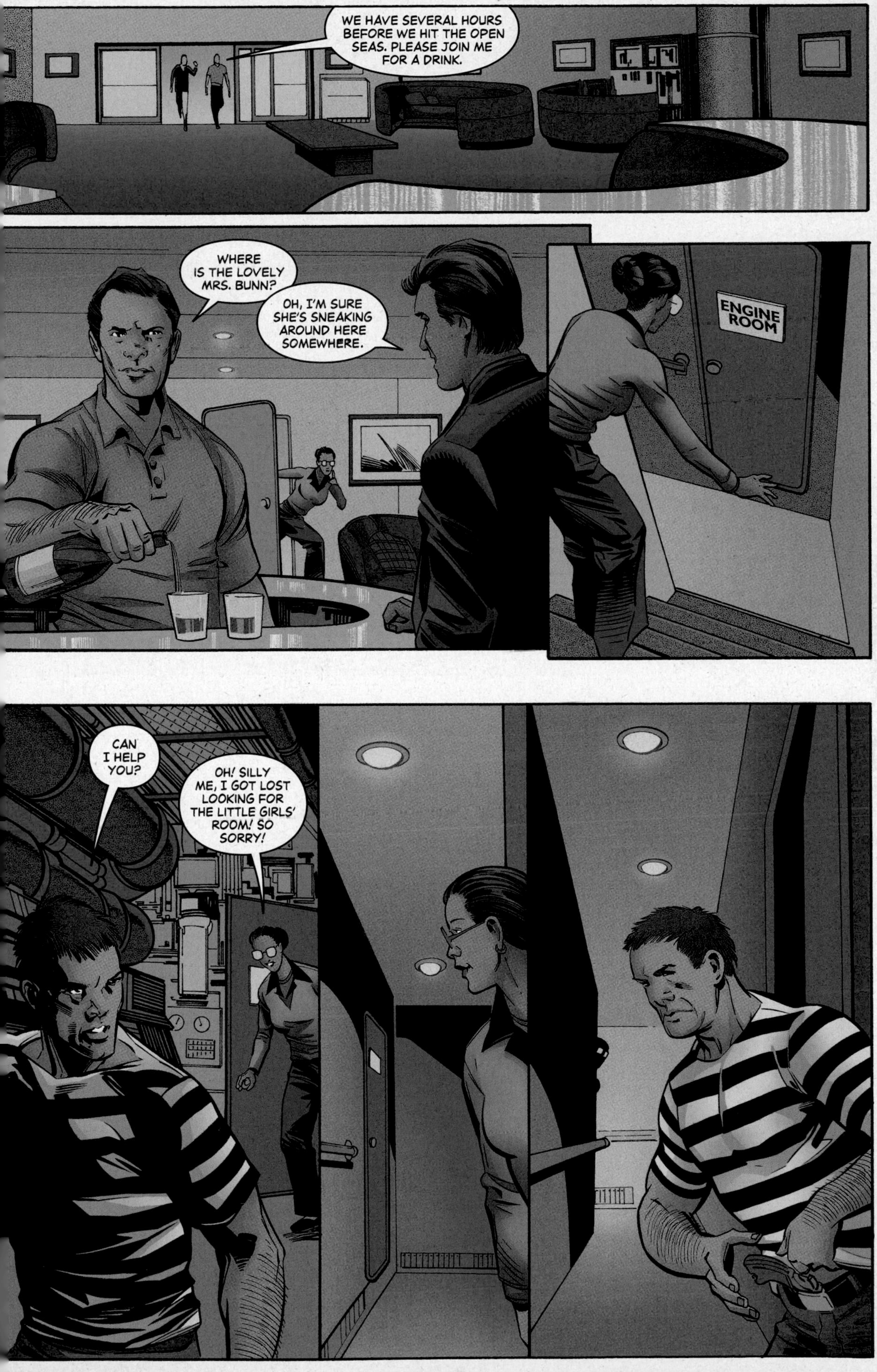
WE HAVE SEVERAL HOURS BEFORE WE HIT THE OPEN SEAS. PLEASE JOIN ME FOR A DRINK.
WHERE IS THE LOVELY MRS. BUNN?
OH, I'M SURE SHE'S SNEAKING AROUND HERE SOMEWHERE.
ENGINE ROOM
CAN I HELP YOU?
OH! SILLY ME, I GOT LOST LOOKING FOR THE LITTLE GIRLS' ROOM! SO SORRY!

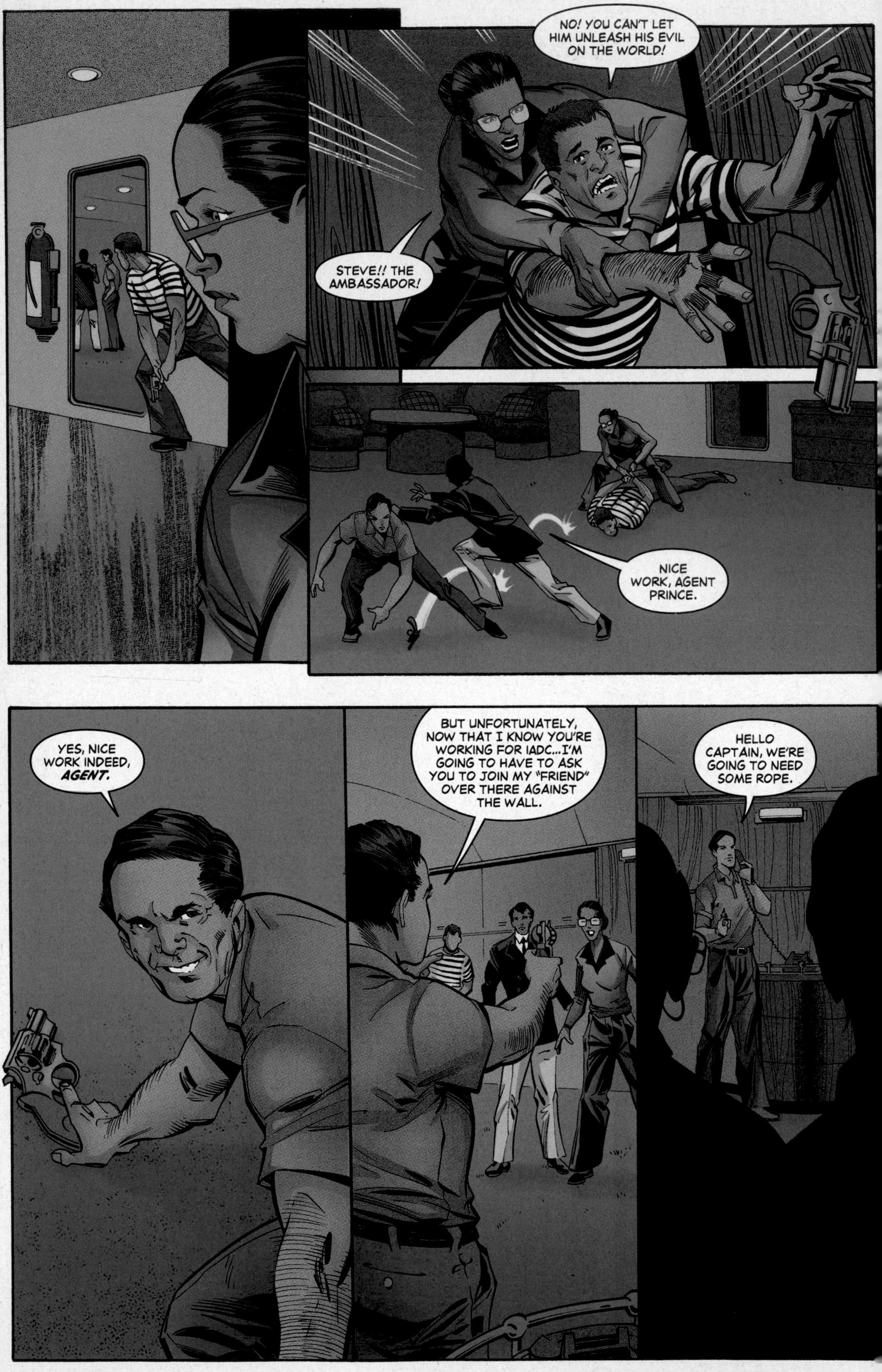
NO! YOU CAN'T LET HIM UNLEASH HIS EVIL ON THE WORLD!
STEVE!! THE AMBASSADOR!
NICE WORK, AGENT PRINCE.
YES, NICE WORK INDEED, ***AGENT.***
BUT UNFORTUNATELY, NOW THAT I KNOW YOU'RE WORKING FOR IADC...I'M GOING TO HAVE TO ASK YOU TO JOIN MY "FRIEND" OVER THERE AGAINST THE WALL.
HELLO CAPTAIN, WE'RE GOING TO NEED SOME ROPE.

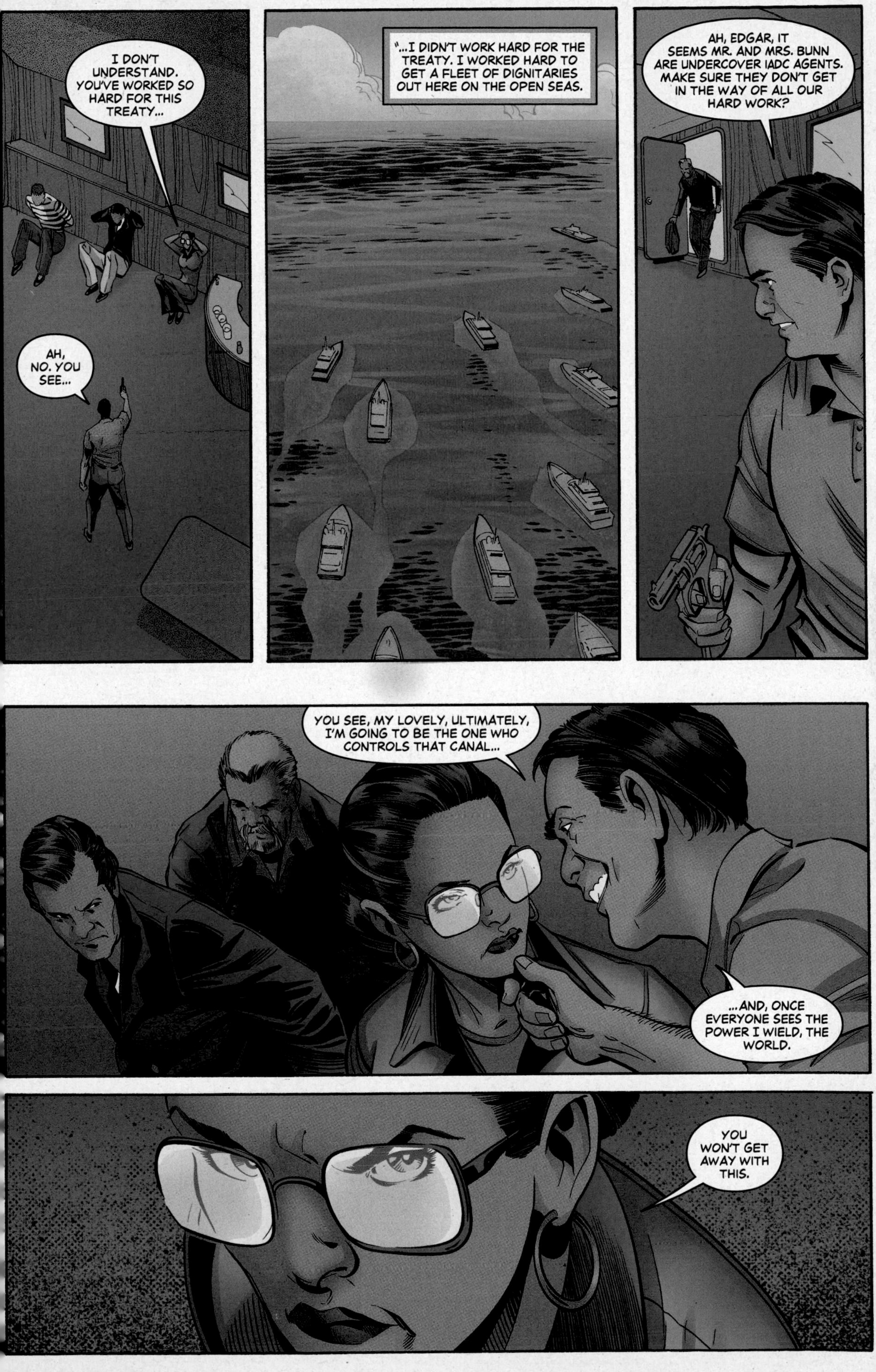
I DON'T UNDERSTAND. YOU'VE WORKED SO HARD FOR THIS TREATY...
AH, NO. YOU SEE...
"...I DIDN'T WORK HARD FOR THE TREATY. I WORKED HARD TO GET A FLEET OF DIGNITARIES OUT HERE ON THE OPEN SEAS.
AH, EDGAR, IT SEEMS MR. AND MRS. BUNN ARE UNDERCOVER IADC AGENTS. MAKE SURE THEY DON'T GET IN THE WAY OF ALL OUR HARD WORK?
YOU SEE, MY LOVELY, ULTIMATELY, I'M GOING TO BE THE ONE WHO CONTROLS THAT CANAL...
...AND, ONCE EVERYONE SEES THE POWER I WIELD, THE WORLD.
YOU WON'T GET AWAY WITH THIS.

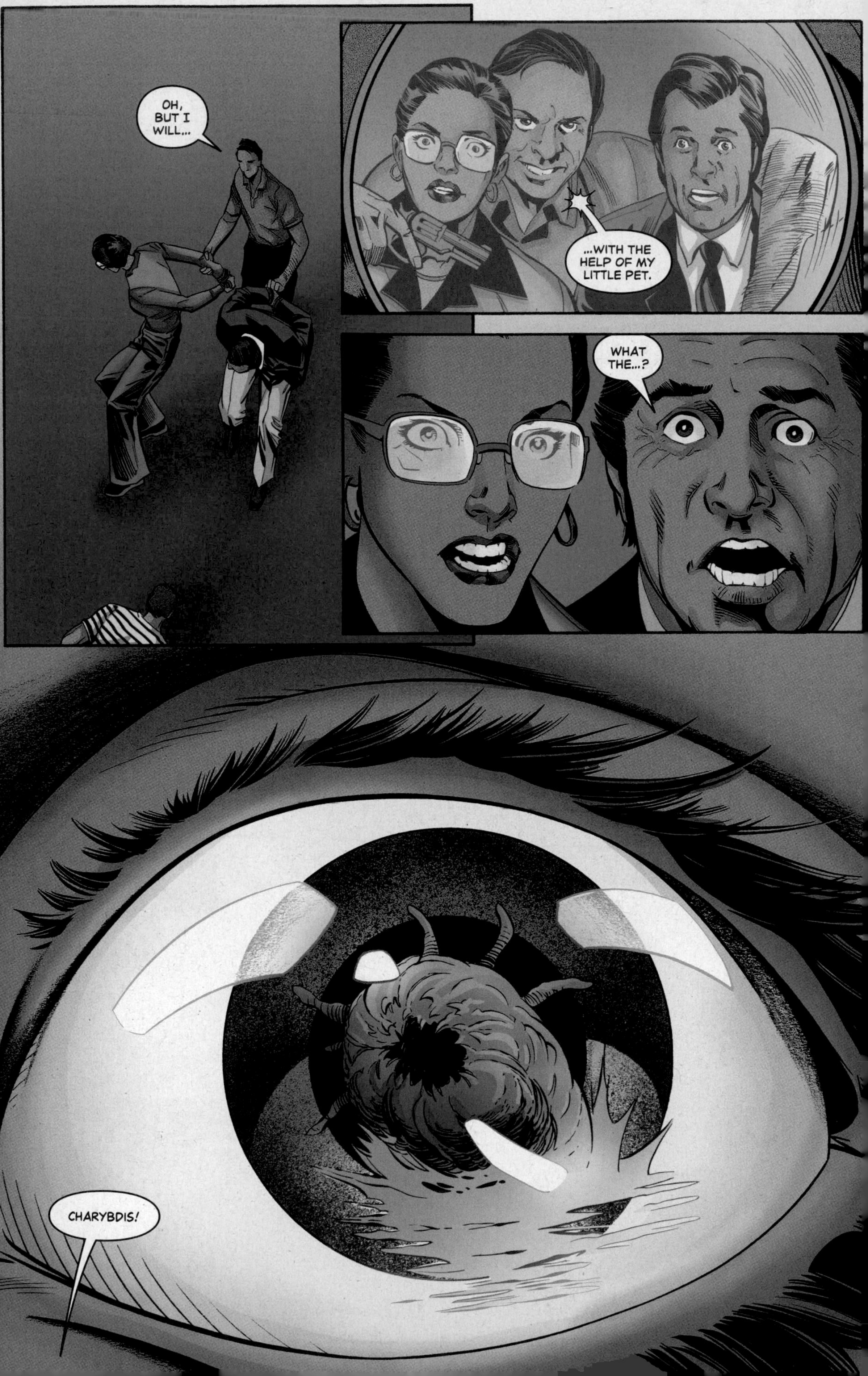
OH, BUT I WILL...
...WITH THE HELP OF MY LITTLE PET.
WHAT THE...?
CHARYBDIS!

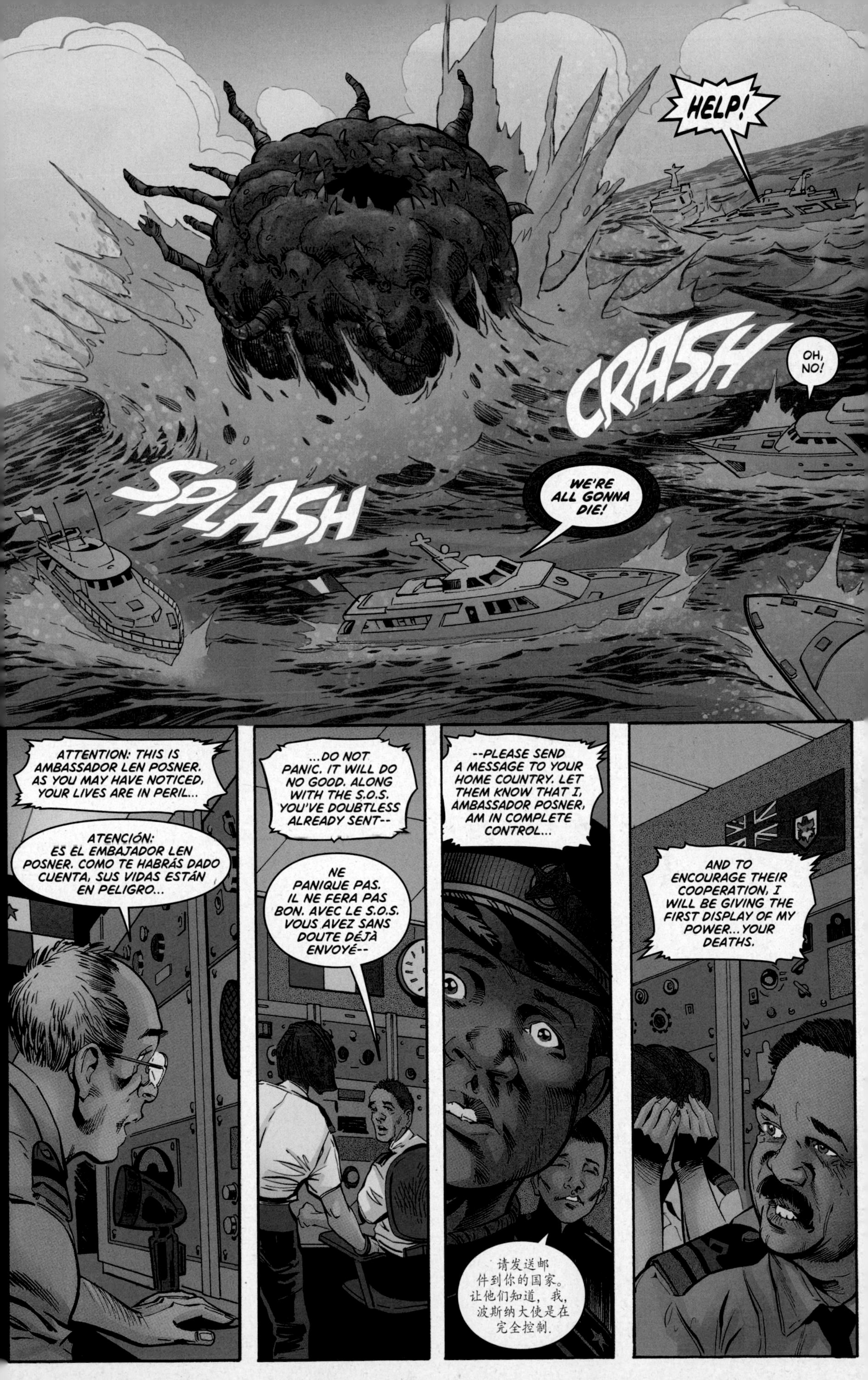
HELP!
CRASH
OH, NO!
SPLASH
WE'RE ALL GONNA DIE!
ATTENTION: THIS IS AMBASSADOR LEN POSNER. AS YOU MAY HAVE NOTICED, YOUR LIVES ARE IN PERIL...
ATENCIÓN: ES EL EMBAJADOR LEN POSNER. COMO TE HABRÁS DADO CUENTA, SUS VIDAS ESTÁN EN PELIGRO...
...DO NOT PANIC. IT WILL DO NO GOOD. ALONG WITH THE S.O.S. YOU'VE DOUBTLESS ALREADY SENT--
NE PANIQUE PAS. IL NE FERA PAS BON. AVEC LE S.O.S. VOUS AVEZ SANS DOUTE DÉJÀ ENVOYÉ--
--PLEASE SEND A MESSAGE TO YOUR HOME COUNTRY. LET THEM KNOW THAT I, AMBASSADOR POSNER, AM IN COMPLETE CONTROL...
请发送邮件到你的国家。让他们知道，我，波斯纳大使是在完全控制.
AND TO ENCOURAGE THEIR COOPERATION, I WILL BE GIVING THE FIRST DISPLAY OF MY POWER...YOUR DEATHS.

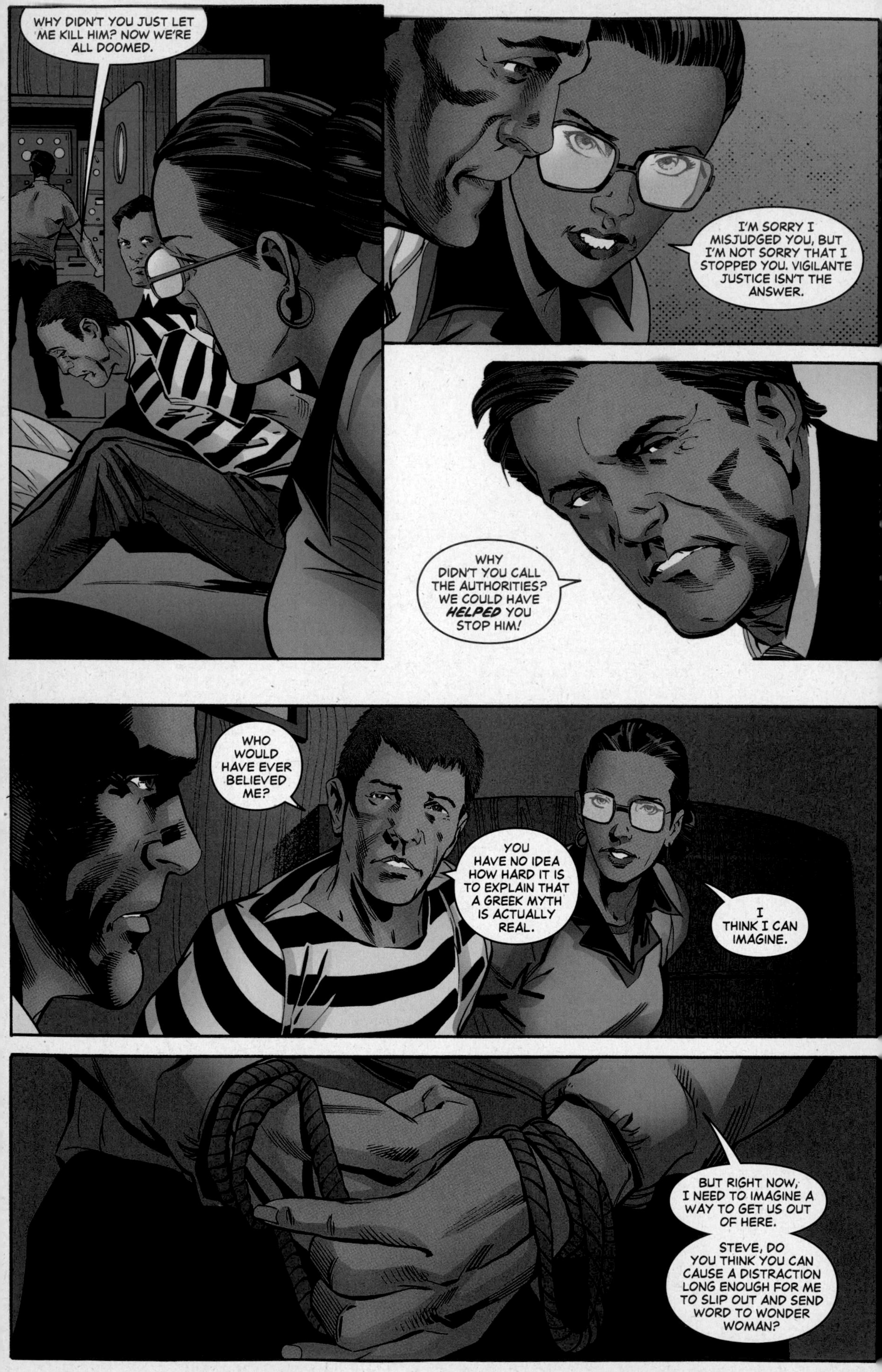
WHY DIDN'T YOU JUST LET ME KILL HIM? NOW WE'RE ALL DOOMED.
I'M SORRY I MISJUDGED YOU, BUT I'M NOT SORRY THAT I STOPPED YOU. VIGILANTE JUSTICE ISN'T THE ANSWER.
WHY DIDN'T YOU CALL THE AUTHORITIES? WE COULD HAVE **HELPED** YOU STOP HIM!
WHO WOULD HAVE EVER BELIEVED ME?
YOU HAVE NO IDEA HOW HARD IT IS TO EXPLAIN THAT A GREEK MYTH IS ACTUALLY REAL.
I THINK I CAN IMAGINE.
BUT RIGHT NOW, I NEED TO IMAGINE A WAY TO GET US OUT OF HERE.
STEVE, DO YOU THINK YOU CAN CAUSE A DISTRACTION LONG ENOUGH FOR ME TO SLIP OUT AND SEND WORD TO WONDER WOMAN?

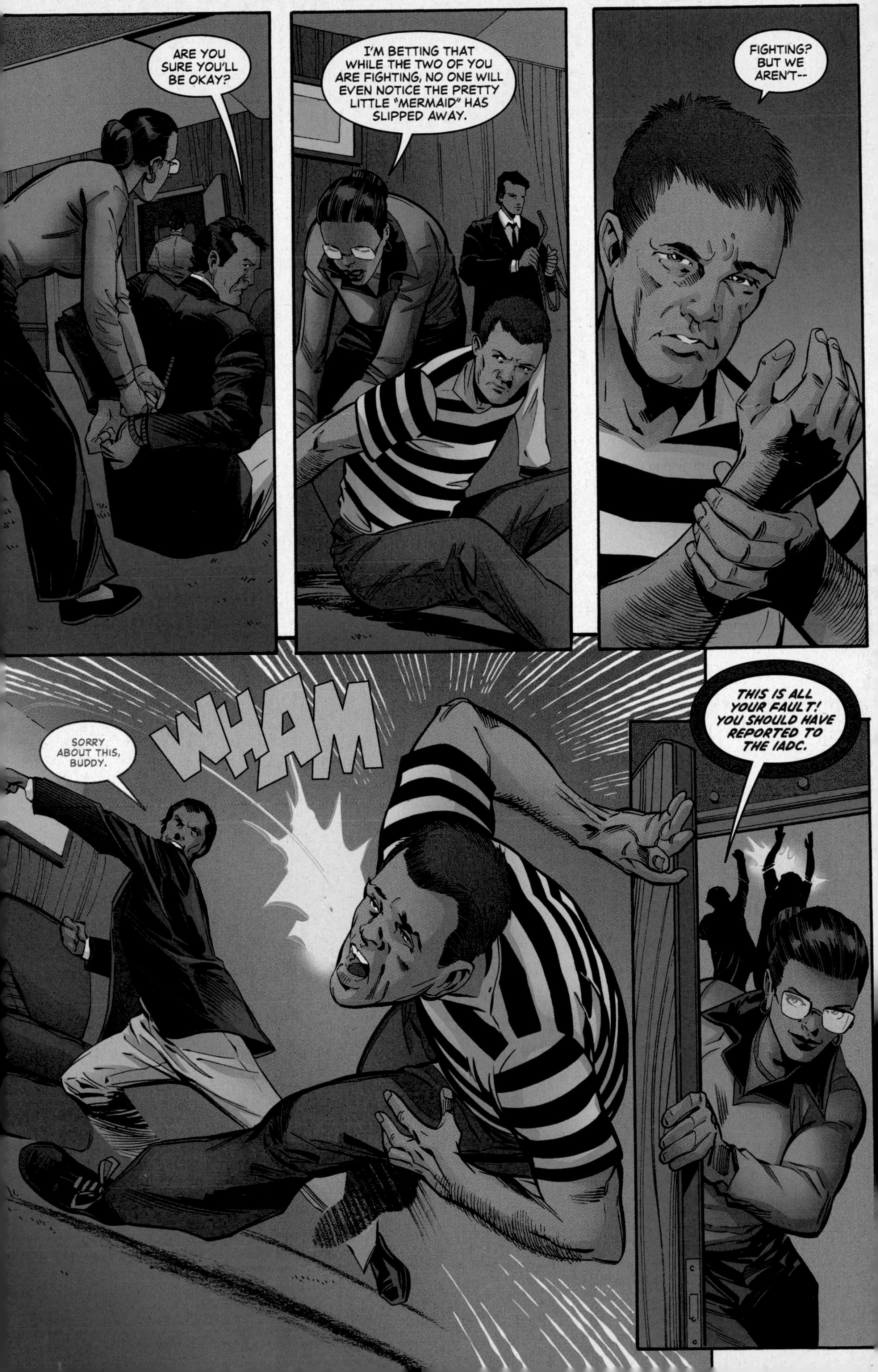
ARE YOU SURE YOU'LL BE OKAY?
I'M BETTING THAT WHILE THE TWO OF YOU ARE FIGHTING, NO ONE WILL EVEN NOTICE THE PRETTY LITTLE "MERMAID" HAS SLIPPED AWAY.
FIGHTING? BUT WE AREN'T--
WHAM
SORRY ABOUT THIS, BUDDY.
THIS IS ALL YOUR FAULT! YOU SHOULD HAVE REPORTED TO THE IADC.

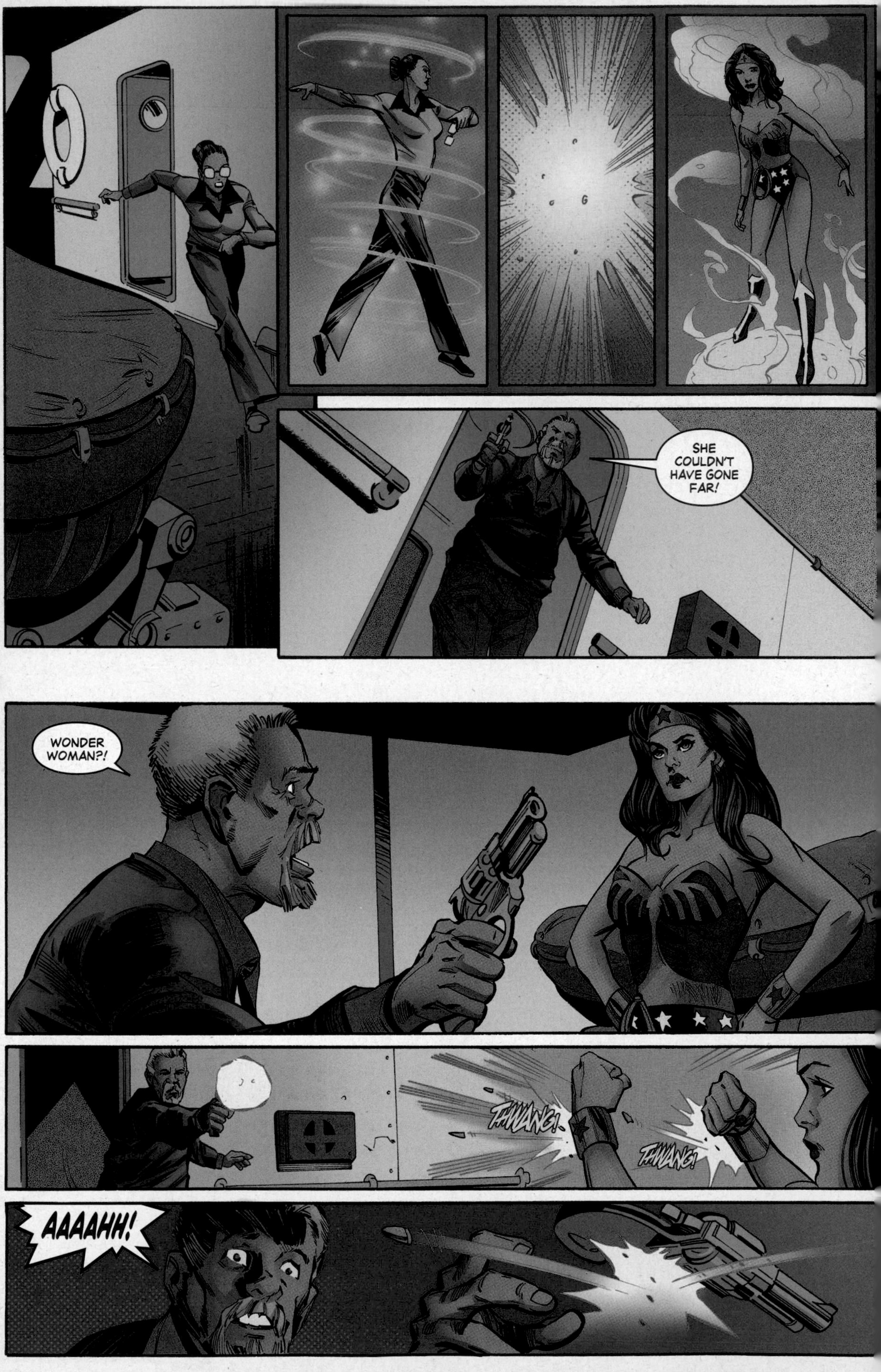
SHE COULDN'T HAVE GONE FAR!
WONDER WOMAN?!
THWANG!
THWANG!
AAAAHH!

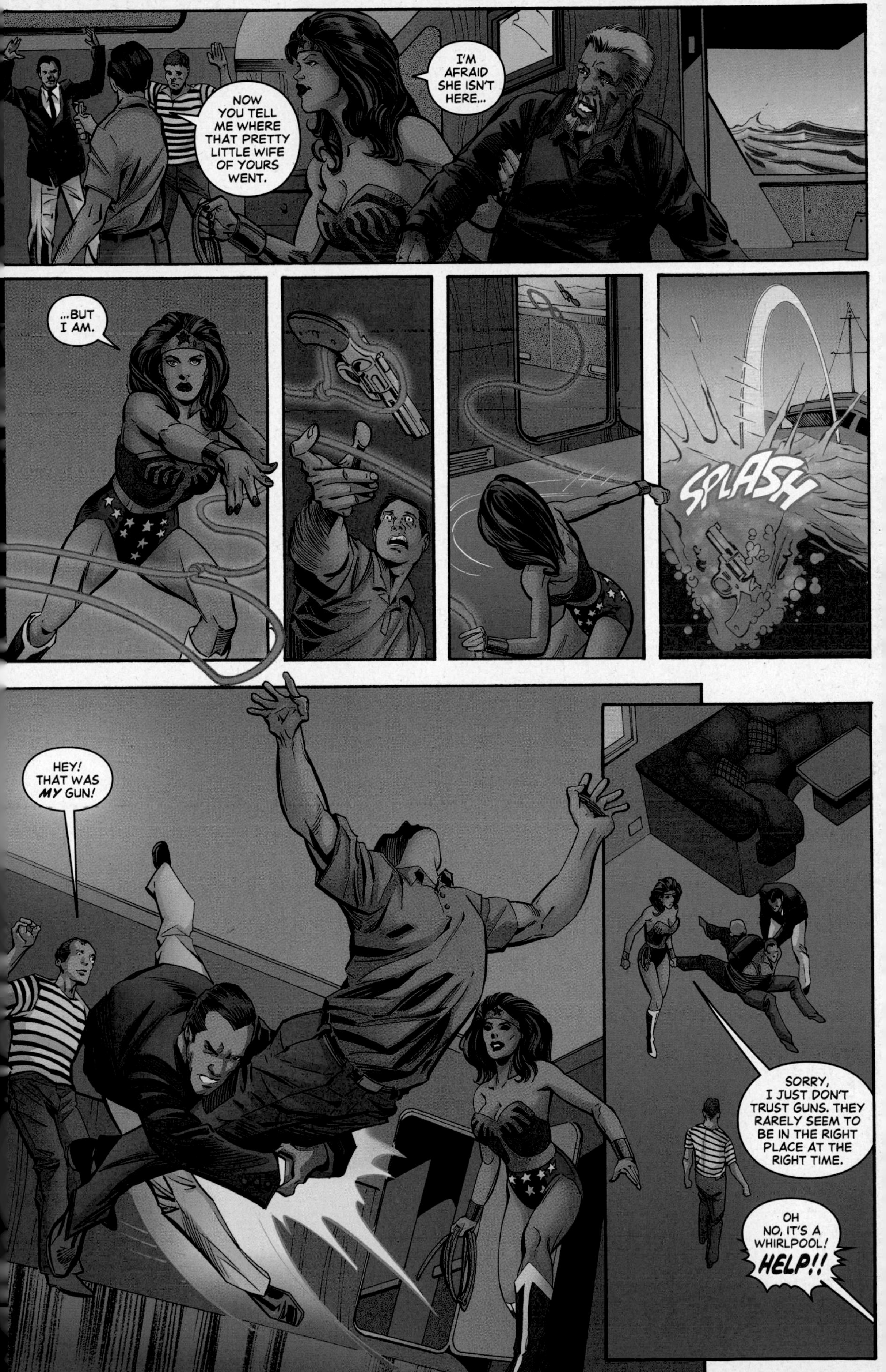
NOW YOU TELL ME WHERE THAT PRETTY LITTLE WIFE OF YOURS WENT.
I'M AFRAID SHE ISN'T HERE...
...BUT I AM.
SPLASH
HEY! THAT WAS *MY* GUN!
SORRY, I JUST DON'T TRUST GUNS. THEY RARELY SEEM TO BE IN THE RIGHT PLACE AT THE RIGHT TIME.
OH NO, IT'S A WHIRLPOOL! **HELP!!**

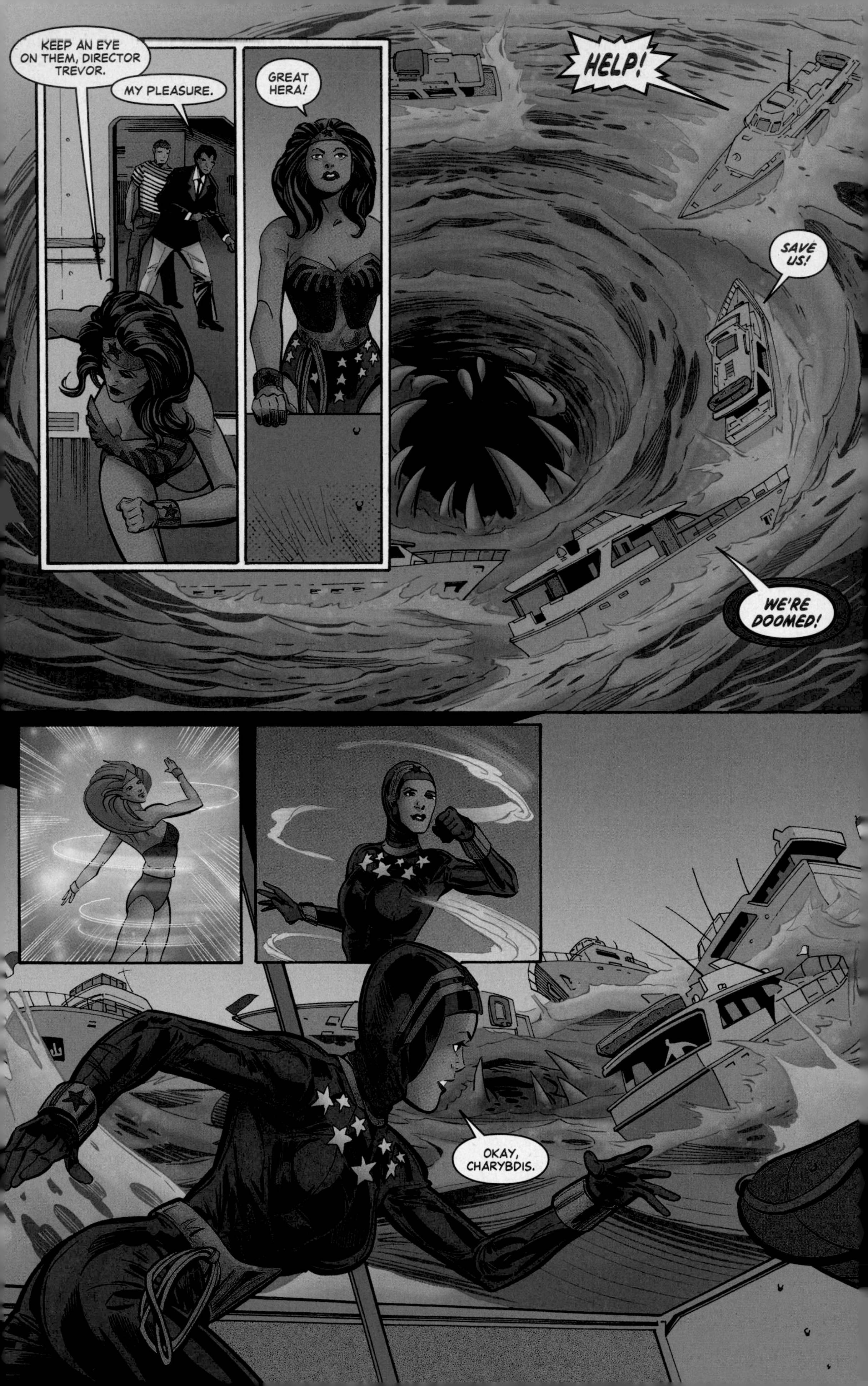
KEEP AN EYE ON THEM, DIRECTOR TREVOR.
MY PLEASURE.
GREAT HERA!
HELP!
SAVE US!
WE'RE DOOMED!
OKAY, CHARYBDIS.

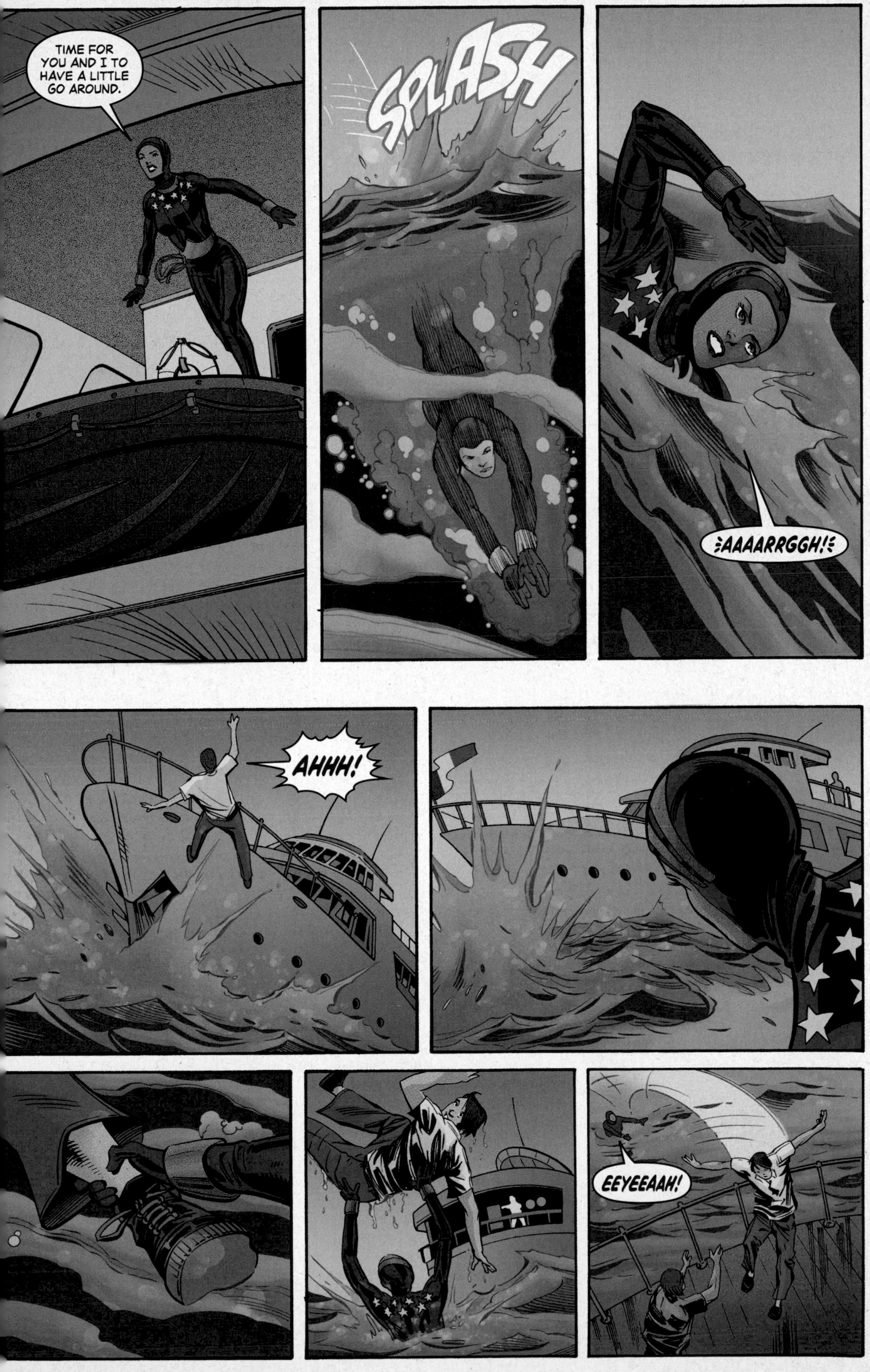
TIME FOR YOU AND I TO HAVE A LITTLE GO AROUND.
SPLASH
AAAARRGGH!
AHHH!
EEYEEAAH!

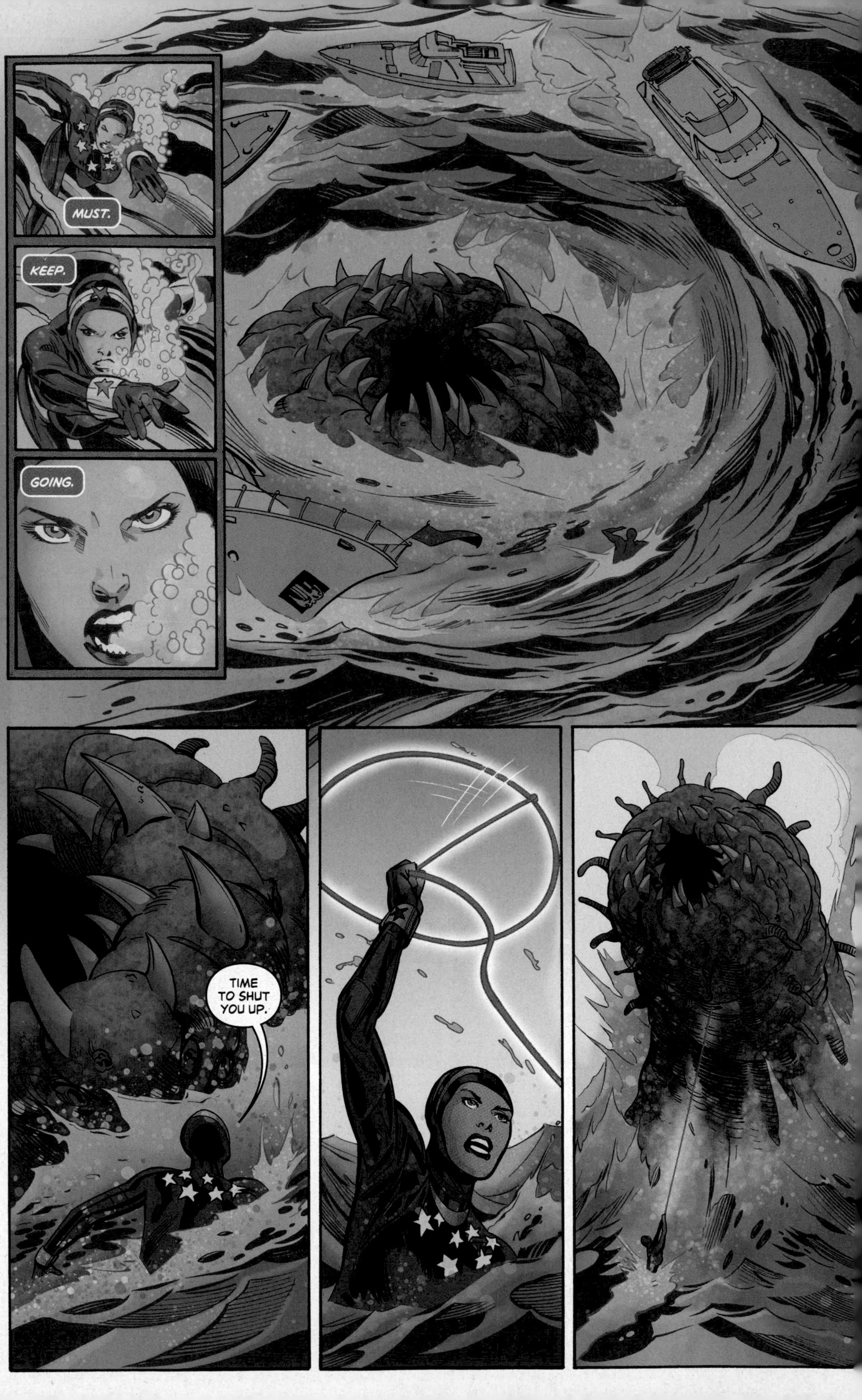
MUST.
KEEP.
GOING.
TIME TO SHUT YOU UP.

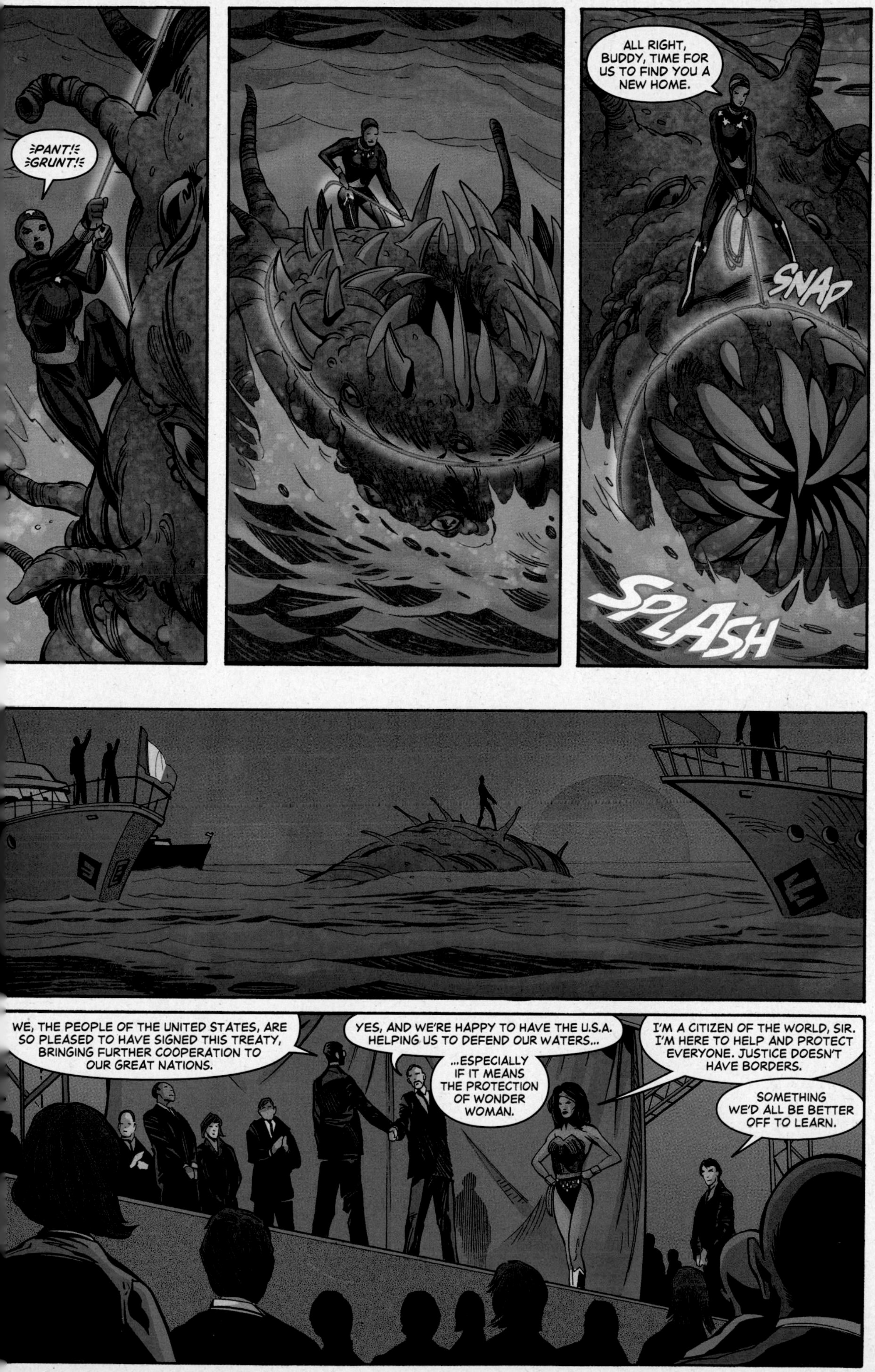

PANT!
GRUNT!
ALL RIGHT, BUDDY, TIME FOR US TO FIND YOU A NEW HOME.
SNAP
SPLASH
WE, THE PEOPLE OF THE UNITED STATES, ARE SO PLEASED TO HAVE SIGNED THIS TREATY, BRINGING FURTHER COOPERATION TO OUR GREAT NATIONS.
YES, AND WE'RE HAPPY TO HAVE THE U.S.A. HELPING US TO DEFEND OUR WATERS...
...ESPECIALLY IF IT MEANS THE PROTECTION OF WONDER WOMAN.
I'M A CITIZEN OF THE WORLD, SIR. I'M HERE TO HELP AND PROTECT EVERYONE. JUSTICE DOESN'T HAVE BORDERS.
SOMETHING WE'D ALL BE BETTER OFF TO LEARN.

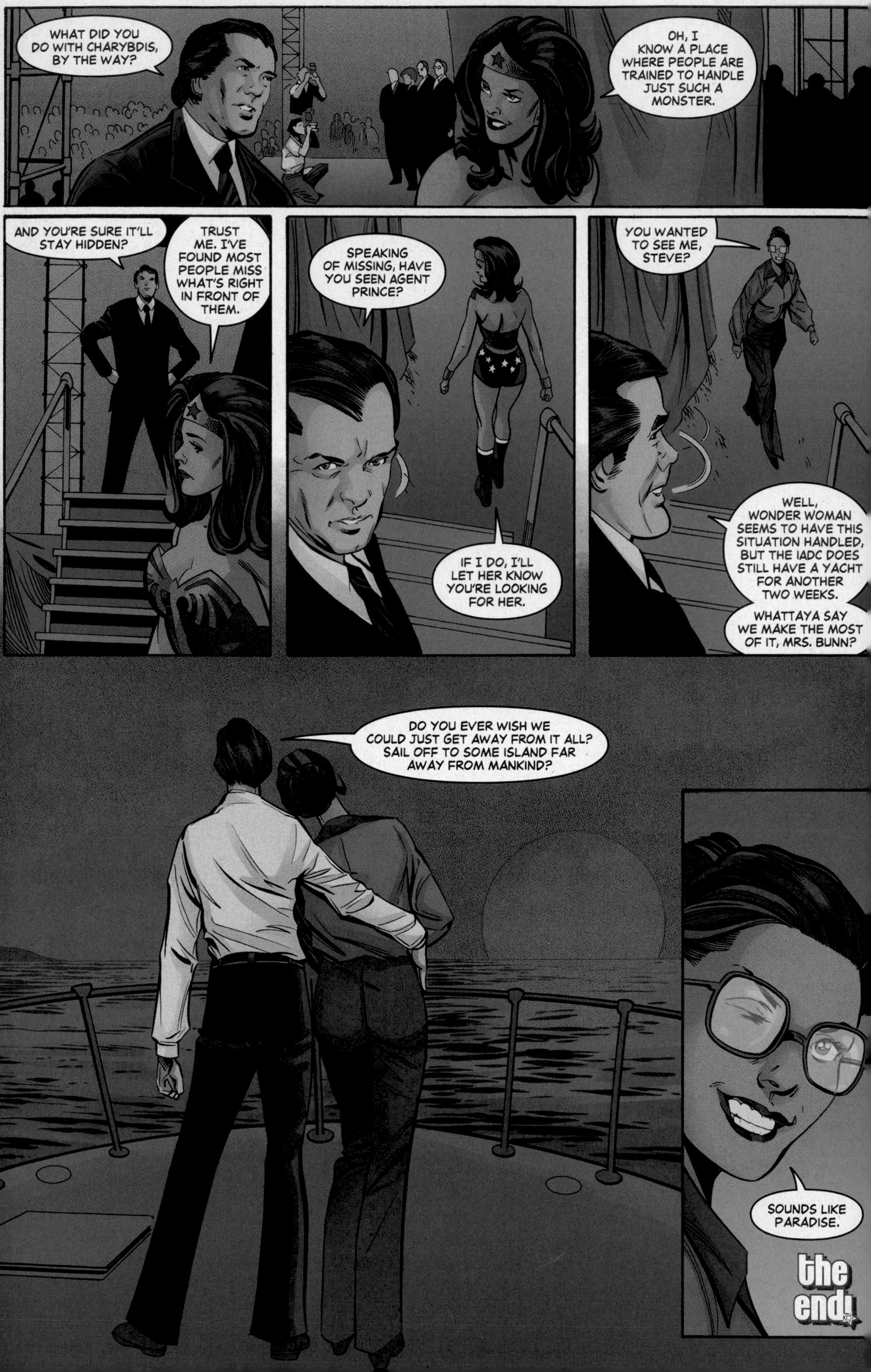
WHAT DID YOU DO WITH CHARYBDIS, BY THE WAY?
OH, I KNOW A PLACE WHERE PEOPLE ARE TRAINED TO HANDLE JUST SUCH A MONSTER.
AND YOU'RE SURE IT'LL STAY HIDDEN?
TRUST ME. I'VE FOUND MOST PEOPLE MISS WHAT'S RIGHT IN FRONT OF THEM.
SPEAKING OF MISSING, HAVE YOU SEEN AGENT PRINCE?
IF I DO, I'LL LET HER KNOW YOU'RE LOOKING FOR HER.
YOU WANTED TO SEE ME, STEVE?
WELL, WONDER WOMAN SEEMS TO HAVE THIS SITUATION HANDLED, BUT THE IADC DOES STILL HAVE A YACHT FOR ANOTHER TWO WEEKS.
WHATTAYA SAY WE MAKE THE MOST OF IT, MRS. BUNN?
DO YOU EVER WISH WE COULD JUST GET AWAY FROM IT ALL? SAIL OFF TO SOME ISLAND FAR AWAY FROM MANKIND?
SOUNDS LIKE PARADISE.
the end!

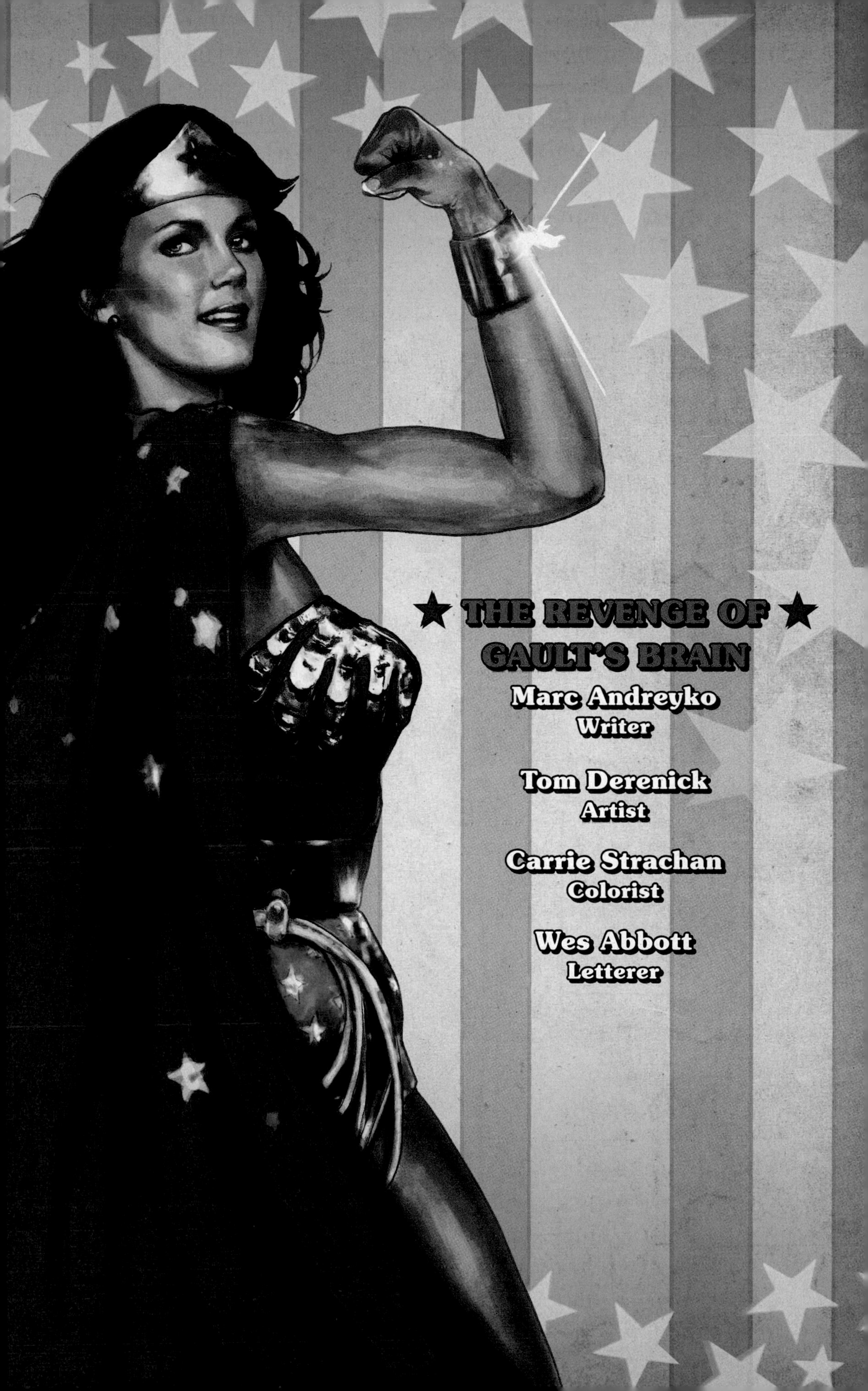

★ THE REVENGE OF GAULT'S BRAIN ★

Marc Andreyko
Writer

Tom Derenick
Artist

Carrie Strachan
Colorist

Wes Abbott
Letterer

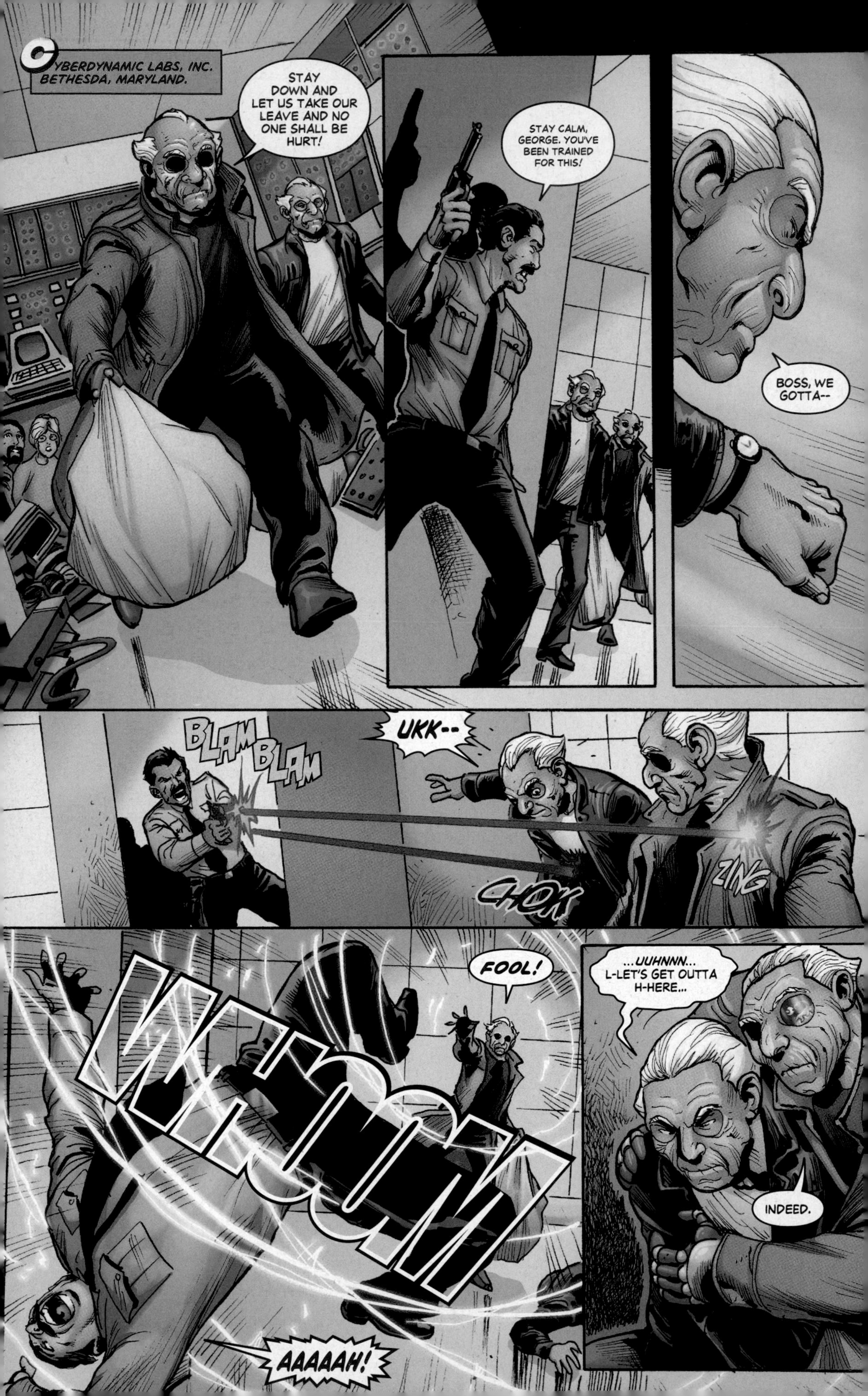
CYBERDYNAMIC LABS, INC.
BETHESDA, MARYLAND.
STAY DOWN AND LET US TAKE OUR LEAVE AND NO ONE SHALL BE HURT!
STAY CALM, GEORGE. YOU'VE BEEN TRAINED FOR THIS!
BOSS, WE GOTTA--
BLAM BLAM
UKK--
CHOK
ZING
WHOOM
FOOL!
AAAAAH!
...UUHNNN... L-LET'S GET OUTTA H-HERE...
INDEED.

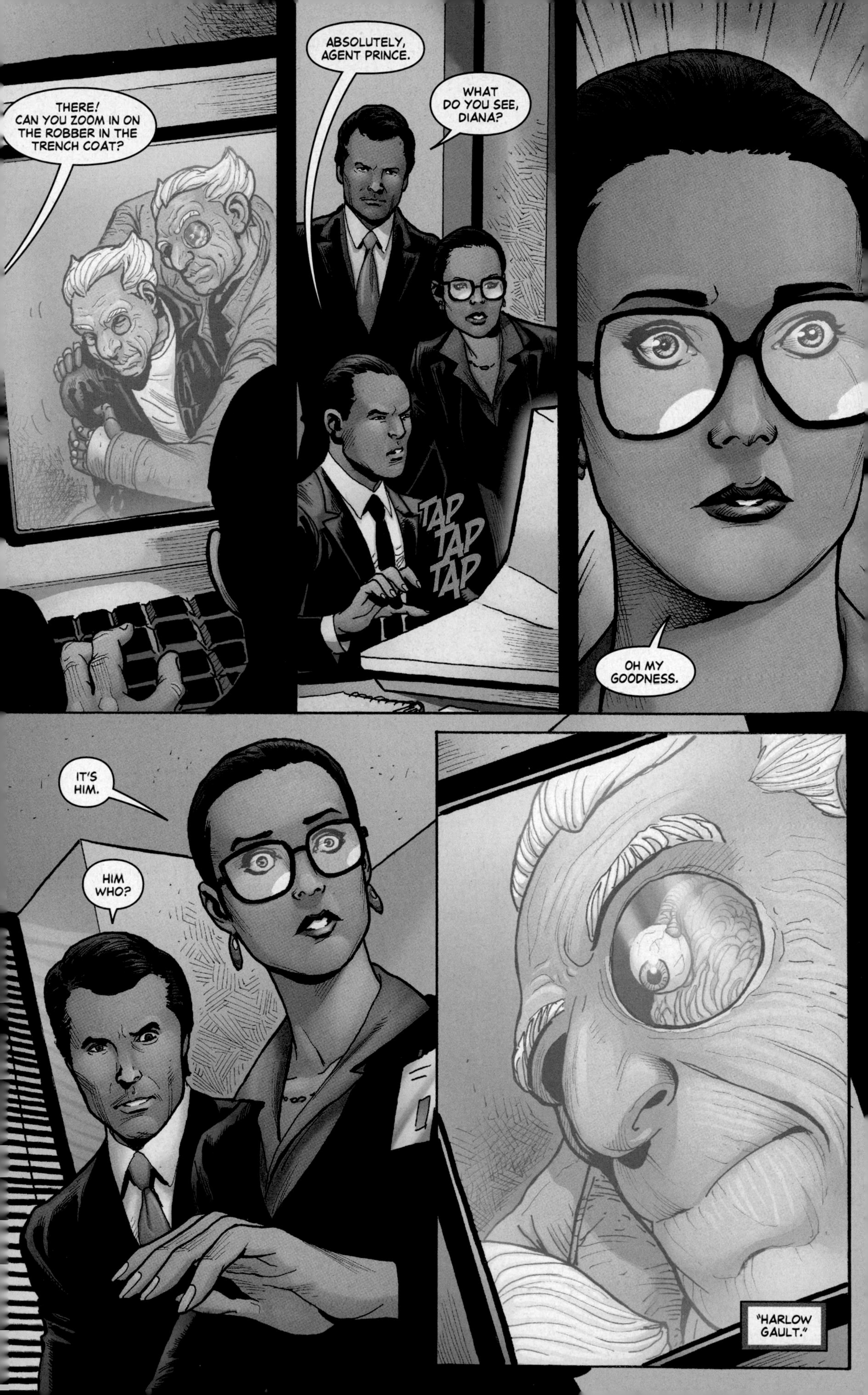
THERE! CAN YOU ZOOM IN ON THE ROBBER IN THE TRENCH COAT?
ABSOLUTELY, AGENT PRINCE.
WHAT DO YOU SEE, DIANA?
TAP TAP TAP
OH MY GOODNESS.
IT'S HIM.
HIM WHO?
"HARLOW GAULT."

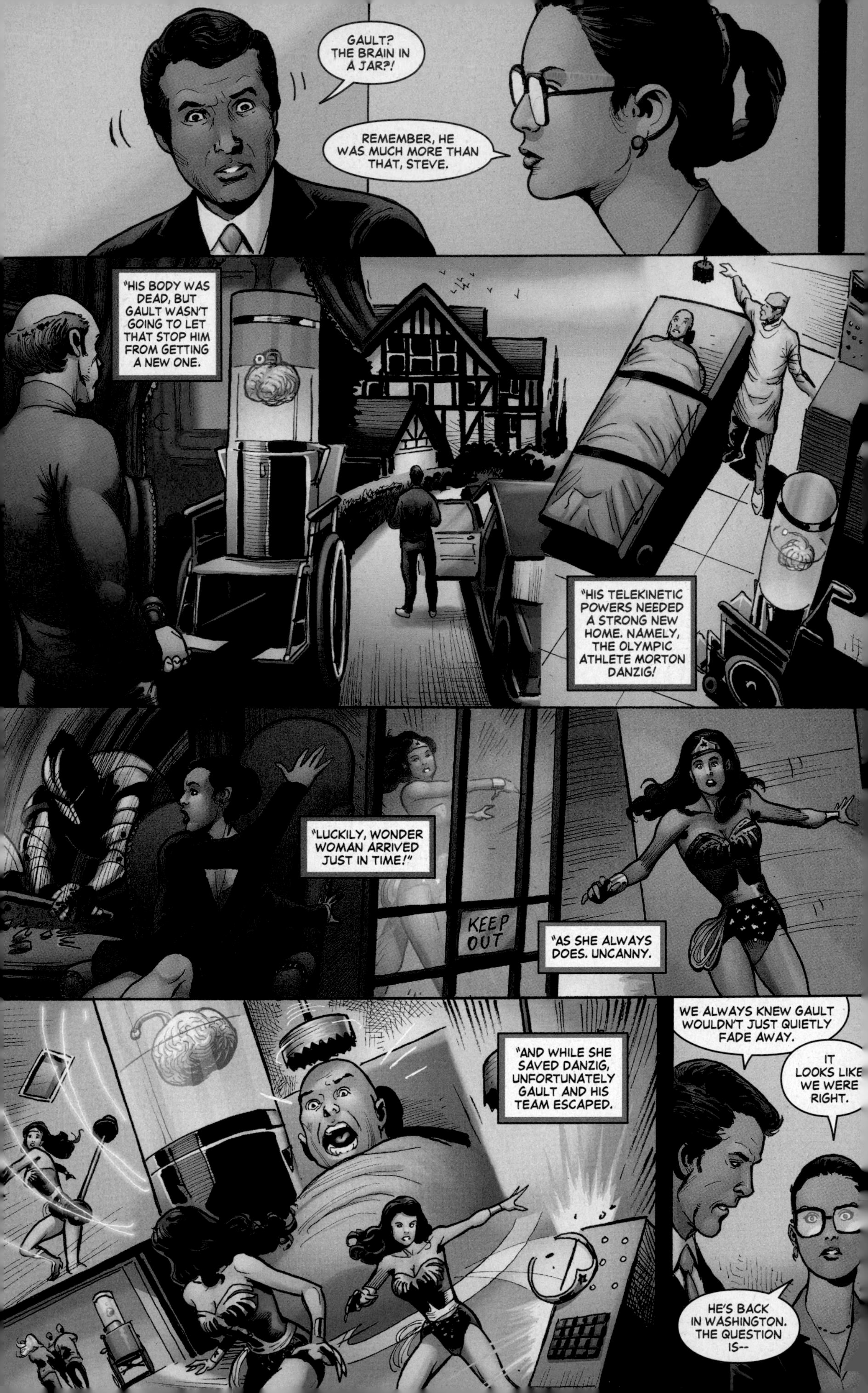
GAULT? THE BRAIN IN A JAR?!
REMEMBER, HE WAS MUCH MORE THAN THAT, STEVE.
"HIS BODY WAS DEAD, BUT GAULT WASN'T GOING TO LET THAT STOP HIM FROM GETTING A NEW ONE.
"HIS TELEKINETIC POWERS NEEDED A STRONG NEW HOME. NAMELY, THE OLYMPIC ATHLETE MORTON DANZIG!
"LUCKILY, WONDER WOMAN ARRIVED JUST IN TIME!"
KEEP OUT
"AS SHE ALWAYS DOES. UNCANNY.
"AND WHILE SHE SAVED DANZIG, UNFORTUNATELY GAULT AND HIS TEAM ESCAPED.
WE ALWAYS KNEW GAULT WOULDN'T JUST QUIETLY FADE AWAY.
IT LOOKS LIKE WE WERE RIGHT.
HE'S BACK IN WASHINGTON. THE QUESTION IS--

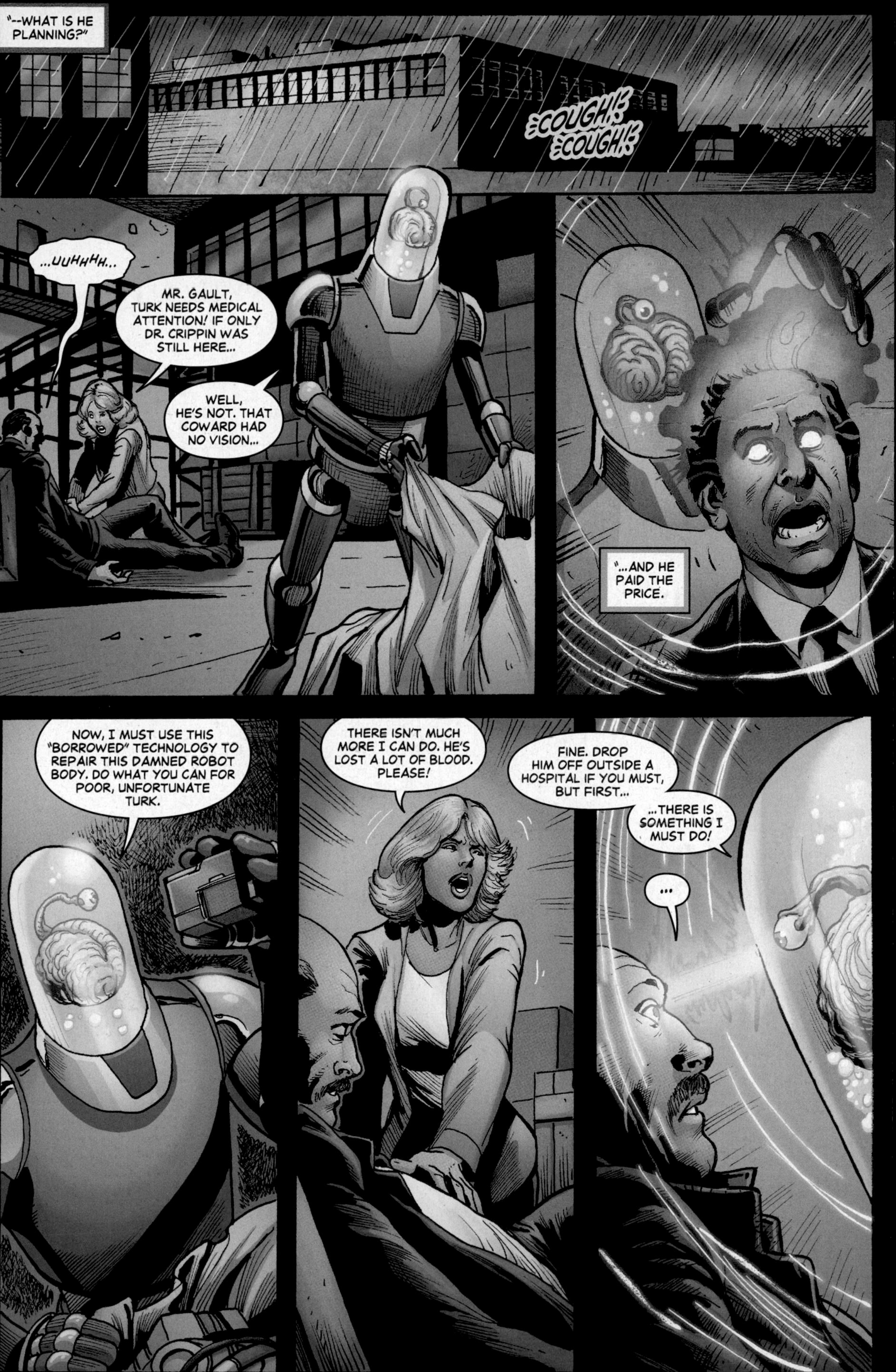
"--WHAT IS HE PLANNING?"
COUGH! COUGH!
...UUHHHH...
MR. GAULT, TURK NEEDS MEDICAL ATTENTION! IF ONLY DR. CRIPPIN WAS STILL HERE...
WELL, HE'S NOT. THAT COWARD HAD NO VISION...
"...AND HE PAID THE PRICE.
NOW, I MUST USE THIS "BORROWED" TECHNOLOGY TO REPAIR THIS DAMNED ROBOT BODY. DO WHAT YOU CAN FOR POOR, UNFORTUNATE TURK.
THERE ISN'T MUCH MORE I CAN DO. HE'S LOST A LOT OF BLOOD. PLEASE!
FINE. DROP HIM OFF OUTSIDE A HOSPITAL IF YOU MUST, BUT FIRST...
...THERE IS SOMETHING I MUST DO!
...

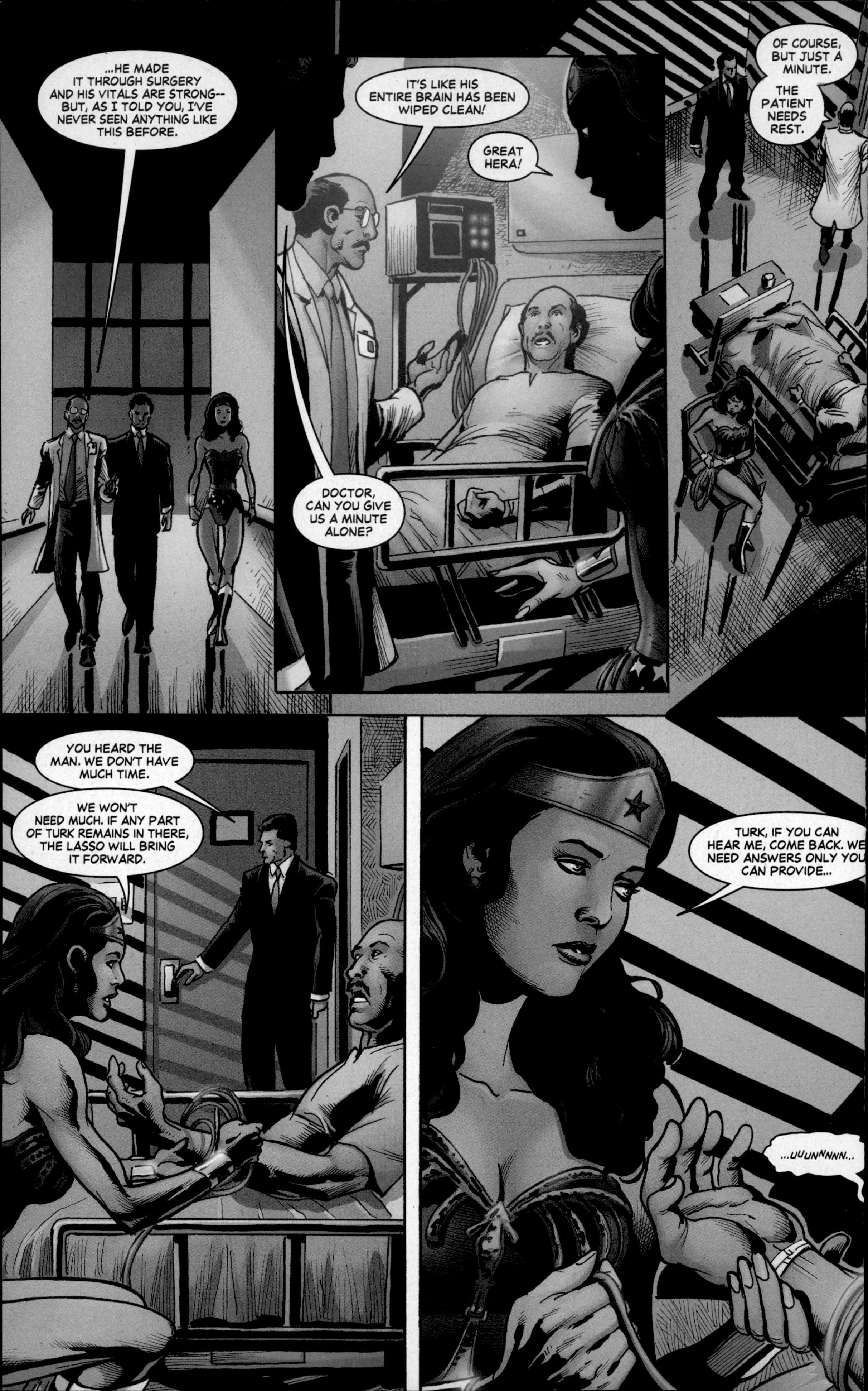
...HE MADE IT THROUGH SURGERY AND HIS VITALS ARE STRONG-- BUT, AS I TOLD YOU, I'VE NEVER SEEN ANYTHING LIKE THIS BEFORE.
IT'S LIKE HIS ENTIRE BRAIN HAS BEEN WIPED CLEAN!
GREAT HERA!
DOCTOR, CAN YOU GIVE US A MINUTE ALONE?
OF COURSE, BUT JUST A MINUTE.
THE PATIENT NEEDS REST.
YOU HEARD THE MAN. WE DON'T HAVE MUCH TIME.
WE WON'T NEED MUCH. IF ANY PART OF TURK REMAINS IN THERE, THE LASSO WILL BRING IT FORWARD.
TURK, IF YOU CAN HEAR ME, COME BACK. WE NEED ANSWERS ONLY YOU CAN PROVIDE...
...UUUNNNNN...

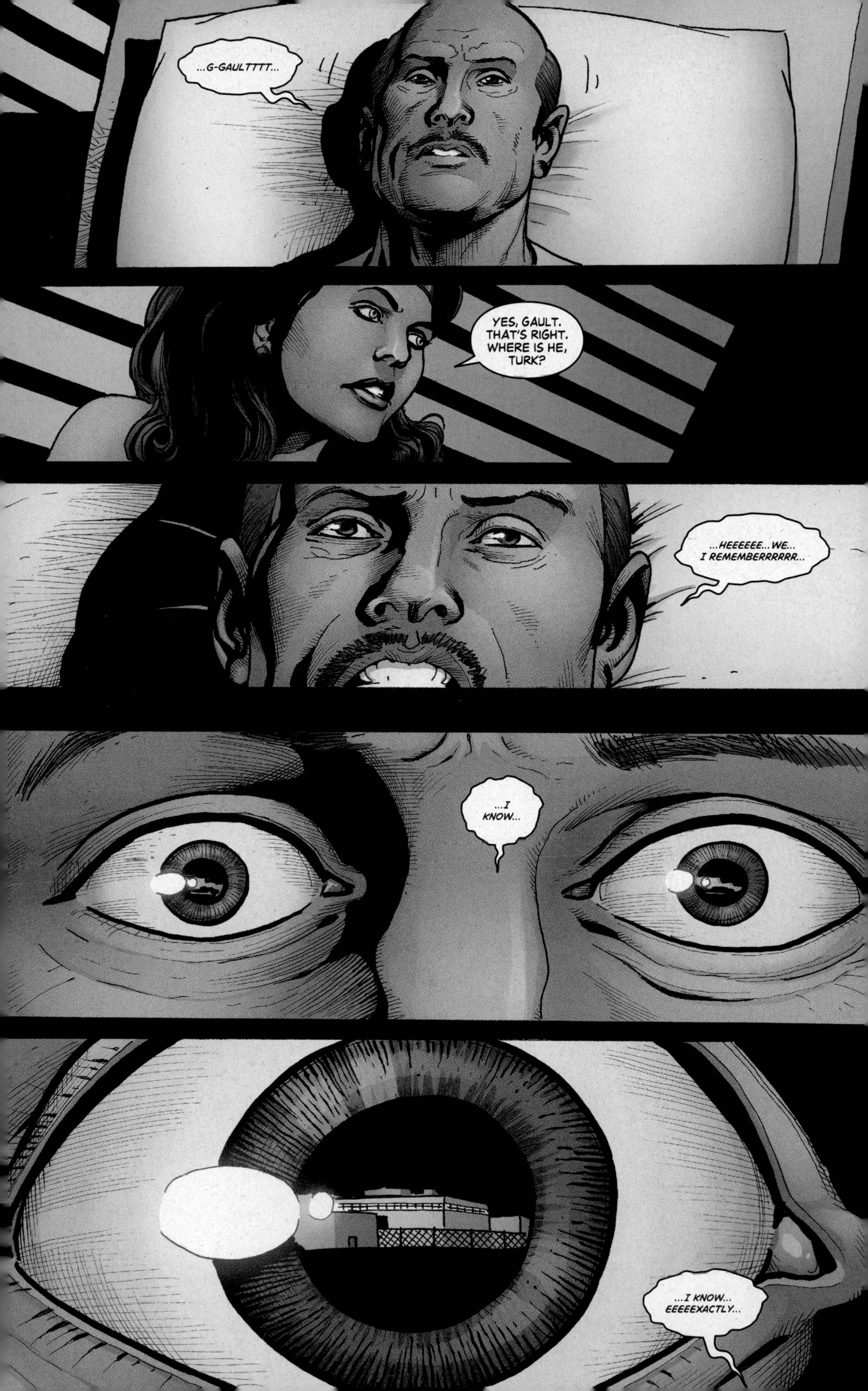
...G-GAULTTTT...
YES, GAULT. THAT'S RIGHT. WHERE IS HE, TURK?
...HEEEEEE...WE... I REMEMBERRRRRR...
...I KNOW...
...I KNOW... EEEEEXACTLY...

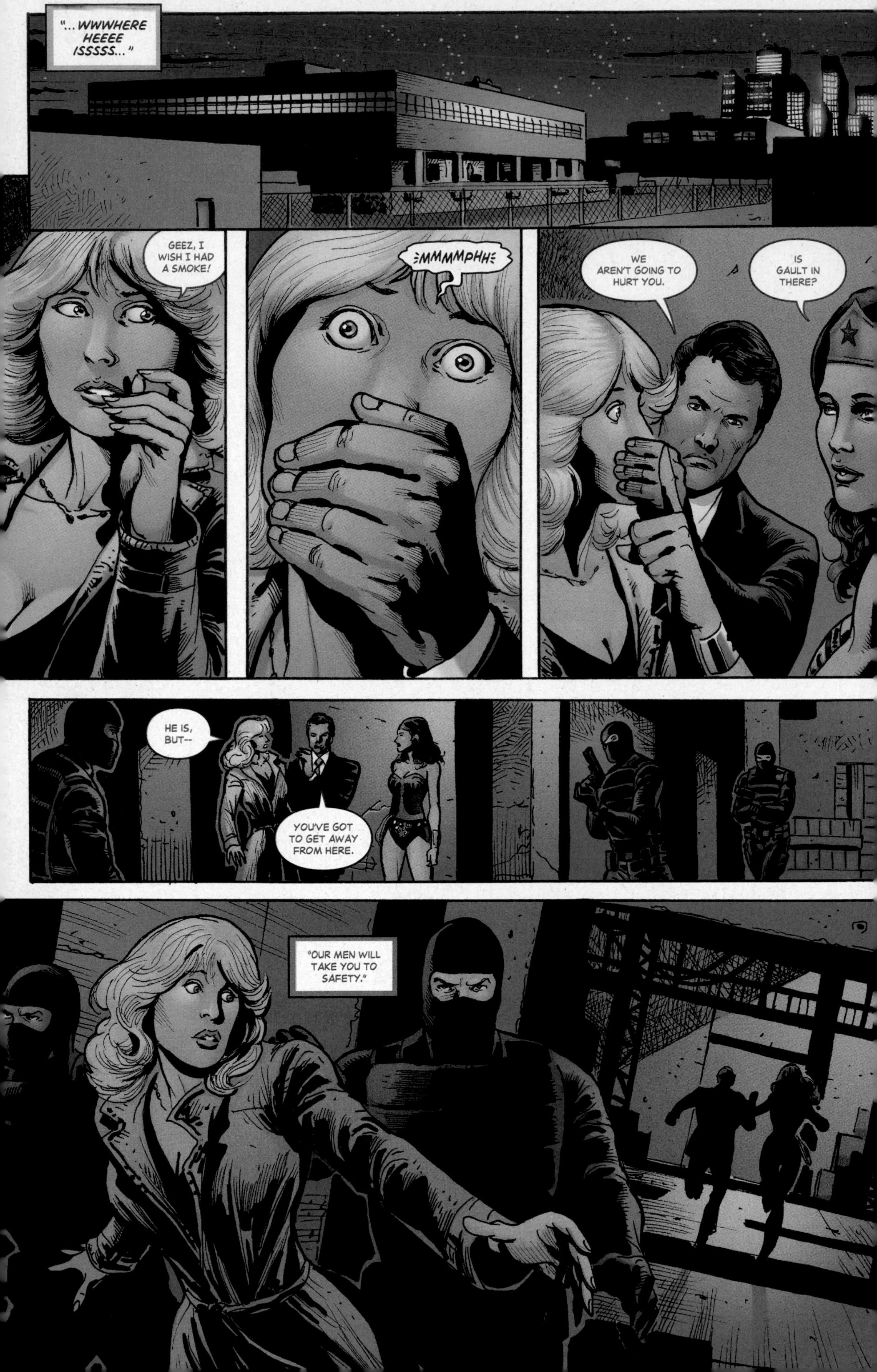
"...WWWHERE HEEEE ISSSSS..."
GEEZ, I WISH I HAD A SMOKE!
MMMMPHH
WE AREN'T GOING TO HURT YOU.
IS GAULT IN THERE?
HE IS, BUT--
YOU'VE GOT TO GET AWAY FROM HERE.
"OUR MEN WILL TAKE YOU TO SAFETY."

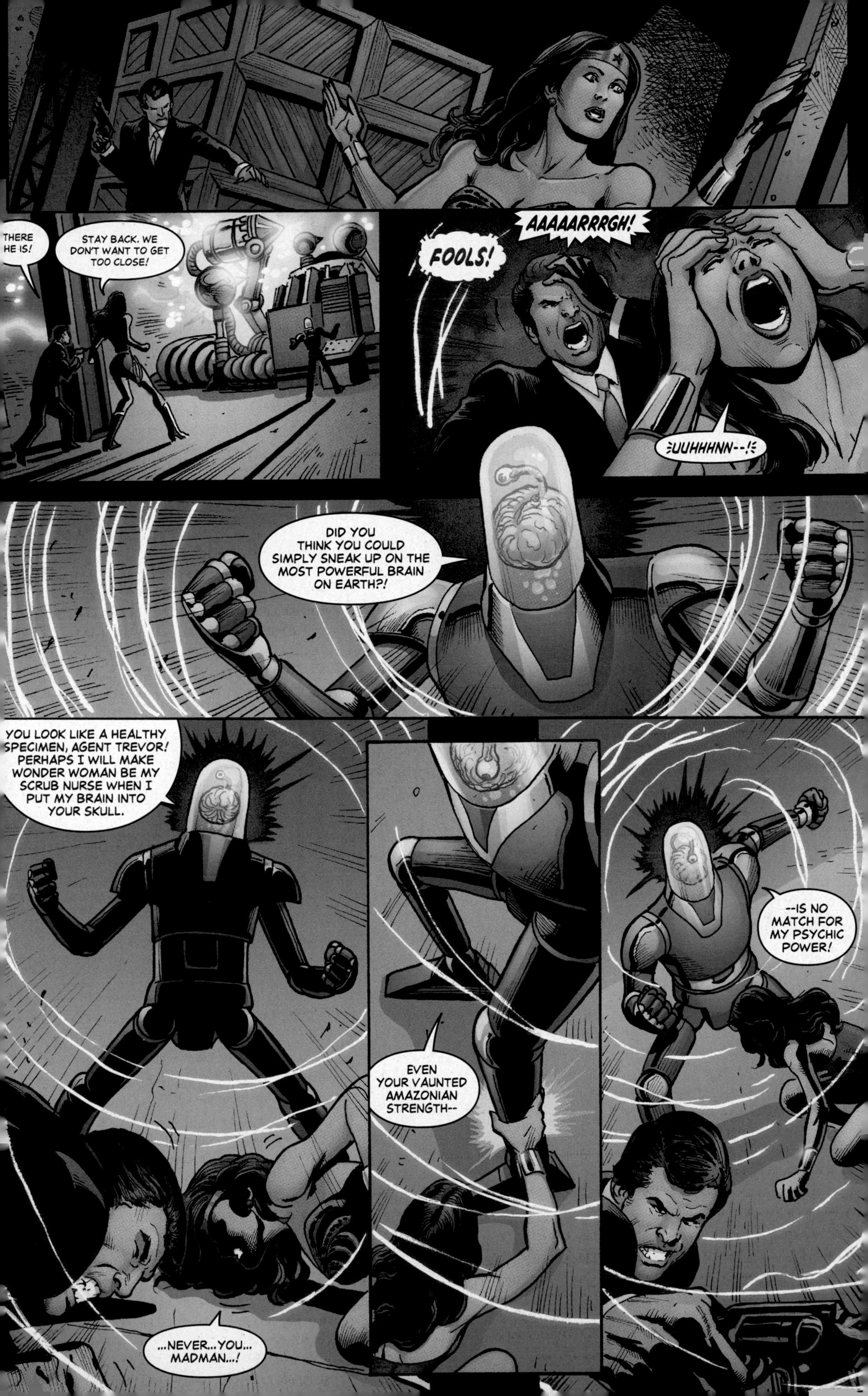
THERE HE IS!
STAY BACK. WE DON'T WANT TO GET TOO CLOSE!
AAAAARRRGH!
FOOLS!
UUHHHNN--!
DID YOU THINK YOU COULD SIMPLY SNEAK UP ON THE MOST POWERFUL BRAIN ON EARTH?!
YOU LOOK LIKE A HEALTHY SPECIMEN, AGENT TREVOR! PERHAPS I WILL MAKE WONDER WOMAN BE MY SCRUB NURSE WHEN I PUT MY BRAIN INTO YOUR SKULL.
...NEVER...YOU... MADMAN...!
EVEN YOUR VAUNTED AMAZONIAN STRENGTH--
--IS NO MATCH FOR MY PSYCHIC POWER!

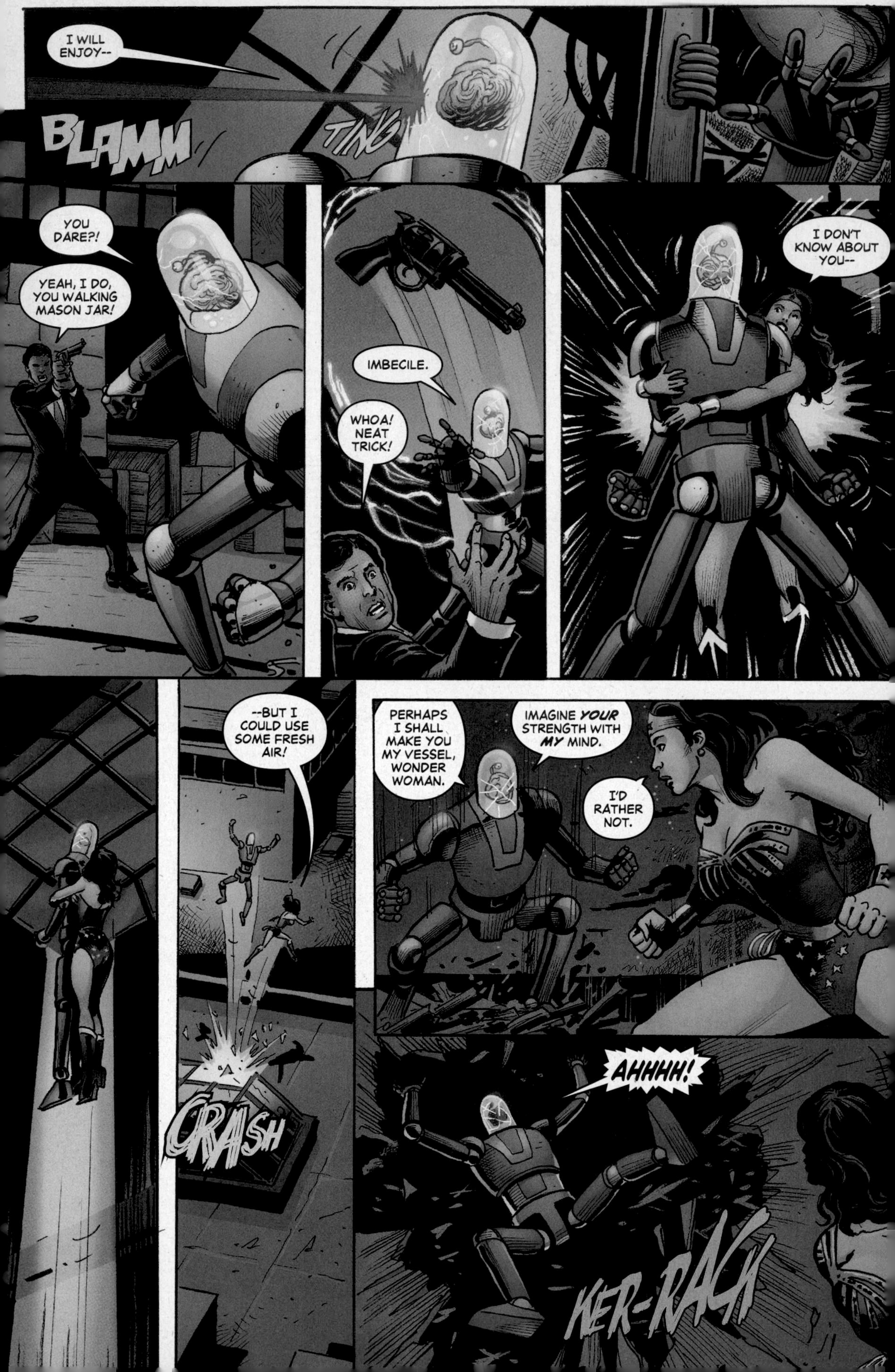
I WILL ENJOY--
BLAMM
TING
YOU DARE?!
YEAH, I DO, YOU WALKING MASON JAR!
IMBECILE.
WHOA! NEAT TRICK!
I DON'T KNOW ABOUT YOU--
--BUT I COULD USE SOME FRESH AIR!
CRASH
PERHAPS I SHALL MAKE YOU MY VESSEL, WONDER WOMAN.
IMAGINE *YOUR* STRENGTH WITH *MY* MIND.
I'D RATHER NOT.
AHHHH!
KER-RACK

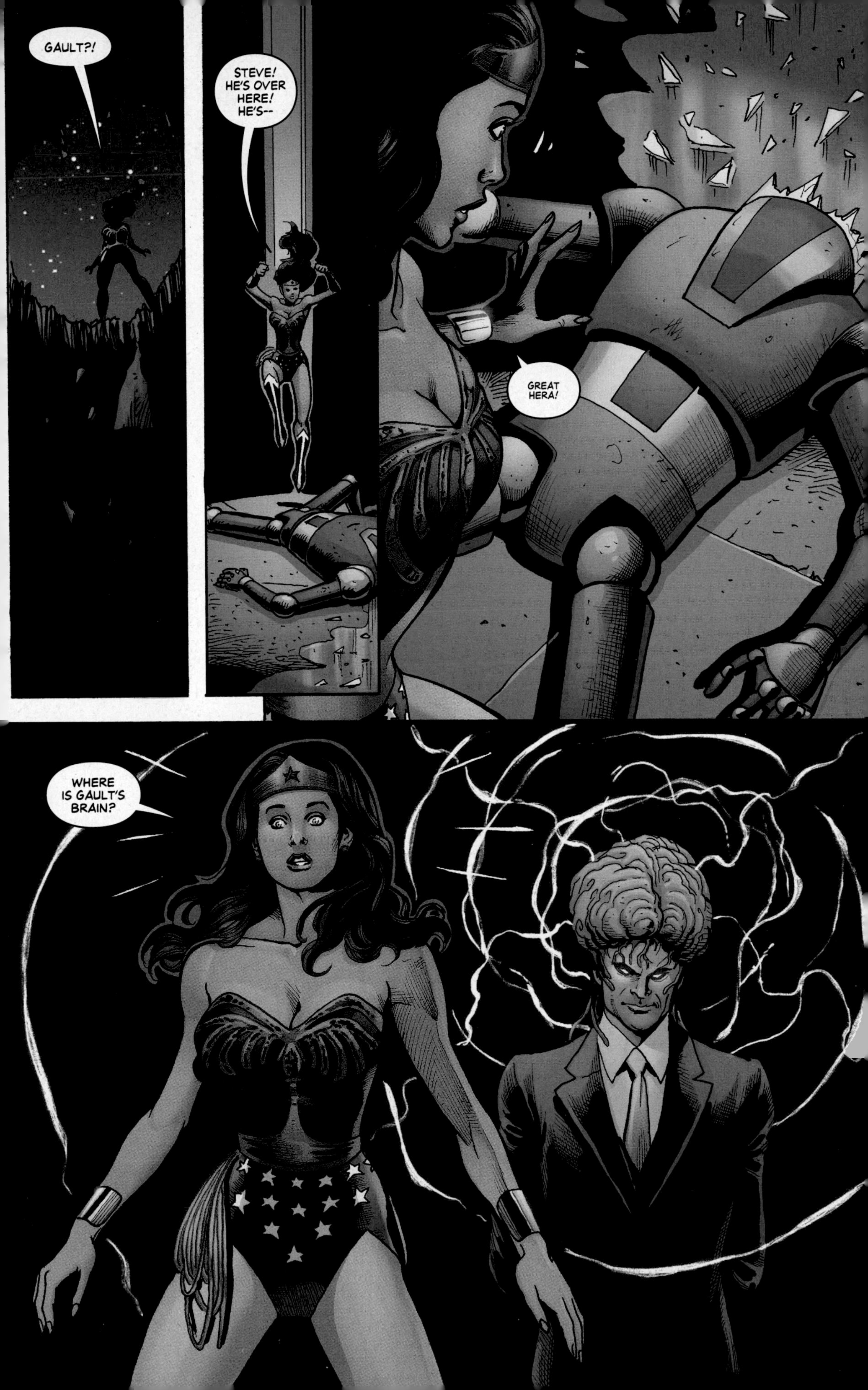
GAULT?!
STEVE! HE'S OVER HERE! HE'S--
GREAT HERA!
WHERE IS GAULT'S BRAIN?

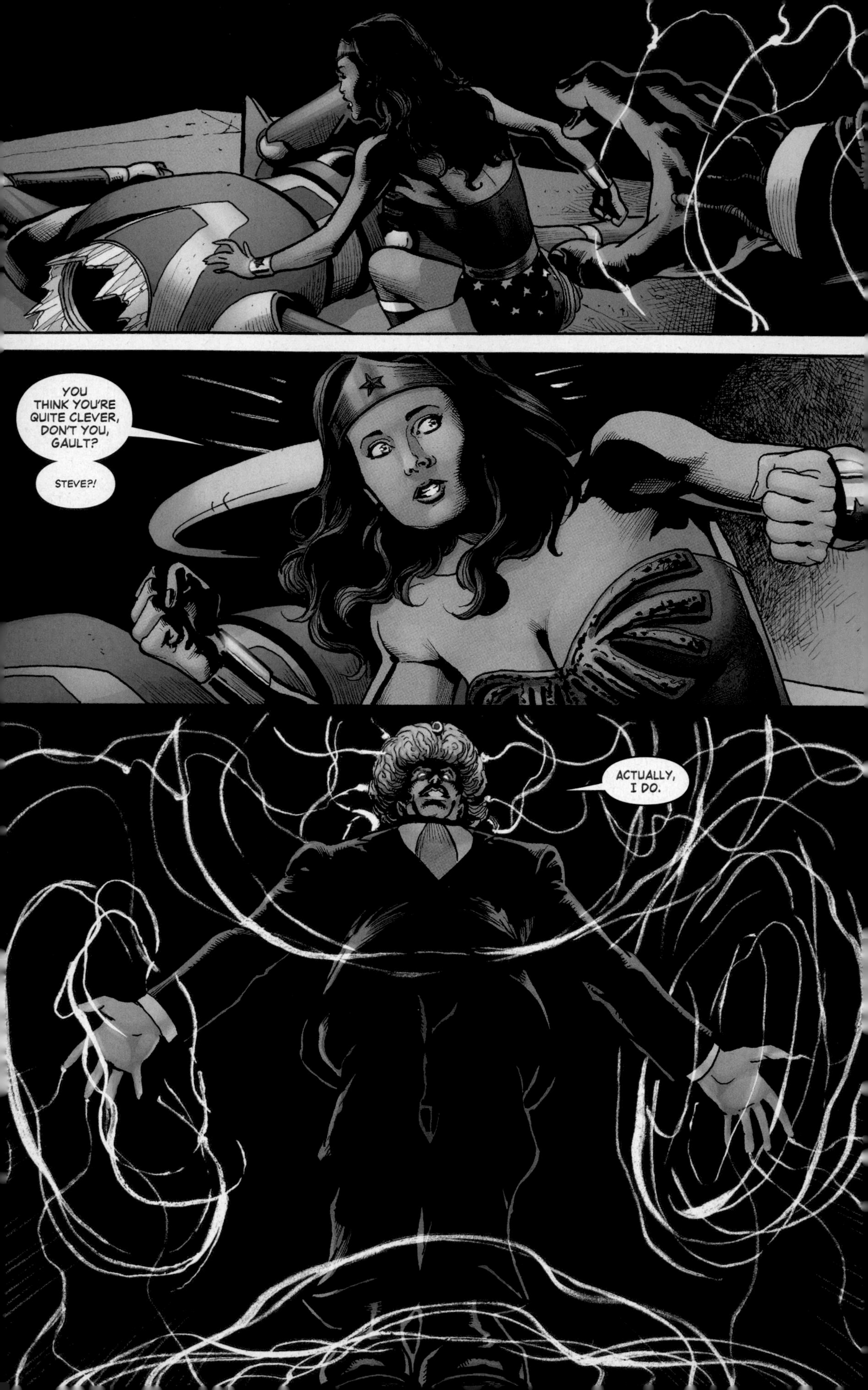
YOU THINK YOU'RE QUITE CLEVER, DON'T YOU, GAULT?
STEVE?!
ACTUALLY, I DO.

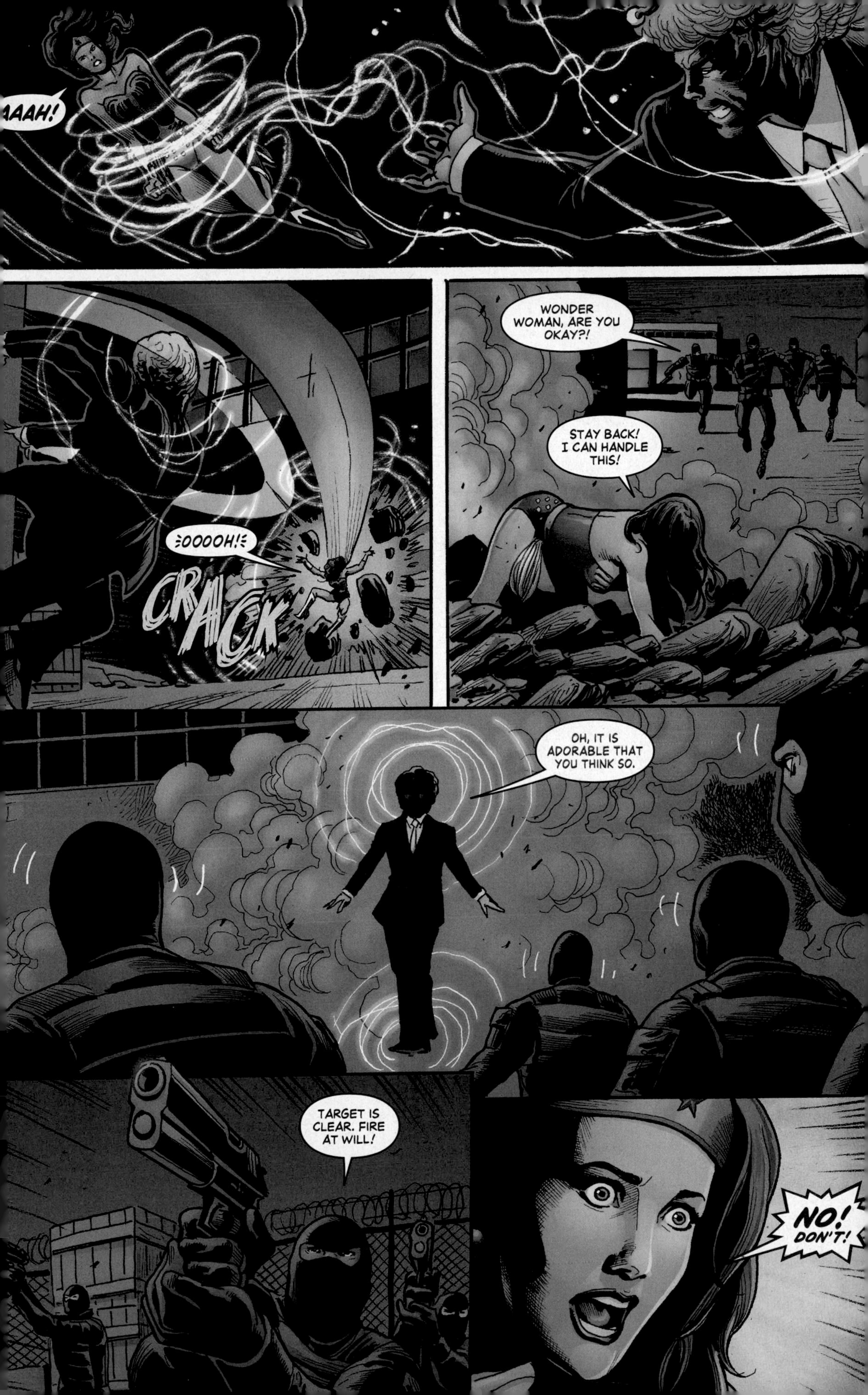
AAAH!
OOOOH!
CRACK
WONDER WOMAN, ARE YOU OKAY?!
STAY BACK! I CAN HANDLE THIS!
OH, IT IS ADORABLE THAT YOU THINK SO.
TARGET IS CLEAR. FIRE AT WILL!
NO! DON'T!

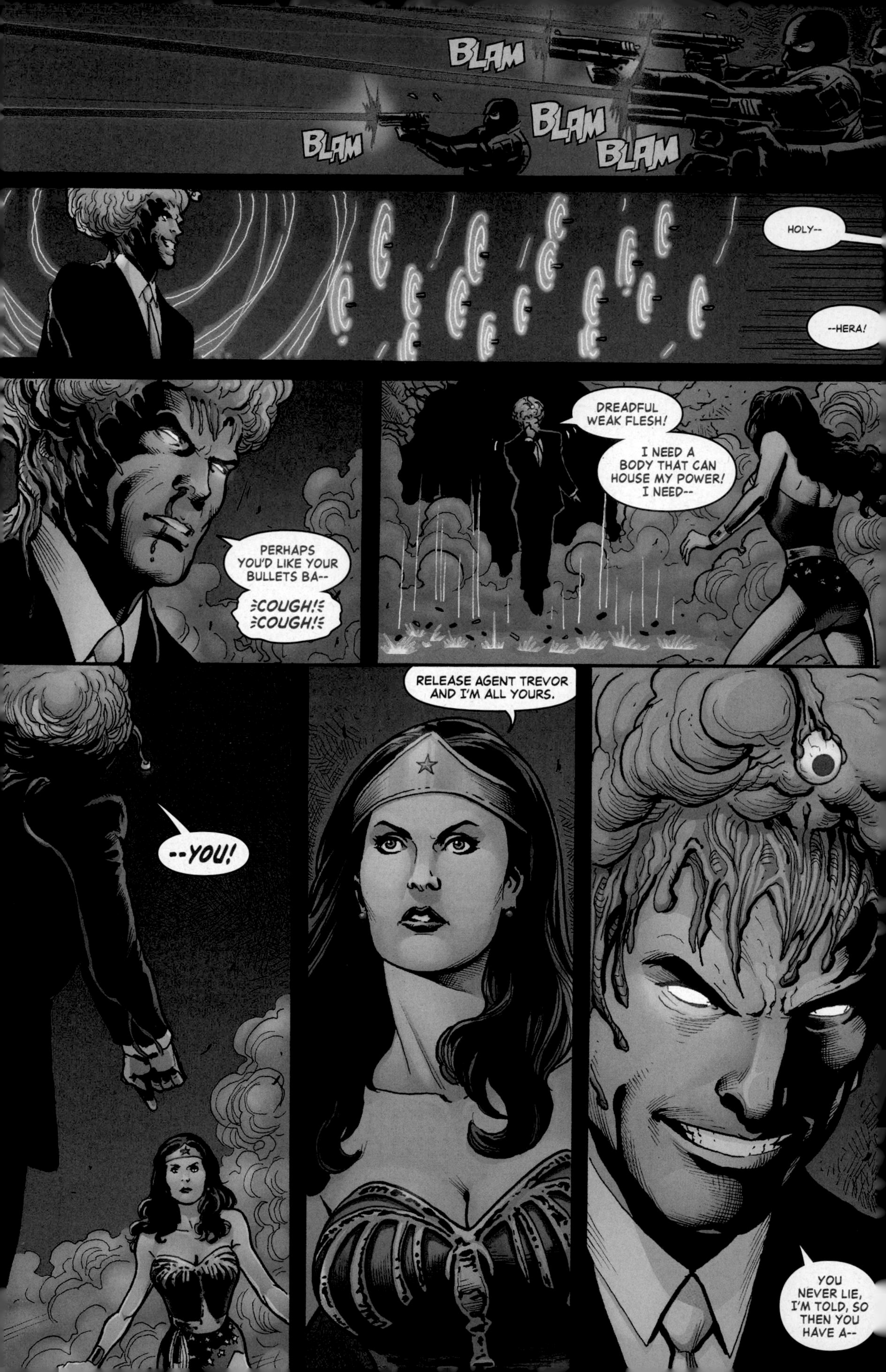
BLAM
BLAM
BLAM
BLAM
HOLY--
--HERA!
PERHAPS YOU'D LIKE YOUR BULLETS BA--
COUGH! COUGH!
DREADFUL WEAK FLESH!
I NEED A BODY THAT CAN HOUSE MY POWER! I NEED--
--YOU!
RELEASE AGENT TREVOR AND I'M ALL YOURS.
YOU NEVER LIE, I'M TOLD, SO THEN YOU HAVE A--

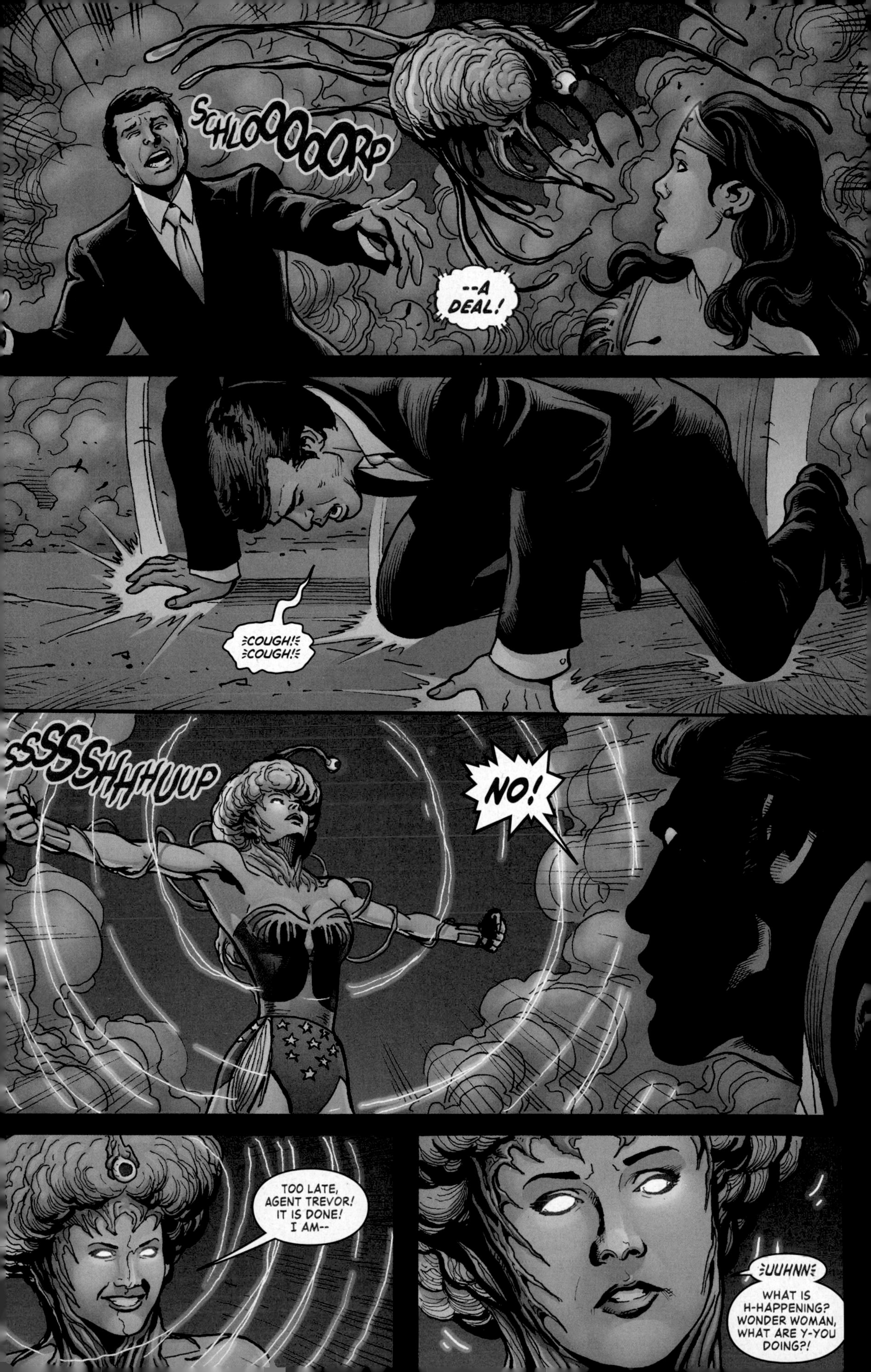
SCHLOOOOOORP
--A DEAL!
COUGH! COUGH!
SSSSHHHUUP
NO!
TOO LATE, AGENT TREVOR! IT IS DONE! I AM--
UUHNN
WHAT IS H-HAPPENING? WONDER WOMAN, WHAT ARE Y-YOU DOING?!

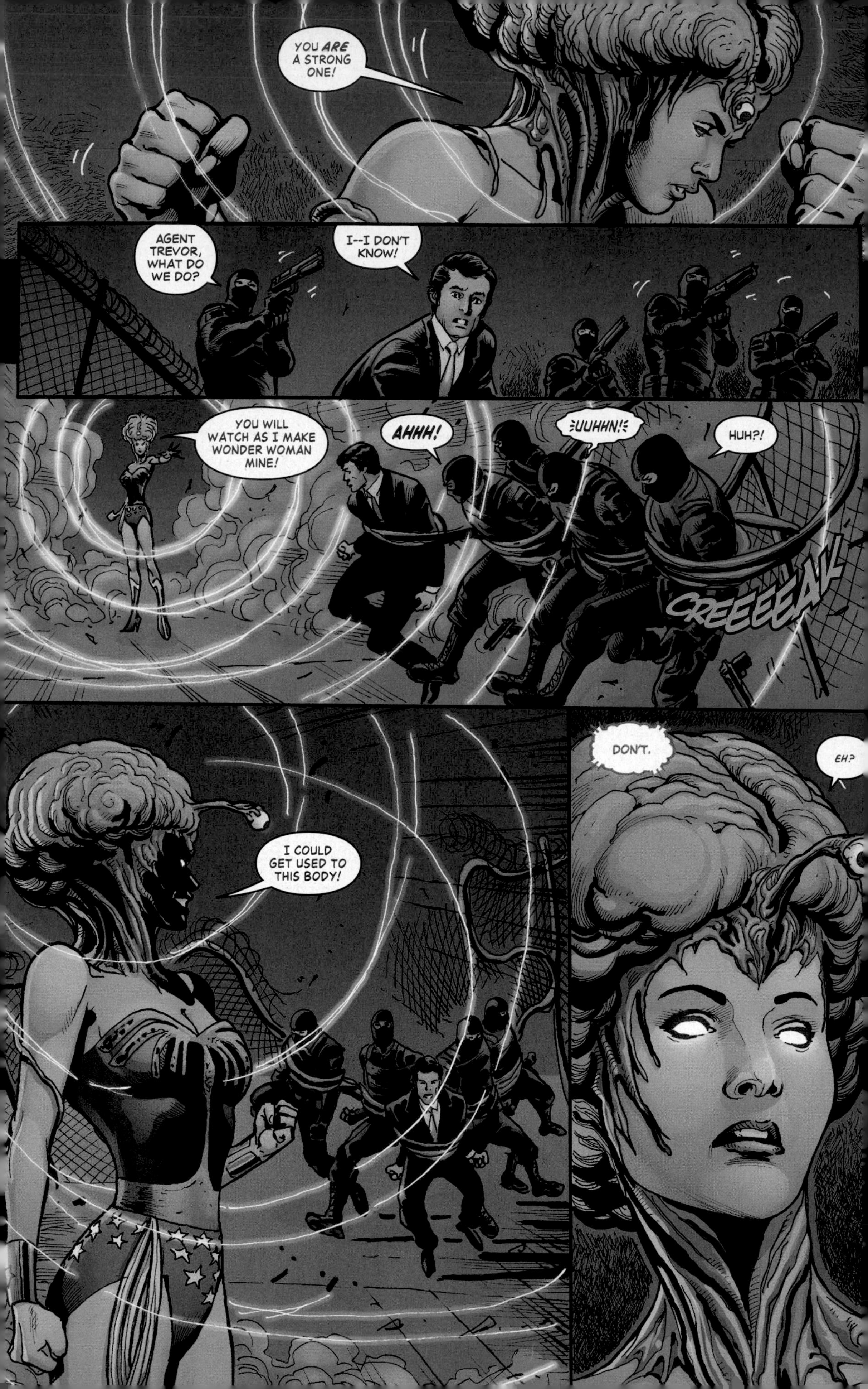
YOU ARE A STRONG ONE!
AGENT TREVOR, WHAT DO WE DO?
I--I DON'T KNOW!
YOU WILL WATCH AS I MAKE WONDER WOMAN MINE!
AHHH!
UUHHN!
HUH?!
CREEEEAK
I COULD GET USED TO THIS BODY!
DON'T.
EH?

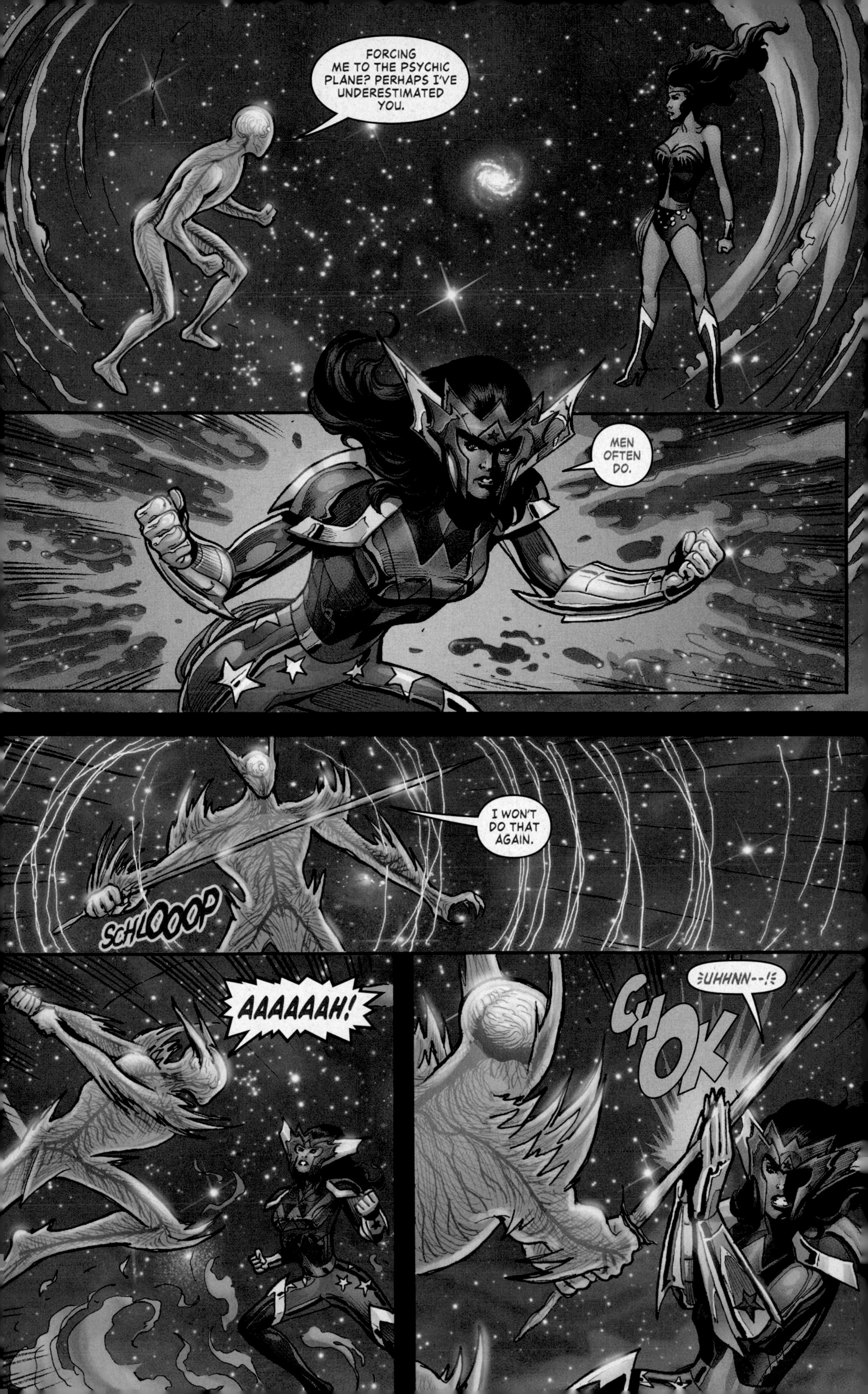
FORCING ME TO THE PSYCHIC PLANE? PERHAPS I'VE UNDERESTIMATED YOU.
MEN OFTEN DO.
I WON'T DO THAT AGAIN.
SCHLOOOP
AAAAAAH!
CHOK
UHHNN--!

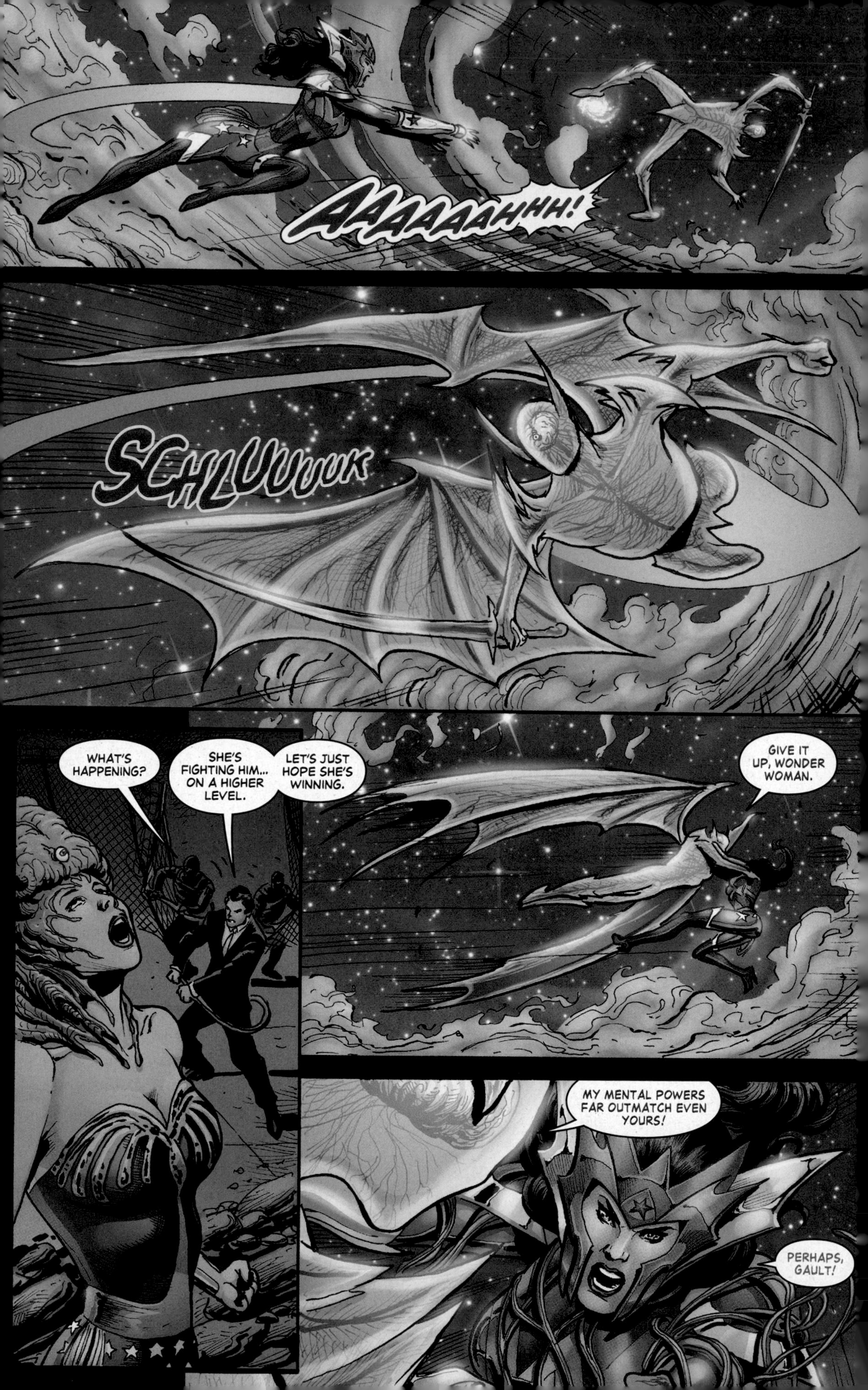
AAAAAAHHH!
SCHLUUUUK
WHAT'S HAPPENING?
SHE'S FIGHTING HIM... ON A HIGHER LEVEL.
LET'S JUST HOPE SHE'S WINNING.
GIVE IT UP, WONDER WOMAN.
MY MENTAL POWERS FAR OUTMATCH EVEN YOURS!
PERHAPS, GAULT!

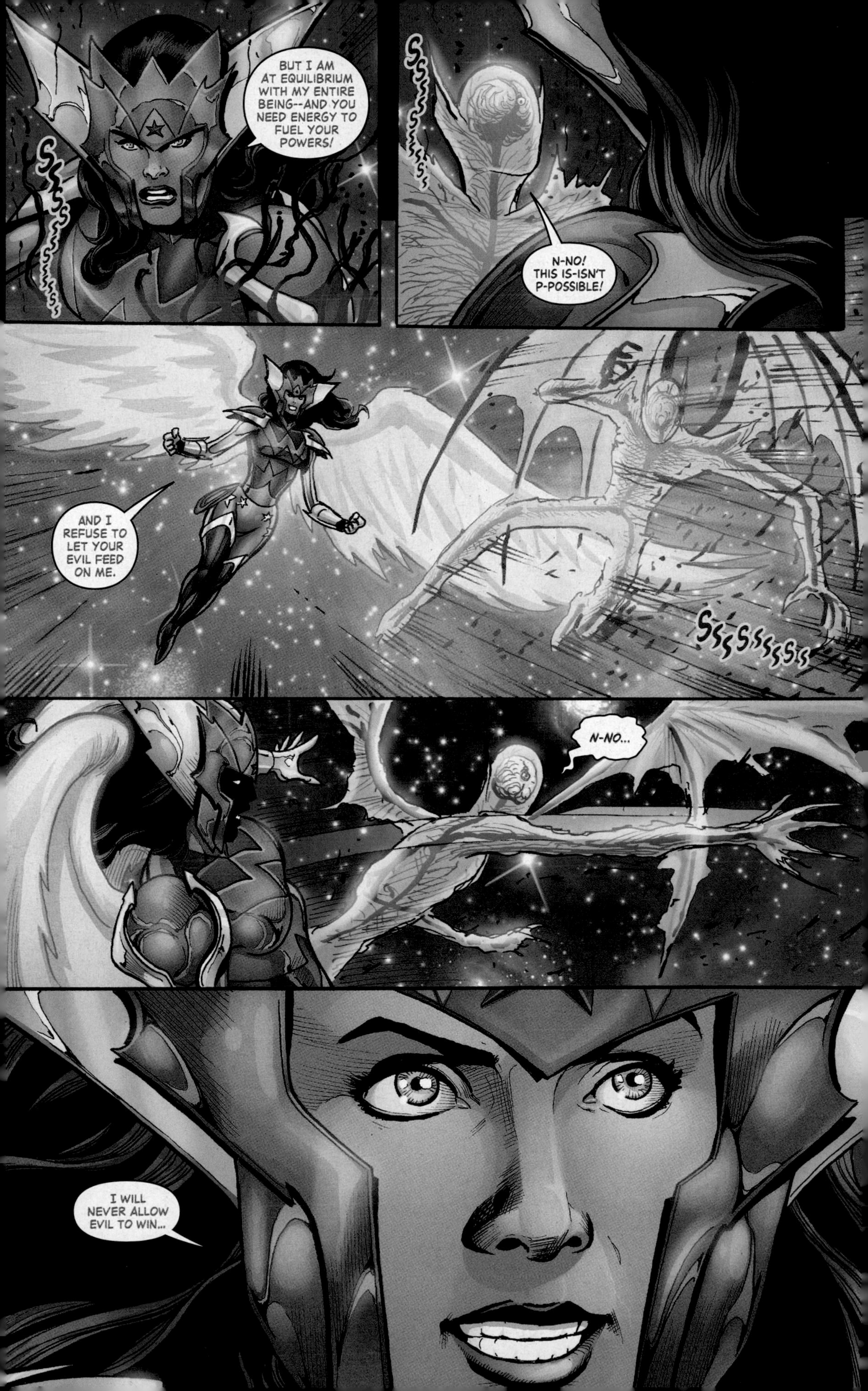
BUT I AM AT EQUILIBRIUM WITH MY ENTIRE BEING--AND YOU NEED ENERGY TO FUEL YOUR POWERS!
SSSSSSSSS
SSSSSSSS
N-NO! THIS IS-ISN'T P-POSSIBLE!
AND I REFUSE TO LET YOUR EVIL FEED ON ME.
SSSSSSSSS
N-NO...
I WILL NEVER ALLOW EVIL TO WIN...

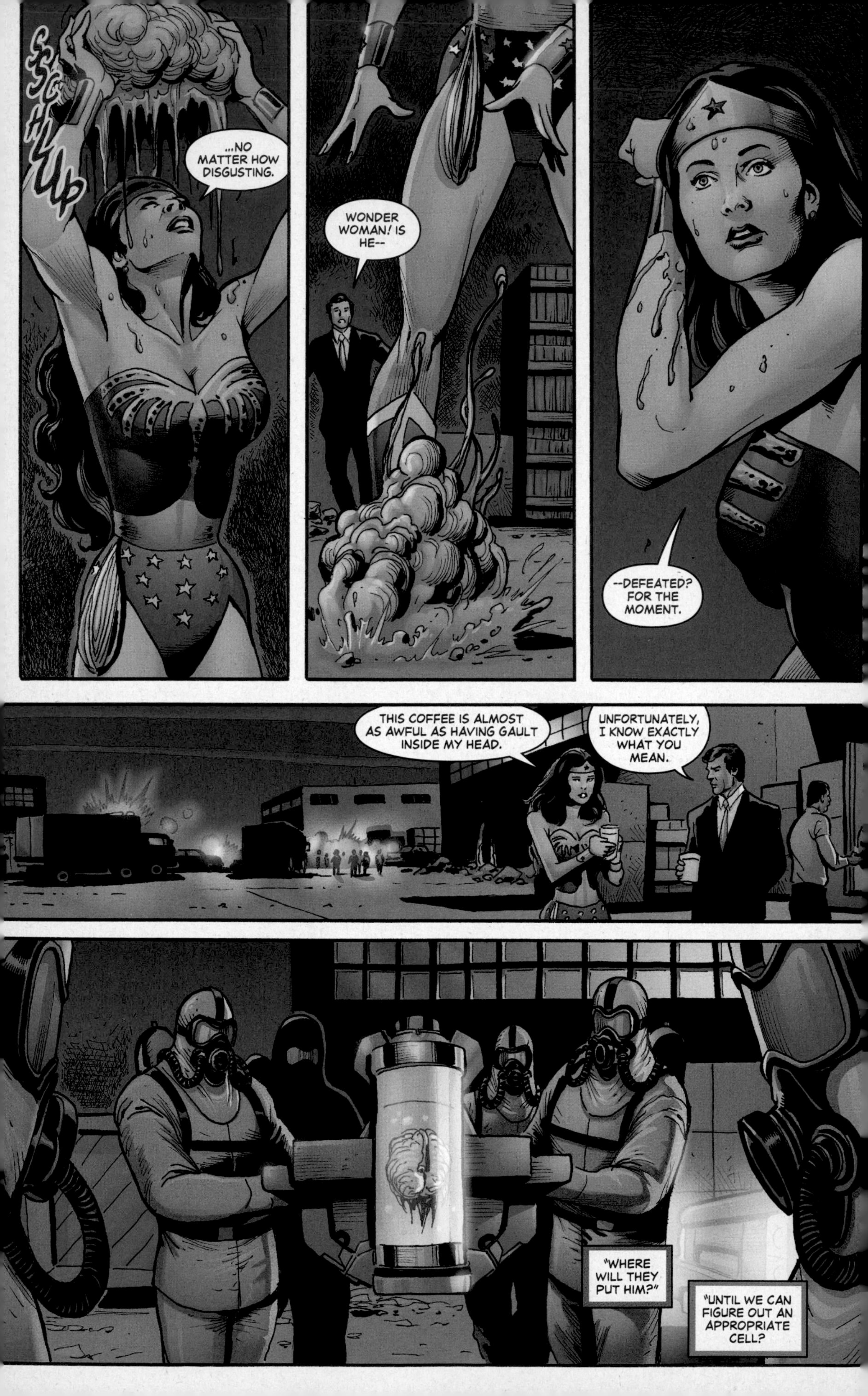

ESCHHLLUP
...NO MATTER HOW DISGUSTING.
WONDER WOMAN! IS HE--
--DEFEATED? FOR THE MOMENT.
THIS COFFEE IS ALMOST AS AWFUL AS HAVING GAULT INSIDE MY HEAD.
UNFORTUNATELY, I KNOW EXACTLY WHAT YOU MEAN.
"WHERE WILL THEY PUT HIM?"
"UNTIL WE CAN FIGURE OUT AN APPROPRIATE CELL?

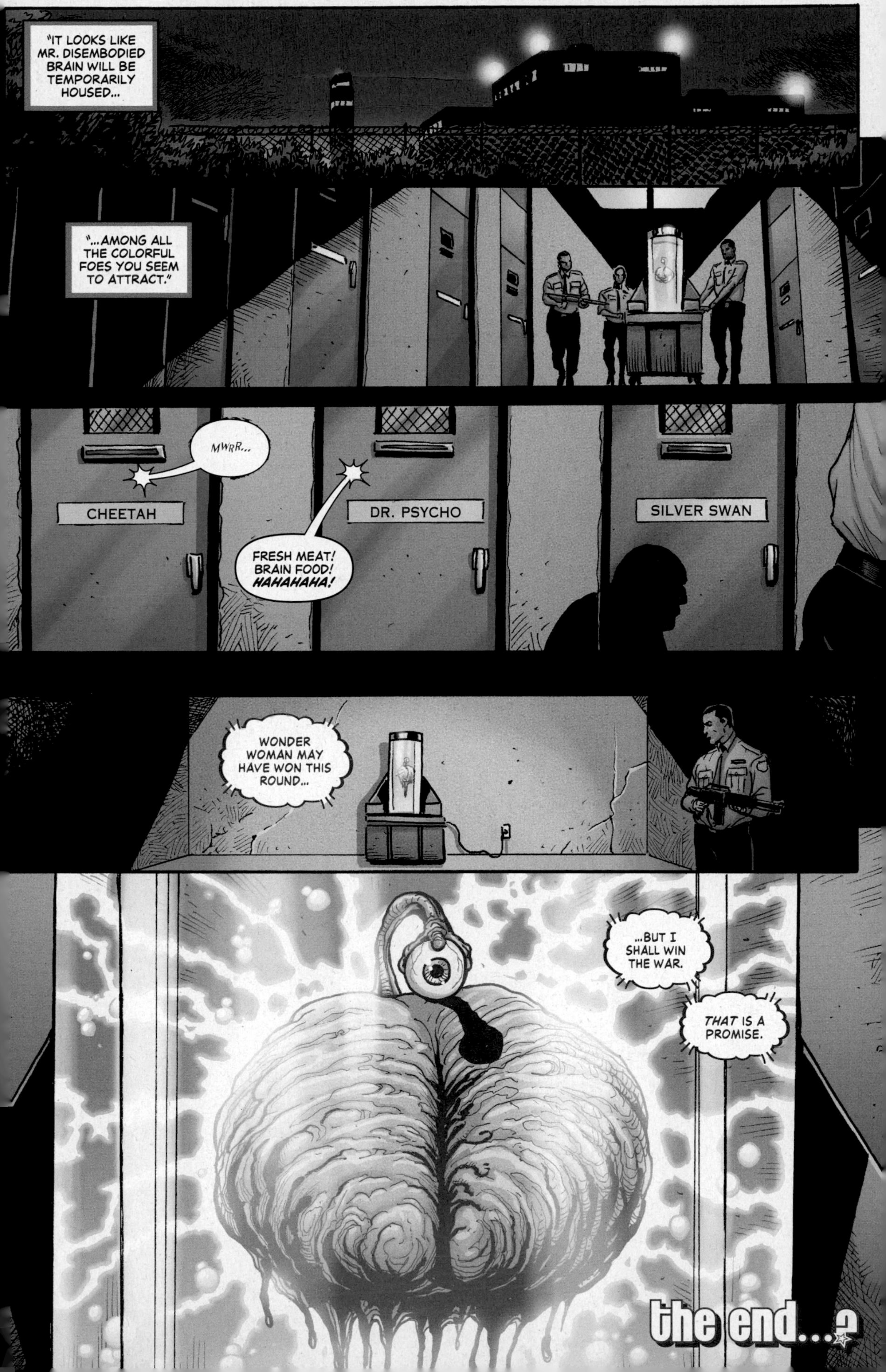
"IT LOOKS LIKE MR. DISEMBODIED BRAIN WILL BE TEMPORARILY HOUSED...
"...AMONG ALL THE COLORFUL FOES YOU SEEM TO ATTRACT."
CHEETAH
MWRR...
DR. PSYCHO
FRESH MEAT! BRAIN FOOD! HAHAHAHA!
SILVER SWAN
WONDER WOMAN MAY HAVE WON THIS ROUND...
...BUT I SHALL WIN THE WAR.
THAT IS A PROMISE.
the end...?

★ WORLDS COLLIDE ★

Amy Chu
Writer

Dario Brizuela
Artist

Jenn Manley Lee
Colorist

Wes Abbott
Letterer

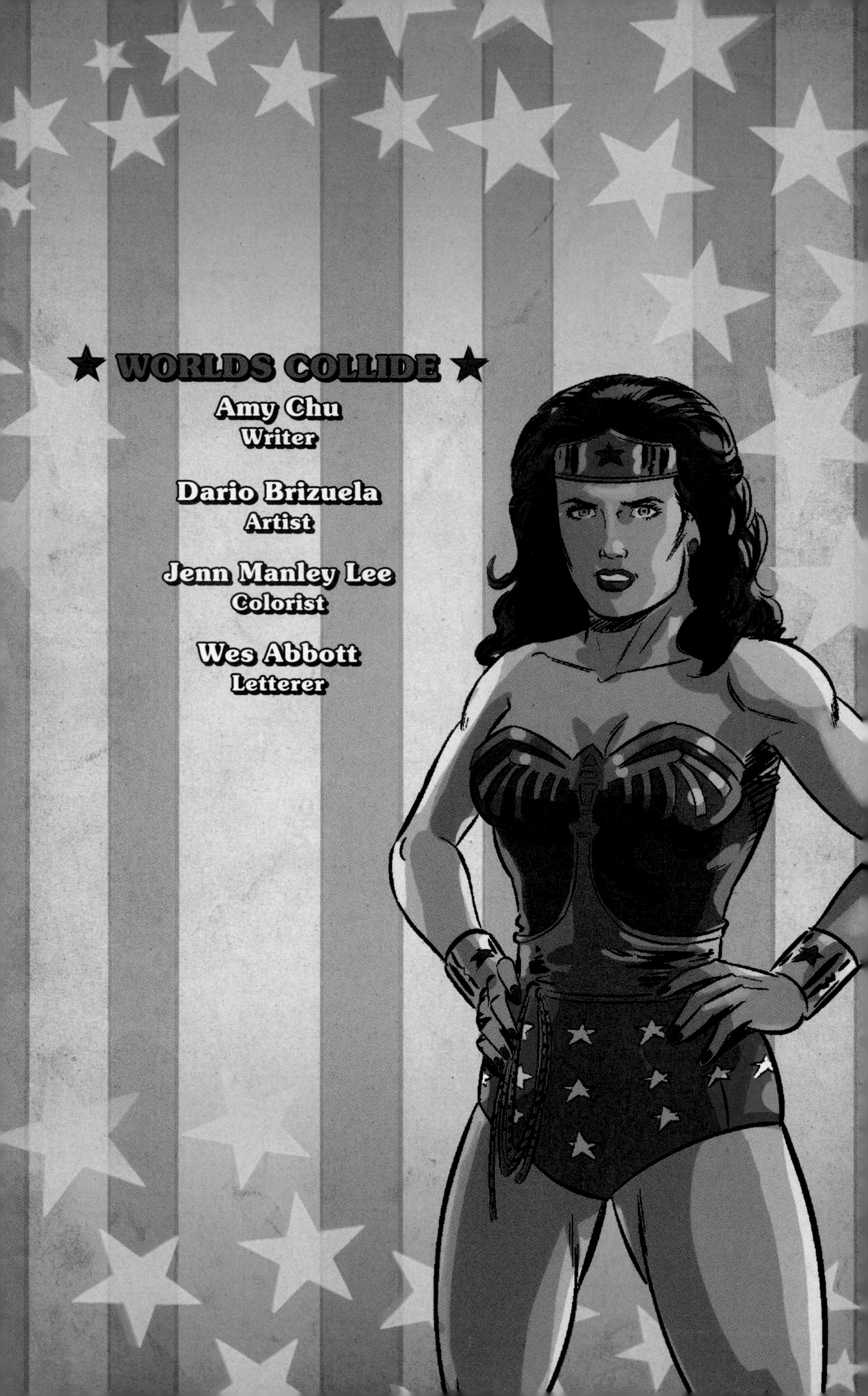

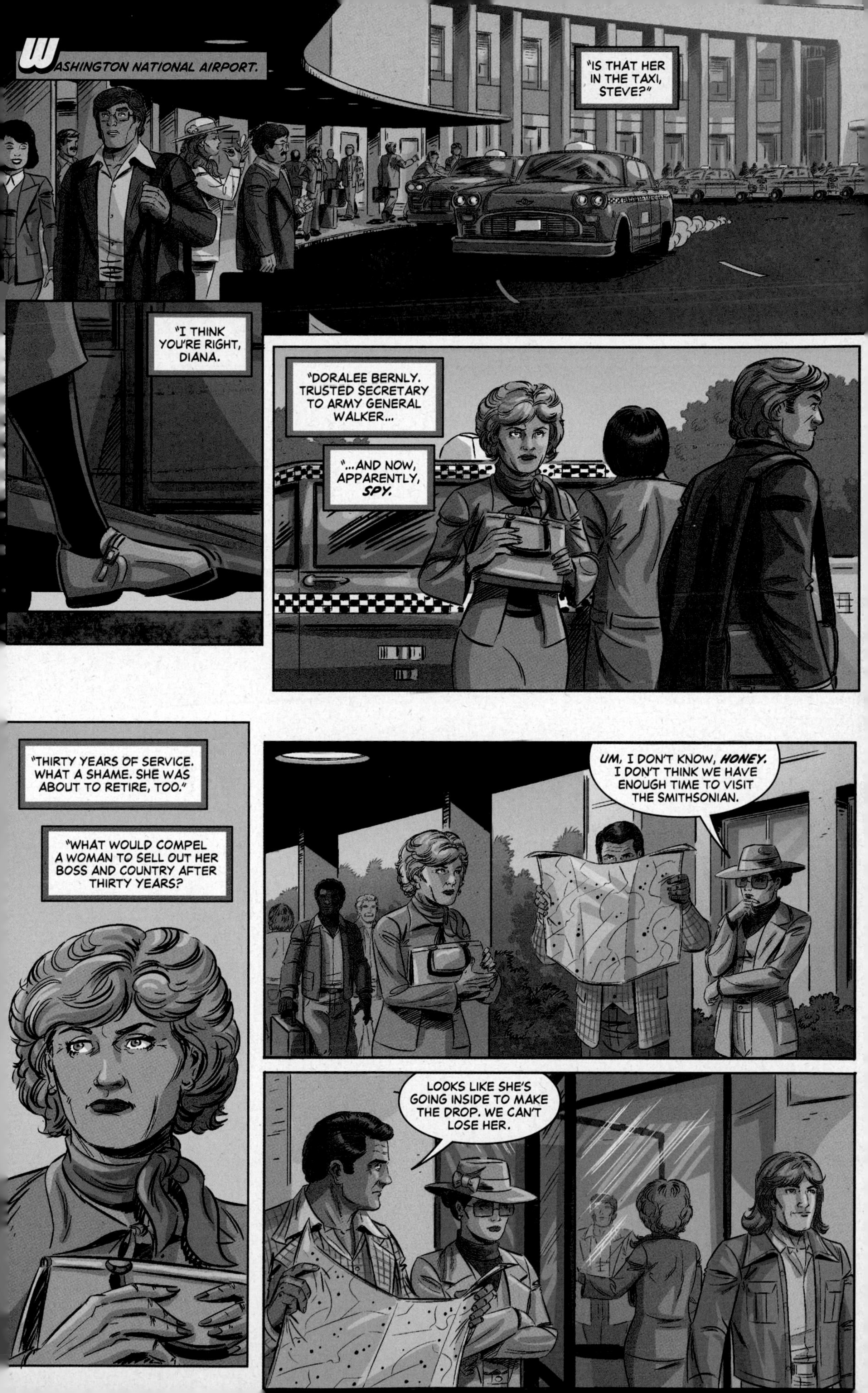
WASHINGTON NATIONAL AIRPORT.
"IS THAT HER IN THE TAXI, STEVE?"
"I THINK YOU'RE RIGHT, DIANA.
"DORALEE BERNLY. TRUSTED SECRETARY TO ARMY GENERAL WALKER...
"...AND NOW, APPARENTLY, SPY.
"THIRTY YEARS OF SERVICE. WHAT A SHAME. SHE WAS ABOUT TO RETIRE, TOO."
"WHAT WOULD COMPEL A WOMAN TO SELL OUT HER BOSS AND COUNTRY AFTER THIRTY YEARS?
UM, I DON'T KNOW, HONEY. I DON'T THINK WE HAVE ENOUGH TIME TO VISIT THE SMITHSONIAN.
LOOKS LIKE SHE'S GOING INSIDE TO MAKE THE DROP. WE CAN'T LOSE HER.

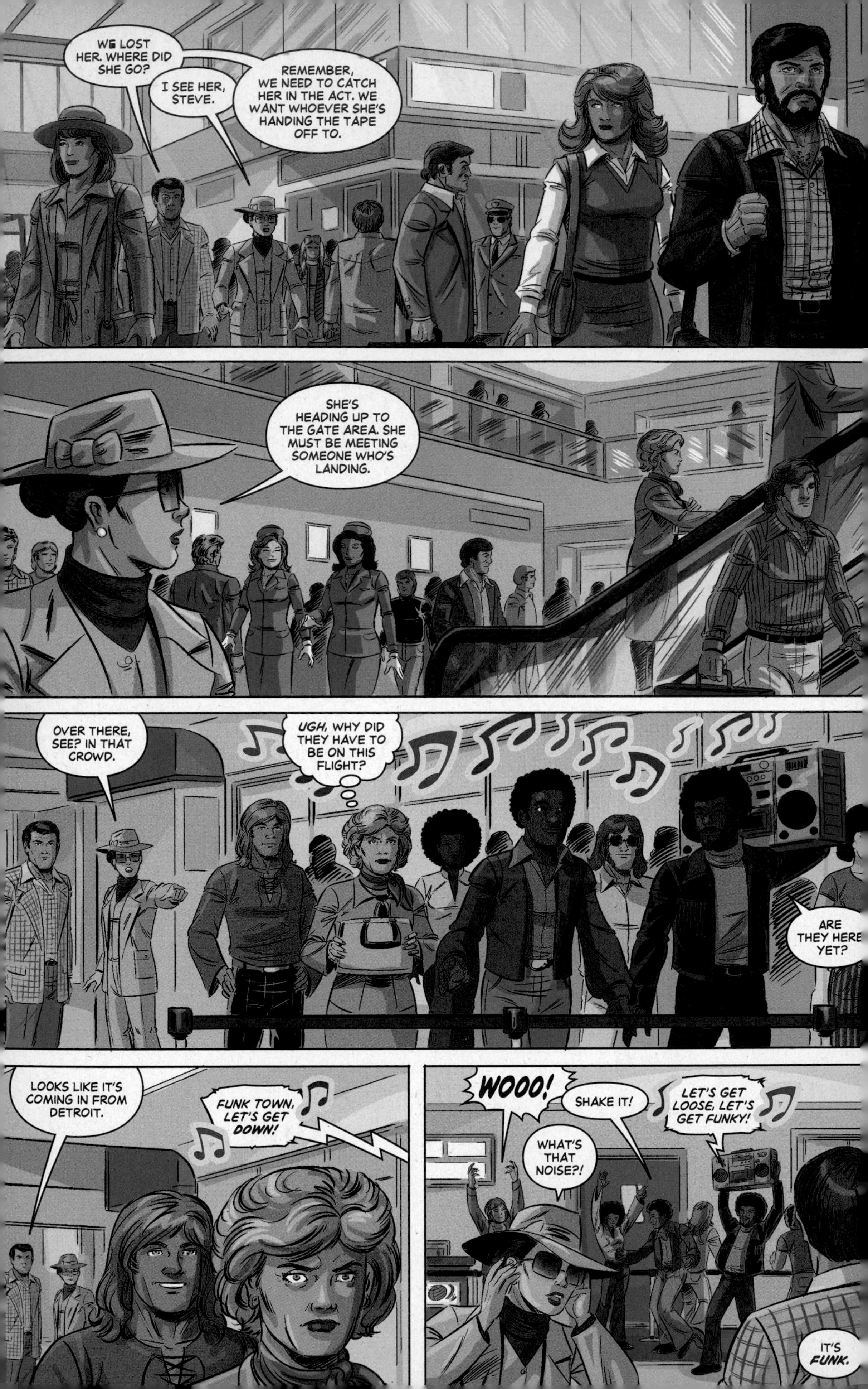
WE LOST HER. WHERE DID SHE GO?
I SEE HER, STEVE.
REMEMBER, WE NEED TO CATCH HER IN THE ACT. WE WANT WHOEVER SHE'S HANDING THE TAPE OFF TO.
SHE'S HEADING UP TO THE GATE AREA. SHE MUST BE MEETING SOMEONE WHO'S LANDING.
OVER THERE, SEE? IN THAT CROWD.
UGH, WHY DID THEY HAVE TO BE ON THIS FLIGHT?
ARE THEY HERE YET?
LOOKS LIKE IT'S COMING IN FROM DETROIT.
FUNK TOWN, LET'S GET DOWN!
WOOO!
SHAKE IT!
LET'S GET LOOSE, LET'S GET FUNKY!
WHAT'S THAT NOISE?!
IT'S FUNK.

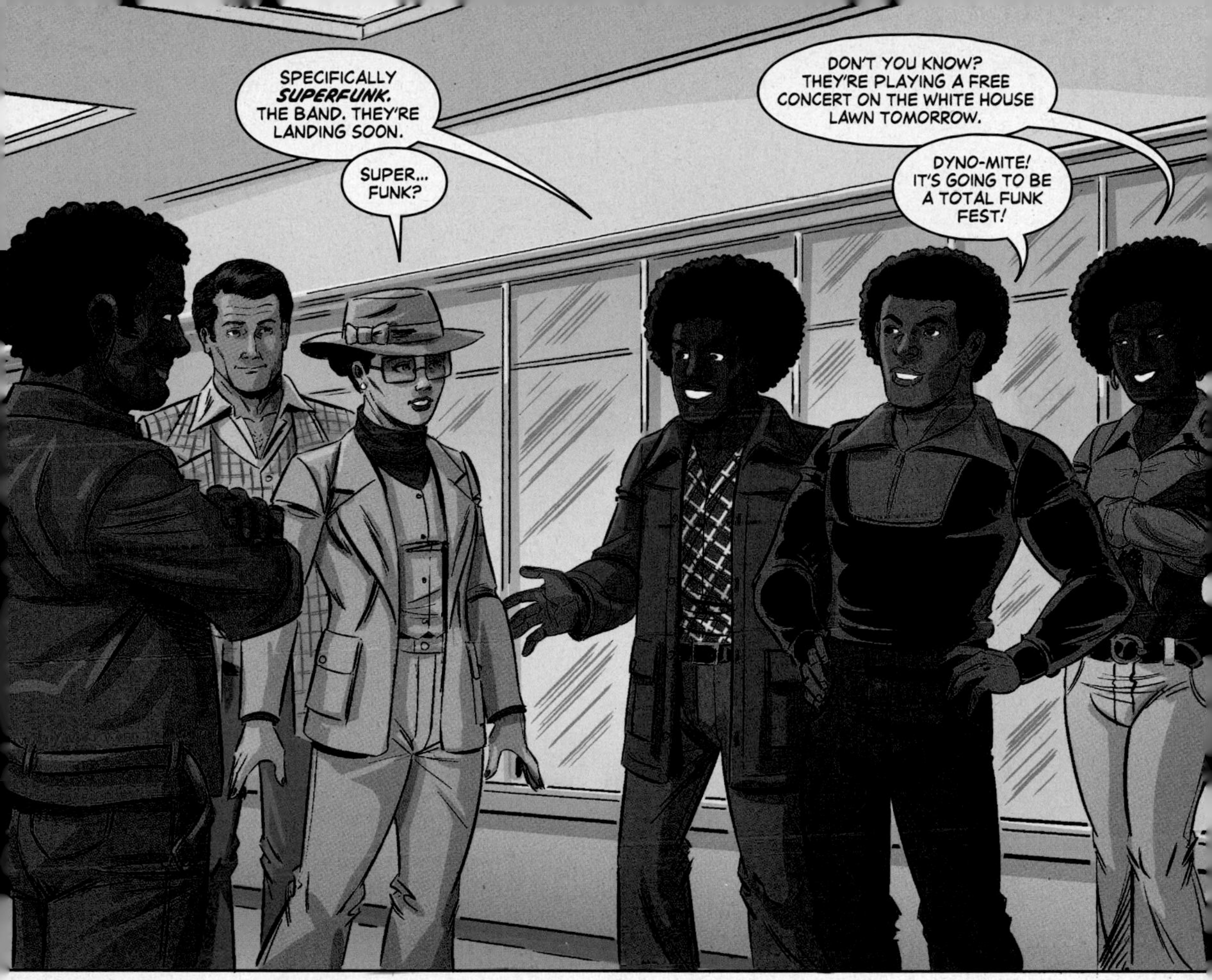
SPECIFICALLY **SUPERFUNK.** THE BAND. THEY'RE LANDING SOON.
SUPER... FUNK?
DON'T YOU KNOW? THEY'RE PLAYING A FREE CONCERT ON THE WHITE HOUSE LAWN TOMORROW.
DYNO-MITE! IT'S GOING TO BE A TOTAL FUNK FEST!

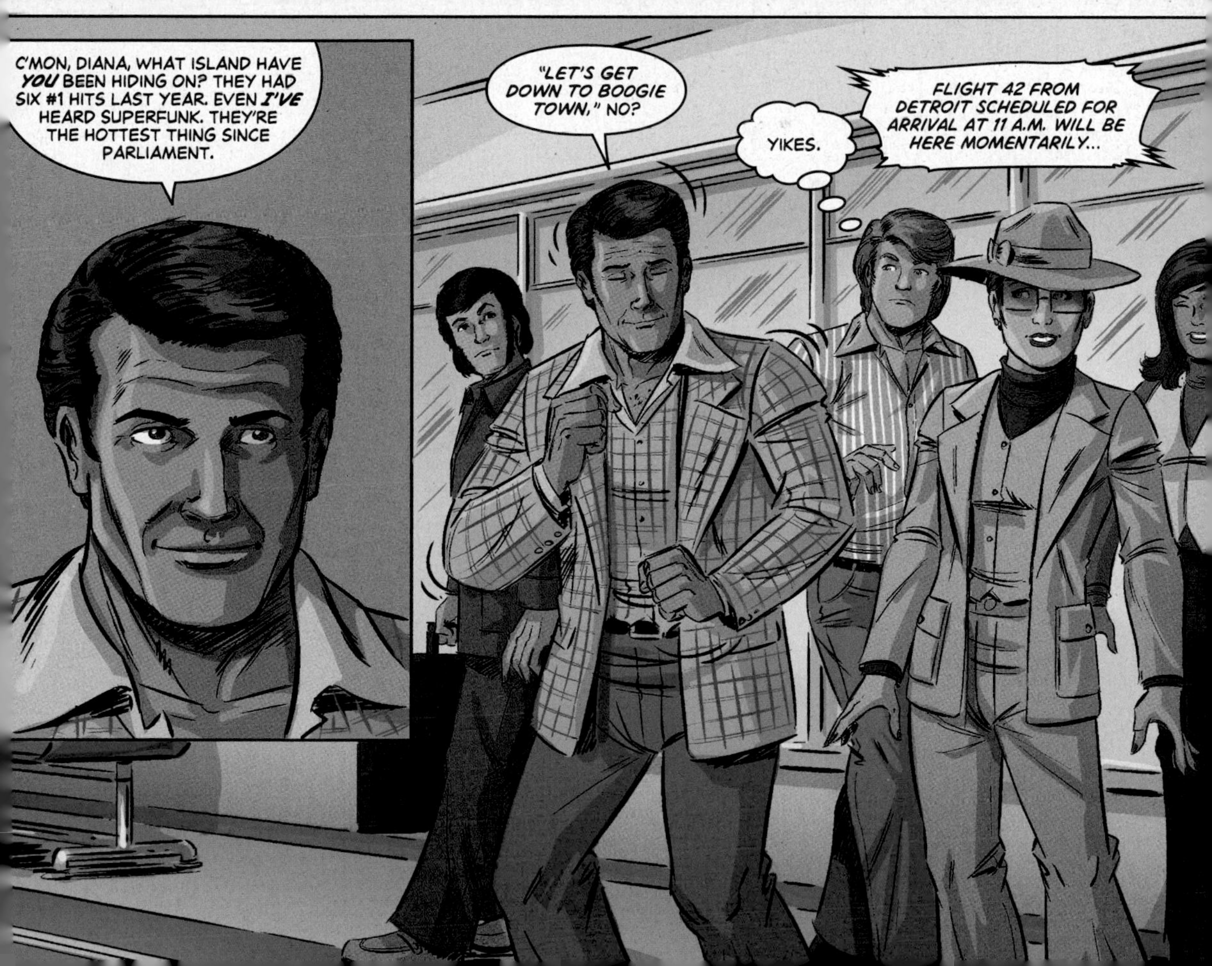
C'MON, DIANA, WHAT ISLAND HAVE ***YOU*** BEEN HIDING ON? THEY HAD SIX #1 HITS LAST YEAR. EVEN ***I'VE*** HEARD SUPERFUNK. THEY'RE THE HOTTEST THING SINCE PARLIAMENT.
"LET'S GET DOWN TO BOOGIE TOWN," NO?
YIKES.
FLIGHT 42 FROM DETROIT SCHEDULED FOR ARRIVAL AT 11 A.M. WILL BE HERE MOMENTARILY...

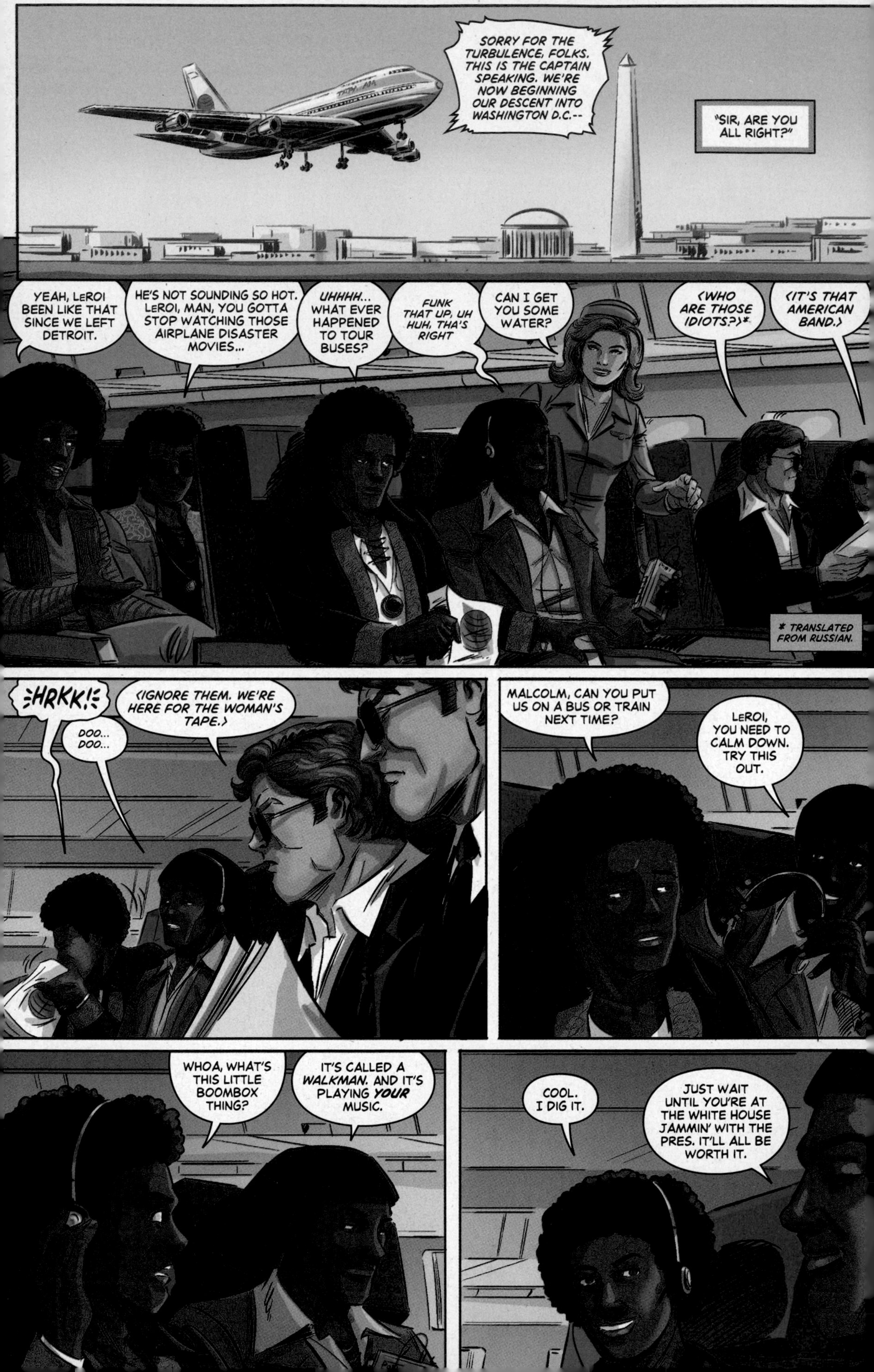
SORRY FOR THE TURBULENCE, FOLKS. THIS IS THE CAPTAIN SPEAKING. WE'RE NOW BEGINNING OUR DESCENT INTO WASHINGTON D.C.--
"SIR, ARE YOU ALL RIGHT?"
YEAH, LeROI BEEN LIKE THAT SINCE WE LEFT DETROIT.
HE'S NOT SOUNDING SO HOT. LeROI, MAN, YOU GOTTA STOP WATCHING THOSE AIRPLANE DISASTER MOVIES...
UHHHH... WHAT EVER HAPPENED TO TOUR BUSES?
FUNK THAT UP, UH HUH, THA'S RIGHT
CAN I GET YOU SOME WATER?
‹WHO ARE THOSE IDIOTS?›*
‹IT'S THAT AMERICAN BAND.›
* TRANSLATED FROM RUSSIAN.
HRKK!
DOO... DOO...
‹IGNORE THEM. WE'RE HERE FOR THE WOMAN'S TAPE.›
MALCOLM, CAN YOU PUT US ON A BUS OR TRAIN NEXT TIME?
LeROI, YOU NEED TO CALM DOWN. TRY THIS OUT.
WHOA, WHAT'S THIS LITTLE BOOMBOX THING?
IT'S CALLED A WALKMAN. AND IT'S PLAYING YOUR MUSIC.
COOL. I DIG IT.
JUST WAIT UNTIL YOU'RE AT THE WHITE HOUSE JAMMIN' WITH THE PRES. IT'LL ALL BE WORTH IT.

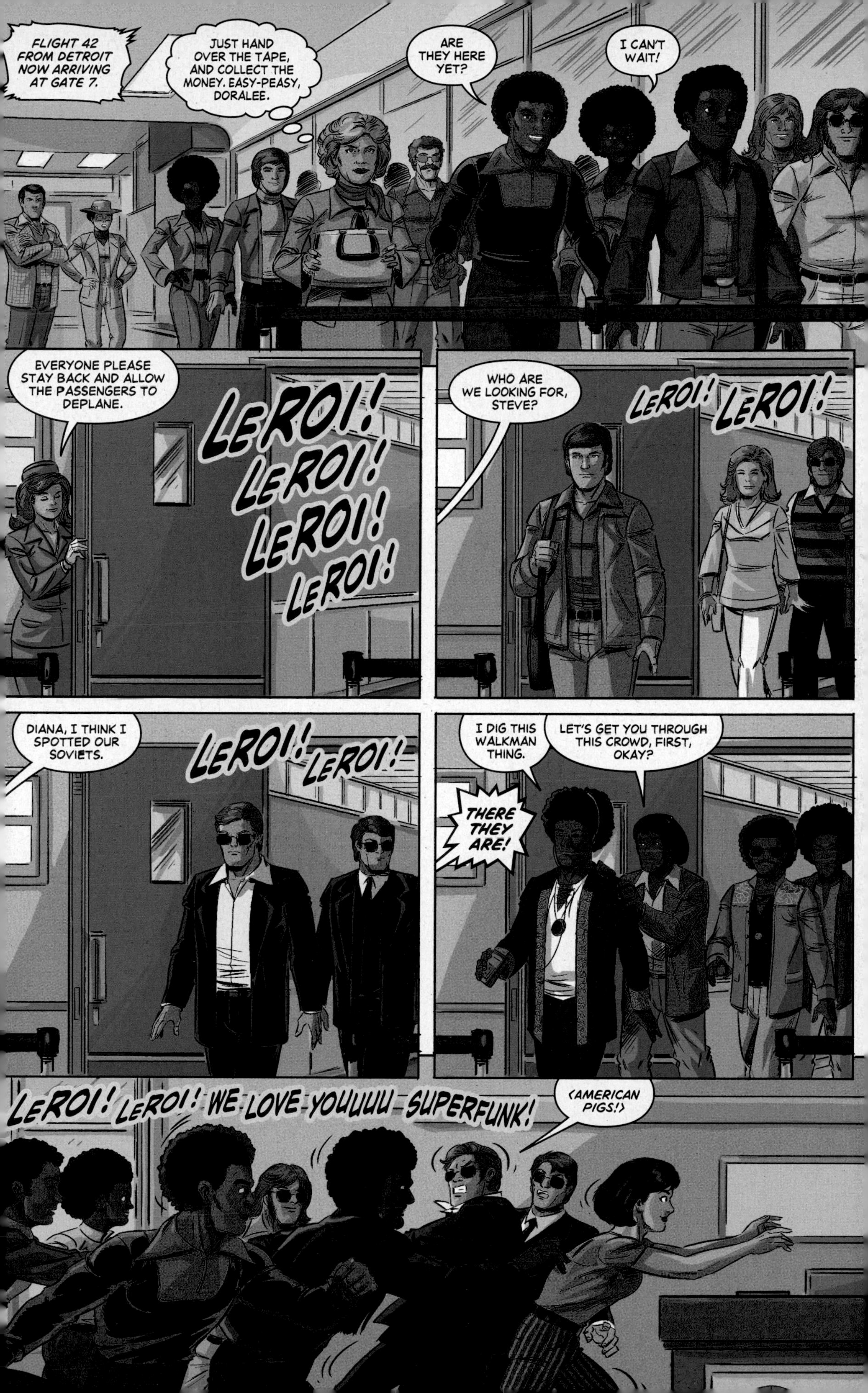
FLIGHT 42 FROM DETROIT NOW ARRIVING AT GATE 7.
JUST HAND OVER THE TAPE, AND COLLECT THE MONEY. EASY-PEASY, DORALEE.
ARE THEY HERE YET?
I CAN'T WAIT!
EVERYONE PLEASE STAY BACK AND ALLOW THE PASSENGERS TO DEPLANE.
LEROI! LEROI! LEROI! LEROI!
WHO ARE WE LOOKING FOR, STEVE?
LEROI! LEROI!
DIANA, I THINK I SPOTTED OUR SOVIETS.
LEROI! LEROI!
I DIG THIS WALKMAN THING.
LET'S GET YOU THROUGH THIS CROWD, FIRST, OKAY?
THERE THEY ARE!
LEROI! LEROI! WE LOVE YOUUUU SUPERFUNK!
<AMERICAN PIGS!>

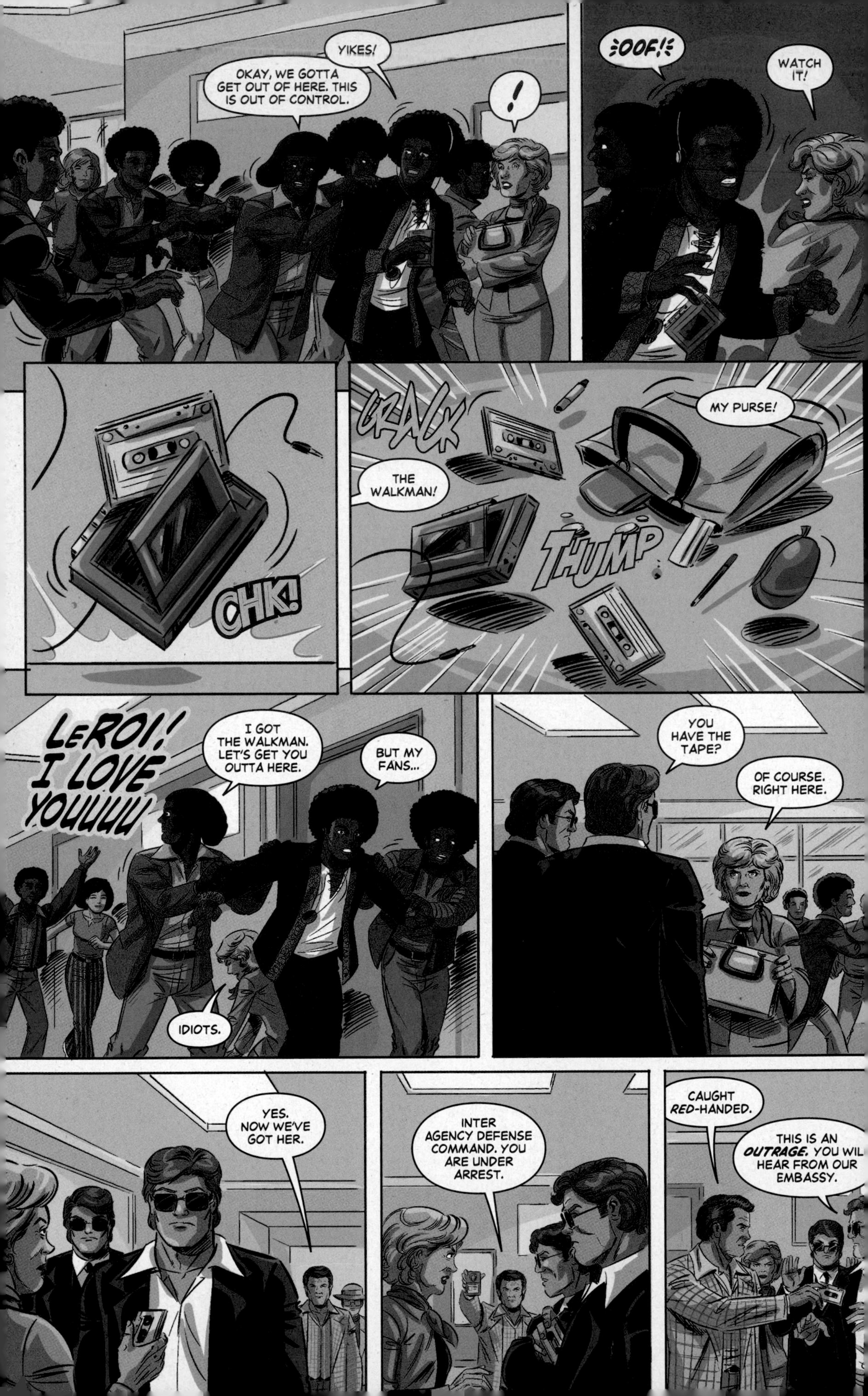
OKAY, WE GOTTA GET OUT OF HERE. THIS IS OUT OF CONTROL.
YIKES!
!
OOF!
WATCH IT!
CHK!
CRACK
MY PURSE!
THE WALKMAN!
THUMP
LeROI! I LOVE YOUUUU
I GOT THE WALKMAN. LET'S GET YOU OUTTA HERE.
BUT MY FANS...
IDIOTS.
YOU HAVE THE TAPE?
OF COURSE. RIGHT HERE.
YES. NOW WE'VE GOT HER.
INTER AGENCY DEFENSE COMMAND. YOU ARE UNDER ARREST.
CAUGHT RED-HANDED.
THIS IS AN OUTRAGE. YOU WIL HEAR FROM OUR EMBASSY.

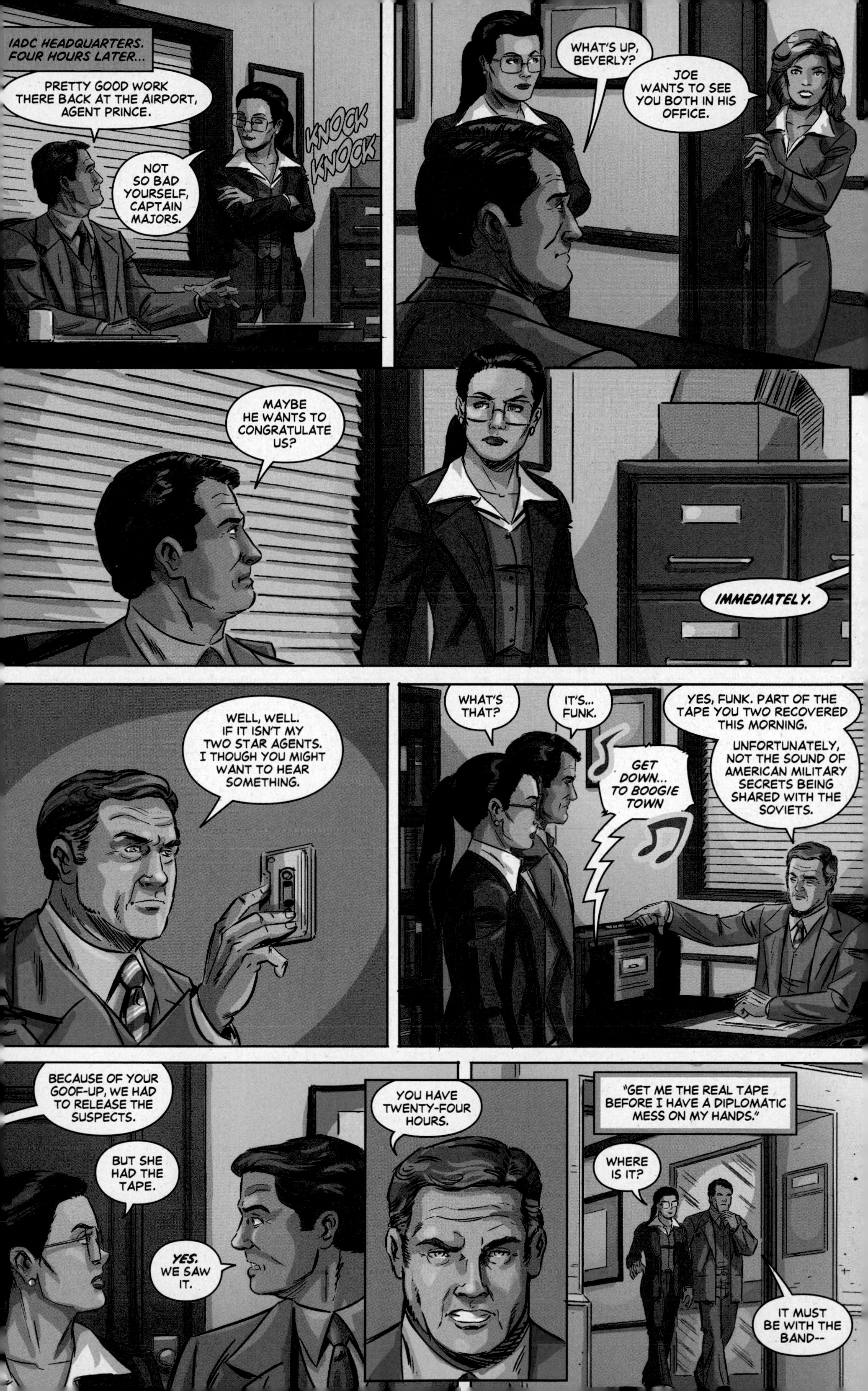
IADC HEADQUARTERS. FOUR HOURS LATER...
PRETTY GOOD WORK THERE BACK AT THE AIRPORT, AGENT PRINCE.
NOT SO BAD YOURSELF, CAPTAIN MAJORS.
KNOCK KNOCK
WHAT'S UP, BEVERLY?
JOE WANTS TO SEE YOU BOTH IN HIS OFFICE.
MAYBE HE WANTS TO CONGRATULATE US?
IMMEDIATELY.
WELL, WELL. IF IT ISN'T MY TWO STAR AGENTS. I THOUGH YOU MIGHT WANT TO HEAR SOMETHING.
WHAT'S THAT?
IT'S... FUNK.
GET DOWN... TO BOOGIE TOWN
YES, FUNK. PART OF THE TAPE YOU TWO RECOVERED THIS MORNING.
UNFORTUNATELY, NOT THE SOUND OF AMERICAN MILITARY SECRETS BEING SHARED WITH THE SOVIETS.
BECAUSE OF YOUR GOOF-UP, WE HAD TO RELEASE THE SUSPECTS.
BUT SHE HAD THE TAPE.
YES. WE SAW IT.
YOU HAVE TWENTY-FOUR HOURS.
"GET ME THE REAL TAPE BEFORE I HAVE A DIPLOMATIC MESS ON MY HANDS."
WHERE IS IT?
IT MUST BE WITH THE BAND--

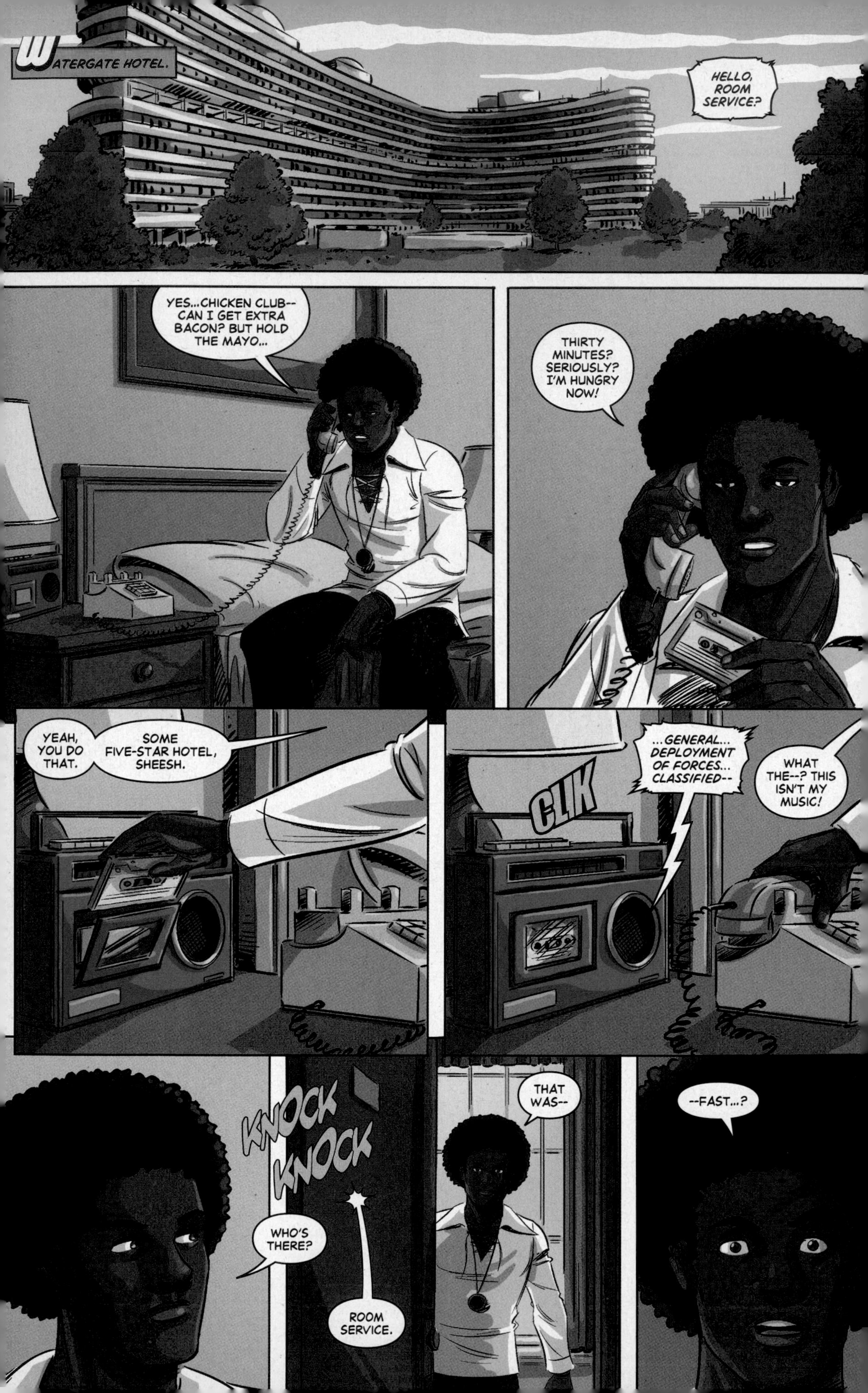
WATERGATE HOTEL.
HELLO, ROOM SERVICE?
YES...CHICKEN CLUB-- CAN I GET EXTRA BACON? BUT HOLD THE MAYO...
THIRTY MINUTES? SERIOUSLY? I'M HUNGRY NOW!
YEAH, YOU DO THAT.
SOME FIVE-STAR HOTEL, SHEESH.
CLIK
...GENERAL... DEPLOYMENT OF FORCES... CLASSIFIED--
WHAT THE--? THIS ISN'T MY MUSIC!
KNOCK KNOCK
WHO'S THERE?
ROOM SERVICE.
THAT WAS--
--FAST...?

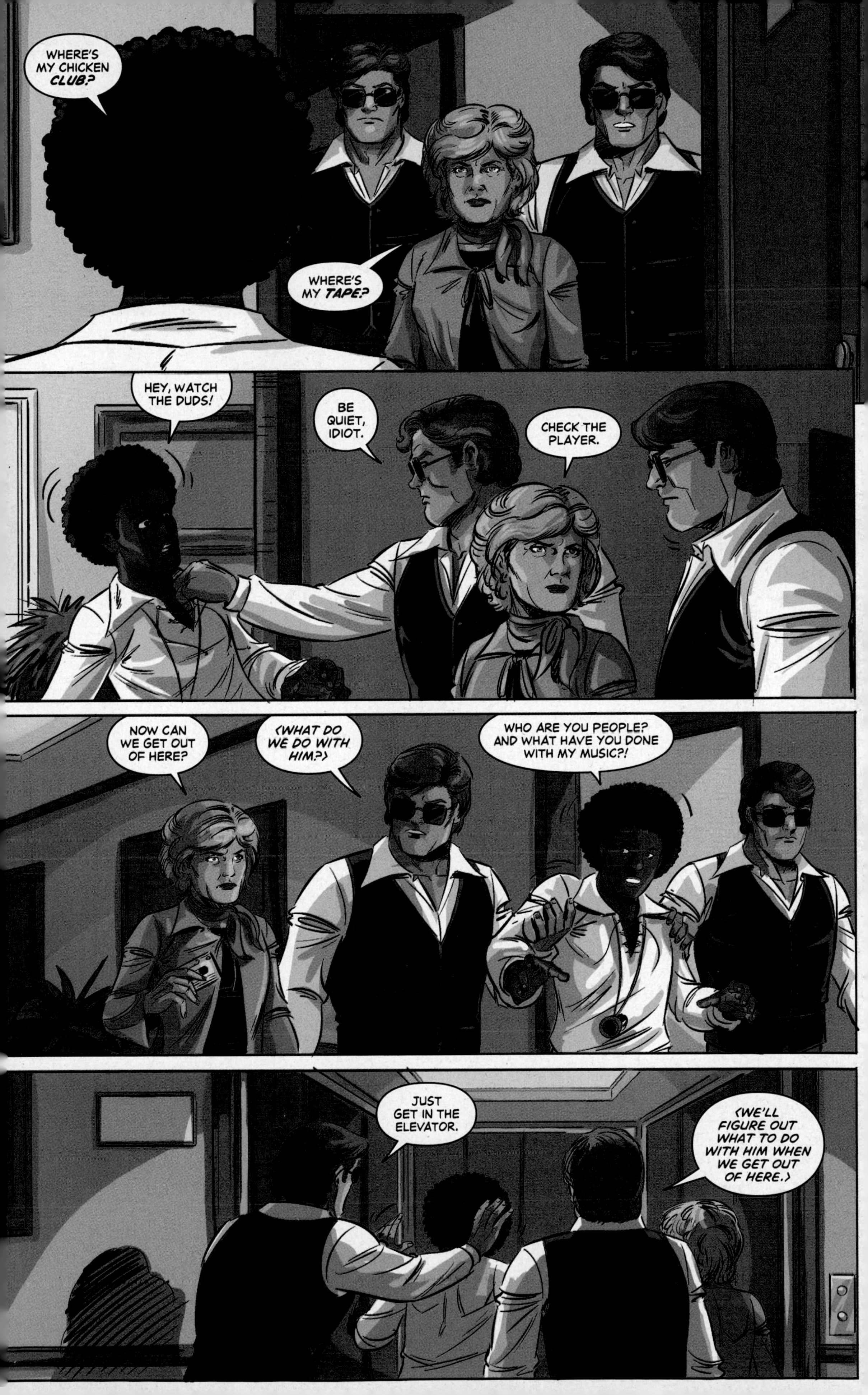
WHERE'S MY CHICKEN *CLUB?*
WHERE'S MY *TAPE?*
HEY, WATCH THE DUDS!
BE QUIET, IDIOT.
CHECK THE PLAYER.
NOW CAN WE GET OUT OF HERE?
<*WHAT DO WE DO WITH HIM?*>
WHO ARE YOU PEOPLE? AND WHAT HAVE YOU DONE WITH MY MUSIC?!
JUST GET IN THE ELEVATOR.
<*WE'LL FIGURE OUT WHAT TO DO WITH HIM WHEN WE GET OUT OF HERE.*>

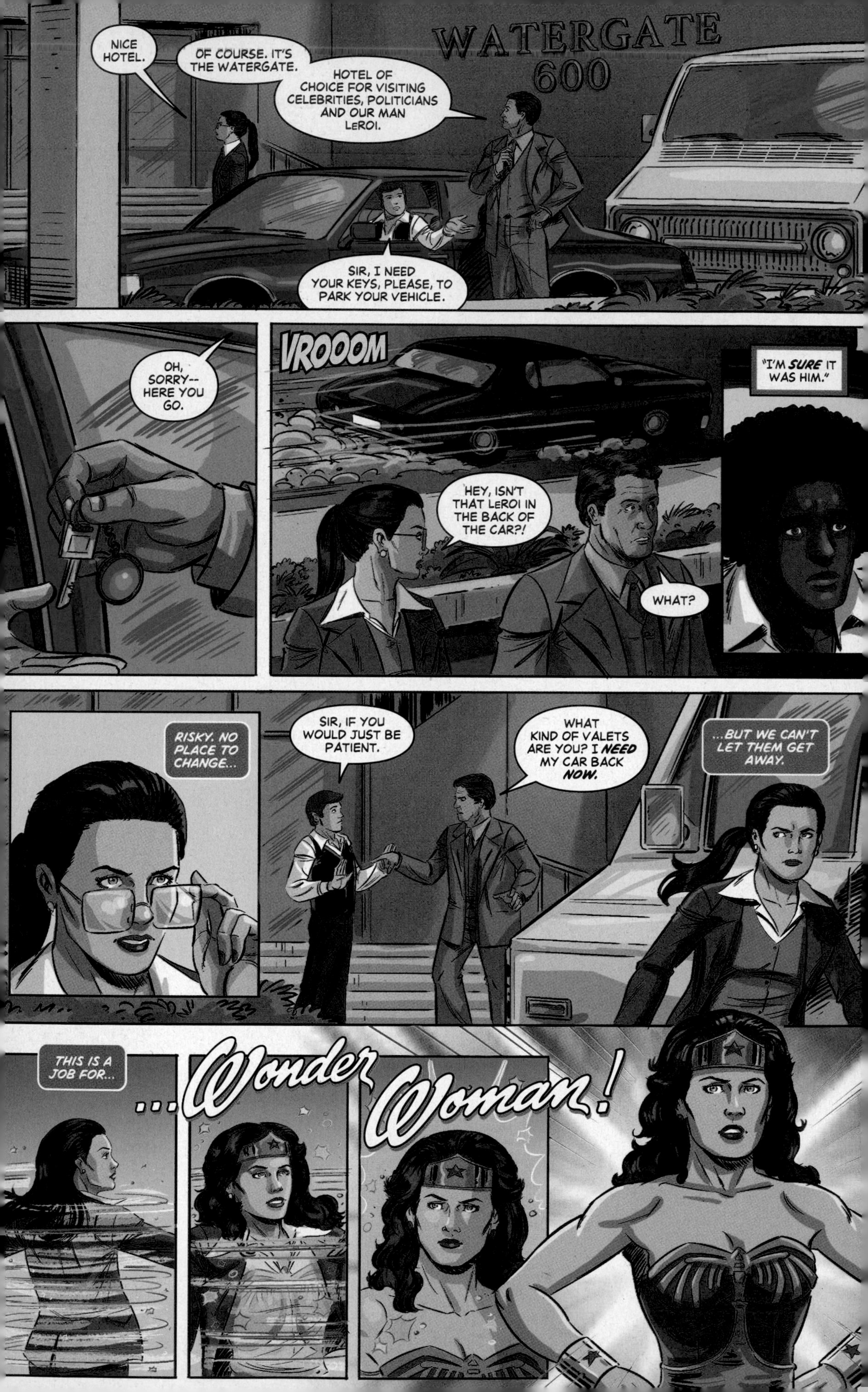
WATERGATE 600
NICE HOTEL.
OF COURSE. IT'S THE WATERGATE.
HOTEL OF CHOICE FOR VISITING CELEBRITIES, POLITICIANS AND OUR MAN LeROI.
SIR, I NEED YOUR KEYS, PLEASE, TO PARK YOUR VEHICLE.
OH, SORRY-- HERE YOU GO.
VROOOM
HEY, ISN'T THAT LeROI IN THE BACK OF THE CAR?!
WHAT?
"I'M SURE IT WAS HIM."
RISKY. NO PLACE TO CHANGE...
SIR, IF YOU WOULD JUST BE PATIENT.
WHAT KIND OF VALETS ARE YOU? I NEED MY CAR BACK NOW.
...BUT WE CAN'T LET THEM GET AWAY.
THIS IS A JOB FOR...
...Wonder Woman!

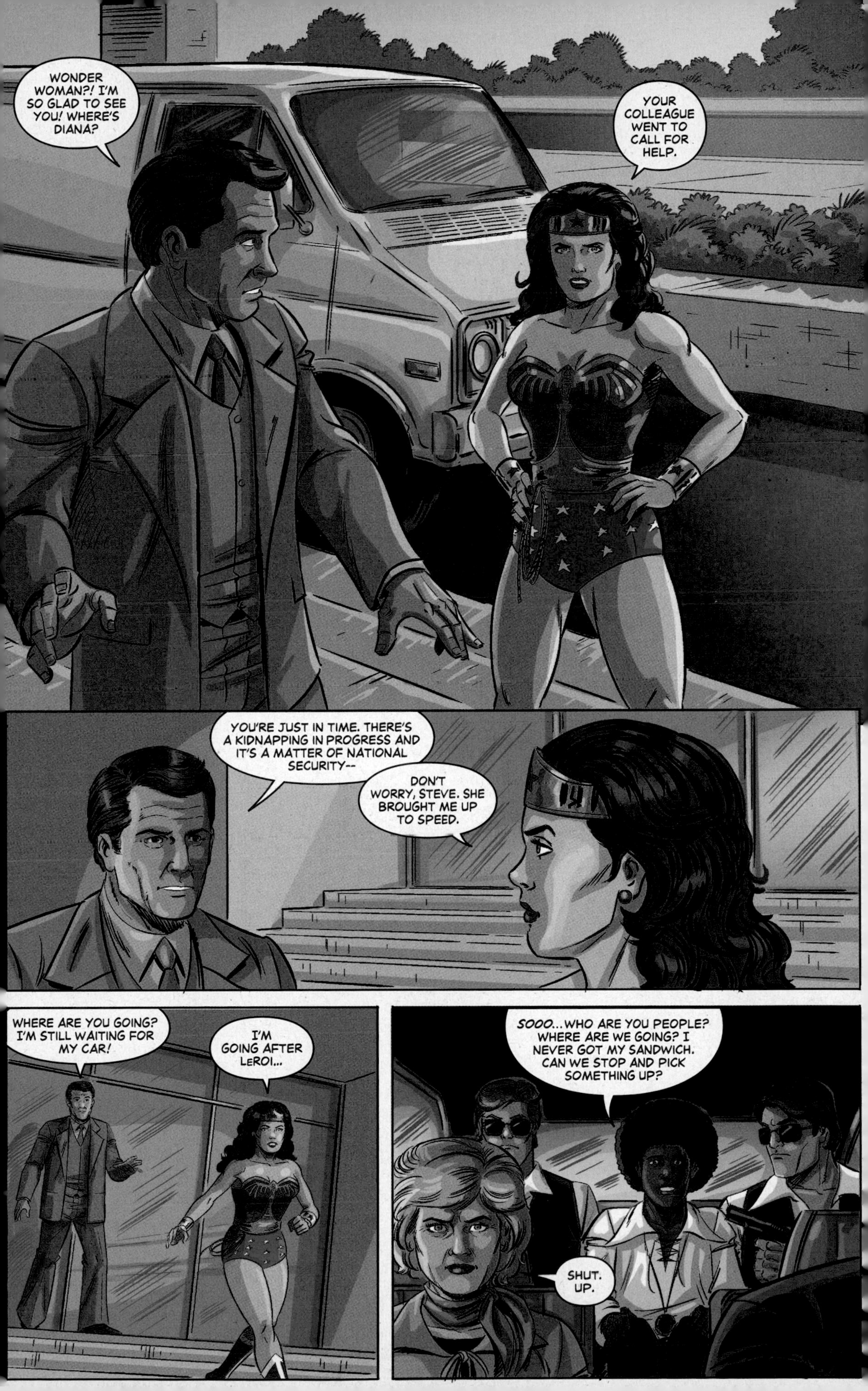
WONDER WOMAN?! I'M SO GLAD TO SEE YOU! WHERE'S DIANA?
YOUR COLLEAGUE WENT TO CALL FOR HELP.
YOU'RE JUST IN TIME. THERE'S A KIDNAPPING IN PROGRESS AND IT'S A MATTER OF NATIONAL SECURITY--
DON'T WORRY, STEVE. SHE BROUGHT ME UP TO SPEED.
WHERE ARE YOU GOING? I'M STILL WAITING FOR MY CAR!
I'M GOING AFTER LEROI...
SOOO...WHO ARE YOU PEOPLE? WHERE ARE WE GOING? I NEVER GOT MY SANDWICH. CAN WE STOP AND PICK SOMETHING UP?
SHUT. UP.

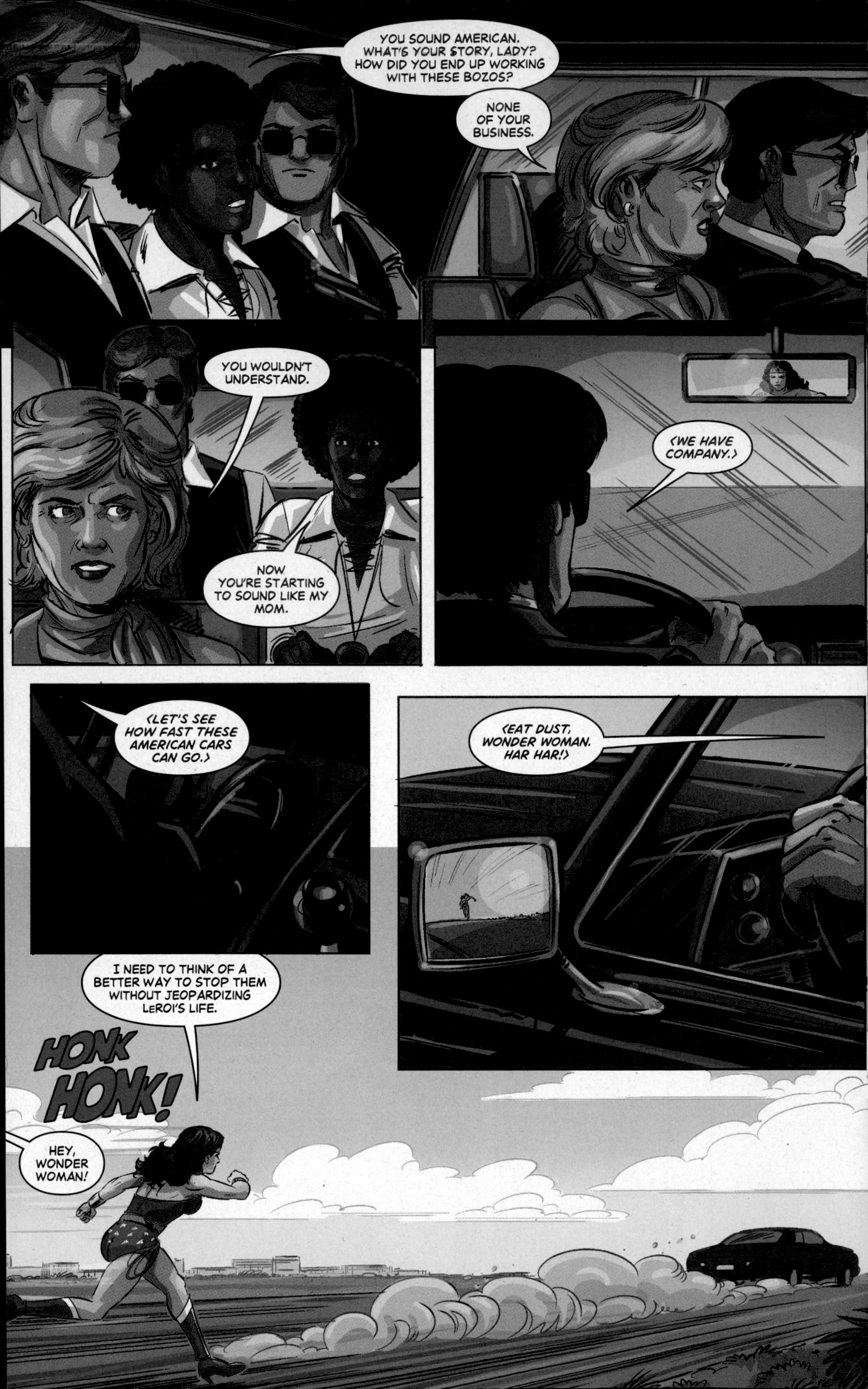
YOU SOUND AMERICAN. WHAT'S YOUR STORY, LADY? HOW DID YOU END UP WORKING WITH THESE BOZOS?
NONE OF YOUR BUSINESS.
YOU WOULDN'T UNDERSTAND.
NOW YOU'RE STARTING TO SOUND LIKE MY MOM.
‹WE HAVE COMPANY.›
‹LET'S SEE HOW FAST THESE AMERICAN CARS CAN GO.›
‹EAT DUST, WONDER WOMAN. HAR HAR!›
I NEED TO THINK OF A BETTER WAY TO STOP THEM WITHOUT JEOPARDIZING LEROI'S LIFE.
HONK HONK!
HEY, WONDER WOMAN!

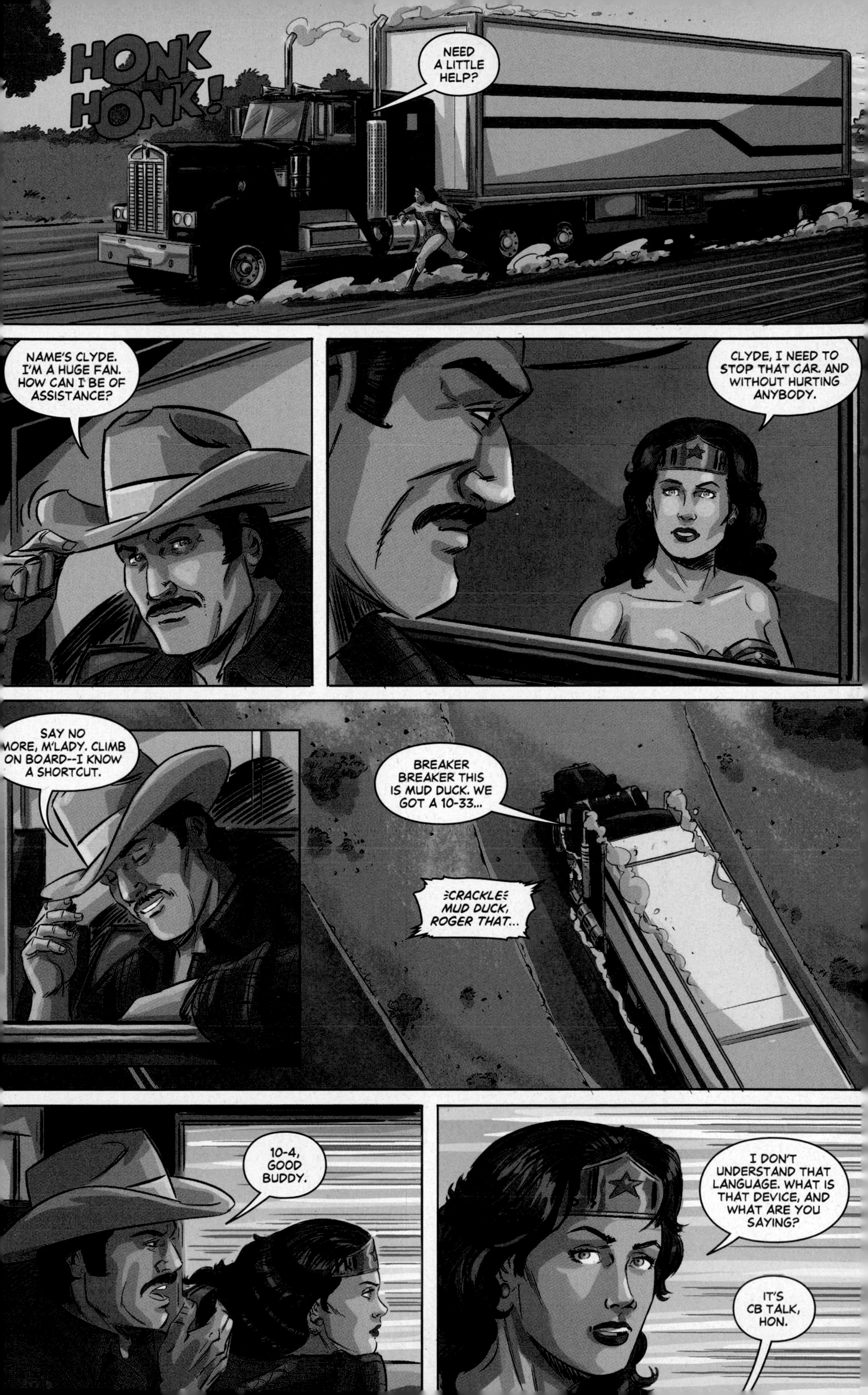
HONK HONK!
NEED A LITTLE HELP?
NAME'S CLYDE. I'M A HUGE FAN. HOW CAN I BE OF ASSISTANCE?
CLYDE, I NEED TO STOP THAT CAR. AND WITHOUT HURTING ANYBODY.
SAY NO MORE, M'LADY. CLIMB ON BOARD--I KNOW A SHORTCUT.
BREAKER BREAKER THIS IS MUD DUCK. WE GOT A 10-33...
CRACKLE MUD DUCK, ROGER THAT...
10-4, GOOD BUDDY.
I DON'T UNDERSTAND THAT LANGUAGE. WHAT IS THAT DEVICE, AND WHAT ARE YOU SAYING?
IT'S CB TALK, HON.

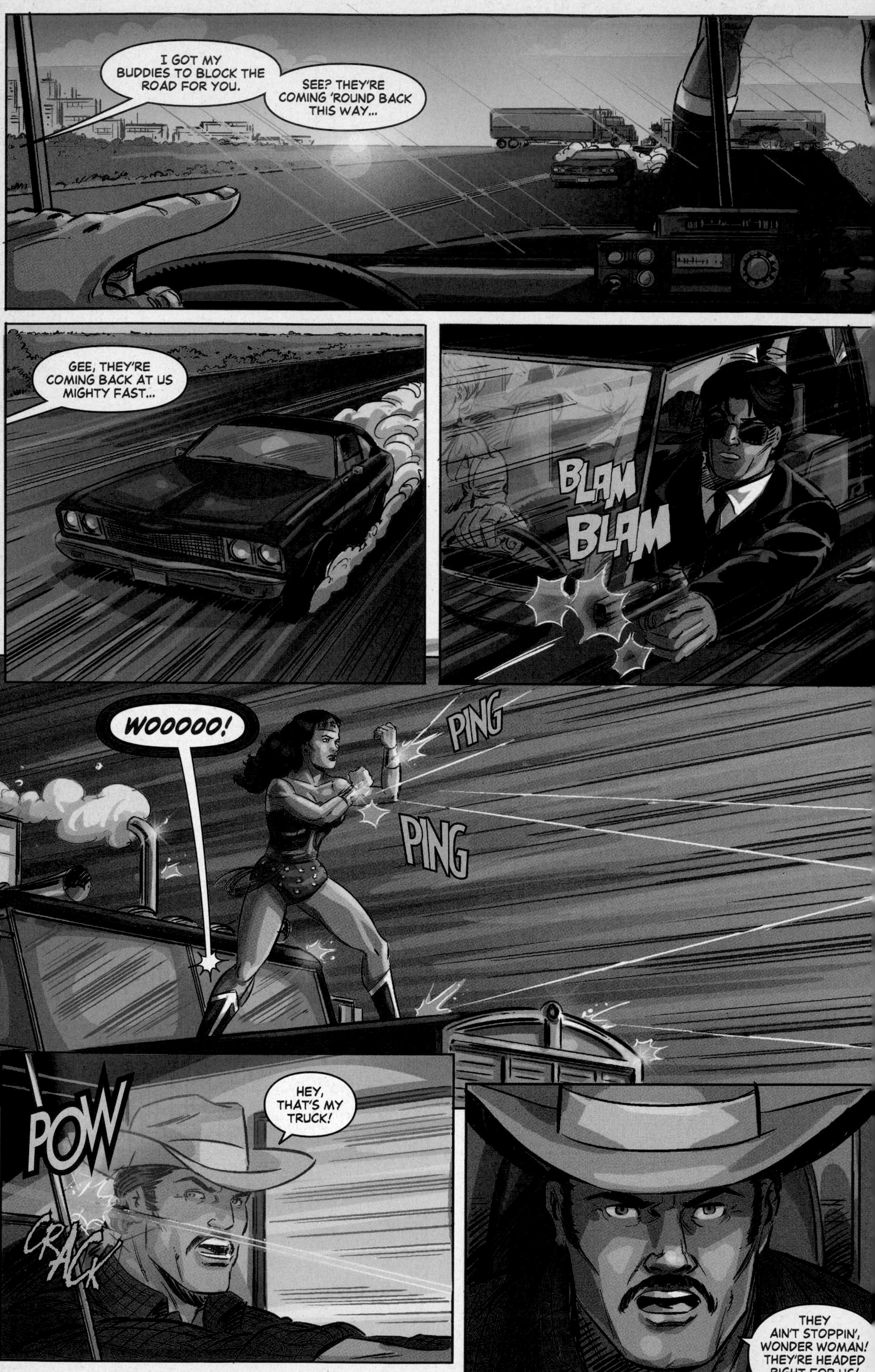
I GOT MY BUDDIES TO BLOCK THE ROAD FOR YOU.
SEE? THEY'RE COMING 'ROUND BACK THIS WAY...
GEE, THEY'RE COMING BACK AT US MIGHTY FAST...
BLAM
BLAM
WOOOOO!
PING
PING
POW
CRACK
HEY, THAT'S MY TRUCK!
THEY AIN'T STOPPIN', WONDER WOMAN! THEY'RE HEADED RIGHT FOR US!

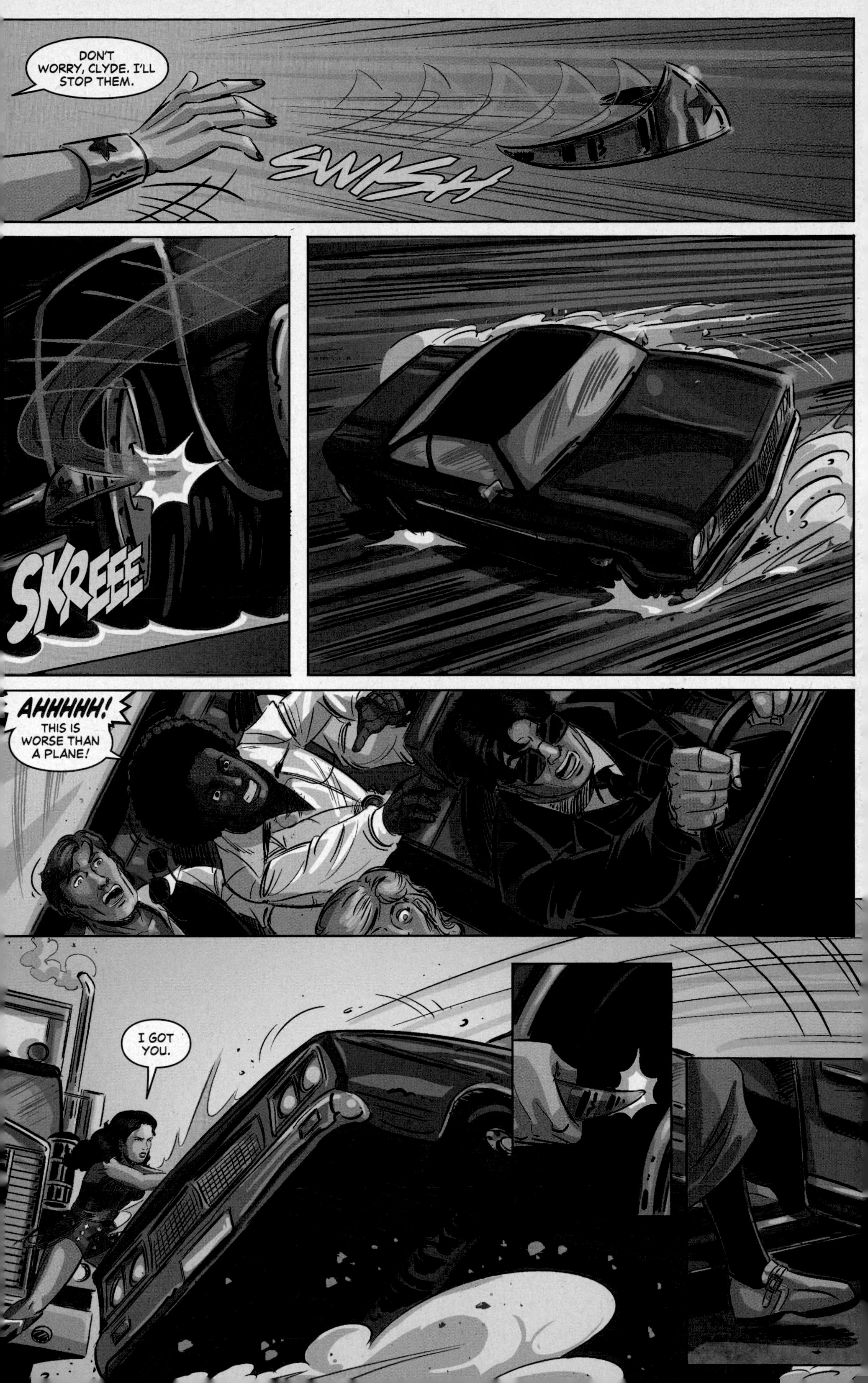
DON'T WORRY, CLYDE. I'LL STOP THEM.
SWISH
SKREEE
AHHHHH! THIS IS WORSE THAN A PLANE!
I GOT YOU.

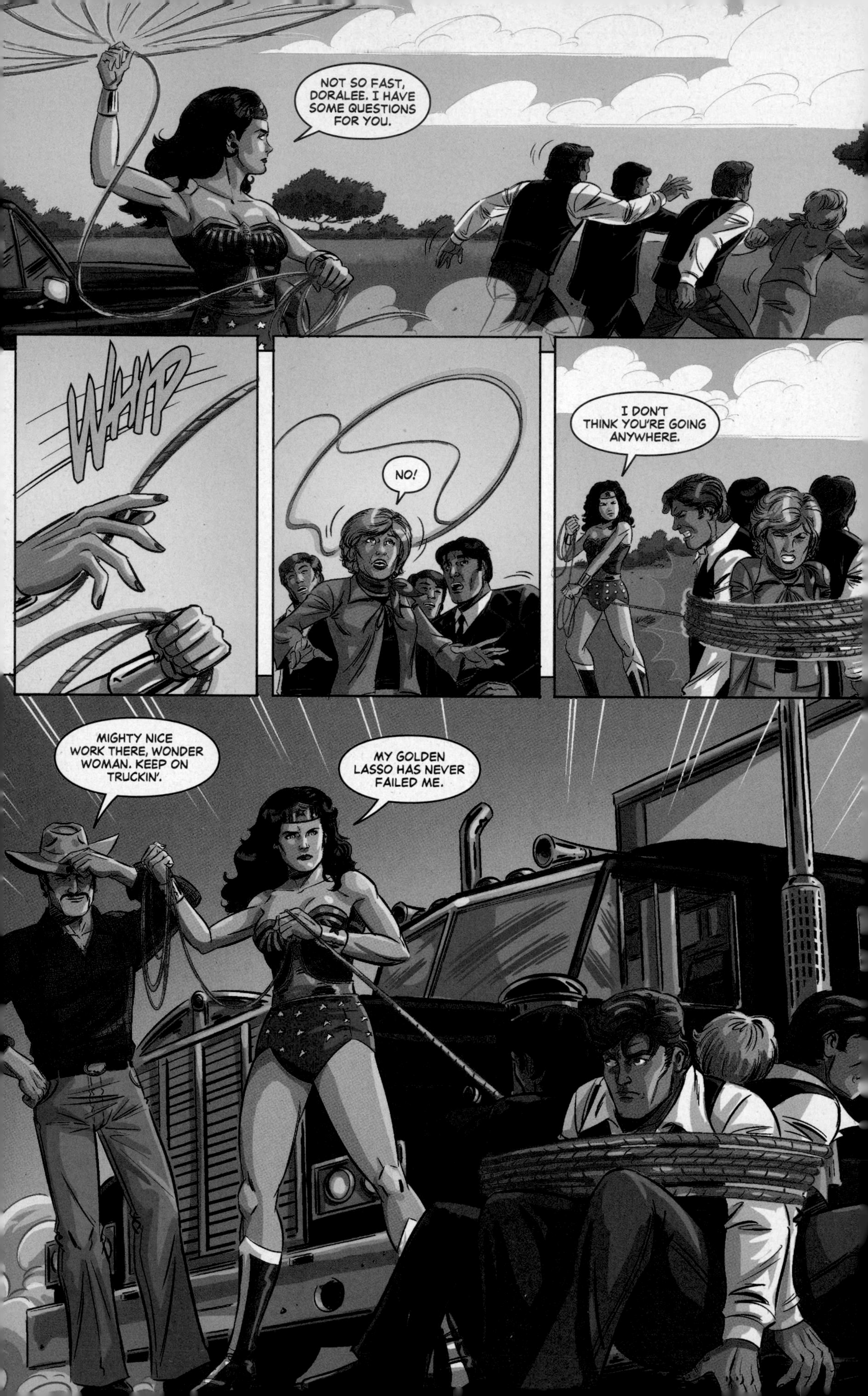
NOT SO FAST, DORALEE. I HAVE SOME QUESTIONS FOR YOU.
WHIP
NO!
I DON'T THINK YOU'RE GOING ANYWHERE.
MIGHTY NICE WORK THERE, WONDER WOMAN. KEEP ON TRUCKIN'.
MY GOLDEN LASSO HAS NEVER FAILED ME.

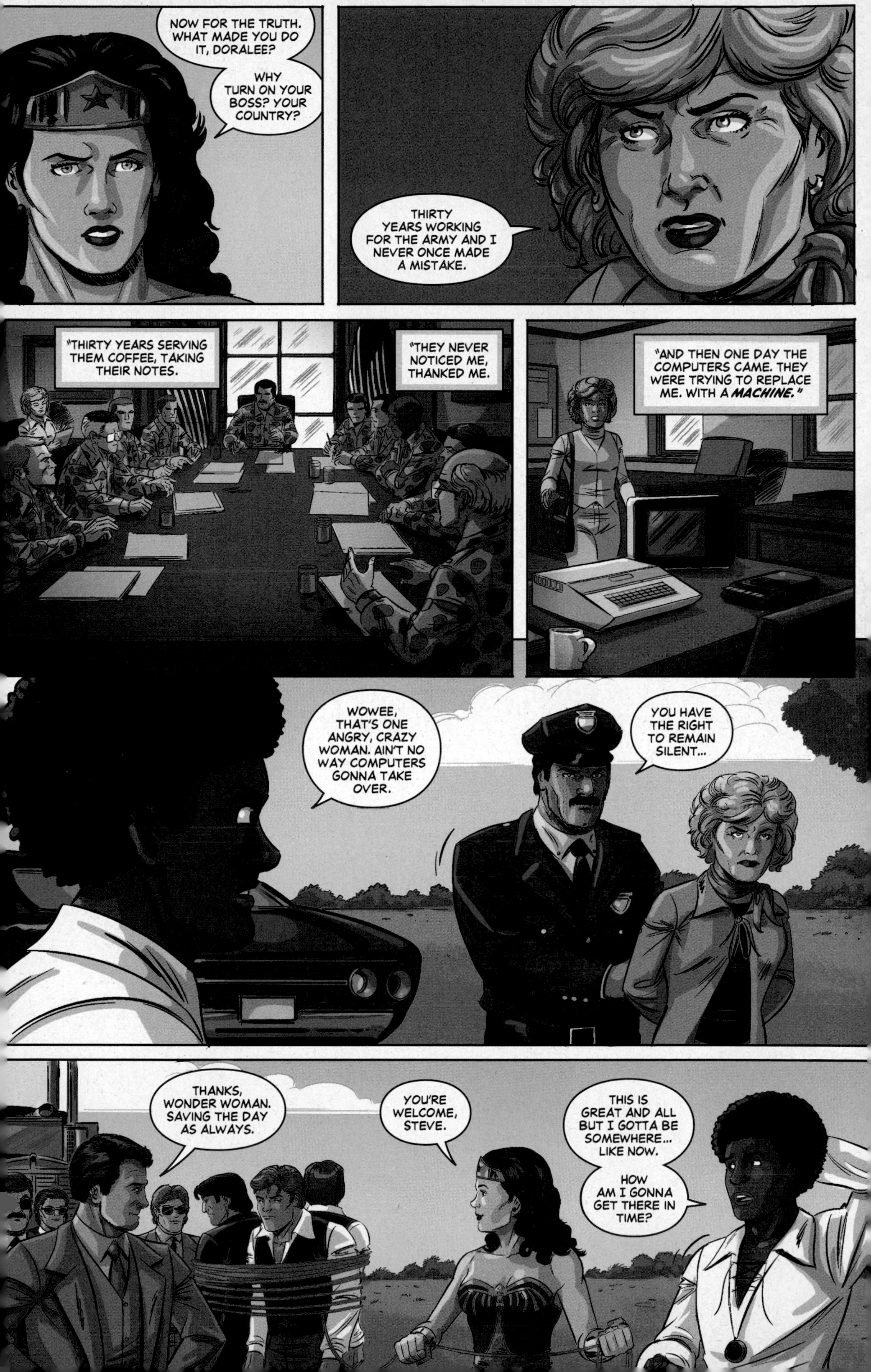
NOW FOR THE TRUTH. WHAT MADE YOU DO IT, DORALEE?
WHY TURN ON YOUR BOSS? YOUR COUNTRY?
THIRTY YEARS WORKING FOR THE ARMY AND I NEVER ONCE MADE A MISTAKE.
"THIRTY YEARS SERVING THEM COFFEE, TAKING THEIR NOTES.
"THEY NEVER NOTICED ME, THANKED ME.
"AND THEN ONE DAY THE COMPUTERS CAME. THEY WERE TRYING TO REPLACE ME. WITH A MACHINE."
WOWEE, THAT'S ONE ANGRY, CRAZY WOMAN. AIN'T NO WAY COMPUTERS GONNA TAKE OVER.
YOU HAVE THE RIGHT TO REMAIN SILENT...
THANKS, WONDER WOMAN. SAVING THE DAY AS ALWAYS.
YOU'RE WELCOME, STEVE.
THIS IS GREAT AND ALL BUT I GOTTA BE SOMEWHERE... LIKE NOW.
HOW AM I GONNA GET THERE IN TIME?

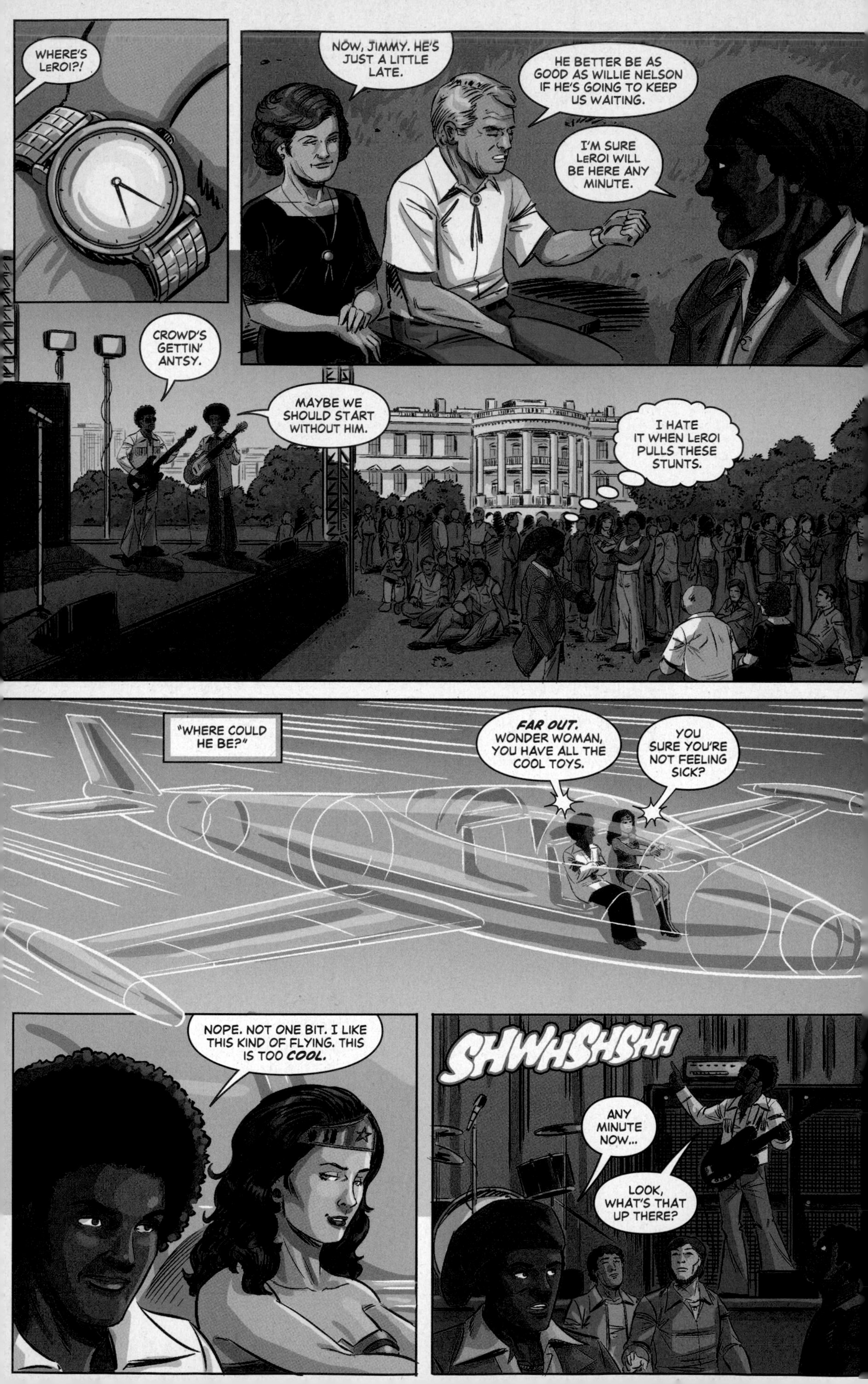
WHERE'S LEROI?!
NOW, JIMMY. HE'S JUST A LITTLE LATE.
HE BETTER BE AS GOOD AS WILLIE NELSON IF HE'S GOING TO KEEP US WAITING.
I'M SURE LEROI WILL BE HERE ANY MINUTE.
CROWD'S GETTIN' ANTSY.
MAYBE WE SHOULD START WITHOUT HIM.
I HATE IT WHEN LEROI PULLS THESE STUNTS.
"WHERE COULD HE BE?"
FAR OUT. WONDER WOMAN, YOU HAVE ALL THE COOL TOYS.
YOU SURE YOU'RE NOT FEELING SICK?
NOPE. NOT ONE BIT. I LIKE THIS KIND OF FLYING. THIS IS TOO *COOL.*
SHWHSHSHH
ANY MINUTE NOW...
LOOK, WHAT'S THAT UP THERE?

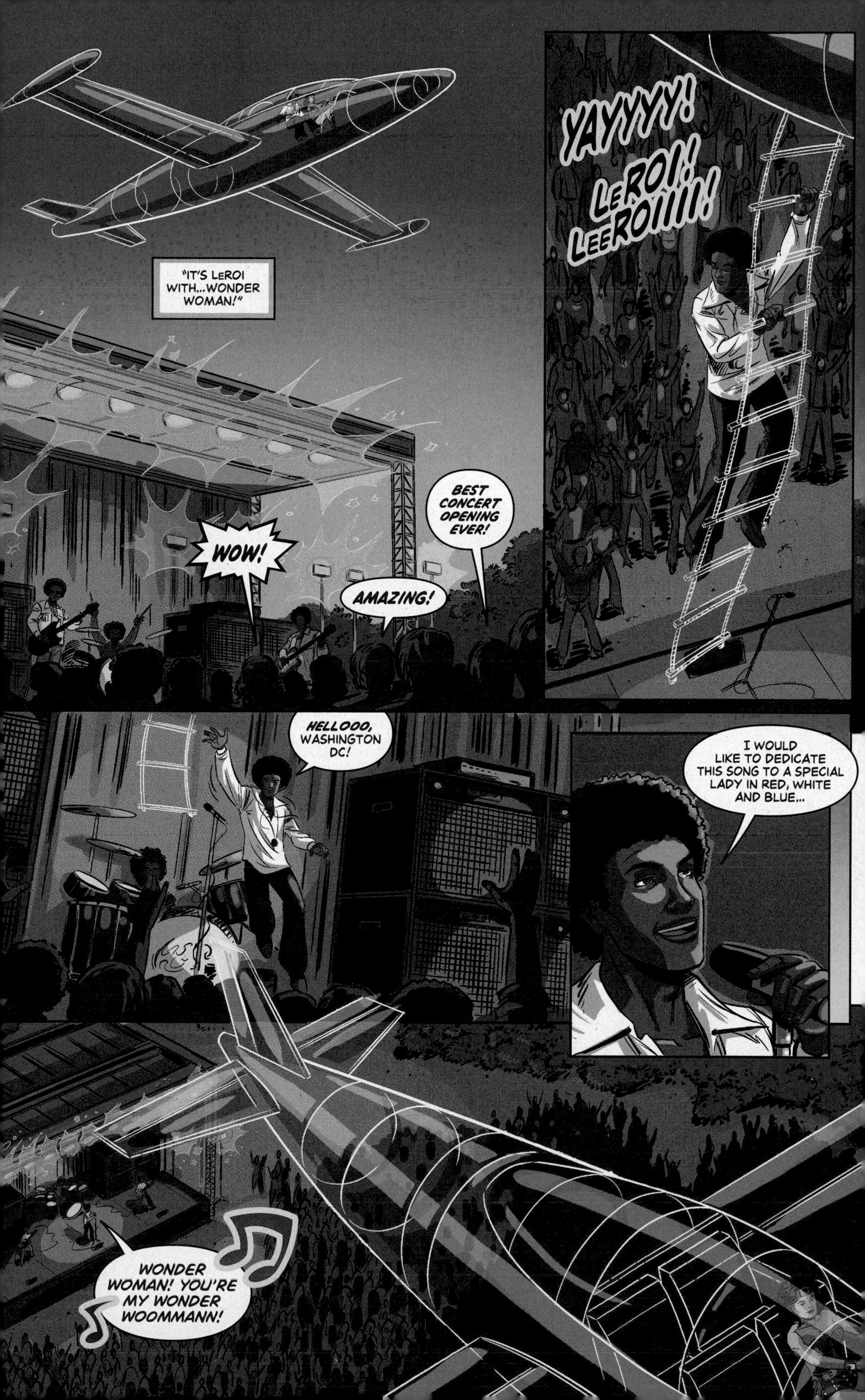
"IT'S LeROI WITH...WONDER WOMAN!"
WOW!
AMAZING!
BEST CONCERT OPENING EVER!
YAYYYY!
LeROI! LeeROIIIII!
HELLOOO, WASHINGTON DC!
I WOULD LIKE TO DEDICATE THIS SONG TO A SPECIAL LADY IN RED, WHITE AND BLUE...
WONDER WOMAN! YOU'RE MY WONDER WOOMMANN!

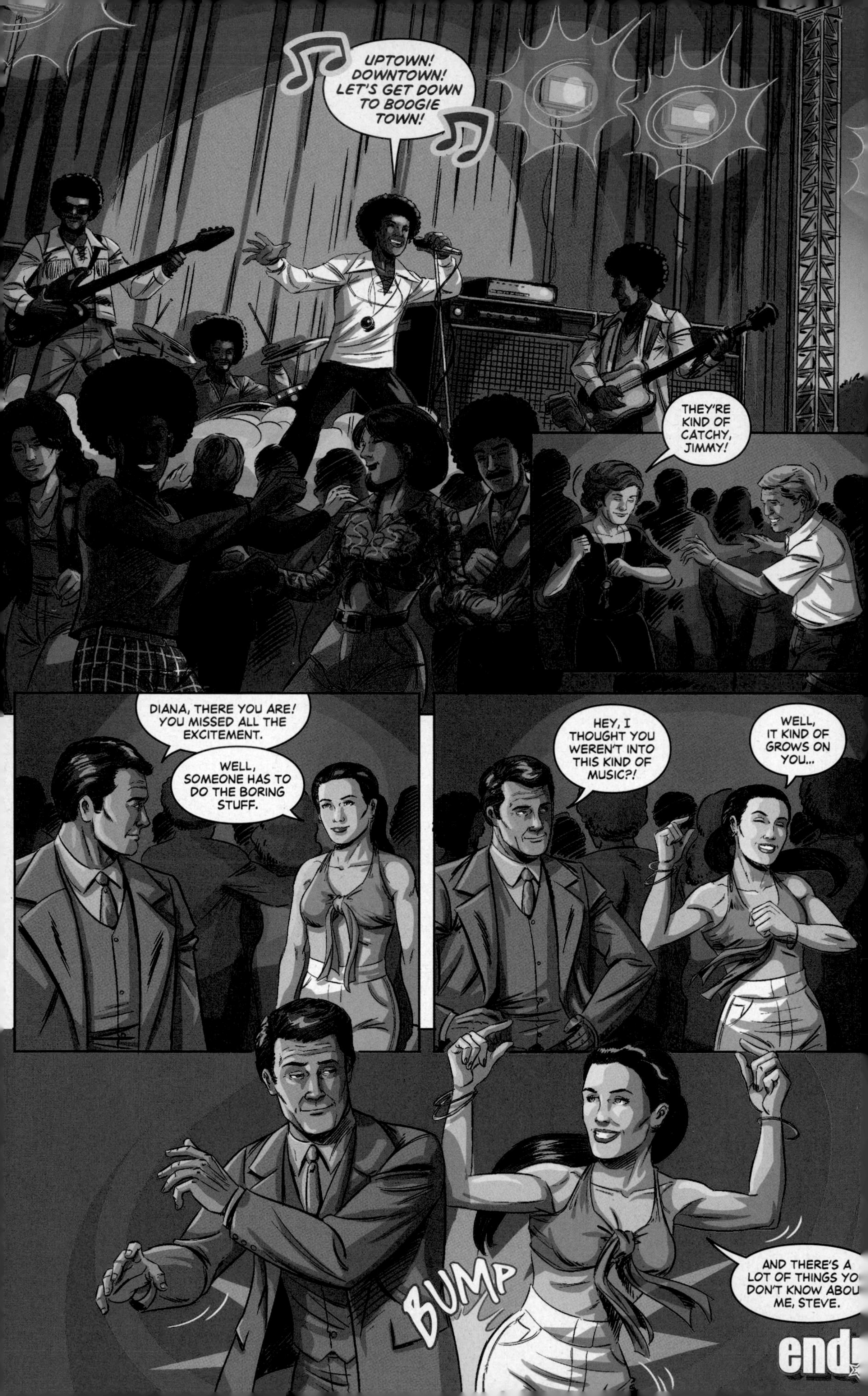
UPTOWN! DOWNTOWN! LET'S GET DOWN TO BOOGIE TOWN!
THEY'RE KIND OF CATCHY, JIMMY!
DIANA, THERE YOU ARE! YOU MISSED ALL THE EXCITEMENT.
WELL, SOMEONE HAS TO DO THE BORING STUFF.
HEY, I THOUGHT YOU WEREN'T INTO THIS KIND OF MUSIC?!
WELL, IT KIND OF GROWS ON YOU...
BUMP
AND THERE'S A LOT OF THINGS YO DON'T KNOW ABOU ME, STEVE.
end

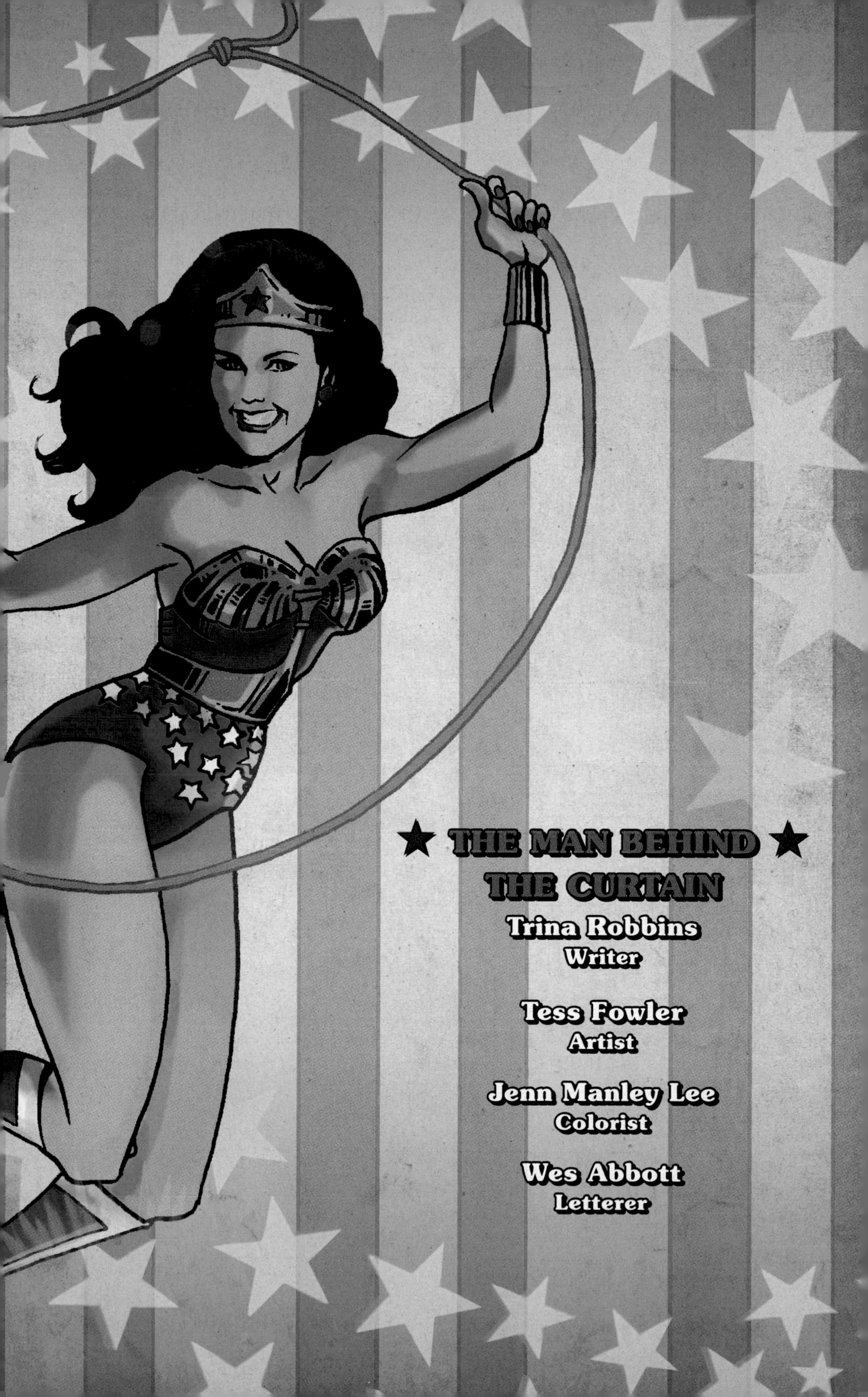

★ THE MAN BEHIND THE CURTAIN ★

Trina Robbins
Writer

Tess Fowler
Artist

Jenn Manley Lee
Colorist

Wes Abbott
Letterer

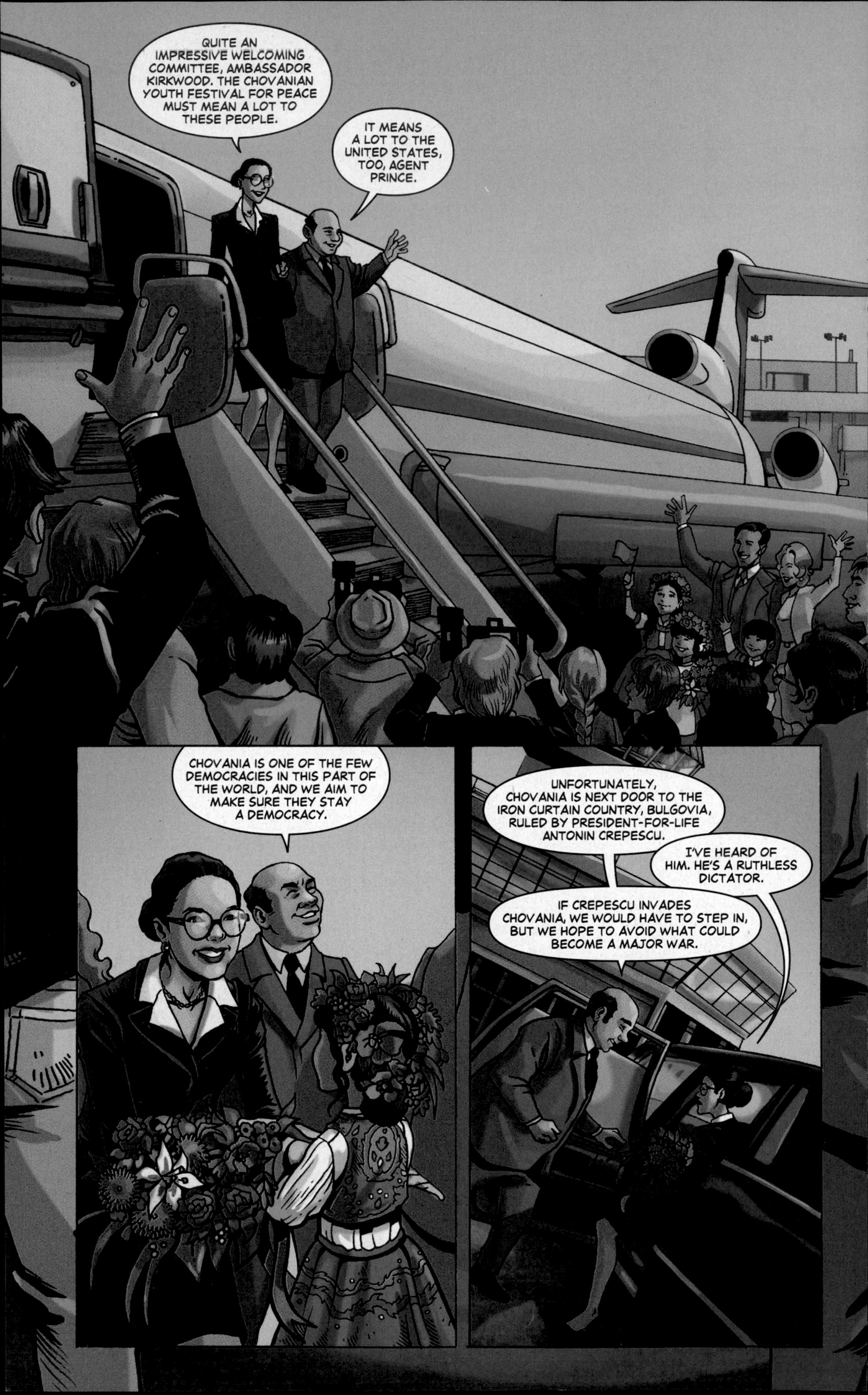
QUITE AN IMPRESSIVE WELCOMING COMMITTEE, AMBASSADOR KIRKWOOD. THE CHOVANIAN YOUTH FESTIVAL FOR PEACE MUST MEAN A LOT TO THESE PEOPLE.
IT MEANS A LOT TO THE UNITED STATES, TOO, AGENT PRINCE.
CHOVANIA IS ONE OF THE FEW DEMOCRACIES IN THIS PART OF THE WORLD, AND WE AIM TO MAKE SURE THEY STAY A DEMOCRACY.
UNFORTUNATELY, CHOVANIA IS NEXT DOOR TO THE IRON CURTAIN COUNTRY, BULGOVIA, RULED BY PRESIDENT-FOR-LIFE ANTONIN CREPESCU.
I'VE HEARD OF HIM. HE'S A RUTHLESS DICTATOR.
IF CREPESCU INVADES CHOVANIA, WE WOULD HAVE TO STEP IN, BUT WE HOPE TO AVOID WHAT COULD BECOME A MAJOR WAR.

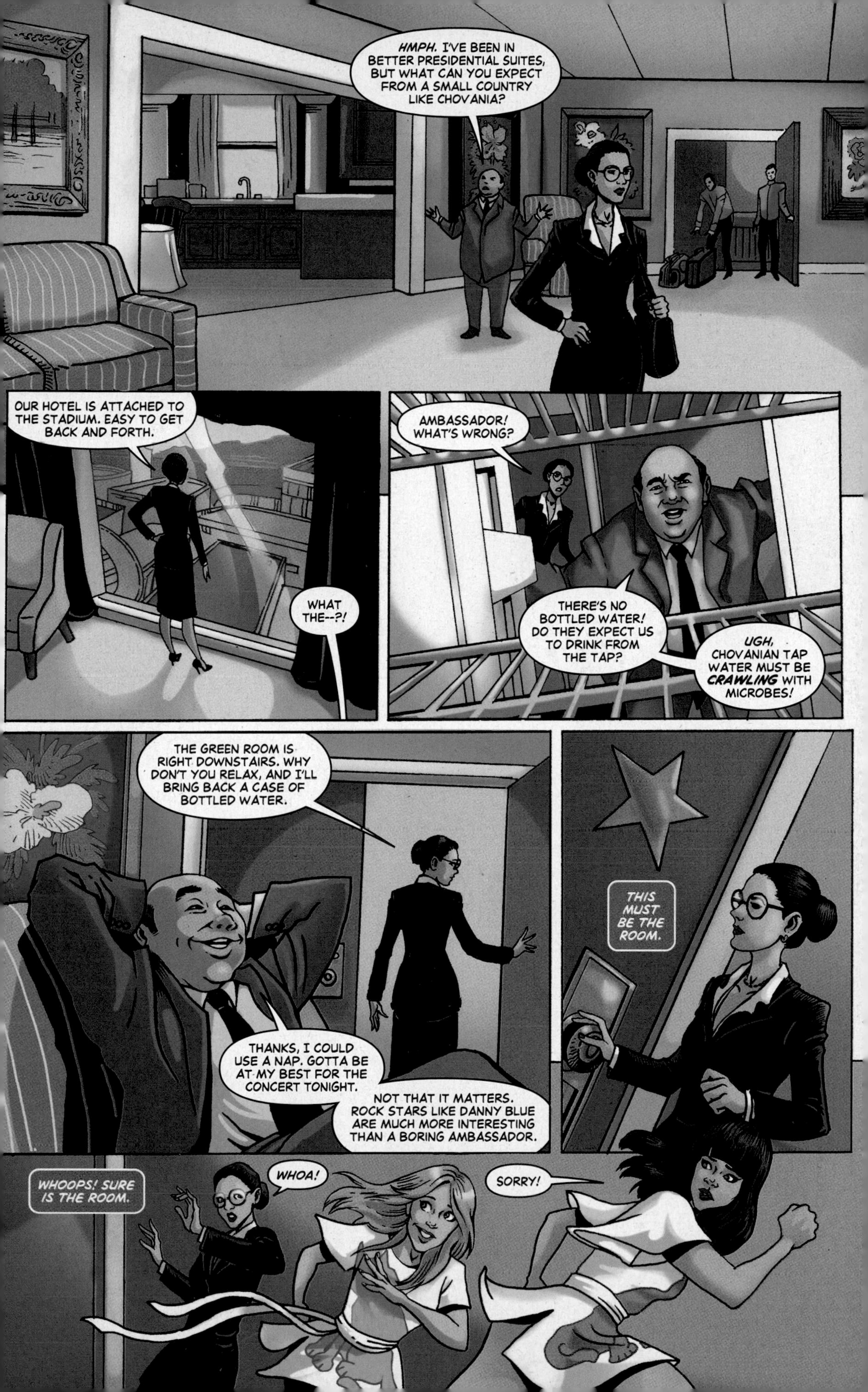
HMPH. I'VE BEEN IN BETTER PRESIDENTIAL SUITES, BUT WHAT CAN YOU EXPECT FROM A SMALL COUNTRY LIKE CHOVANIA?
OUR HOTEL IS ATTACHED TO THE STADIUM. EASY TO GET BACK AND FORTH.
WHAT THE--?!
AMBASSADOR! WHAT'S WRONG?
THERE'S NO BOTTLED WATER! DO THEY EXPECT US TO DRINK FROM THE TAP?
UGH, CHOVANIAN TAP WATER MUST BE CRAWLING WITH MICROBES!
THE GREEN ROOM IS RIGHT DOWNSTAIRS. WHY DON'T YOU RELAX, AND I'LL BRING BACK A CASE OF BOTTLED WATER.
THANKS, I COULD USE A NAP. GOTTA BE AT MY BEST FOR THE CONCERT TONIGHT.
NOT THAT IT MATTERS. ROCK STARS LIKE DANNY BLUE ARE MUCH MORE INTERESTING THAN A BORING AMBASSADOR.
THIS MUST BE THE ROOM.
WHOOPS! SURE IS THE ROOM.
WHOA!
SORRY!

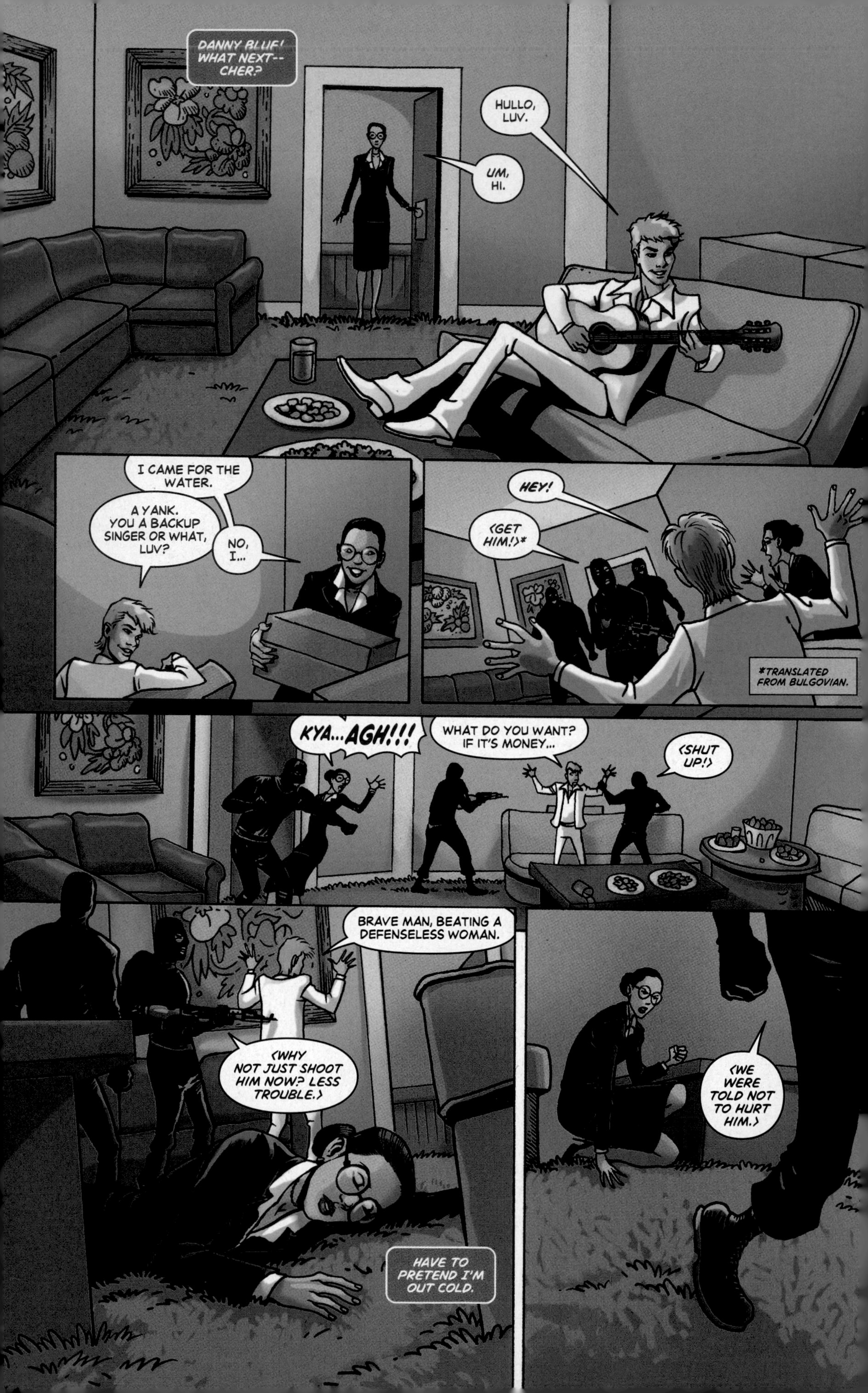
DANNY BLUE! WHAT NEXT-- CHER?
HULLO, LUV.
UM, HI.
I CAME FOR THE WATER.
A YANK. YOU A BACKUP SINGER OR WHAT, LUV?
NO, I...
HEY!
<GET HIM!>*
*TRANSLATED FROM BULGOVIAN.
KYA...AGH!!!
WHAT DO YOU WANT? IF IT'S MONEY...
<SHUT UP!>
BRAVE MAN, BEATING A DEFENSELESS WOMAN.
<WHY NOT JUST SHOOT HIM NOW? LESS TROUBLE.>
HAVE TO PRETEND I'M OUT COLD.
<WE WERE TOLD NOT TO HURT HIM.>

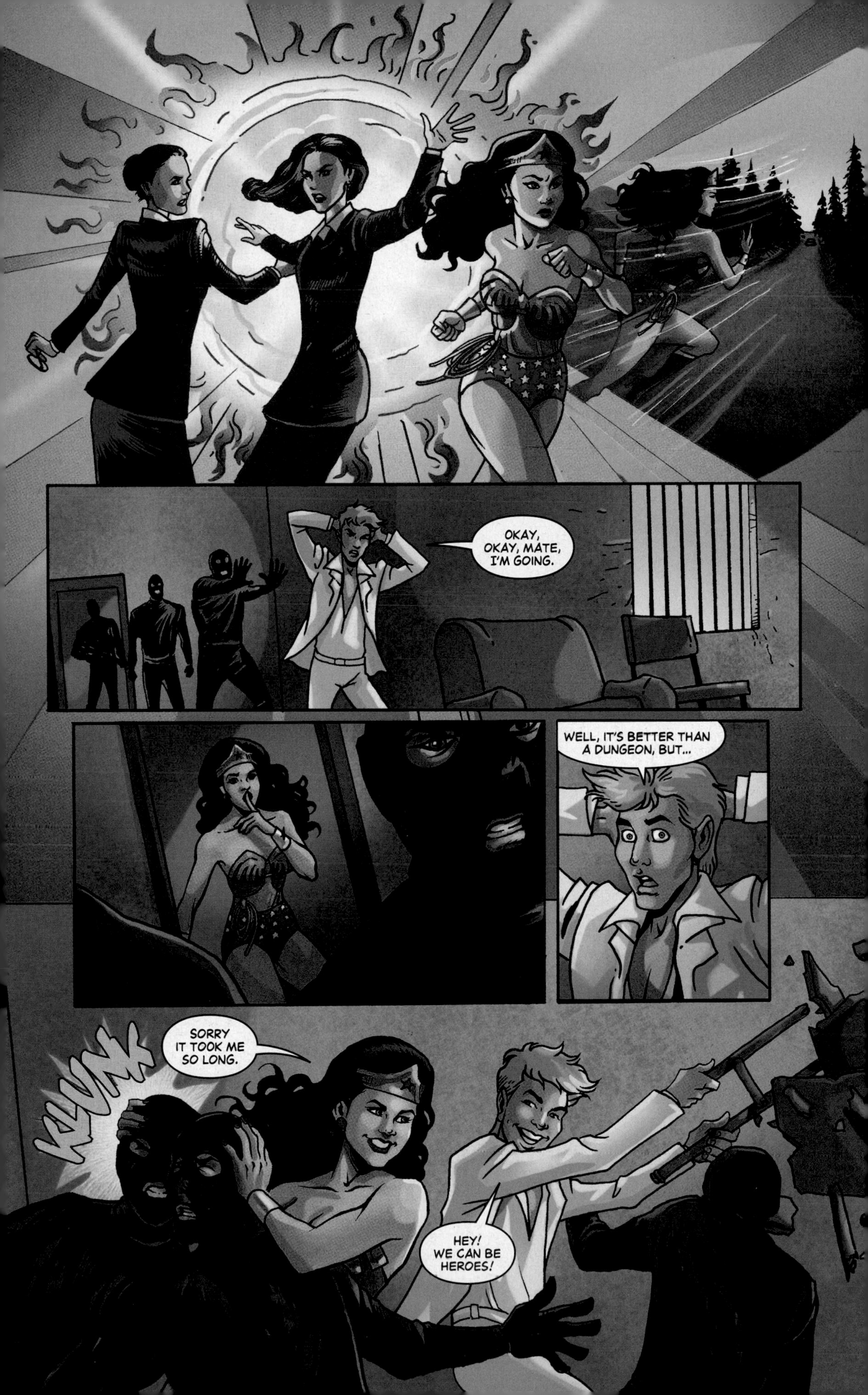
OKAY, OKAY, MATE, I'M GOING.
WELL, IT'S BETTER THAN A DUNGEON, BUT...
KLUNK
SORRY IT TOOK ME SO LONG.
HEY! WE CAN BE HEROES!

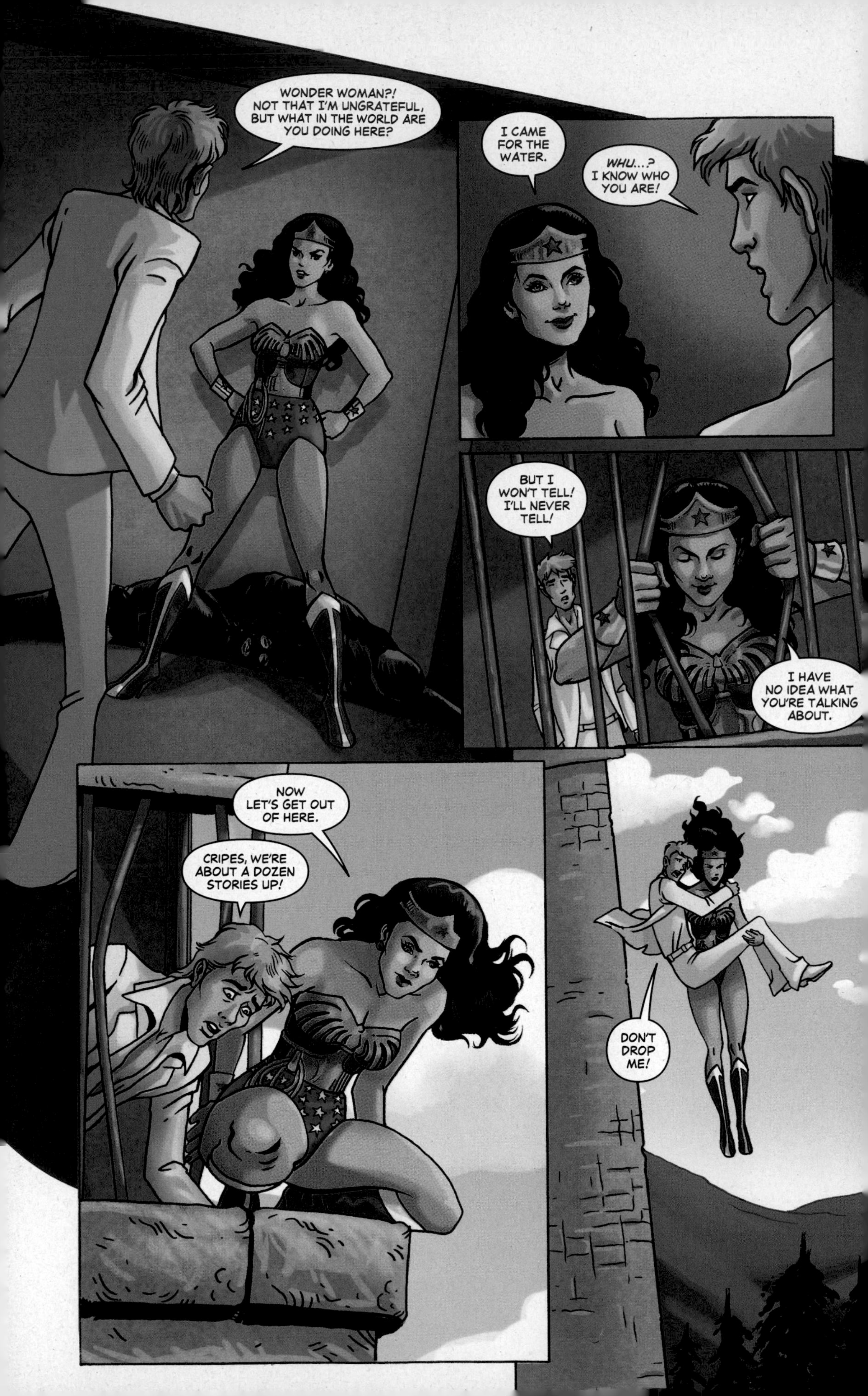
WONDER WOMAN?! NOT THAT I'M UNGRATEFUL, BUT WHAT IN THE WORLD ARE YOU DOING HERE?
I CAME FOR THE WATER.
WHU...? I KNOW WHO YOU ARE!
BUT I WON'T TELL! I'LL NEVER TELL!
I HAVE NO IDEA WHAT YOU'RE TALKING ABOUT.
NOW LET'S GET OUT OF HERE.
CRIPES, WE'RE ABOUT A DOZEN STORIES UP!
DON'T DROP ME!

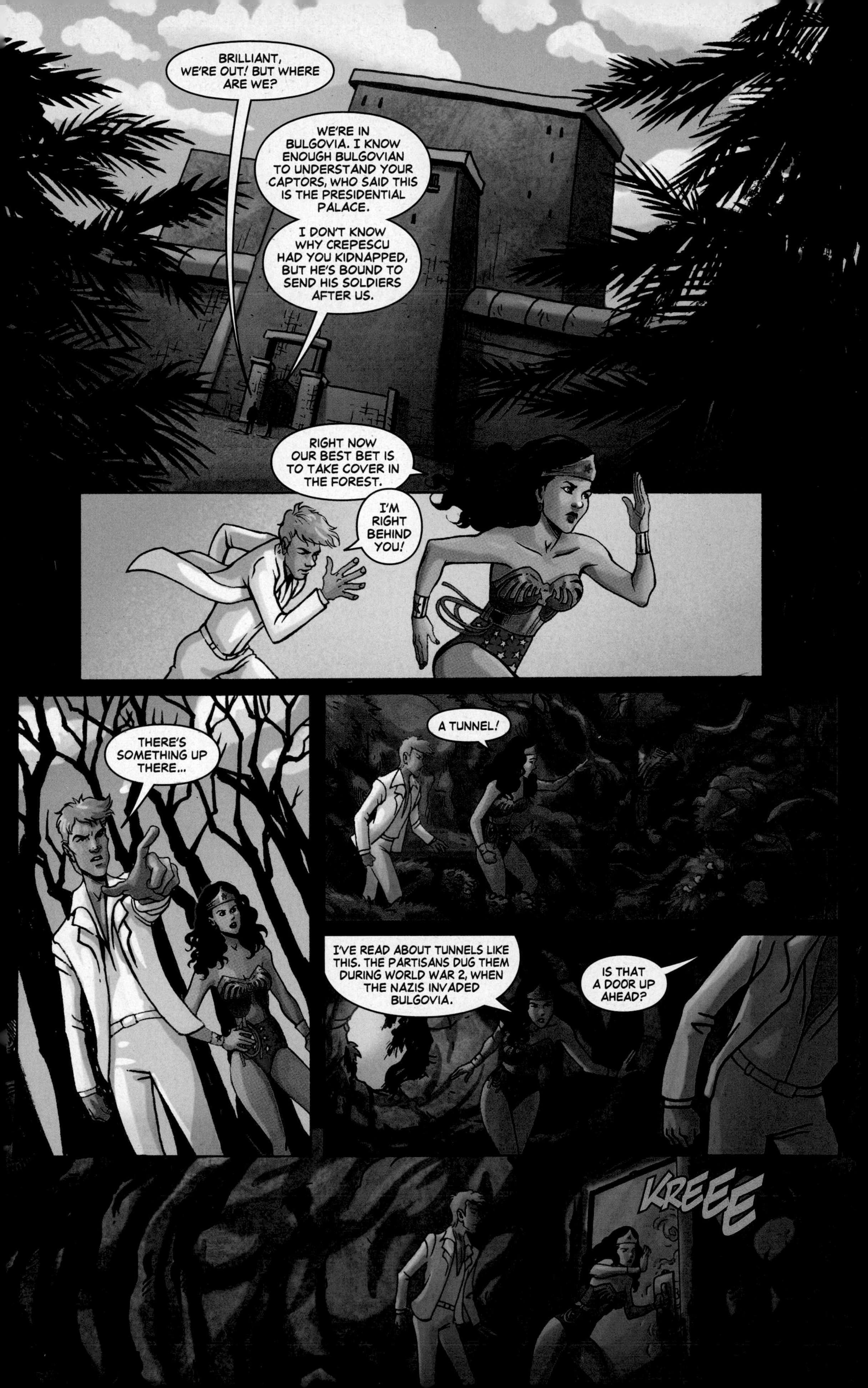
BRILLIANT, WE'RE OUT! BUT WHERE ARE WE?
WE'RE IN BULGOVIA. I KNOW ENOUGH BULGOVIAN TO UNDERSTAND YOUR CAPTORS, WHO SAID THIS IS THE PRESIDENTIAL PALACE.
I DON'T KNOW WHY CREPESCU HAD YOU KIDNAPPED, BUT HE'S BOUND TO SEND HIS SOLDIERS AFTER US.
RIGHT NOW OUR BEST BET IS TO TAKE COVER IN THE FOREST.
I'M RIGHT BEHIND YOU!
THERE'S SOMETHING UP THERE...
A TUNNEL!
I'VE READ ABOUT TUNNELS LIKE THIS. THE PARTISANS DUG THEM DURING WORLD WAR 2, WHEN THE NAZIS INVADED BULGOVIA.
IS THAT A DOOR UP AHEAD?
KREEE

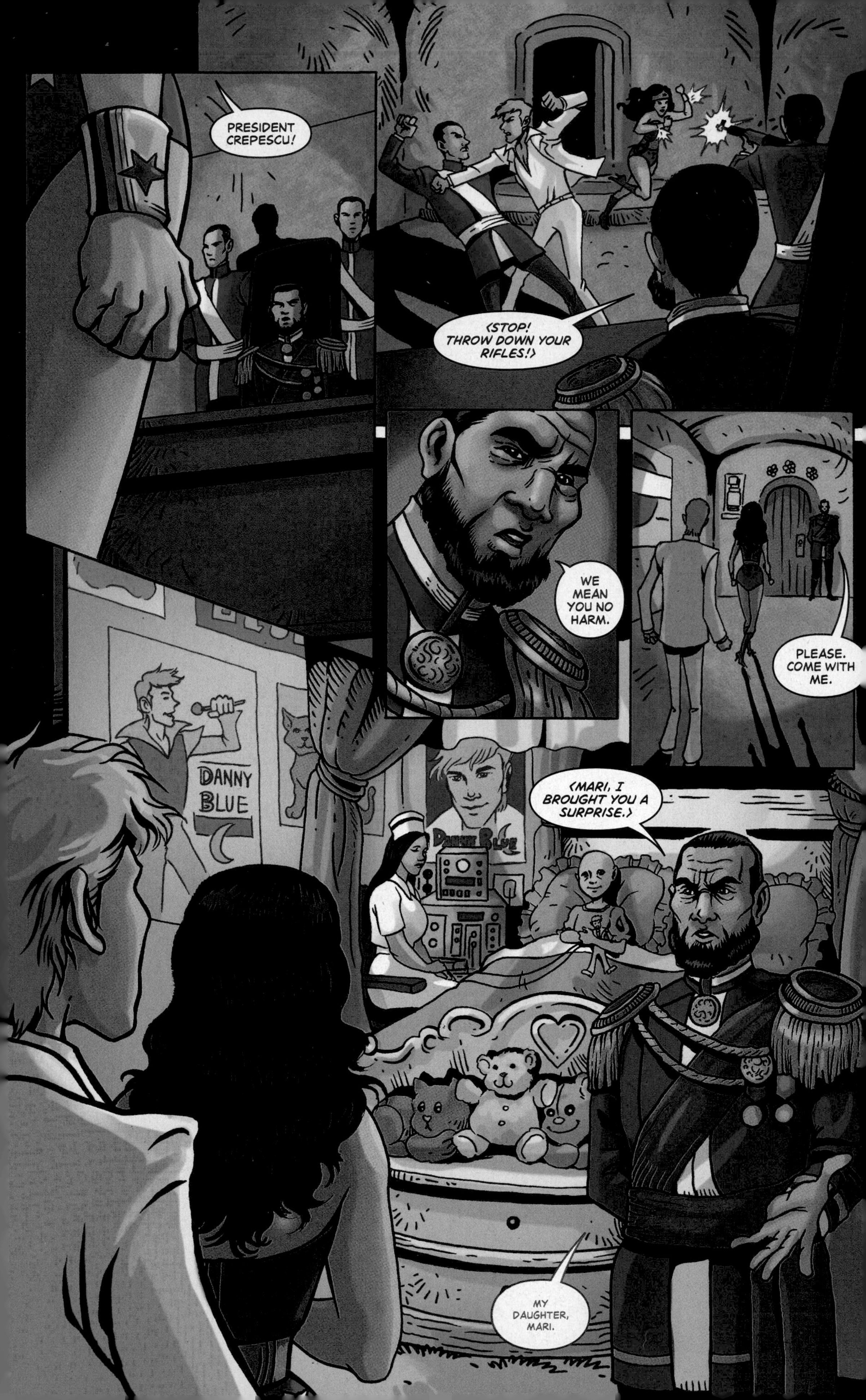
PRESIDENT CREPESCU!
‹STOP! THROW DOWN YOUR RIFLES!›
WE MEAN YOU NO HARM.
PLEASE. COME WITH ME.
DANNY BLUE
‹MARI, I BROUGHT YOU A SURPRISE.›
MY DAUGHTER, MARI.

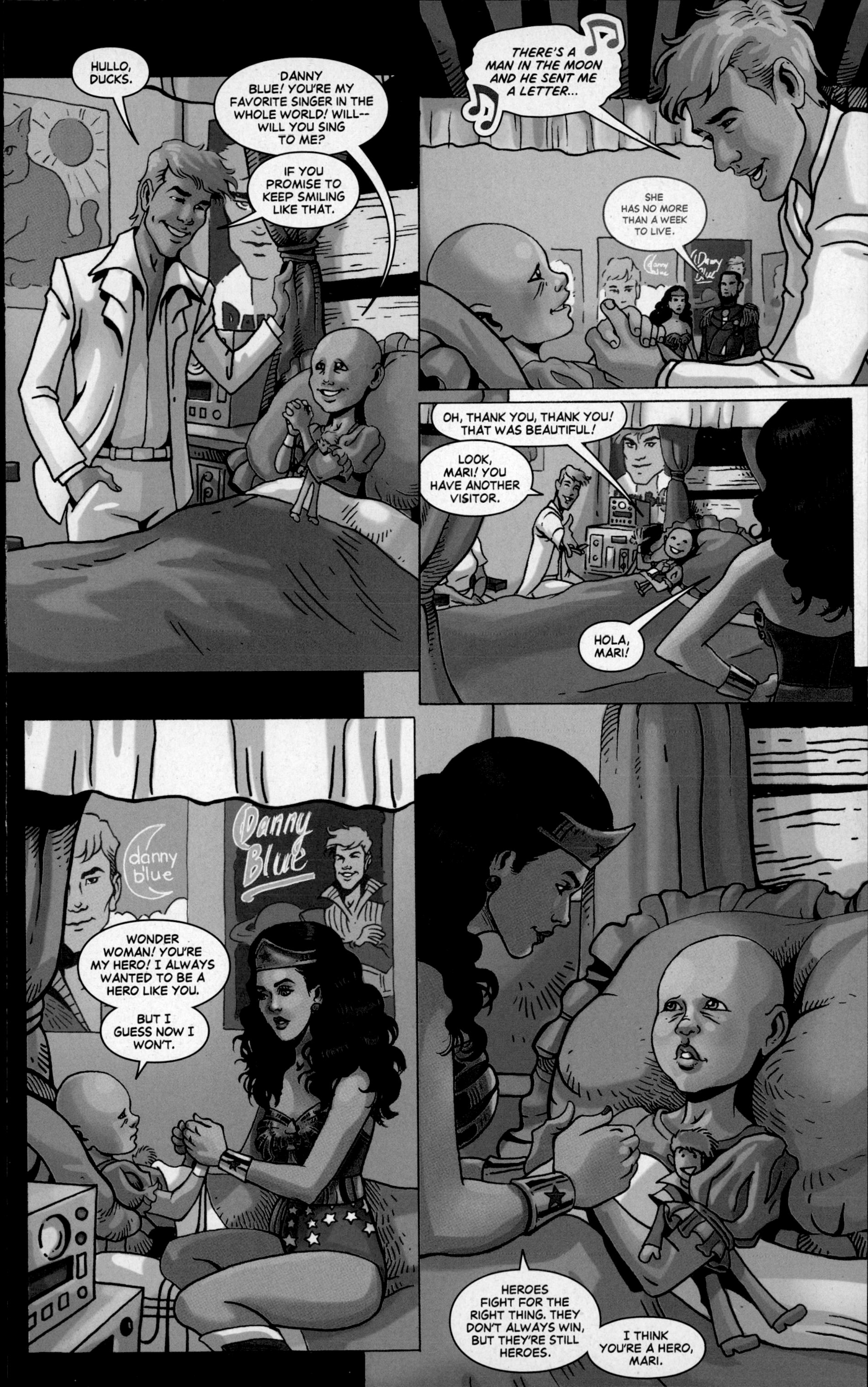
HULLO, DUCKS.
DANNY BLUE! YOU'RE MY FAVORITE SINGER IN THE WHOLE WORLD! WILL-- WILL YOU SING TO ME?
IF YOU PROMISE TO KEEP SMILING LIKE THAT.
THERE'S A MAN IN THE MOON AND HE SENT ME A LETTER...
SHE HAS NO MORE THAN A WEEK TO LIVE.
Danny Blue
OH, THANK YOU, THANK YOU! THAT WAS BEAUTIFUL!
LOOK, MARI! YOU HAVE ANOTHER VISITOR.
HOLA, MARI!
danny blue
Danny Blue
WONDER WOMAN! YOU'RE MY HERO! I ALWAYS WANTED TO BE A HERO LIKE YOU.
BUT I GUESS NOW I WON'T.
HEROES FIGHT FOR THE RIGHT THING. THEY DON'T ALWAYS WIN, BUT THEY'RE STILL HEROES.
I THINK YOU'RE A HERO, MARI.

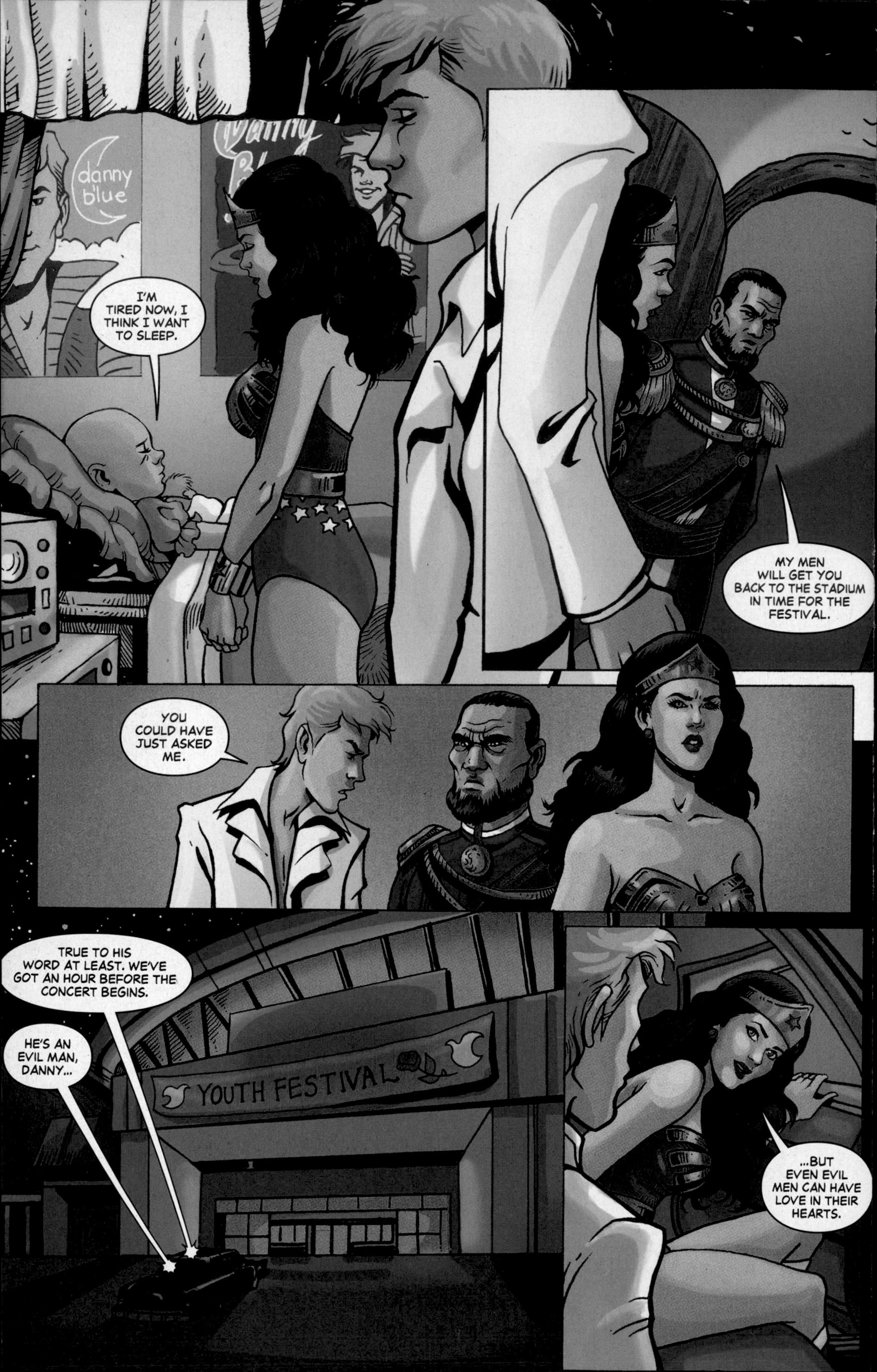

danny b'lue
I'M TIRED NOW, I THINK I WANT TO SLEEP.
MY MEN WILL GET YOU BACK TO THE STADIUM IN TIME FOR THE FESTIVAL.
YOU COULD HAVE JUST ASKED ME.
TRUE TO HIS WORD AT LEAST. WE'VE GOT AN HOUR BEFORE THE CONCERT BEGINS.
HE'S AN EVIL MAN, DANNY...
YOUTH FESTIVAL
...BUT EVEN EVIL MEN CAN HAVE LOVE IN THEIR HEARTS.

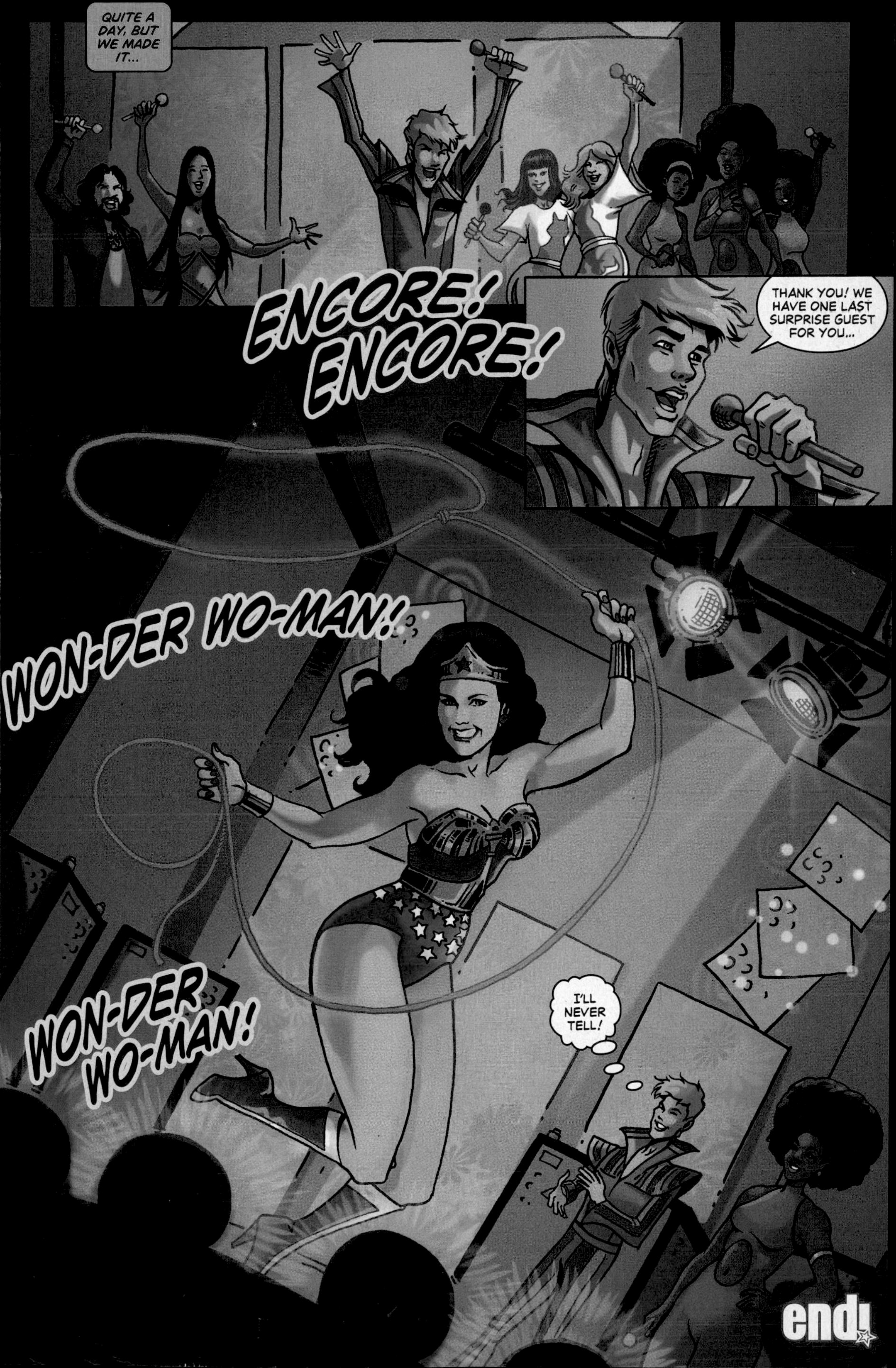
QUITE A DAY, BUT WE MADE IT...
ENCORE! ENCORE!
THANK YOU! WE HAVE ONE LAST SURPRISE GUEST FOR YOU...
WON-DER WO-MAN!
WON-DER WO-MAN!
I'LL NEVER TELL!
end!

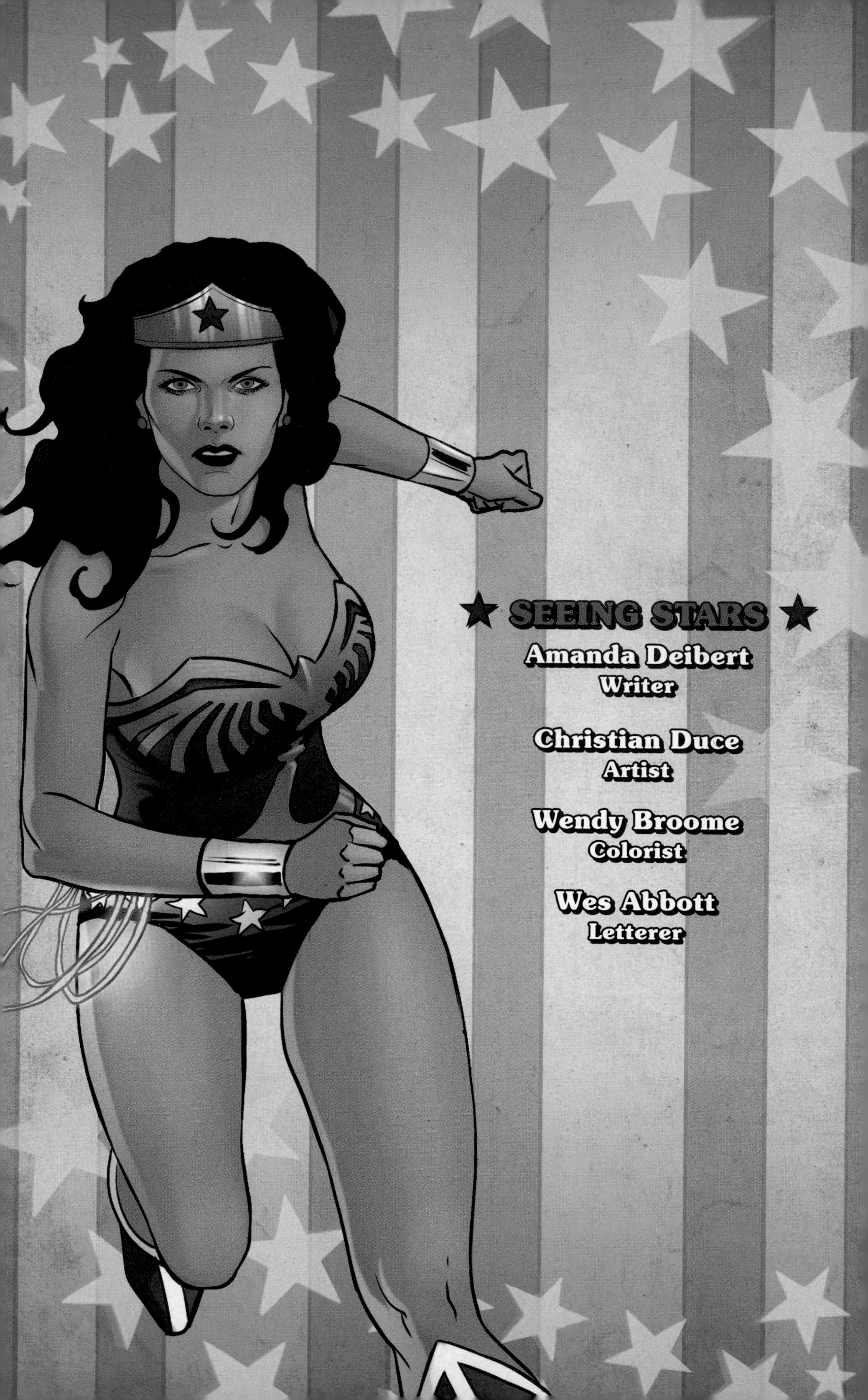
★ SEEING STARS ★
Amanda Deibert
Writer
Christian Duce
Artist
Wendy Broome
Colorist
Wes Abbott
Letterer

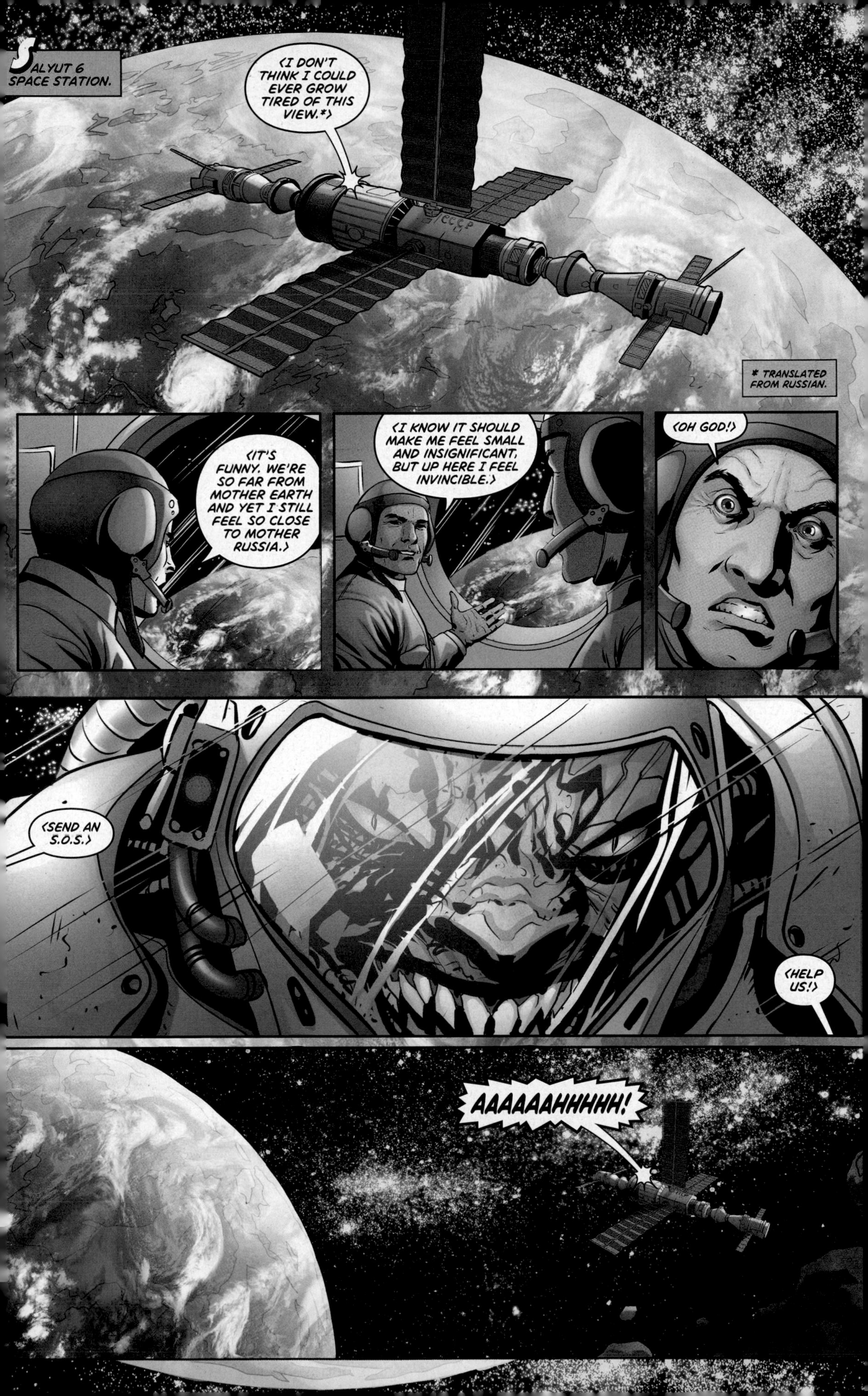
SALYUT 6 SPACE STATION.
<I DON'T THINK I COULD EVER GROW TIRED OF THIS VIEW.*>
* TRANSLATED FROM RUSSIAN.
<IT'S FUNNY. WE'RE SO FAR FROM MOTHER EARTH AND YET I STILL FEEL SO CLOSE TO MOTHER RUSSIA.>
<I KNOW IT SHOULD MAKE ME FEEL SMALL AND INSIGNIFICANT, BUT UP HERE I FEEL INVINCIBLE.>
<OH GOD!>
<SEND AN S.O.S.>
<HELP US!>
AAAAAAHHHHH!

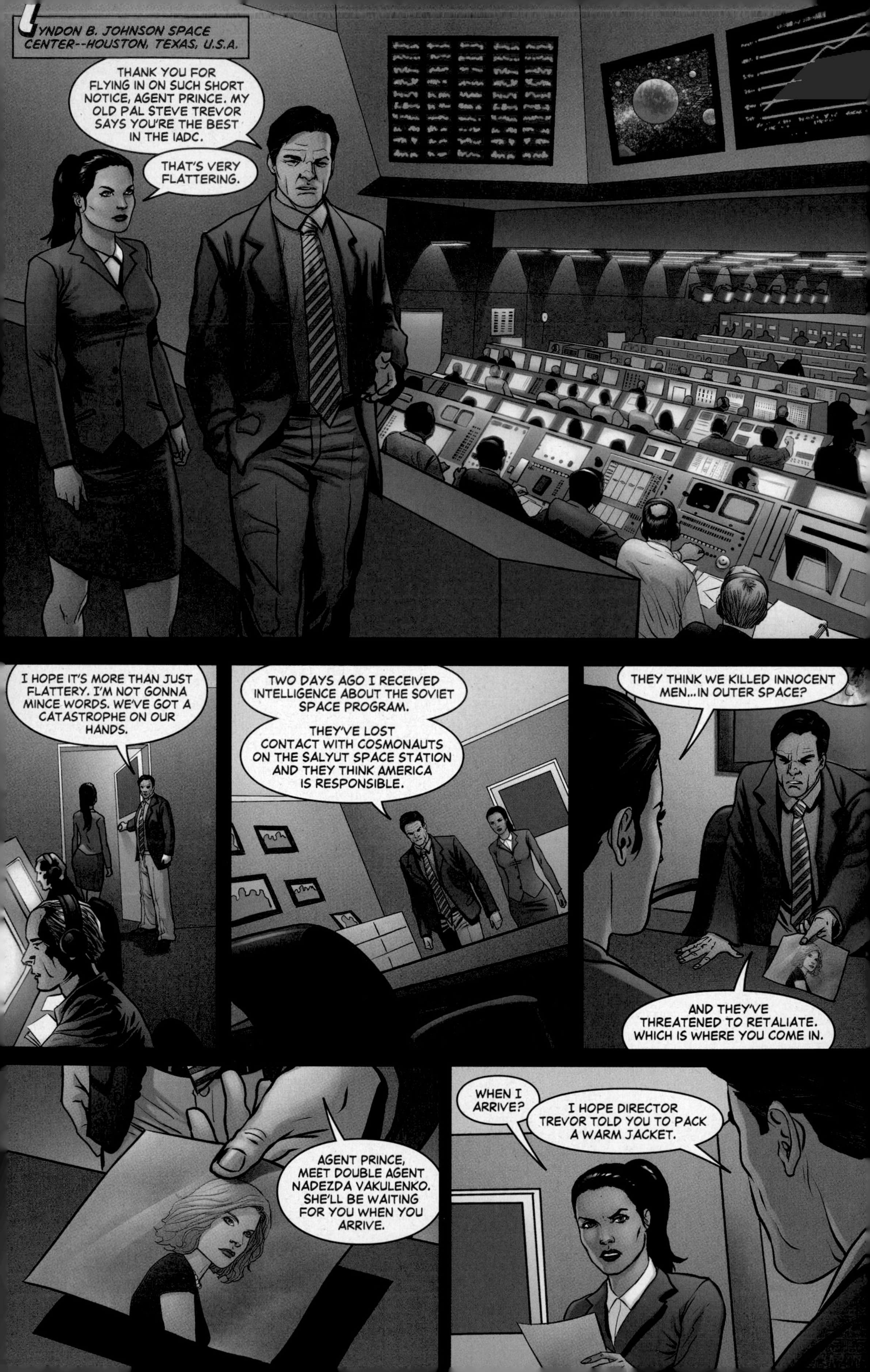
LYNDON B. JOHNSON SPACE CENTER--HOUSTON, TEXAS, U.S.A.
THANK YOU FOR FLYING IN ON SUCH SHORT NOTICE, AGENT PRINCE. MY OLD PAL STEVE TREVOR SAYS YOU'RE THE BEST IN THE IADC.
THAT'S VERY FLATTERING.
I HOPE IT'S MORE THAN JUST FLATTERY. I'M NOT GONNA MINCE WORDS. WE'VE GOT A CATASTROPHE ON OUR HANDS.
TWO DAYS AGO I RECEIVED INTELLIGENCE ABOUT THE SOVIET SPACE PROGRAM.
THEY'VE LOST CONTACT WITH COSMONAUTS ON THE SALYUT SPACE STATION AND THEY THINK AMERICA IS RESPONSIBLE.
THEY THINK WE KILLED INNOCENT MEN...IN OUTER SPACE?
AND THEY'VE THREATENED TO RETALIATE. WHICH IS WHERE YOU COME IN.
AGENT PRINCE, MEET DOUBLE AGENT NADEZDA VAKULENKO. SHE'LL BE WAITING FOR YOU WHEN YOU ARRIVE.
WHEN I ARRIVE?
I HOPE DIRECTOR TREVOR TOLD YOU TO PACK A WARM JACKET.

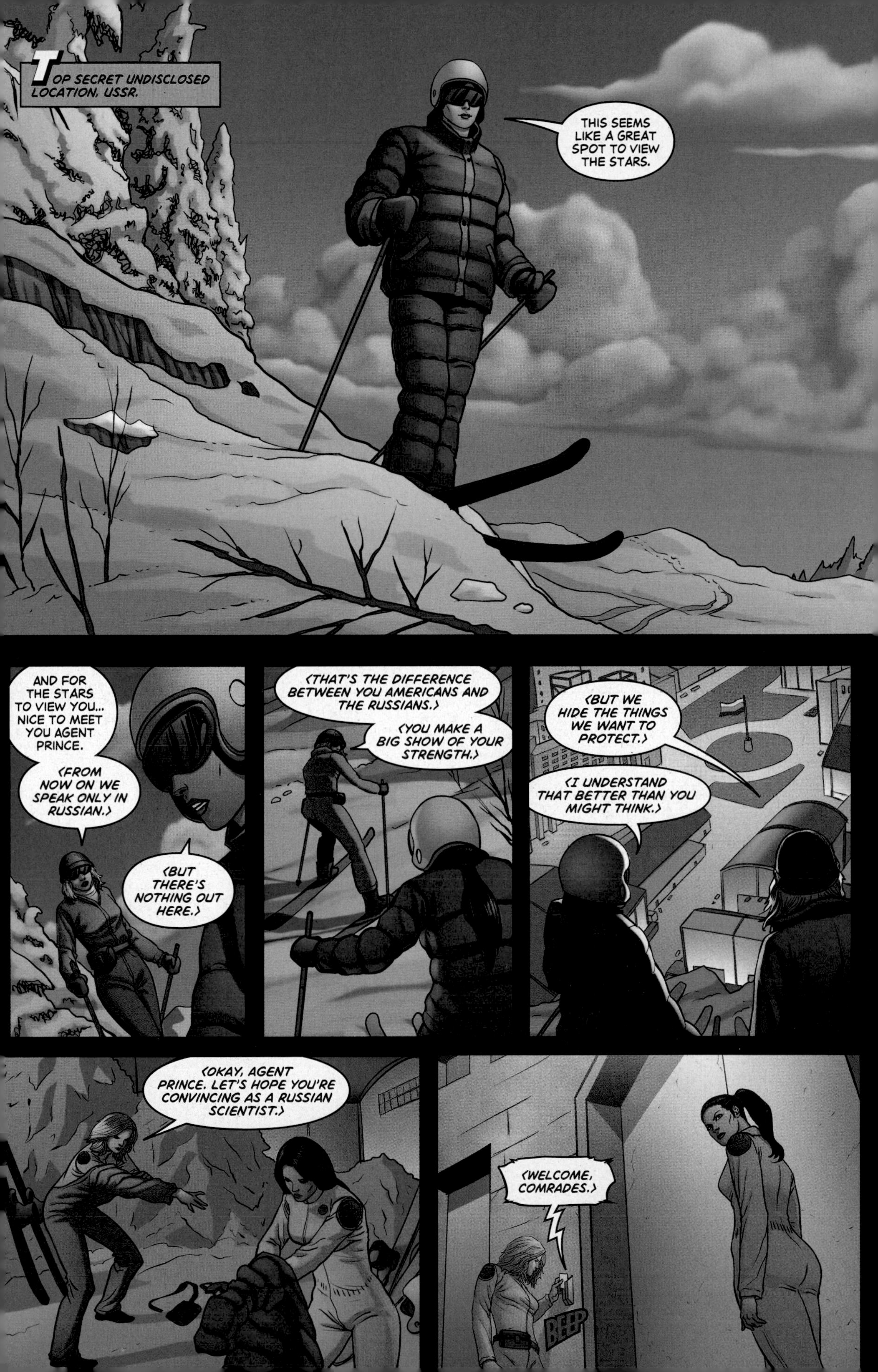
TOP SECRET UNDISCLOSED LOCATION, USSR.
THIS SEEMS LIKE A GREAT SPOT TO VIEW THE STARS.
AND FOR THE STARS TO VIEW YOU... NICE TO MEET YOU AGENT PRINCE.
‹FROM NOW ON WE SPEAK ONLY IN RUSSIAN.›
‹BUT THERE'S NOTHING OUT HERE.›
‹THAT'S THE DIFFERENCE BETWEEN YOU AMERICANS AND THE RUSSIANS.›
‹YOU MAKE A BIG SHOW OF YOUR STRENGTH.›
‹BUT WE HIDE THE THINGS WE WANT TO PROTECT.›
‹I UNDERSTAND THAT BETTER THAN YOU MIGHT THINK.›
‹OKAY, AGENT PRINCE. LET'S HOPE YOU'RE CONVINCING AS A RUSSIAN SCIENTIST.›
‹WELCOME, COMRADES.›
BEEP

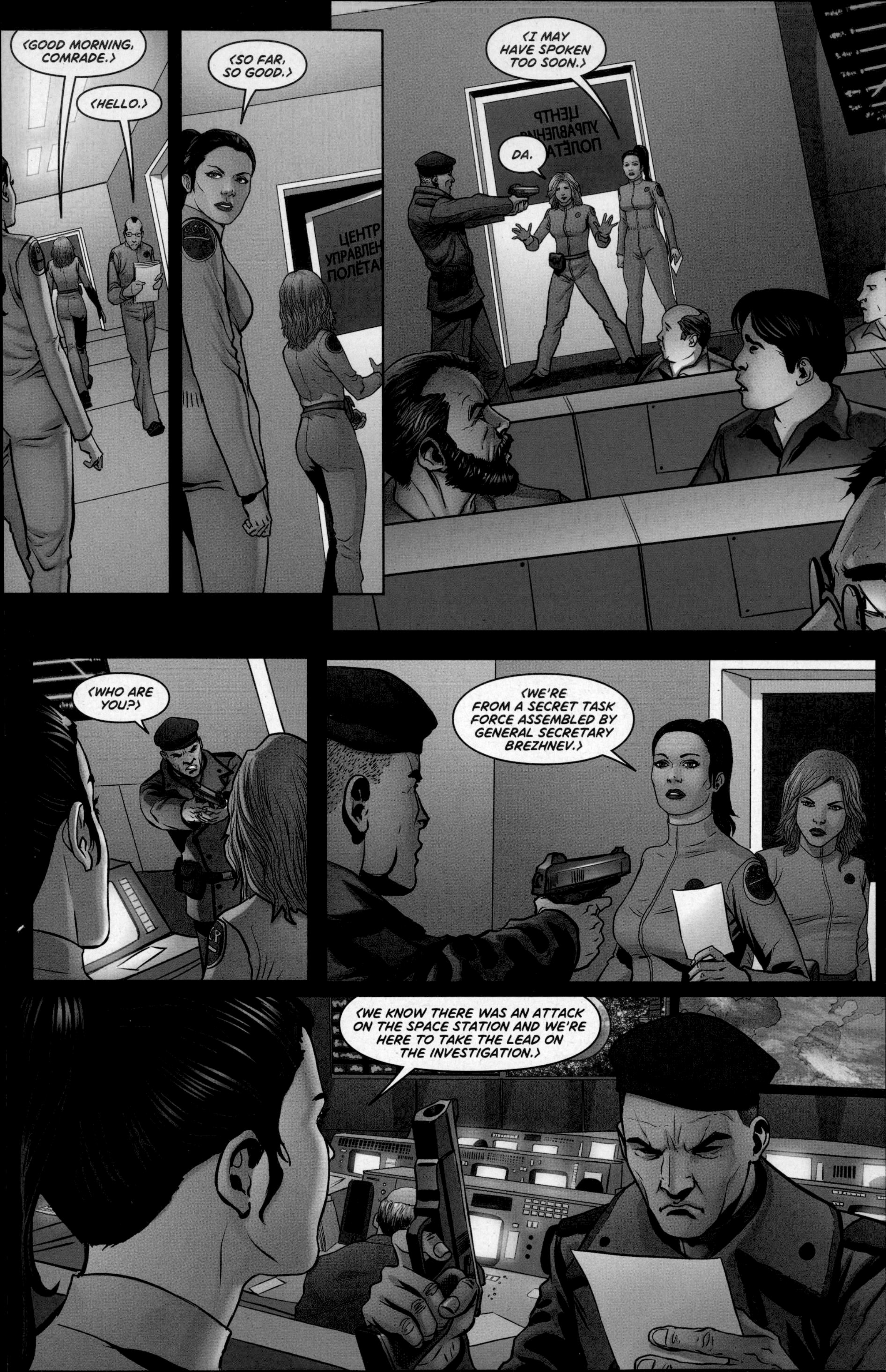

<GOOD MORNING, COMRADE.>
<HELLO.>
<SO FAR, SO GOOD.>
ЦЕНТР УПРАВЛЕНИ ПОЛЁТА
<I MAY HAVE SPOKEN TOO SOON.>
DA.
<WHO ARE YOU?>
<WE'RE FROM A SECRET TASK FORCE ASSEMBLED BY GENERAL SECRETARY BREZHNEV.>
<WE KNOW THERE WAS AN ATTACK ON THE SPACE STATION AND WE'RE HERE TO TAKE THE LEAD ON THE INVESTIGATION.>

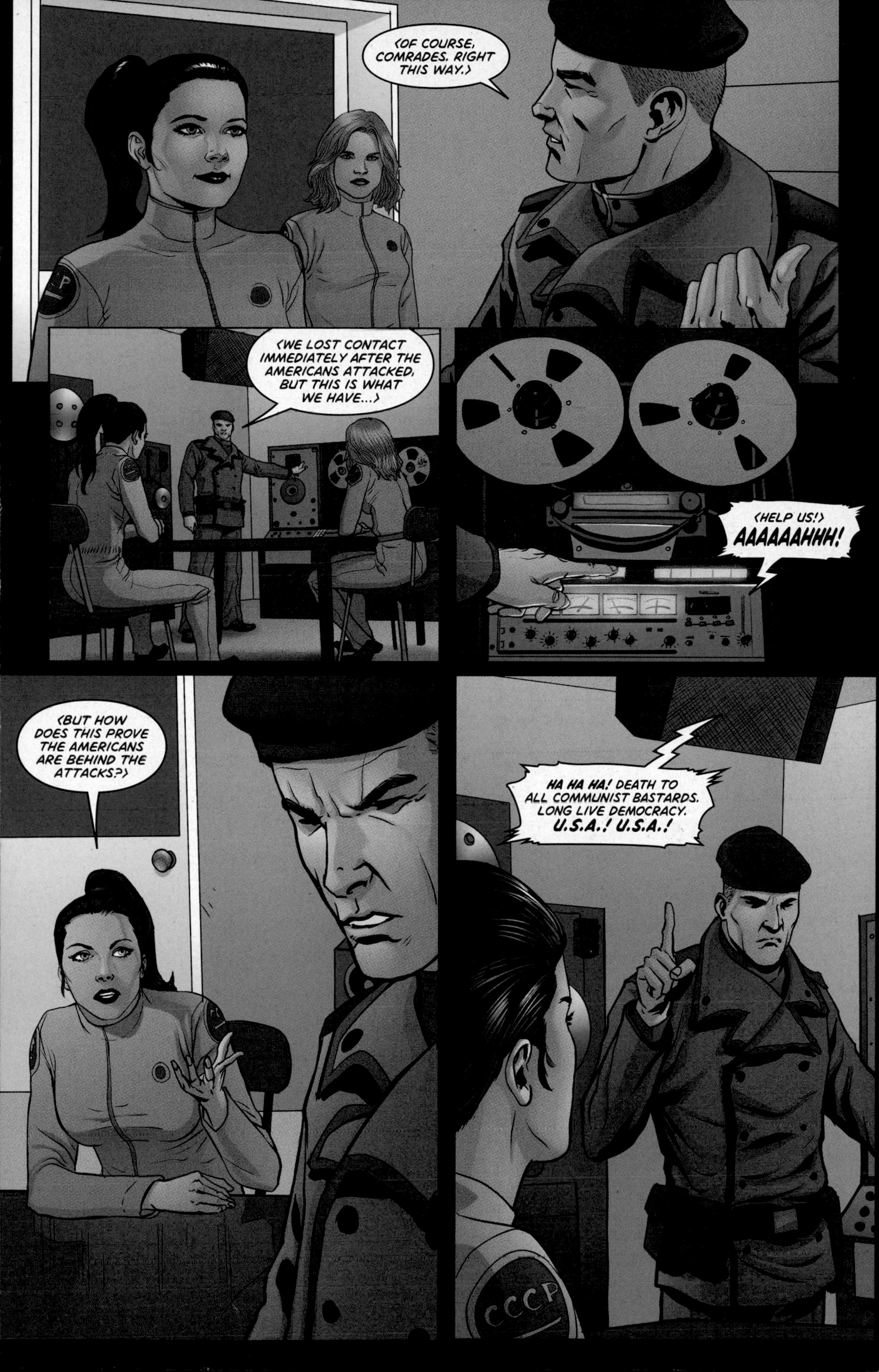
⟨OF COURSE, COMRADES. RIGHT THIS WAY.⟩
⟨WE LOST CONTACT IMMEDIATELY AFTER THE AMERICANS ATTACKED, BUT THIS IS WHAT WE HAVE...⟩
⟨HELP US!⟩ AAAAAAHHH!
⟨BUT HOW DOES THIS PROVE THE AMERICANS ARE BEHIND THE ATTACKS?⟩
HA HA HA! DEATH TO ALL COMMUNIST BASTARDS. LONG LIVE DEMOCRACY. U.S.A.! U.S.A.!
CCCP

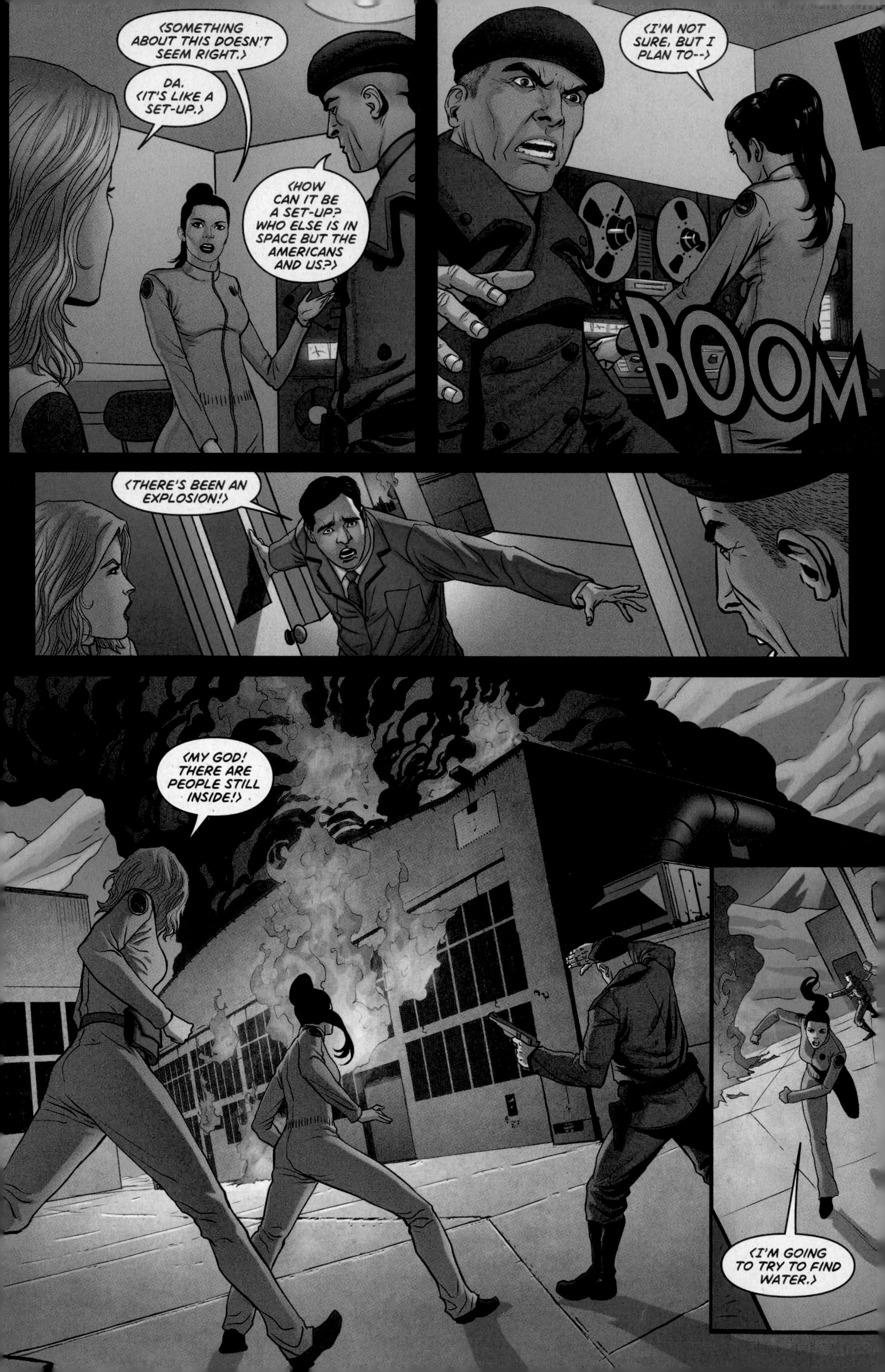

‹SOMETHING ABOUT THIS DOESN'T SEEM RIGHT.›
DA. ‹IT'S LIKE A SET-UP.›
‹HOW CAN IT BE A SET-UP? WHO ELSE IS IN SPACE BUT THE AMERICANS AND US?›
‹I'M NOT SURE, BUT I PLAN TO--›
BOOM
‹THERE'S BEEN AN EXPLOSION!›
‹MY GOD! THERE ARE PEOPLE STILL INSIDE!›
‹I'M GOING TO TRY TO FIND WATER.›

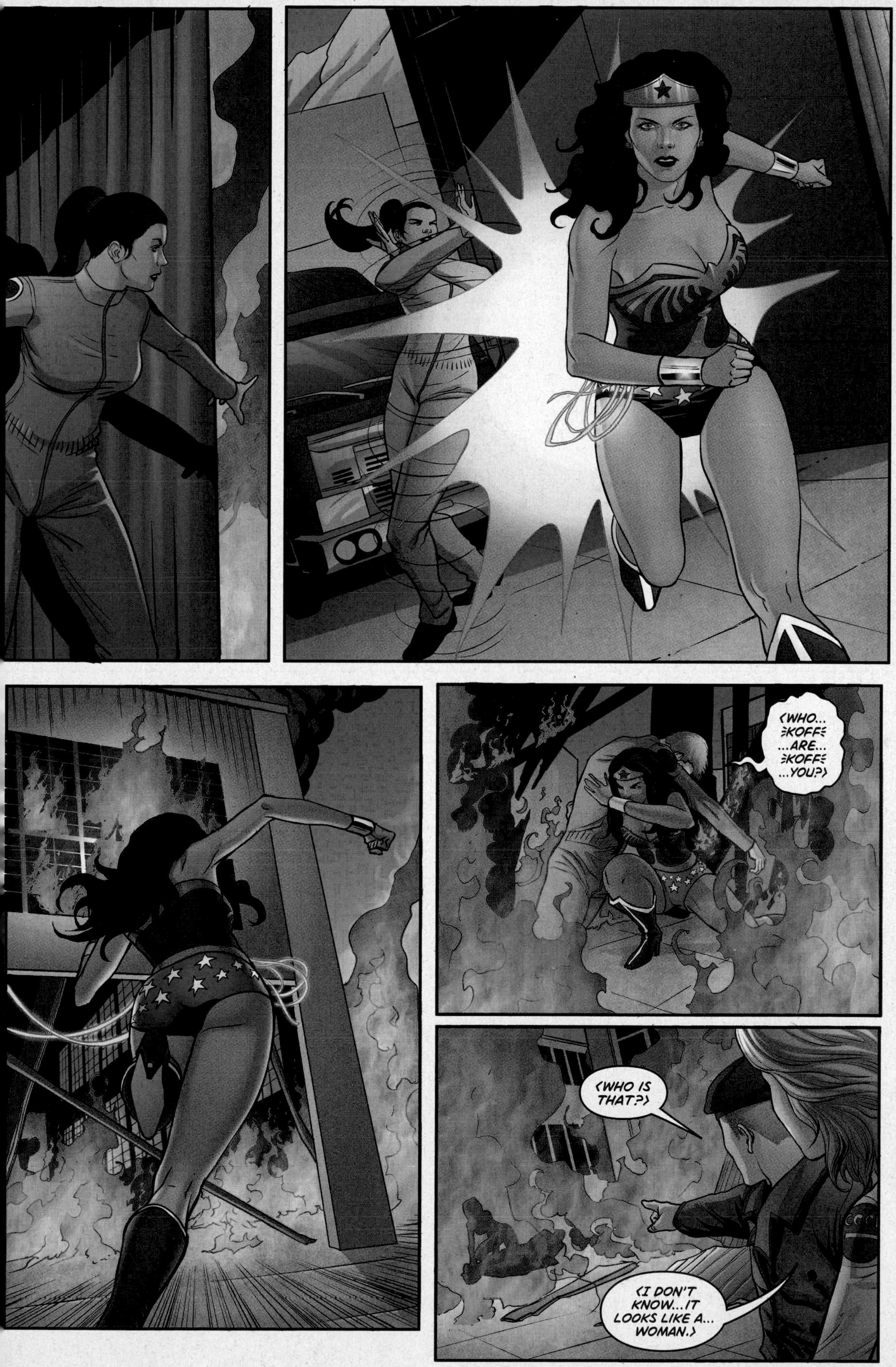

‹WHO... KOFF ...ARE... KOFF ...YOU?›
‹WHO IS THAT?›
‹I DON'T KNOW...IT LOOKS LIKE A... WOMAN.›

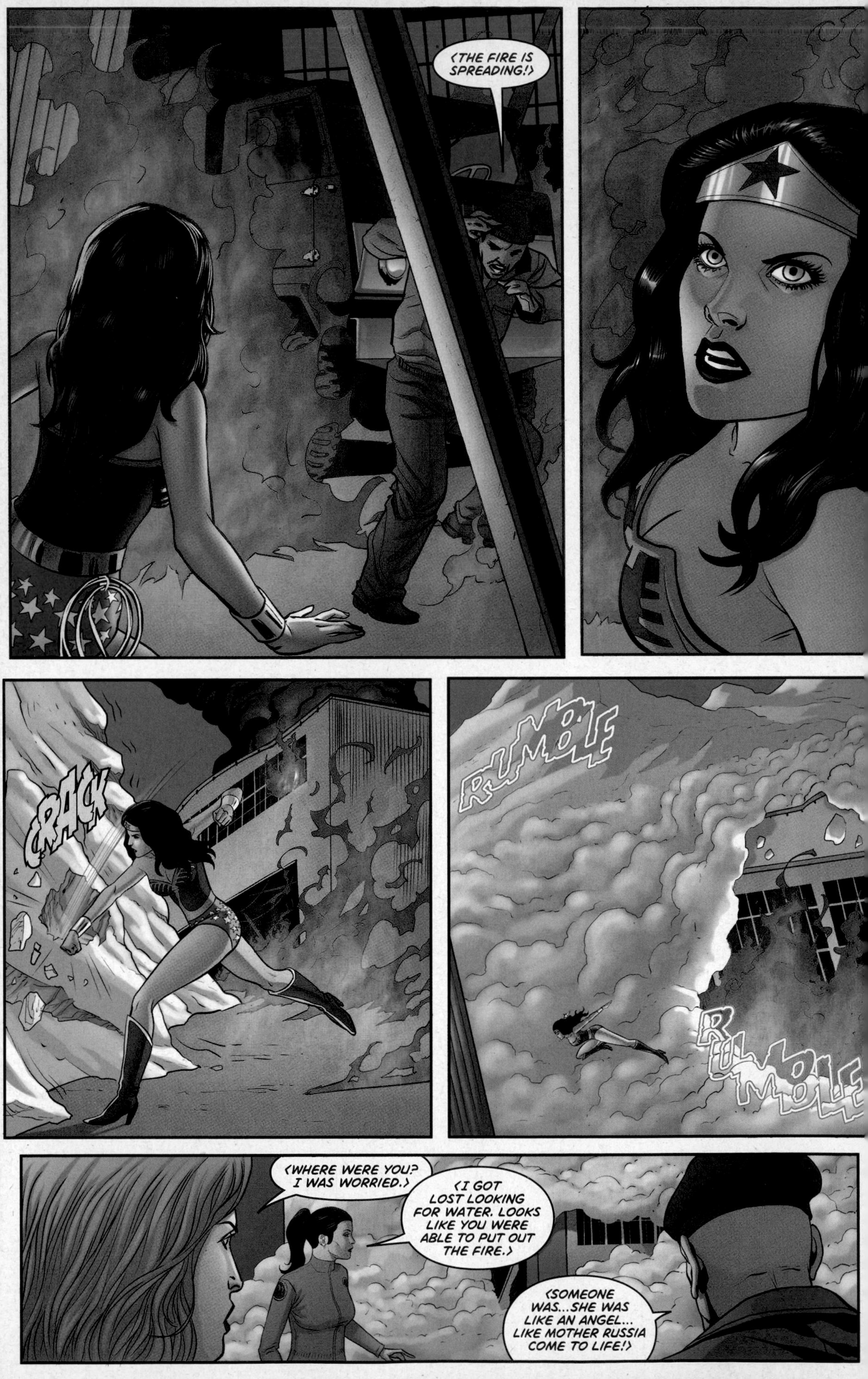
‹THE FIRE IS SPREADING!›
CRACK
RUMBLE
RUMBLE
‹WHERE WERE YOU? I WAS WORRIED.›
‹I GOT LOST LOOKING FOR WATER. LOOKS LIKE YOU WERE ABLE TO PUT OUT THE FIRE.›
‹SOMEONE WAS...SHE WAS LIKE AN ANGEL... LIKE MOTHER RUSSIA COME TO LIFE!›

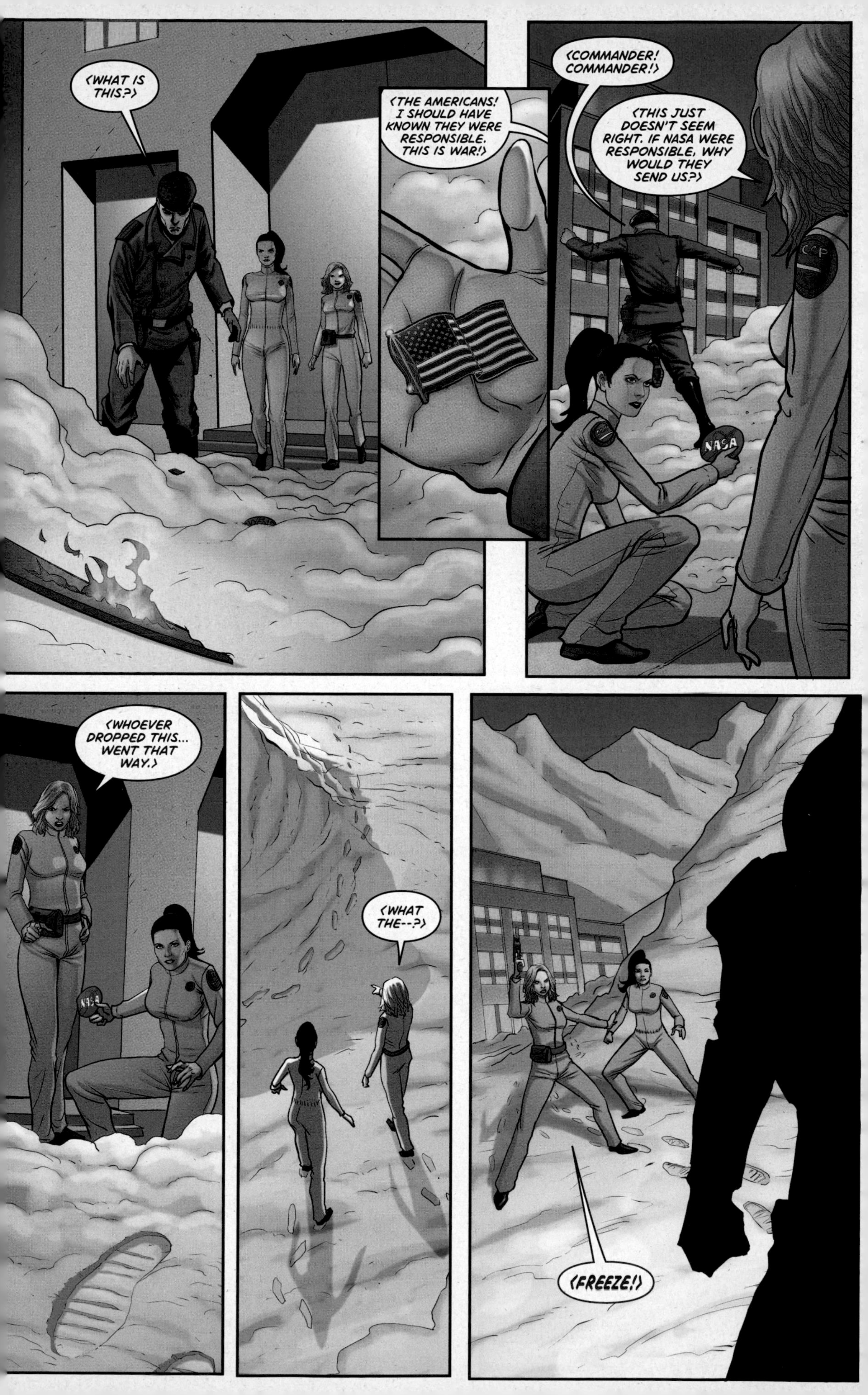

<WHAT IS THIS?>
<THE AMERICANS! I SHOULD HAVE KNOWN THEY WERE RESPONSIBLE. THIS IS WAR!>
<COMMANDER! COMMANDER!>
<THIS JUST DOESN'T SEEM RIGHT. IF NASA WERE RESPONSIBLE, WHY WOULD THEY SEND US?>
NASA
<WHOEVER DROPPED THIS... WENT THAT WAY.>
<WHAT THE--?>
<FREEZE!>

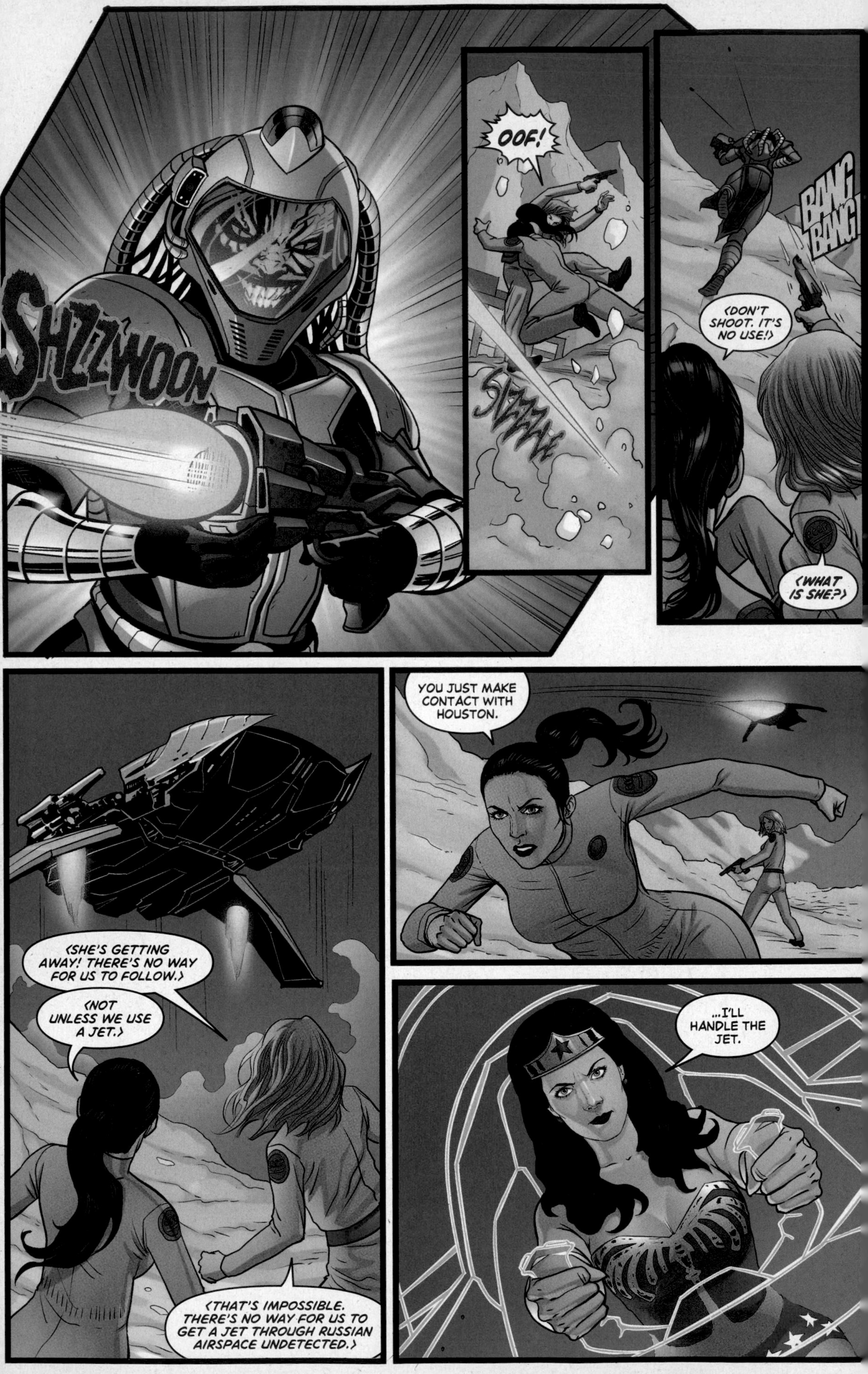
SHZZWOON
OOF!
SZZZZZ
BANG BANG!
‹DON'T SHOOT. IT'S NO USE!›
‹WHAT IS SHE?›
‹SHE'S GETTING AWAY! THERE'S NO WAY FOR US TO FOLLOW.›
‹NOT UNLESS WE USE A JET.›
‹THAT'S IMPOSSIBLE. THERE'S NO WAY FOR US TO GET A JET THROUGH RUSSIAN AIRSPACE UNDETECTED.›
YOU JUST MAKE CONTACT WITH HOUSTON.
...I'LL HANDLE THE JET.

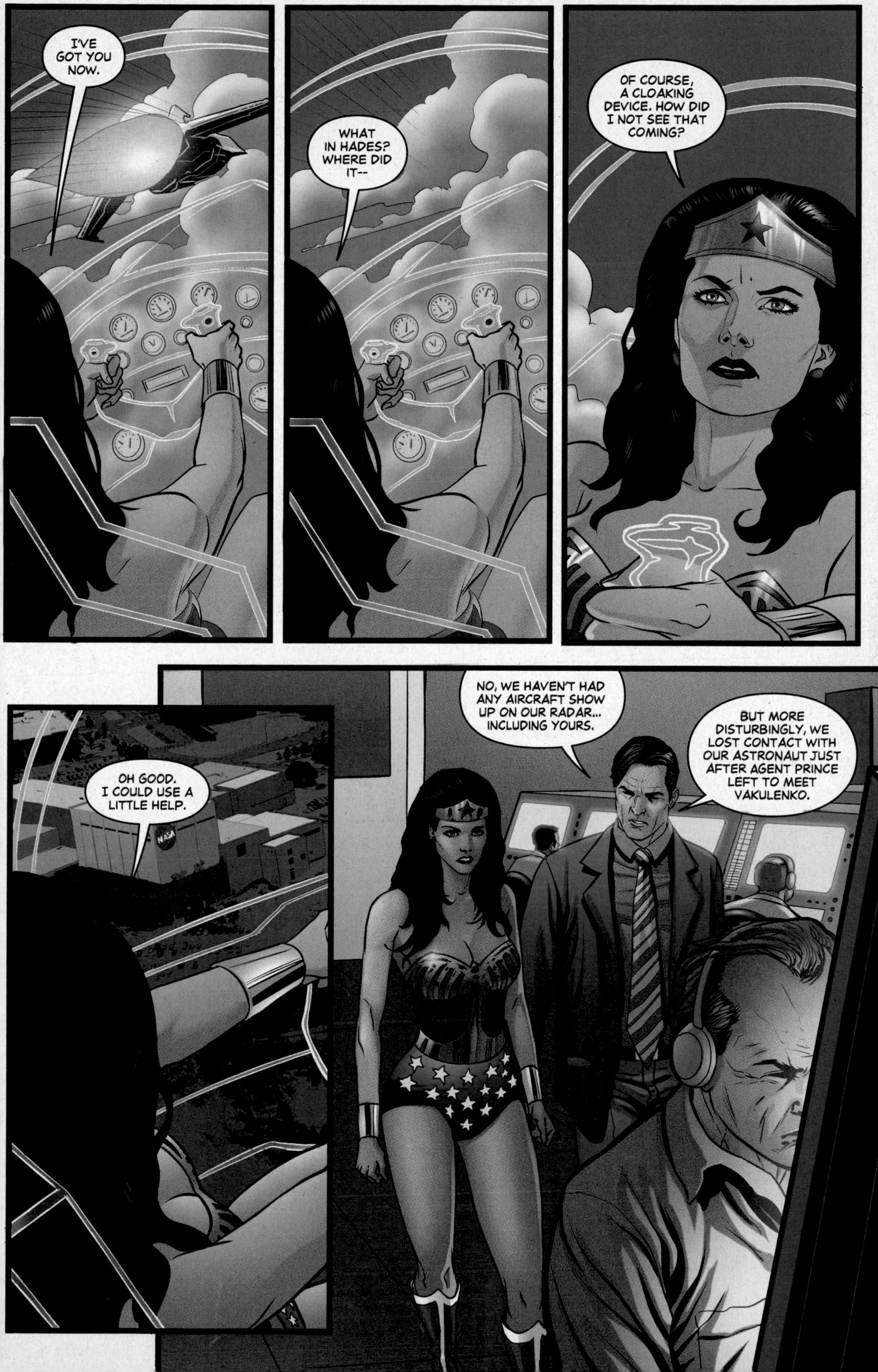
I'VE GOT YOU NOW.
WHAT IN HADES? WHERE DID IT--
OF COURSE, A CLOAKING DEVICE. HOW DID I NOT SEE THAT COMING?
OH GOOD. I COULD USE A LITTLE HELP.
NASA
NO, WE HAVEN'T HAD ANY AIRCRAFT SHOW UP ON OUR RADAR... INCLUDING YOURS.
BUT MORE DISTURBINGLY, WE LOST CONTACT WITH OUR ASTRONAUT JUST AFTER AGENT PRINCE LEFT TO MEET VAKULENKO.

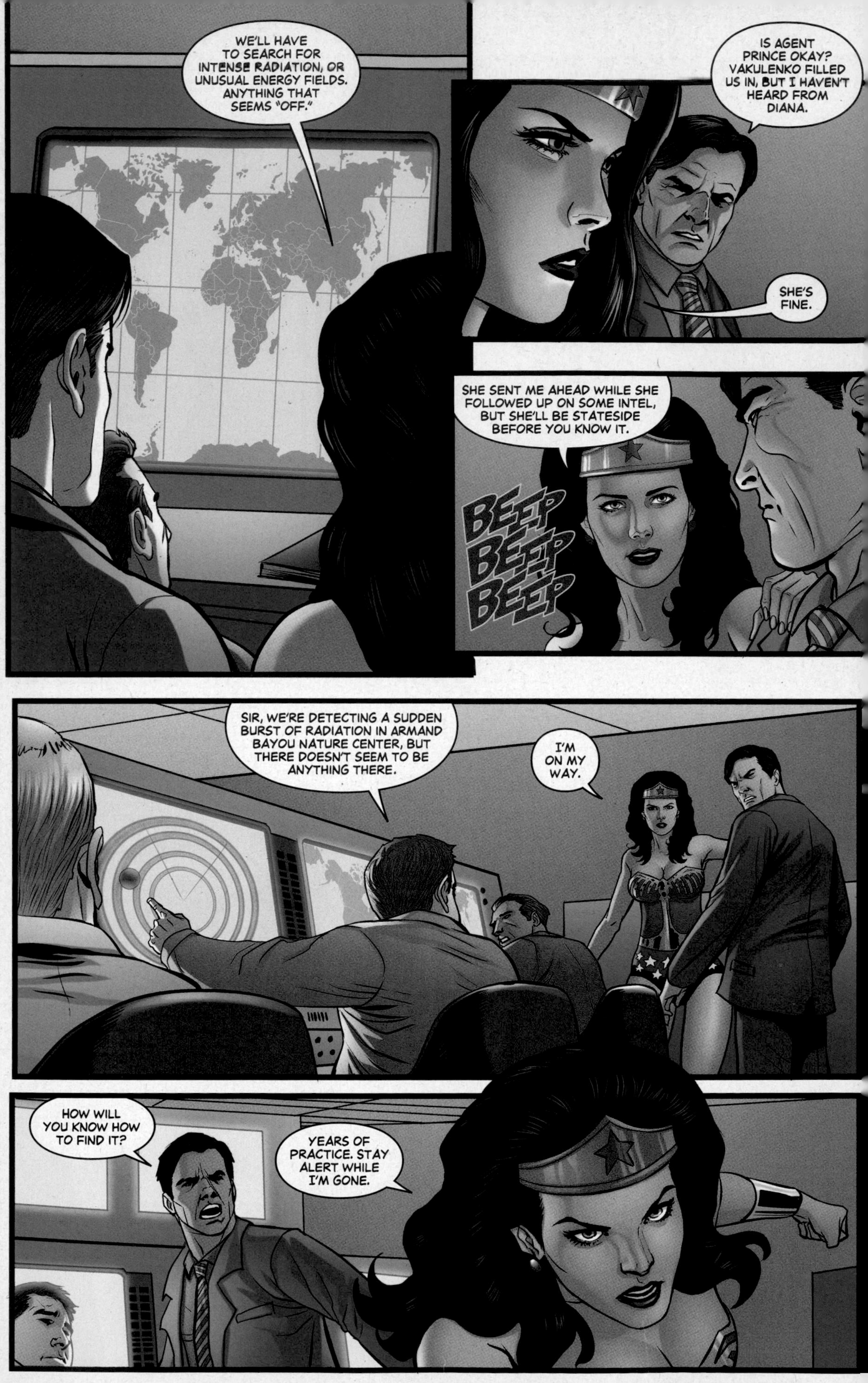
WE'LL HAVE TO SEARCH FOR INTENSE RADIATION, OR UNUSUAL ENERGY FIELDS. ANYTHING THAT SEEMS "OFF."
IS AGENT PRINCE OKAY? VAKULENKO FILLED US IN, BUT I HAVEN'T HEARD FROM DIANA.
SHE'S FINE.
SHE SENT ME AHEAD WHILE SHE FOLLOWED UP ON SOME INTEL, BUT SHE'LL BE STATESIDE BEFORE YOU KNOW IT.
BEEP BEEP BEEP
SIR, WE'RE DETECTING A SUDDEN BURST OF RADIATION IN ARMAND BAYOU NATURE CENTER, BUT THERE DOESN'T SEEM TO BE ANYTHING THERE.
I'M ON MY WAY.
HOW WILL YOU KNOW HOW TO FIND IT?
YEARS OF PRACTICE. STAY ALERT WHILE I'M GONE.

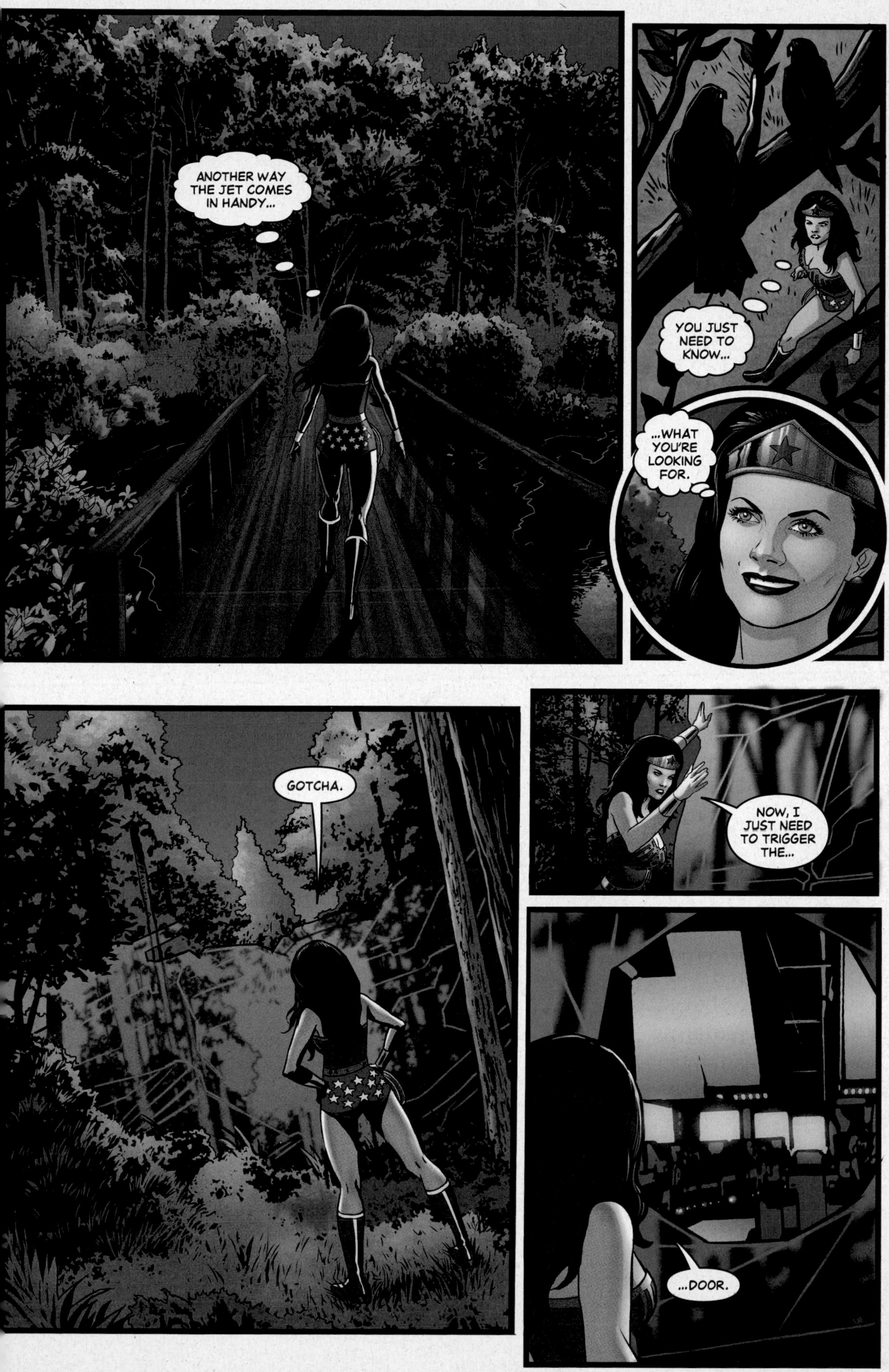
ANOTHER WAY THE JET COMES IN HANDY...
YOU JUST NEED TO KNOW...
...WHAT YOU'RE LOOKING FOR.
GOTCHA.
NOW, I JUST NEED TO TRIGGER THE...
...DOOR.

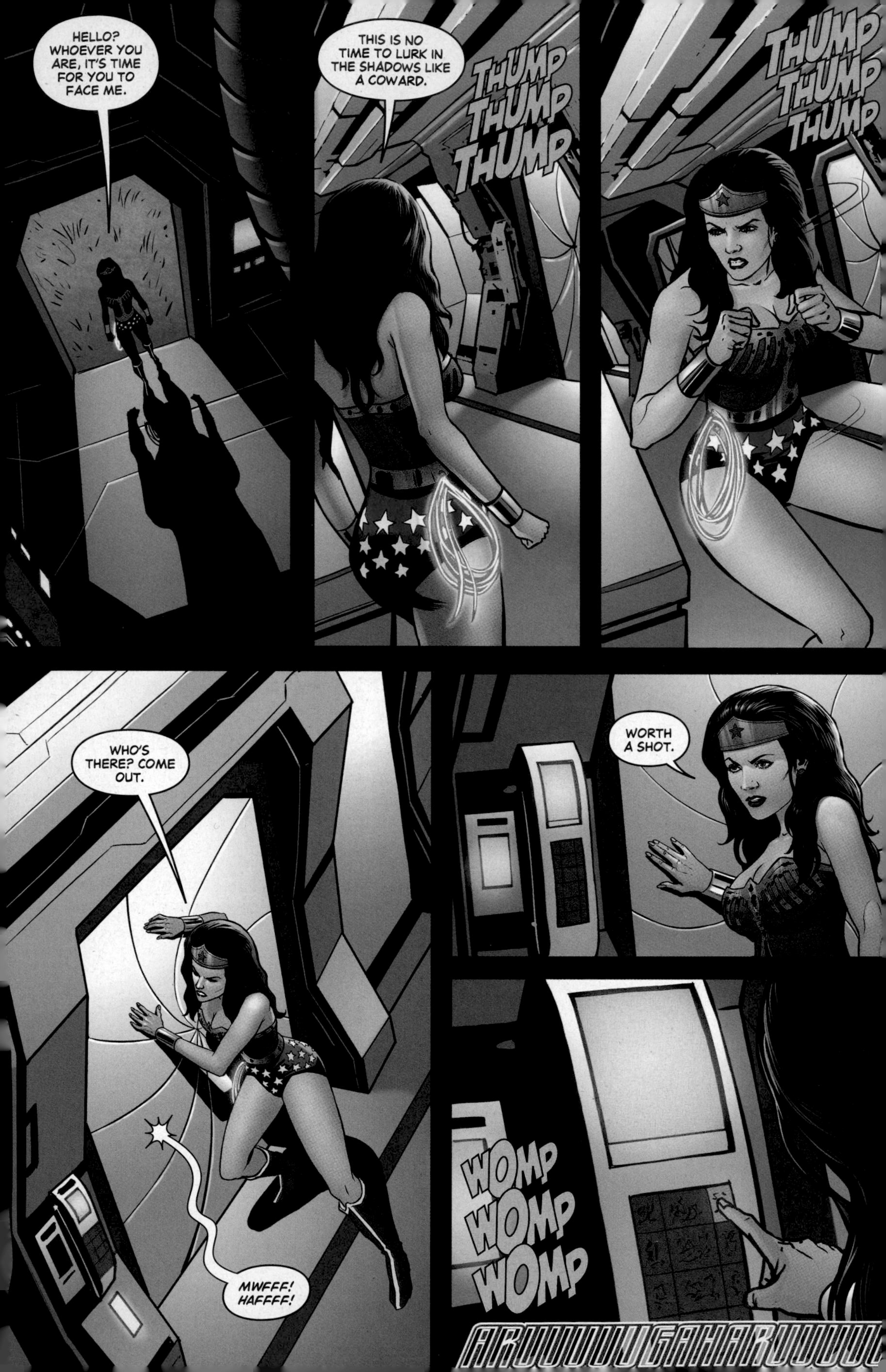
HELLO? WHOEVER YOU ARE, IT'S TIME FOR YOU TO FACE ME.
THIS IS NO TIME TO LURK IN THE SHADOWS LIKE A COWARD.
THUMP THUMP THUMP
THUMP THUMP THUMP
WHO'S THERE? COME OUT.
MWFFF! HAFFFF!
WORTH A SHOT.
WOMP WOMP WOMP

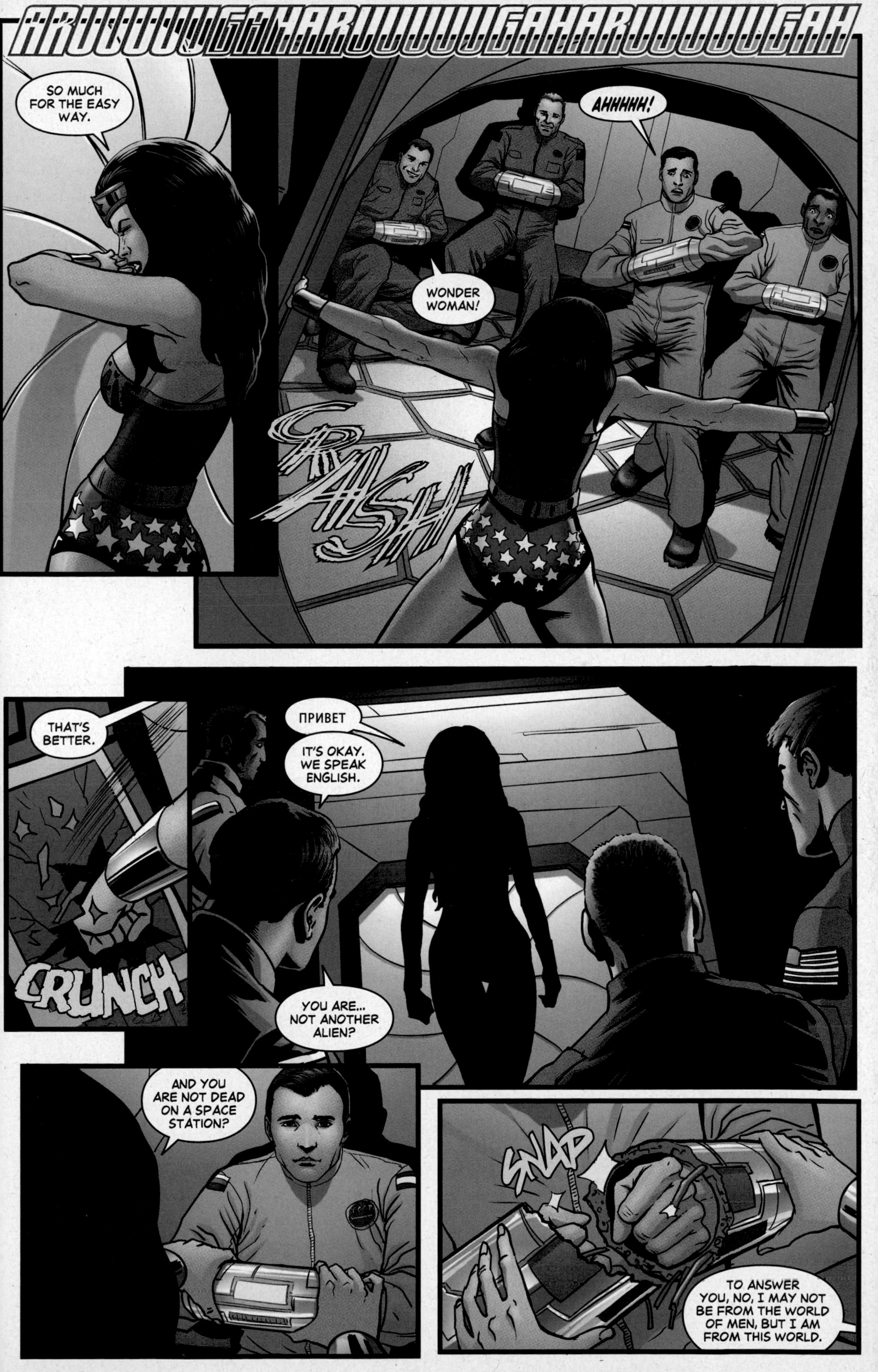
ARUUUUUGAH ARUUUUUUGAH ARUUUUUUGAH
SO MUCH FOR THE EASY WAY.
CRASH
AHHHHH!
WONDER WOMAN!
THAT'S BETTER.
CRUNCH
ПРИВЕТ
IT'S OKAY. WE SPEAK ENGLISH.
YOU ARE... NOT ANOTHER ALIEN?
AND YOU ARE NOT DEAD ON A SPACE STATION?
SNAP
TO ANSWER YOU, NO, I MAY NOT BE FROM THE WORLD OF MEN, BUT I AM FROM THIS WORLD.

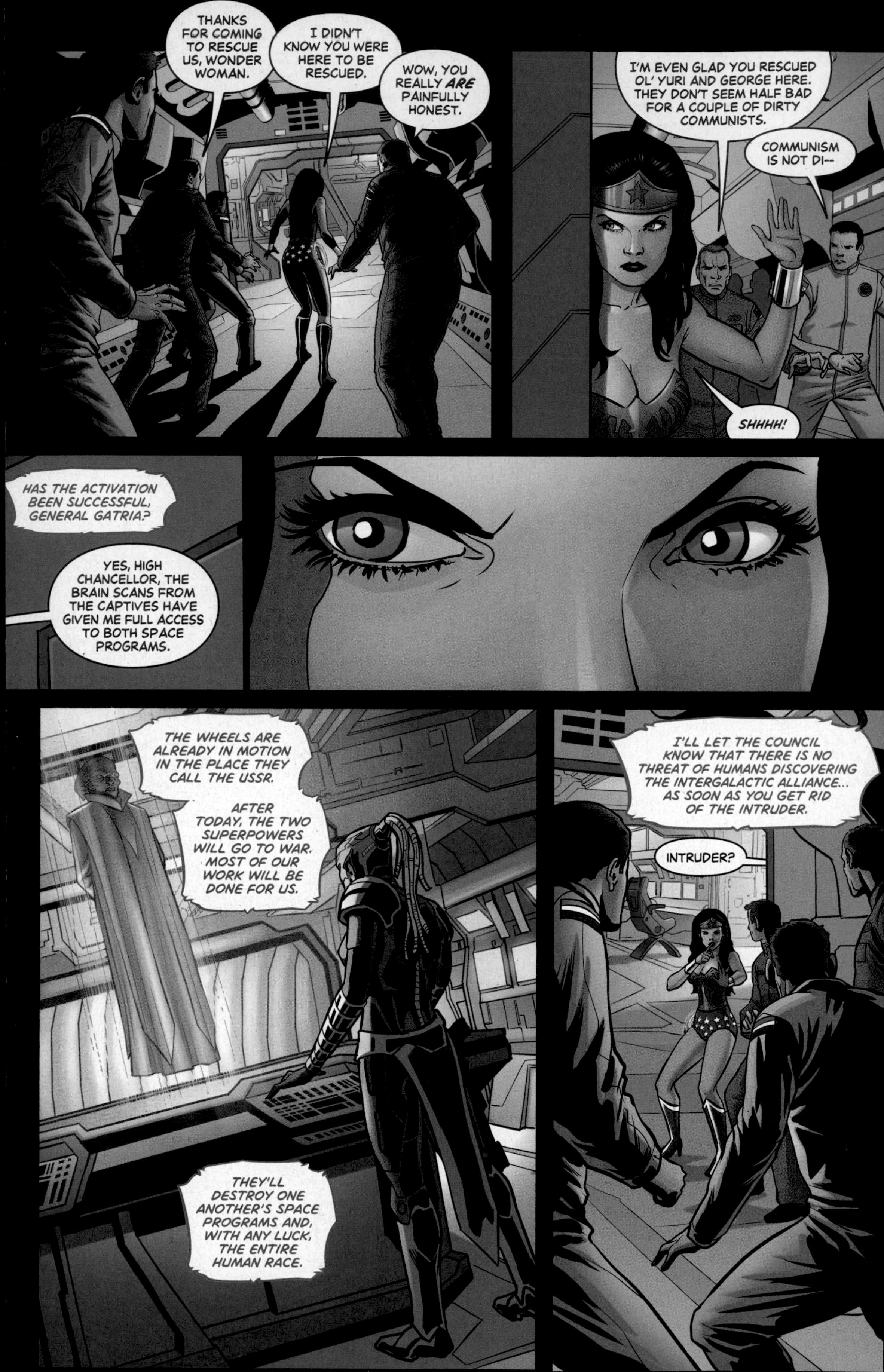
THANKS FOR COMING TO RESCUE US, WONDER WOMAN.
I DIDN'T KNOW YOU WERE HERE TO BE RESCUED.
WOW, YOU REALLY ARE PAINFULLY HONEST.
I'M EVEN GLAD YOU RESCUED OL' YURI AND GEORGE HERE. THEY DON'T SEEM HALF BAD FOR A COUPLE OF DIRTY COMMUNISTS.
COMMUNISM IS NOT DI--
SHHHH!
HAS THE ACTIVATION BEEN SUCCESSFUL, GENERAL GATRIA?
YES, HIGH CHANCELLOR, THE BRAIN SCANS FROM THE CAPTIVES HAVE GIVEN ME FULL ACCESS TO BOTH SPACE PROGRAMS.
THE WHEELS ARE ALREADY IN MOTION IN THE PLACE THEY CALL THE USSR.
AFTER TODAY, THE TWO SUPERPOWERS WILL GO TO WAR. MOST OF OUR WORK WILL BE DONE FOR US.
THEY'LL DESTROY ONE ANOTHER'S SPACE PROGRAMS AND, WITH ANY LUCK, THE ENTIRE HUMAN RACE.
I'LL LET THE COUNCIL KNOW THAT THERE IS NO THREAT OF HUMANS DISCOVERING THE INTERGALACTIC ALLIANCE... AS SOON AS YOU GET RID OF THE INTRUDER.
INTRUDER?

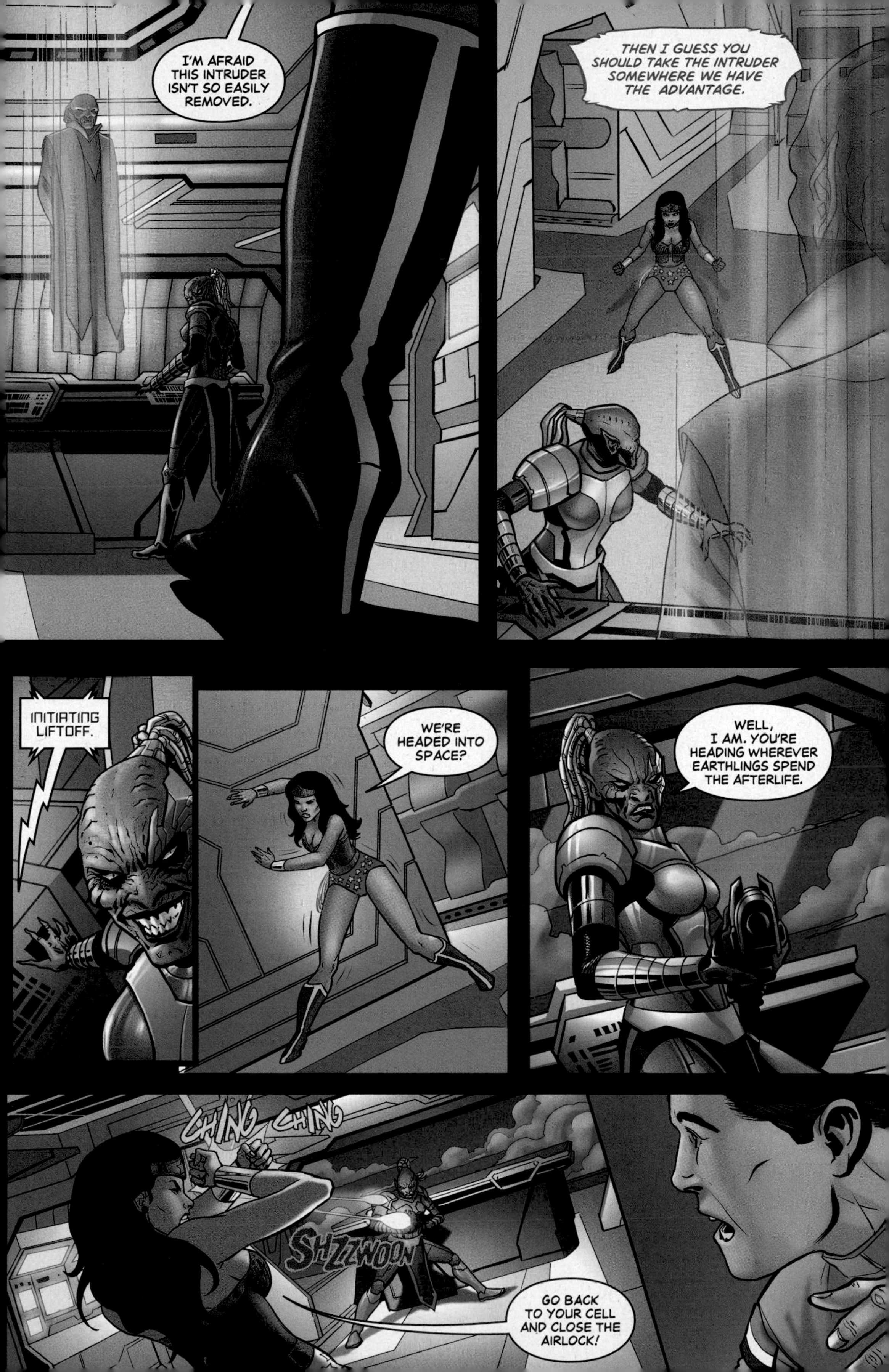
I'M AFRAID THIS INTRUDER ISN'T SO EASILY REMOVED.
THEN I GUESS YOU SHOULD TAKE THE INTRUDER SOMEWHERE WE HAVE THE ADVANTAGE.
INITIATING LIFTOFF.
WE'RE HEADED INTO SPACE?
WELL, I AM. YOU'RE HEADING WHEREVER EARTHLINGS SPEND THE AFTERLIFE.
CHING CHING
SHZZWOON
GO BACK TO YOUR CELL AND CLOSE THE AIRLOCK!

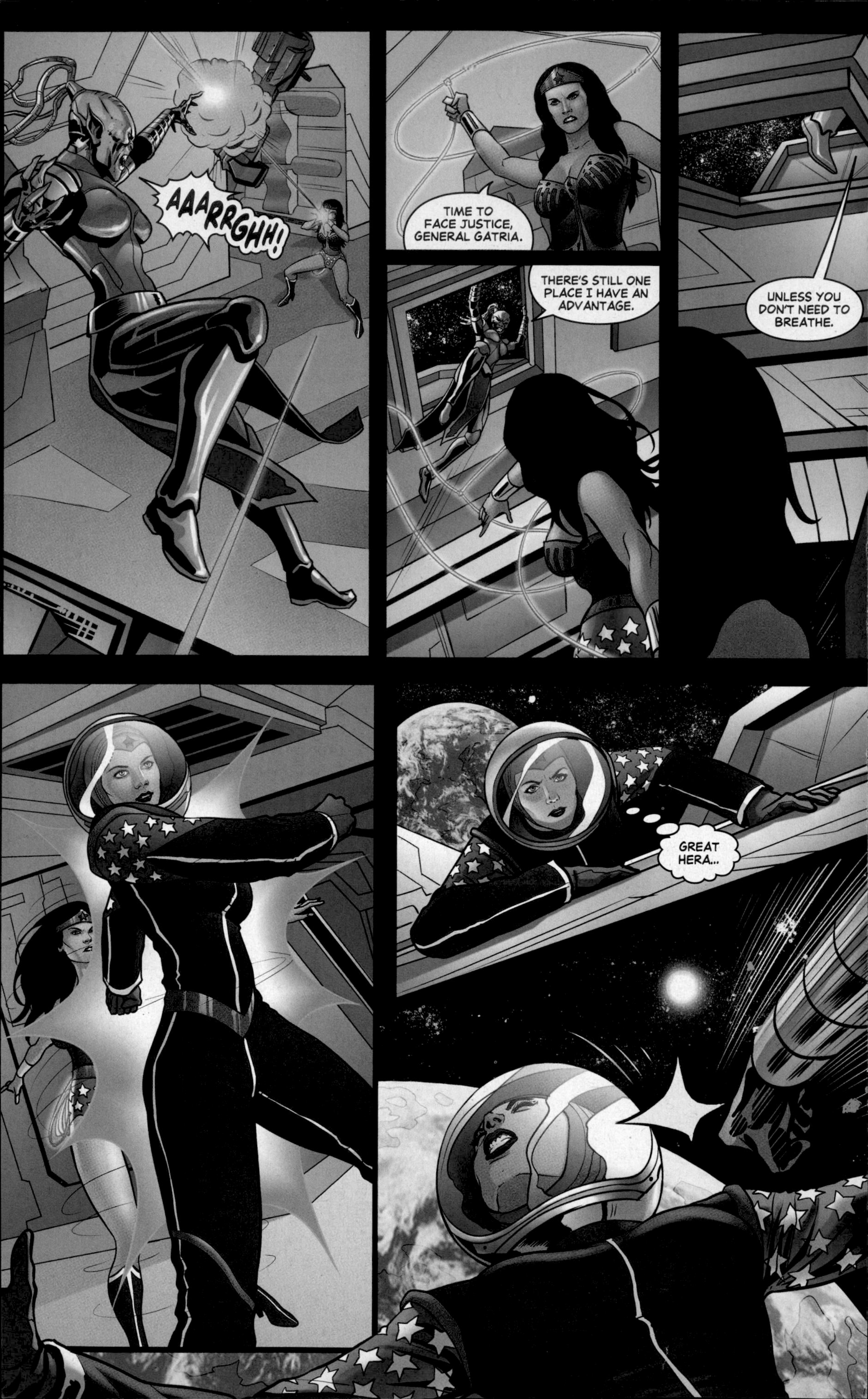
AAARRGHH!
TIME TO FACE JUSTICE, GENERAL GATRIA.
THERE'S STILL ONE PLACE I HAVE AN ADVANTAGE.
UNLESS YOU DON'T NEED TO BREATHE.
GREAT HERA...

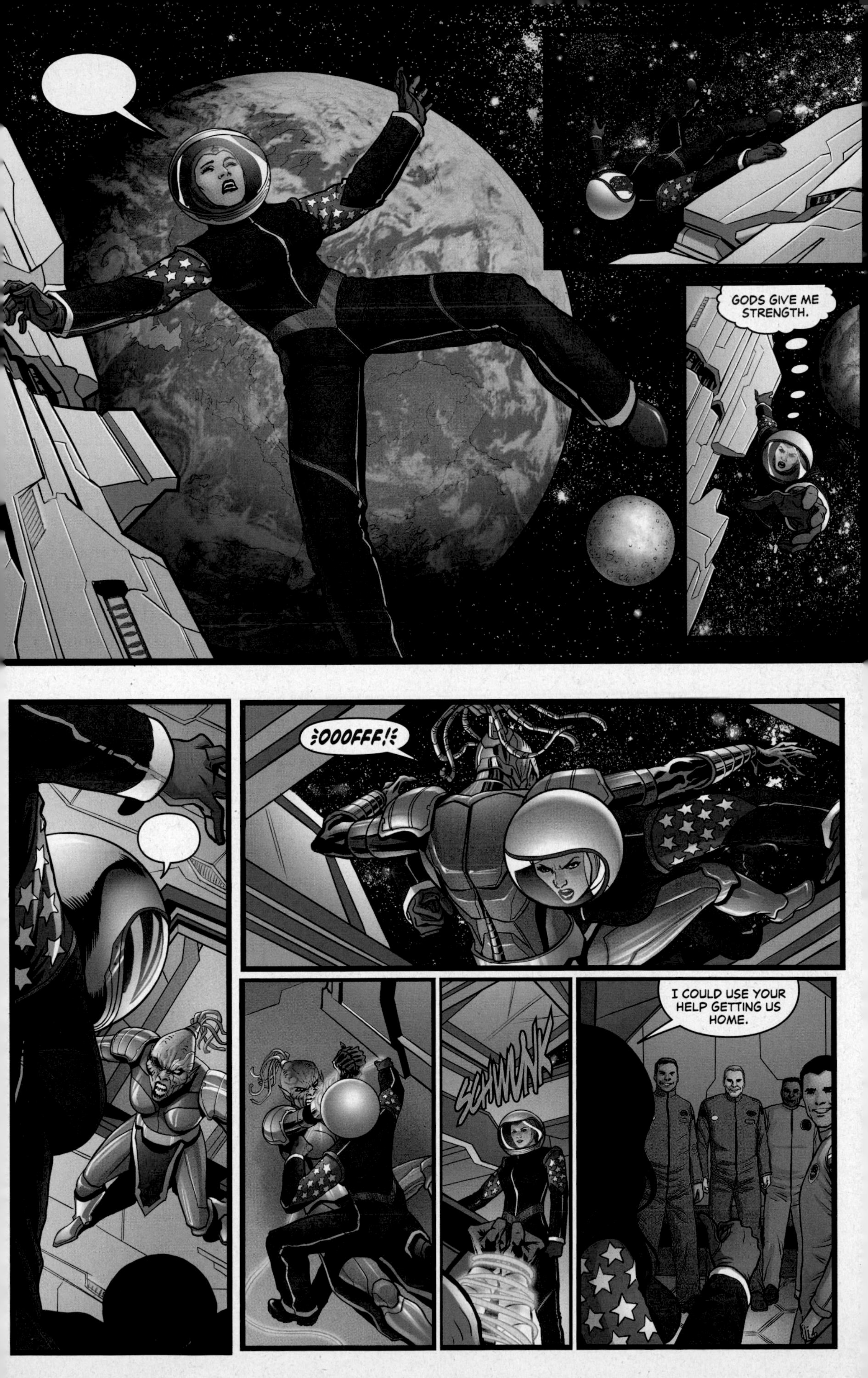
GODS GIVE ME STRENGTH.
OOOFFF!
SCHMUNK
I COULD USE YOUR HELP GETTING US HOME.

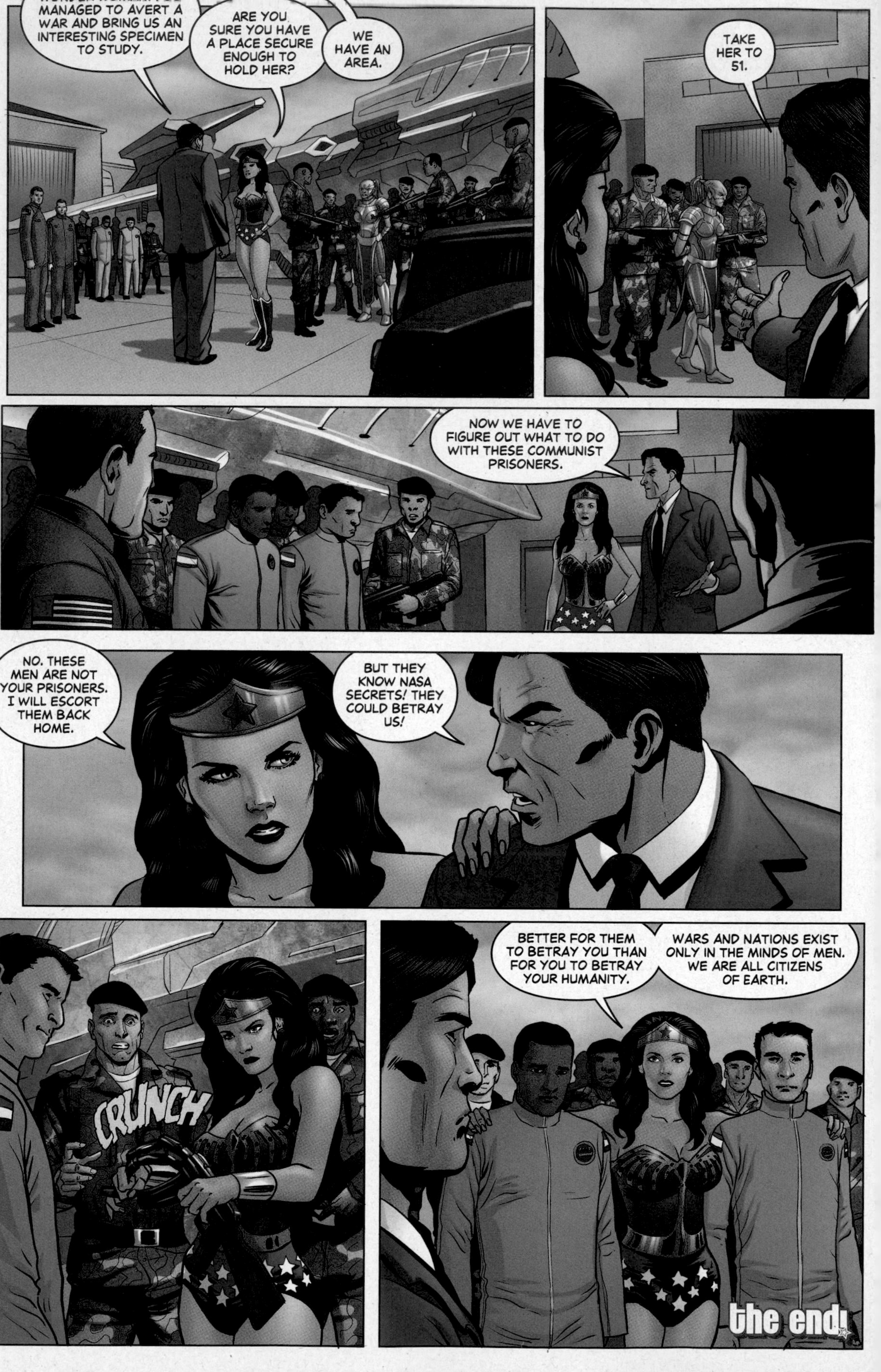
THANK YOU, WONDER WOMAN. YOU MANAGED TO AVERT A WAR AND BRING US AN INTERESTING SPECIMEN TO STUDY.
ARE YOU SURE YOU HAVE A PLACE SECURE ENOUGH TO HOLD HER?
WE HAVE AN AREA.
TAKE HER TO 51.
NOW WE HAVE TO FIGURE OUT WHAT TO DO WITH THESE COMMUNIST PRISONERS.
NO. THESE MEN ARE NOT YOUR PRISONERS. I WILL ESCORT THEM BACK HOME.
BUT THEY KNOW NASA SECRETS! THEY COULD BETRAY US!
CRUNCH
BETTER FOR THEM TO BETRAY YOU THAN FOR YOU TO BETRAY YOUR HUMANITY.
WARS AND NATIONS EXIST ONLY IN THE MINDS OF MEN. WE ARE ALL CITIZENS OF EARTH.
the end!

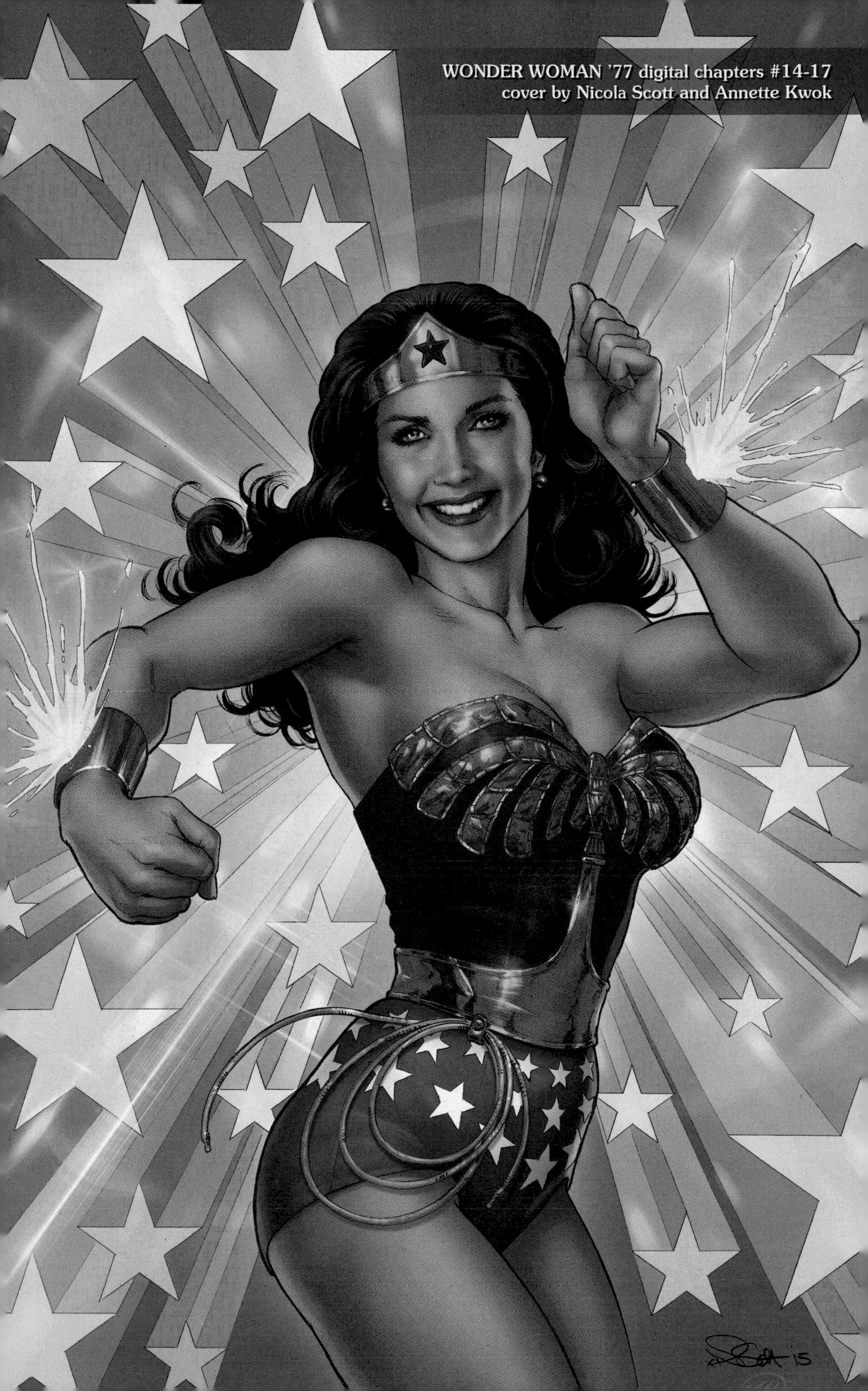

WONDER WOMAN '77 digital chapters #14-17
cover by Nicola Scott and Annette Kwok

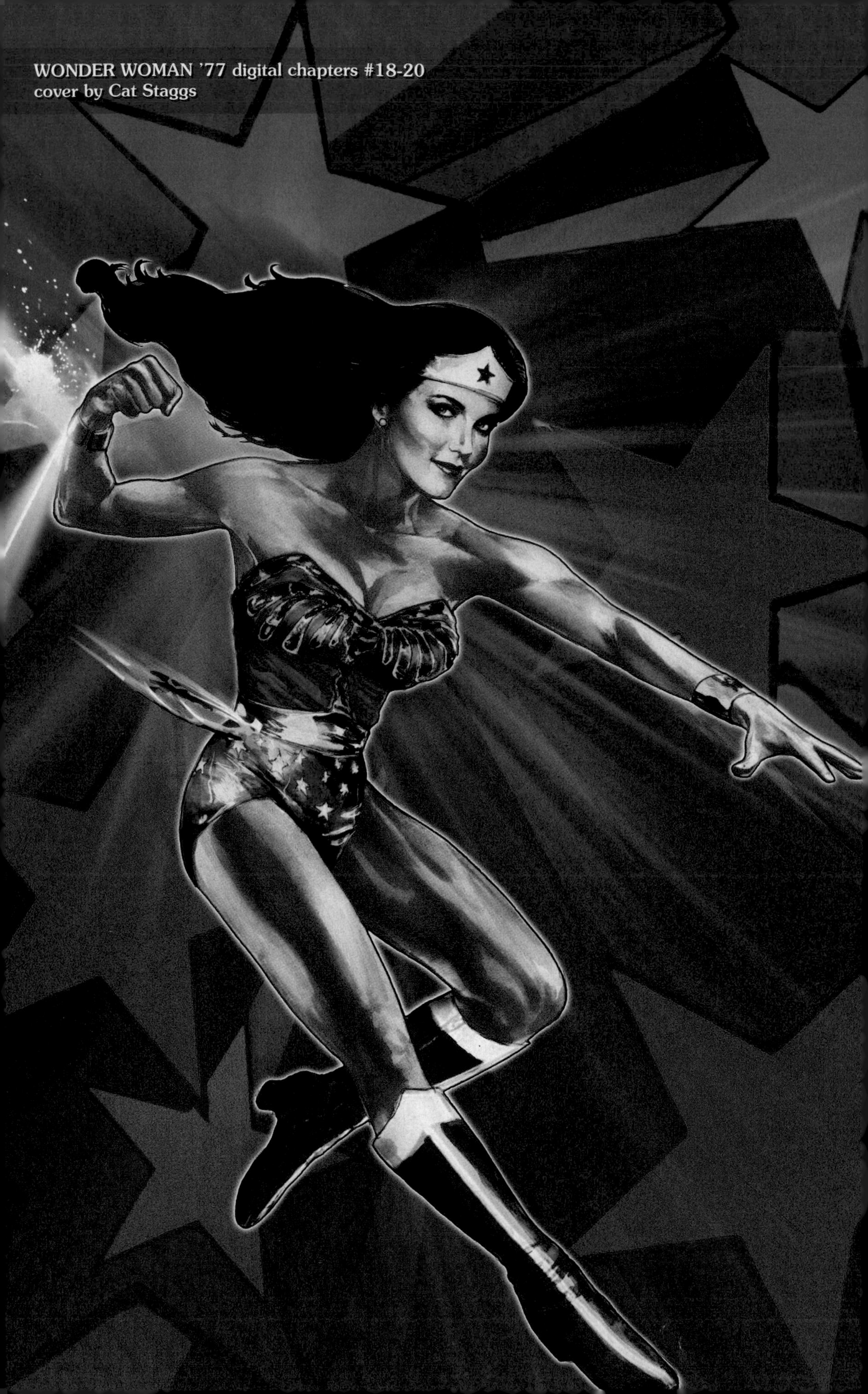

WONDER WOMAN '77 digital chapters #18-20
cover by Cat Staggs

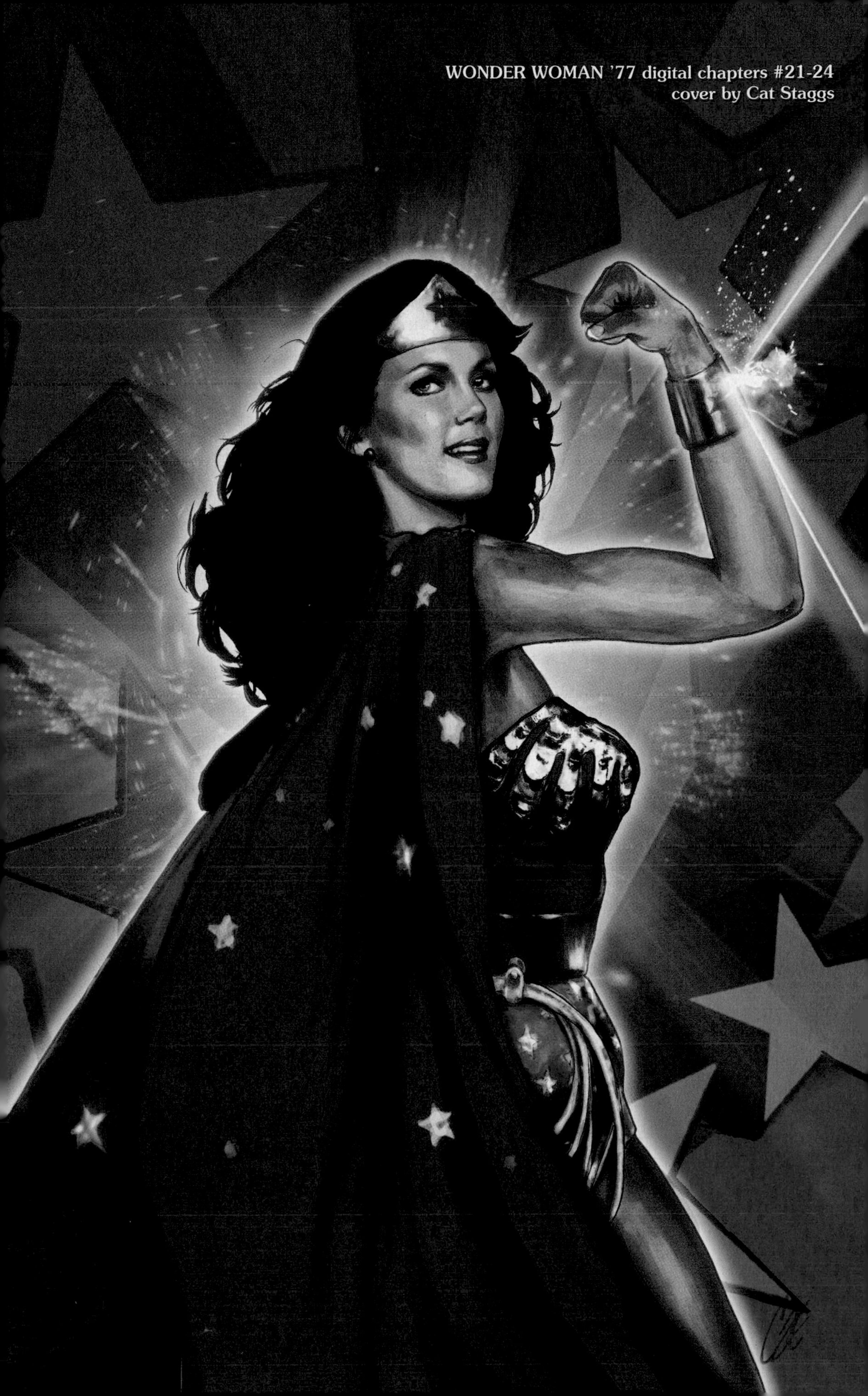

WONDER WOMAN '77 digital chapters #21-24
cover by Cat Staggs

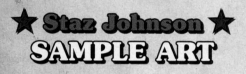

★ Staz Johnson ★ SAMPLE ART

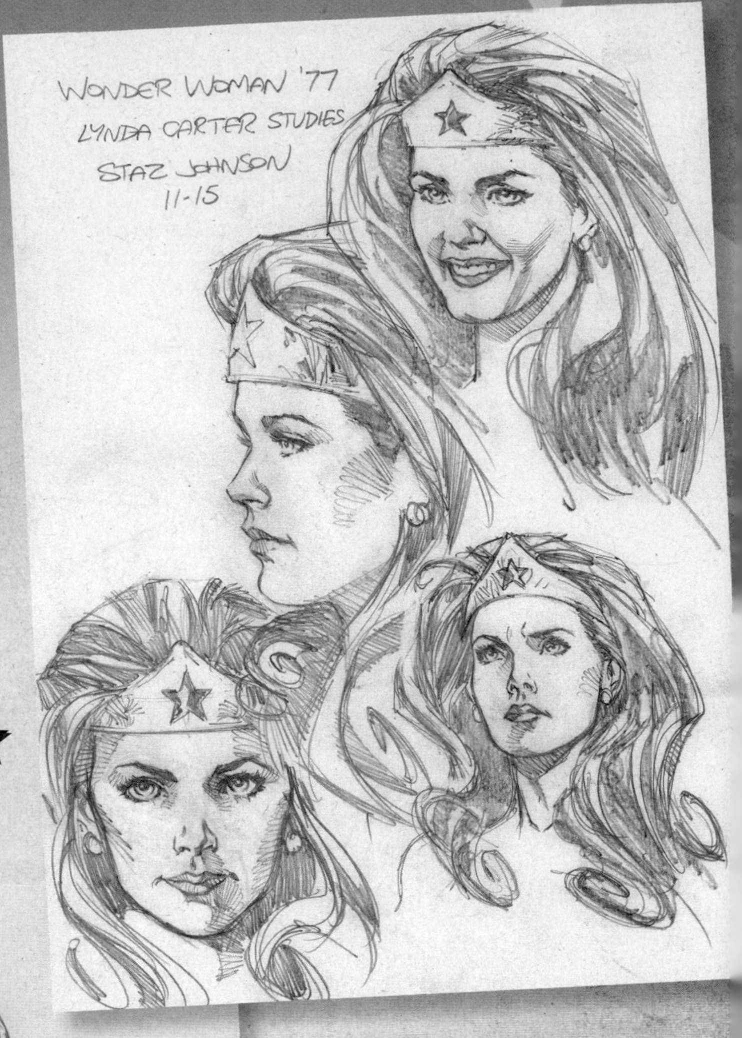
WONDER WOMAN '77
LYNDA CARTER STUDIES
STAZ JOHNSON
11-15

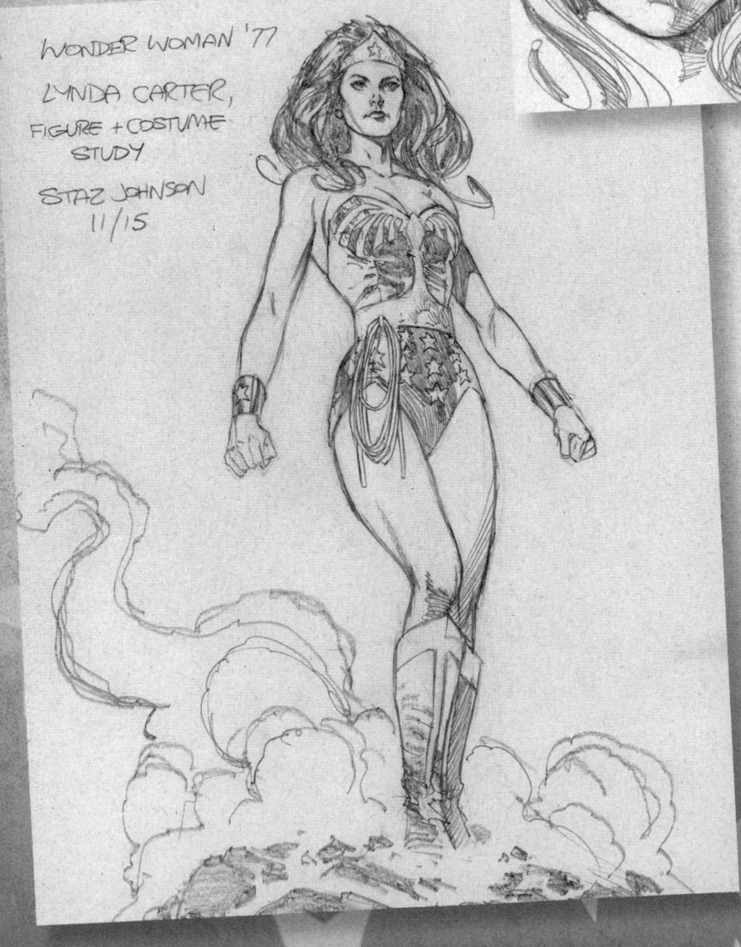
WONDER WOMAN '77
LYNDA CARTER,
FIGURE + COSTUME
STUDY
STAZ JOHNSON
11/15

★ Tom Derenick ★
SKETCHES

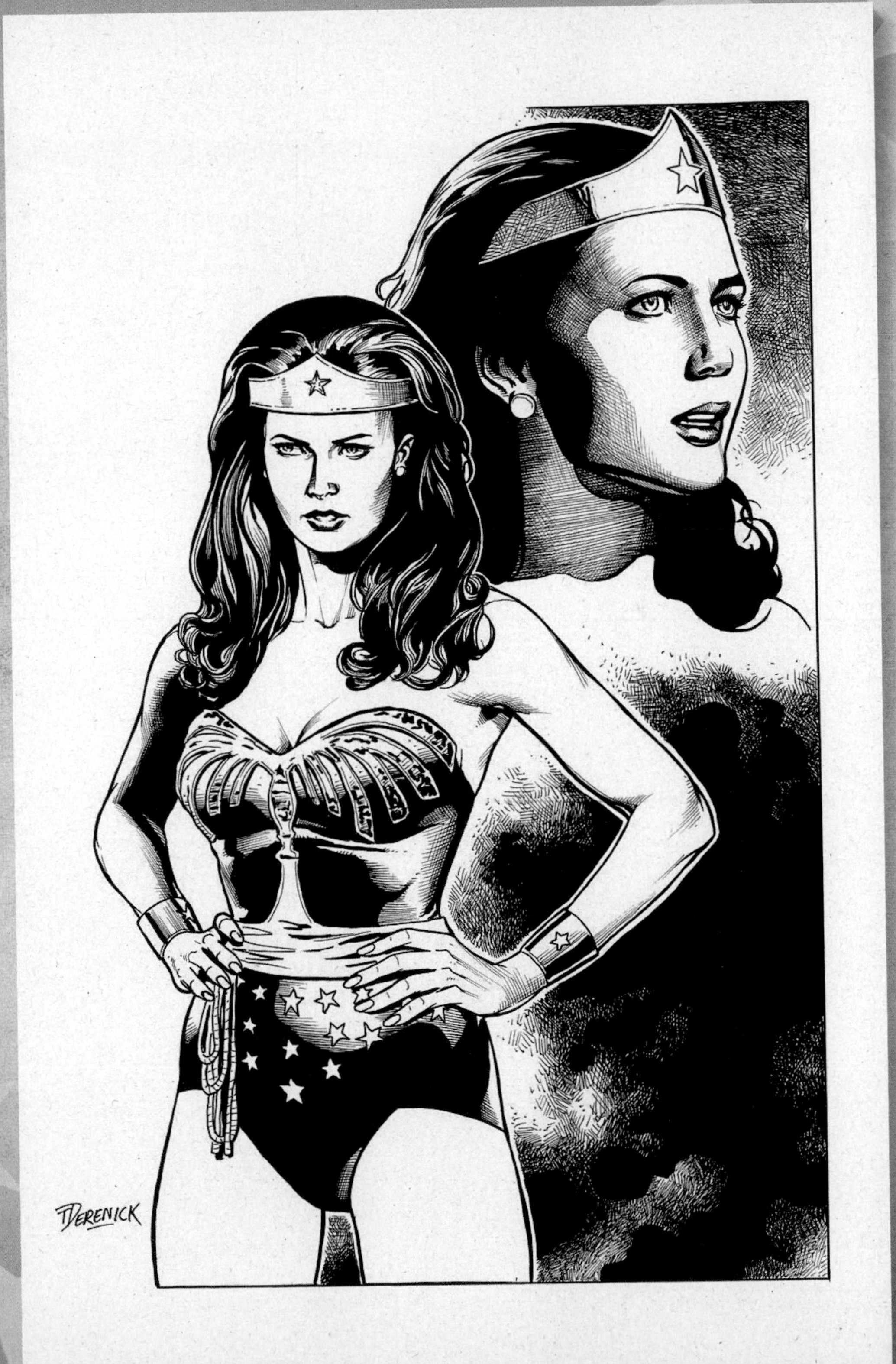

TDERENICK

★ Dario Brizuela ★

SAMPLE ART

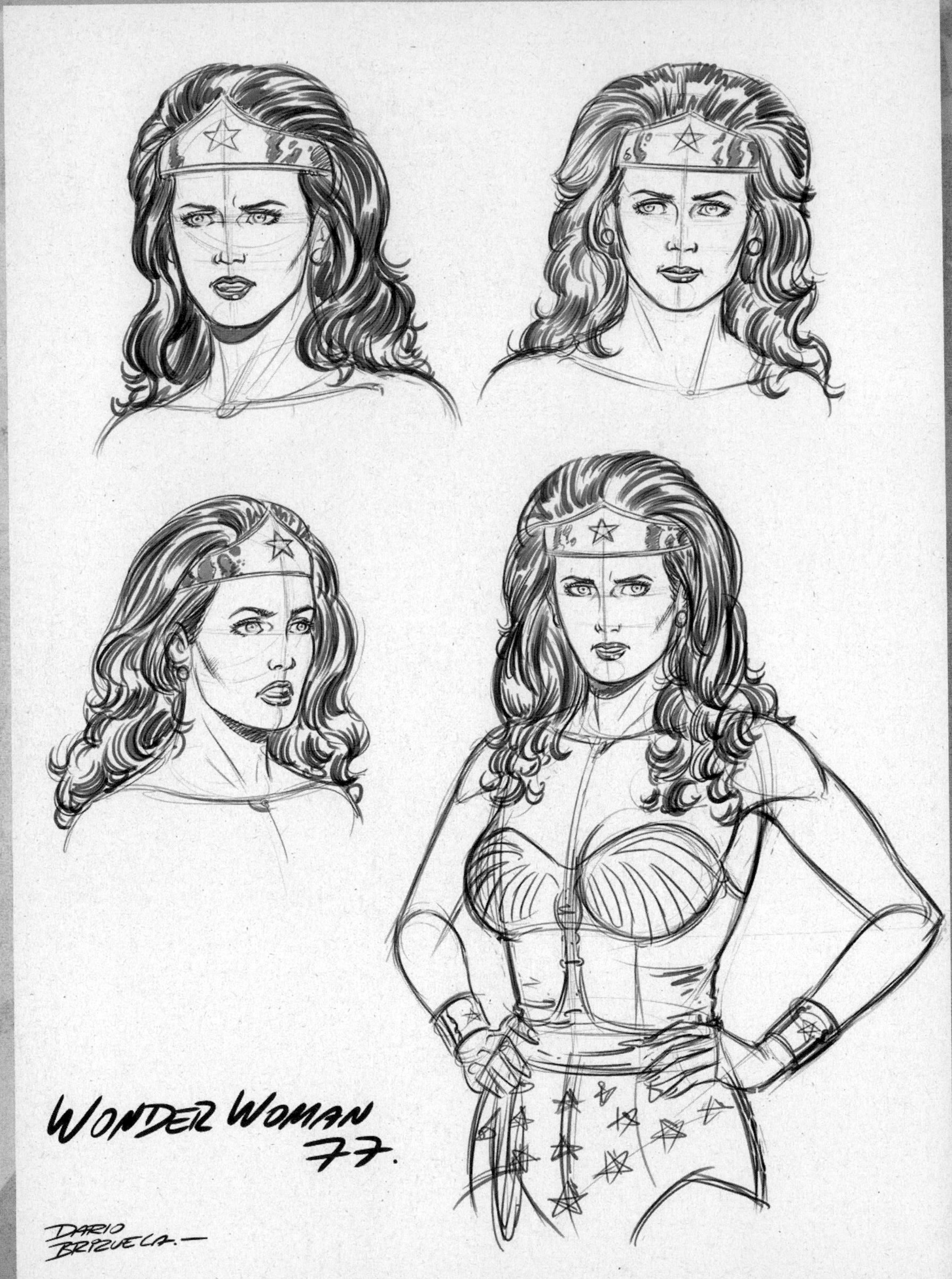

WONDER WOMAN
77.
DARIO
BRIZUELA.—

★ Tess Fowler ★

SKETCHES

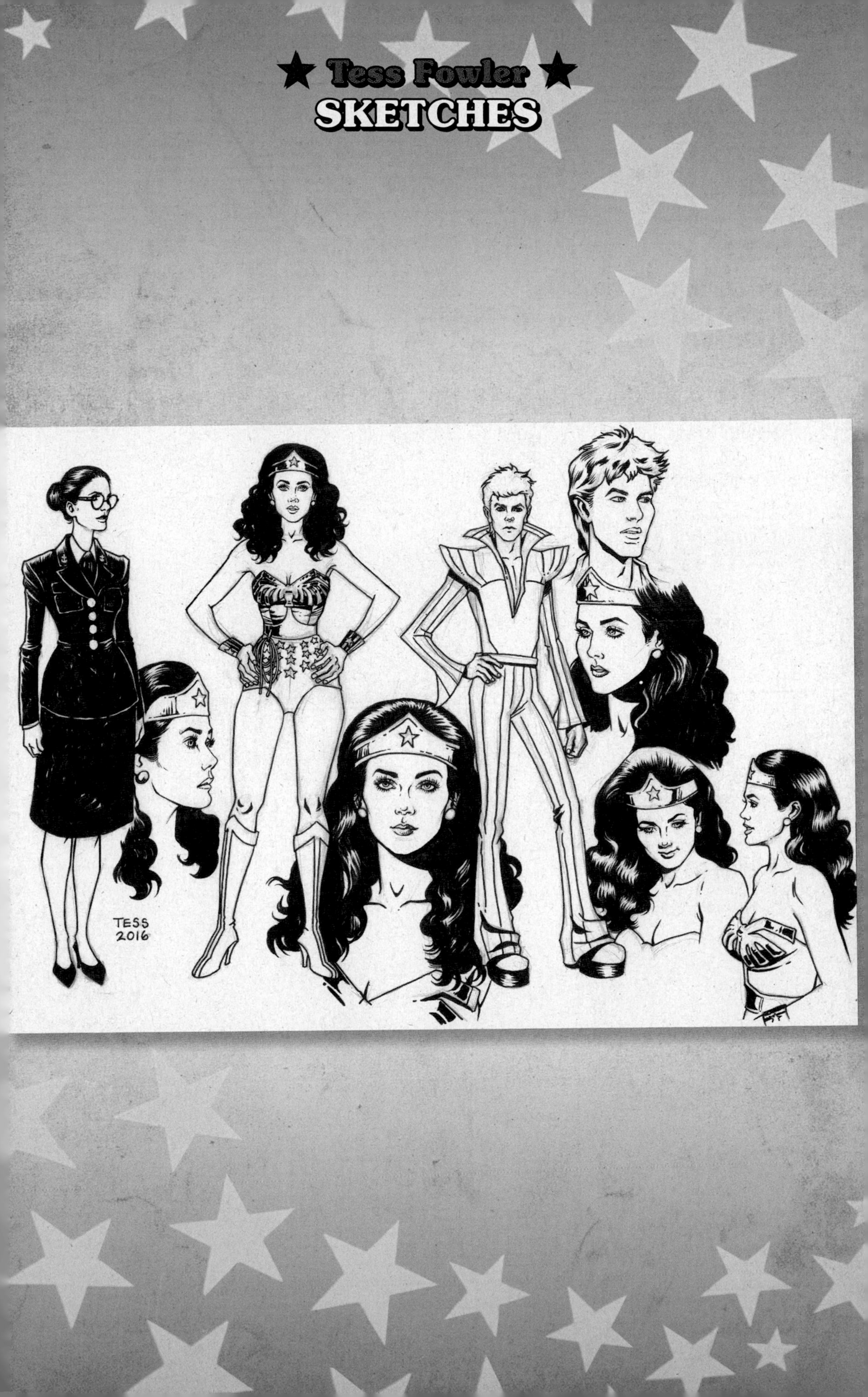
TESS
2016

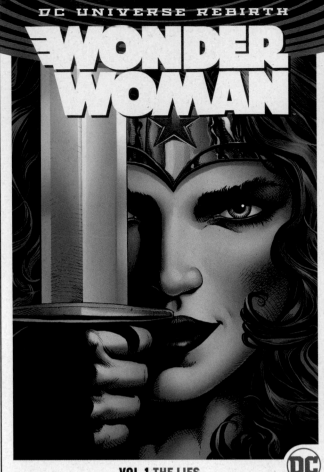